Adobe® AIR™

Create-Modify-Reuse

Adobe® AIR™
Create-Modify-Reuse

Marc Leuchner
Todd Anderson
Matt Wright

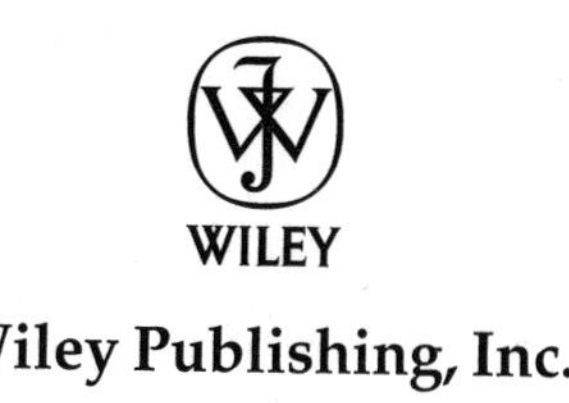

Wiley Publishing, Inc.

Adobe® AIR™
Create-Modify-Reuse

Published by
Wiley Publishing, Inc.
10475 Crosspoint Boulevard
Indianapolis, IN 46256

Published simultaneously in Canada

ISBN: 978-0-470-18207-9

Manufactured in the United States of America

10 9 8 7 6 5 4 3 2 1

Library of Congress Cataloging-in-Publication Data is available from the publisher.

For general information on our other products and services please contact our Customer Care Department within the United States at (800) 762-2974, outside the United States at (317) 572-3993 or fax (317) 572-4002.

Wiley also publishes its books in a variety of electronic formats. Some content that appears in print may not be available in electronic books.

About the Authors

Marc Leuchner is a Senior Flash Developer for the Boston-based advertising group Almighty. His roles and talents within the company primarily revolve around Flash development and interactive design. Over the years, he has worked with clients such as New Balance, ABC, Condé Nast, PUMA, BMW/Mini, Comcast, and GAP, Inc. Marc holds a BFA in New Media/Design from the Rochester Institute of Technology. In his spare time, he writes the technology blog `www.nobien.net/` with co-author Matt Wright.

Todd Anderson is a Senior Software Engineer for Infrared5. With over five years of developing for the Flash Platform in the areas of RIA and game development, Todd has delivered web and desktop solutions for the publishing and entertainment industries for companies including McGraw-Hill, Thomson, Motorola, and Condé Nast. He runs `www.custardbelly.com/blog`, focusing on development of the Flash Platform and game development.

Matthew Wright is a Senior Flash Developer for ROKKAN, a full-service digital agency located in New York City. Since 2005 he has delivered mostly consumer experience Flash sites and applications for a wide array of clients, including Virgin America, the Coca-Cola Company, Atlantic Records, Time Warner, the NBA, and 2K Games. Prior to ROKKAN, he got his start at an interactive agency in Syracuse, New York, called 2ndNature. It was here that he discovered his love for the Flash platform. Outside of work, Matthew contributes to a Flash and technology blog `www.nobien.net`, with friend, colleague, and co-author Marc Leuchner. He has also spoken at FlashForward. Matthew lives in Brooklyn, New York, with his beautiful girlfriend, Chewy.

Credits

Executive Editor
Chris Webb

Development Editor
Brian Herrmann

Technical Editor
Ashley Atkins

Production Editor
Daniel Scribner

Copy Editor
Luann Rouff

Editorial Manager
Mary Beth Wakefield

Production Manager
Tim Tate

Vice President and Executive Group Publisher
Richard Swadley

Vice President and Executive Publisher
Joseph B. Wikert

Project Coordinator, Cover
Lynsey Stanford

Proofreader
Nancy Bell

Indexer
Ron Strauss

Acknowledgments

Marc Leuchner

I would like to thank co-authors Todd Anderson and Matt Wright for their excellence and dedication in writing this book and for being terrific friends. I am excited that you two took charge and made the book your own. To Ash Atkins, your editing and knowledge was greatly needed and well received. To the people at Wiley, Chris Webb, and especially Brian Herrmann, I thank you for the opportunity to write this excellent book. Brian, I know it was sometimes difficult to beat the chapters out of us, but we really appreciate your editing, support, and humor throughout this past year. I would like to thank Joey Lott and Matt Sutton for helping me into the world of writing. And thanks to my family and friends for their support and encouragement over the past year, especially my parents, who have been nothing but supportive in my career. Lastly, I would especially like to thank my girlfriend, Courtney. Your understanding and commitment has meant so much to me, particularly during those busy weekends and sleepless nights.

Todd Anderson

I would like to thank Marc Leuchner and Matt Wright for being excellent co-authors in this endeavor and lending expertise and humor while writing this book. To my family, I could not thank you enough for the huge support and love — my wonderful wife, Carrie, Mom, Dad, Brian, Krissa, Emma, Kelsea, and Cayuga. I would also like to thank my friends and the huge support I get from the Flash community. Big thanks and a shaking fist go out to Ash Atkins, who provided invaluable wisdom during the tech editing process. Lastly, I would like to thank Brian Herrmann, Chris Webb, and the Wiley team for their patience, understanding, and hard work.

Matt Wright

First, I'd like to thank the people at Wiley for giving me the opportunity to write a book on a topic I truly enjoy. In particular, I'd like to thank Chris Webb for trusting me to write my first book on a brand-new technology. It's not often that one gets such an opportunity. Second, I'd like to thank Brian Herrmann and Ash Atkins for being such awesome and helpful editors. Without them this book would have no legs to stand on. I'd also like to send many thanks to my co-authors, Todd Anderson and Marc Leuchner. These two guys are both brilliant and motivating. I only wish we could work together more often. My appreciation also goes out to my family, most importantly my mother and father, for supporting me and my career. Without them I wouldn't be where I am today. Lastly, I'd like to send a huge thank-you to my girlfriend, Chewy, for all her support and patience during the writing of this book.

Contents

Introduction

The release of Adobe Flex 3 featuring the AIR SDK (Software Development Kit) marks the latest advancement in the evolution of Adobe Flash technologies. The initial version of Flash (then FutureSplash) was a program capable of creating animations for the Web. With the later addition and revisions of the ActionScript language, Flash was transformed into a robust development tool that lead to the creation of the Flex framework. The initial two versions of Flex have enabled developers to create rich Internet applications independent of the Flash IDE and with some ease. Version 3 of Flex introduces the capability to create applications specifically for the Adobe AIR runtime, thus moving the Flash family from web-based to desktop-based applications.

With every release of a new Flash technology, there is a mountain of new learning material — books, videos, blogs entries, and so on. Adobe AIR and Flex 3 are no different. In fact, because Adobe released public beta versions of their software, this effect is amplified. People are excited about the new features in Flex 3, especially its integration of the AIR SDK. This excitement has made it easier to find out *how* to use Adobe AIR, but what if you're past that and would like to start building applications? Similarly, some people learn best by dissecting example applications. After all, excitement fuels the need to build something useful with Flex 3 and Adobe AIR. This book attempts to pass this excitement and knowledge on to you.

Who This Book Is For

This book was written with the Flex developer in mind — someone who has experience using Flex 2 to build web application will find the examples in this book easy to follow. However, if you are familiar with object-oriented ActionScript and have a basic knowledge of how Flex works, this book will also be helpful in further learning Flex and ActionScript 3 by example.

Those who are new to, or becoming more familiar with, the Adobe AIR SDK should review the first chapter, as it explains how a basic Flex/AIR project is developed, compiled, and deployed. If you learn better by example, Chapter 2 jumps into creating an AIR application with some moderate techniques.

The advanced user may want to jump right into looking through the code base. All of the code for each example is available on the accompanying website. Feel free to get your feet wet with an application, and use this book as a reference guide or blueprint.

Overall, each chapter in this book is set up to be a self-contained example. Therefore, feel free to skip around in any manner you choose. Each chapter was written with the intention of creating a foundation that you can extend, taking each application to new limits by customizing it and making it your own. They are all built in ways that enable you to easily implement parts of the code base in projects outside of this publication. You're encouraged to select an example application, break it, fix it, add to it, and learn from it.

What This Book Covers

This book consists of 11 applications that demonstrate the features available in the Adobe AIR and Flex 3 SDKs. Each chapter touches on several key features, and collectively they cover most of what the AIR SDK has to offer. By following along with the examples, you will create robust applications using object-oriented concepts and practices.

How This Book Is Structured

This book is structured to be read like an instructional reference manual for reusable applications. Each chapter contains code sets and snippets followed by brief explanations. All the applications have been created with the idea of extensibility, meaning every example should be treated as a foundation from which you can build a larger and better application. After all, this book was created for developers who may have an idea that they don't know how to start, or who need a way to quickly get a project off the ground.

The structure of each chapter is as follows:

- Introduction and overview: what AIR and Flex features will be covered
- Design: the main technical concepts and goals of the application
- Code and code explanation
- Building and deployment: how to compile and package the application
- Summary and modification recommendations

The chapters of the book, the included application, and a brief list of AIR features are as follows:

- Chapter 1, "The Development Environment," provides an overview of setup and the command-line tool.
- Chapter 2, "Simple Text Editor," covers basic file system functionality, including browsing, reading, and writing files.
- Chapter 3, "Simple RSS Reader," covers occasional connectivity and toaster-style alerts.
- Chapter 4, "Music Player," covers recursive file search, browse, copy, read, write files, and chromeless applications.
- Chapter 5, "Mini CMS," covers handling XML, file uploads, writing files, and saving settings.
- Chapter 6, "Image Viewer and Editor," covers creating images files, using the codecs available in the Flex 3 SDK, and native drag-and-drop operations.
- Chapter 7, "HTML and CSS Editor," covers editing the HTML and CSS of a loaded page, and HTML control, including JavaScript integration.
- Chapter 8, "Weather Widget," covers context menus, chromeless apps, customized icons, and system tray/dock interactivity.
- Chapter 9, "Map Application," covers communication with an online API using JavaScript in an HTML control, and communication with a local database.

- Chapter 10, "Blogger Agent," covers publishing posts to your Blogger account or saving them for publishing later when you are connected. Also covered are SQLite DB and LocalEncryptedStore for storing sensitive information.
- Chapter 11, "Slideshow Maker," covers serialization of custom file types and the windowing API.
- Chapter 12, "Video Player," covers Flash 9 and AIR's H.264 and FLV playback support, drag and drop, context and window menus, and full-screen video.

Chapters recommended for those who are new to Flex include 2, 3, 7, 8, and 12.

What You Need to Use This Book

Because Adobe Flex 3 and AIR SDKs are open source, you only need to download the SDKs with compilers and a text editor. However, Flex Builder 3 is certainly recommended. Flex 3 and AIR are available for Windows, Mac OS X, and Linux platforms. Trial versions of Flex Builder 3 and the open-source Flex 3 and AIR SDKs are available at `www.adobe.com`. If you are in need of a good ActionScript editor, try FlashDevelop, a free ActionScript editor, if you do not have Flex Builder or Eclipse (`www.flashdevelop.org`).

Conventions

To help you get the most from the text and keep track of what's happening, we've used a number of conventions throughout the book.

> **Boxes like this one hold important, not-to-be forgotten information that is directly relevant to the surrounding text.**

Notes, tips, hints, tricks, and asides to the current discussion are offset and placed in italics like this.

As for styles in the text:

- New terms and important words are *italicized* when they are introduced.
- Keyboard strokes are shown like this: Ctrl+A.
- Filenames, URLs, and code are shown within the text like so: `persistence.properties`.
- Code is presented in two different ways:

```
A monofont type with no highlighting is used for most code examples.
```

```
Gray highlighting is used to emphasize code that's particularly important in the
present context.
```

Source Code

As you work through the examples in this book, you may choose to either type in all the code manually or use the source code files that accompany the book. All of the source code used in this book is available for download at `www.wrox.com`. Once at the site, simply locate the book's title (either by using the Search box or by using one of the title lists) and click the Download Code link on the book's detail page to obtain all the source code for the book.

Because many books have similar titles, you may find it easiest to search by ISBN; this book's ISBN is 978-0-470-18207-9.

Once you download the code, just decompress it with your favorite compression tool. Alternately, you can go to the main Wrox code download page at `www.wrox.com/dynamic/books/download.aspx` to see the code available for this book and all other Wrox books.

Errata

We make every effort to ensure that there are no errors in the text or in the code. However, no one is perfect, and mistakes do occur. If you find an error in one of our books, such as a spelling mistake or a faulty piece of code, we would be very grateful for your feedback. By sending in errata, you may save another reader hours of frustration, and at the same time you will be helping us provide even higher quality information.

To find the errata page for this book, go to `www.wrox.com` and locate the title using the Search box or one of the title lists. Then, on the book details page, click the Book Errata link. On this page you can view all errata that has been submitted for this book and posted by Wrox editors. A complete book list, including links to each book's errata, is also available at `www.wrox.com/misc-pages/booklist.shtml`.

If you don't spot "your" error on the Book Errata page, go to `www.wrox.com/contact/techsupport.shtml` and complete the form there to send us the error you have found. We'll check the information and, if appropriate, post a message to the book's errata page and fix the problem in subsequent editions of the book.

p2p.wrox.com

For author and peer discussion, join the P2P forums at `p2p.wrox.com`. The forums are a web-based system for you to post messages relating to Wrox books and related technologies and interact with other readers and technology users. The forums offer a subscription feature to e-mail you topics of interest of your choosing when new posts are made to the forums. Wrox authors, editors, other industry experts, and your fellow readers are present on these forums.

At `http://p2p.wrox.com` you will find a number of different forums that will help you not only as you read this book, but also as you develop your own applications. To join the forums, just follow these steps:

1. Go to `p2p.wrox.com` and click the Register link.
2. Read the terms of use and click Agree.

3. Complete the required information to join as well as any optional information you wish to provide and click Submit.

4. You will receive an e-mail with information describing how to verify your account and complete the joining process.

You can read messages in the forums without joining P2P but in order to post your own messages, you must join.

Once you join, you can post new messages and respond to messages other users post. You can read messages at any time on the Web. If you would like to have new messages from a particular forum e-mailed to you, click the Subscribe to This Forum icon by the forum name in the forum listing.

For more information about how to use the Wrox P2P, be sure to read the P2P FAQs for answers to questions about how the forum software works as well as many common questions specific to P2P and Wrox books. To read the FAQs, click the FAQ link on any P2P page.

1

The Development Environment

A reliable development environment will save you loads of time when you are ready to debug and deploy your applications. This chapter explains how to install and use command-line tools in building an AIR (Adobe Integrated Runtime) application. This chapter follows a slightly different format than the following chapters, as it introduces the development process in building applications in AIR, and provides an overview of common tools.

The following section, "SDK Installation," explains where to download and how to install the Flex 3 SDK, which includes all required tools and APIs (Application Programming Interfaces) to build Flex and AIR applications. This section covers the basics of the development environment and provides a brief overview of the command-line tools that are used throughout the book to deploy AIR applications.

The section "Building Your First Application" walks you through the process of building your first AIR application, focusing on how to use the command-line tools to deploy, debug, and package your application for installation.

The section "Installing and Uninstalling" explores the installation process of an AIR application and the storage of application files on a user's machine.

The final section, "Extra Tools," addresses two additional ways for developers to ease the development process: an Apache Ant build scheme to help automate the build process and a simple debug panel to receive basic trace statements from AIR applications.

SDK Installation

Adobe AIR is a cross-platform runtime that runs desktop applications compiled under the AIR framework. By containing two primary web technologies, Flash and HTML, Adobe AIR enables developers to deliver the same Rich Internet Application (RIA) experience to the desktop. It is not assumed that you have an Integrated Development Environment (IDE), such as Adobe FlexBuilder, which combines a text editor, the necessary compilers, a debugger and other useful tools for your AIR applications. Although you are welcome to use any IDE that you choose to facilitate in the development of your applications, all the examples within this book are deployed and packaged using the Software Development Kits (SDKs) discussed in this section and the command line. Later in this chapter you will learn how you can make this process even smoother by using an Apache Ant build scheme, all while building your first AIR application — the ubiquitous *Hello World*.

Necessary Files

First and foremost, you need to install AIR (Adobe Integated Runtime). If it is not already installed on your machine, go to `www.adobe.com/go/air` and download the AIR runtime. Because this is a book on developing AIR applications and not necessarily an overview of the AIR runtime or Flash software itself, it is recommended that you follow the documentation on installing the runtime provided by Adobe, and refer to the manufacturer's guide should you decide to customize your installation of the AIR runtime.

Once the AIR runtime is installed, it is time to start setting up a reliable environment that will enable you to deliver applications without having to think about that aspect of the process during development. You'll be free to code, and when it comes time to debug or deploy, the system will be in place to handle all aspects of those stages.

For this development environment, you need to download the Flex 3 SDK, which includes the AIR API and all the required command-line tools. The AIR SDK is also available for developers creating applications using HTML or AJAX, though the examples in this book are built primarily in Flex.

SDK Installation

This section explains how to download and install the Software Development Kits (SDKs) available from Adobe, as well as how to configure the setup to use the command-line tools found within.

Flex 3 SDK

Download the Adobe Flex 3 SDK from `http://opensource.adobe.com/wiki/display/flexsdk/Flex+SDK`. Once the download is complete, a file titled `flex_sdk_3` (or similar) will be available within the directory to which you downloaded the file. In this case, that was the desktop. Unzip the contents of `flex_sdk_3` into a directory whose location reflects how you work and organize files. For the purposes of the following examples, the Flex 3 SDK was installed at `C:/flex_sdk_3` on Windows and `/Applications/flex_sdk_3` on Mac OS X. If your installation directory is different, then change all references to this installation directory to where you have installed the Flex SDK.

Add a path to your system properties to enable you to call some valuable executables during our development process. The files you are primarily concerned with — since they relate to debugging and deploying — can be found in the `/bin` folder within the Flex SDK installation directory. The executables for the compilers call the Java programs, which can be found in the `/lib` folder within the directory. You have the option of adding the Java programs themselves to your `CLASSPATH` variable, but you will be accessing these native executables themselves — namely, `adt.bat`, `adl.exe`, `mxmlc.exe`, and `amxmlc.bat`. In order to call these directly from the command line without having to provide the full path each time (such as `C:/flex_sdk_3/bin/fdb`), add the `/bin` directory to the `Path` variable.

On Windows:

1. Open System from the Control Panel.
2. Click the Advanced tab from the menu.
3. Click on Environment Variables.
4. Within the System variables grid, navigate to and double-click on Path.
5. In the Variable Value field, if the last character is not a semicolon (;), enter a semicolon and then the path to the `/bin` folder within your Flex SDK installation directory. For the purposes of this example, that would be `;C:\flex_sdk_3\bin`.

On Mac OS X:

1. Open the Terminal and type > **open -e .profile**.
2. If you do not have a `PATH` variable set, add the following line:

```
export PATH:$PATH://Application/flex_sdk_2/bin/
```

If you do have a PATH variable set, add the path to the bin folder after first entering a colon (:) to delimit the paths.

Now you are ready to access the command-line tools directly. These tools require Java to be installed on your machine as well. You probably already have Java installed; if not, download the JRE from `http://java.sun.com` and install it in a directory of your choice. Try to obtain the latest stable release, but note that all the code within this book — including the Apache Ant build scheme — has been tested with Java 1.5 + . Remember where you install the JRE, or remind yourself where it is already installed, as you may need that directory path when you are ready to debug your Hello World application.

Command-Line Tools Overview

Within the `/bin` folder of the Flex SDK installation directory are the command-line tools that you will use for debugging, deploying, and packaging AIR applications. The `.exe` files with the Flex logo icon (a black circle with the text `fx`) are the executable files included with the Flex SDK package. The `.bat` files and `adl.exe` (with the AIR logo icon) are the executable files that come with the AIR SDK.

The `mxmlc` executable is the compiler responsible for generating Shockwave Flash (SWF) files out of MXML and ActionScript code. Its AIR "sister" — the `amxmlc.bat` file — uses the `air-config.xml` file found in the `/frameworks` folder to configure the compiler for AIR. Running `mxmlc` itself uses the `flex-config.xml` file, also in the `/frameworks` folder. The `amxmlc` compiler is invoked for both deploying and debugging the SWF file to be packaged in your AIR application installer. AIR application installer files are created by invoking the ADT batch file (`adt.bat`) found in the `/bin` folder of your installation directory.

In this context, the term *deploy* refers to the creation of the SWF file that will be packaged with your AIR application. By invoking the `amxmlc` compiler with your main `.mxmlc` file as an argument, a SWF file is generated. The SWF file, however, is not launched during this operation, and using the `amxmlc` compiler alone will not enable you to preview the Flash movie running within the AIR runtime environment. Running the AIR Debug Launcher (ADL) will launch the SWF file generated by the `amxmlc` compiler.

In addition, if the `amxmlc` is set to debug mode when compiling the SWF file, you are given the opportunity to debug your applications by running the ADL and Flash Debugger.

When you create an installer file for your AIR application you use the AIR Development Tool (ADT). AIR installer files need to be code signed. It is recommended that you sign your AIR application by linking a certificate from a certificate authority (such as VeriSign and Thawte), as it verifies that you (the publisher) are the signer and that the application has not been maliciously altered — ensuring end users that they are not installing a counterfeit version. You can create a self-signed certificate using the ADT tool as well. Note that when using a self-signed certificate, your identity as the publisher cannot be verified during installation. Moreover, if you later release an update to an existing application with a self-signed certificate, then you need to use the original certificate when creating the installer file. The examples in this book include the process of creating self-signed certificates.

In the next section you'll jump right in and start building in order to see how the development environment you have set up by installing the SDK and setting System Paths to the command line tools will aid your efforts to debug, deploy, and deliver your first AIR application — the familiar *Hello World*.

Building Your First Application

Now that you have the necessary files for deploying and packaging AIR applications, you should carefully consider how you intend to develop your applications. Creating a directory in which you will develop is just as important, as it is where you will spend most of your time in delivering a product.

> *Although the examples in this book use the project directory structure outlined in the following sections, it is not intended to replace any organization techniques you may already have. If the structure used here does not agree with your workflow, you are encouraged to employ your approach and edit accordingly.*

Some IDEs actually create a development directory within the `Documents` directory on your machine — User ➪ My Documents on Windows and User ➪ Documents on Mac. Though that is a viable solution for your development environment, for the purposes of this book, create a folder called `Development` in the root drive on your machine — `C:/` on Windows, the hard drive name on Mac. Within that folder will reside a directory of the type of software you are using to develop your applications, including any subdirectories of the projects therein.

On Windows:

1. Navigate to the root of the `C:/` drive.
2. Create a folder titled `Development`.
3. Within that `Development` folder, create a folder titled `AIR`.

On Mac:

1. Navigate to the hard drive.
2. Create a folder titled `Development`.
3. Within that `Development` folder, create a folder titled `AIR`.

Within this directory — `C:/Development/AIR` or `/Development/AIR` — will reside your AIR project subdirectories. From here on, this will be referred to as the "development directory."

Your first project will create a simple *Hello World* application. There is nothing special about this application and it will not involve much of the AIR API other than the `WindowedApplication` container. It is intended to introduce you to compiling, debugging, and packaging your application.

Within your development directory, create a folder named `HelloWorld`. You need at least two files in order to compile and deploy AIR applications:

- A main file — This can be either an MXML (`.mxml`) or ActionScript (`.as`) file.
- An application descriptor file using the XML markup

Most, if not all, of the examples found in this book have an MXML file as the application's main file. This is the file you will supply as the main file argument to the `amxmlc` compiler when it comes time to compile. In the case of the *Hello World* application, this will be `HelloWorld.mxml`.

The naming convention for the project's application descriptor file used throughout this book appends the string `-app` to the project's name, though you can name the file as you wish. In the case of the *Hello World* application, the application descriptor file is named `HelloWorld-app.xml`. The generated SWF file and the application descriptor will be used to deploy and preview your application prior to packaging. To create an AIR installer, you will need a signed certificate, the generated SWF, the application descriptor file, and any ancillary files required (such as graphics files).

Because the Flex and AIR command-line tools are available within the SDK you have installed, you are not reliant on an IDE and can continue development by firing up your favorite text editor.

Code and Code Explanation

Open your favorite editor and create a new document. Then, complete the following steps:

1. Enter the following markup (alternatively, you can find this example in the code files for this chapter on the accompanying website):

```
<?xml version="1.0" encoding="UTF-8"?>
<application xmlns="http://ns.adobe.com/air/application/1.0">
    <id>com.aircmr.HelloWorld</id>
    <version>0.1</version>
    <filename>HelloWorld</filename>
    <name>Hello World</name>
    <description>An AIR app to say Hello</description>

    <initialWindow>
        <content>HelloWorld.swf</content>
        <title>Hello World</title>
        <systemChrome>standard</systemChrome>
        <transparent>false</transparent>
        <visible>true</visible>
    </initialWindow>
```

```
        <installFolder>AIRCMR/HelloWorld</installFolder>
        <programMenuFolder>AIRCMR</programMenuFolder>
    </application>
```

2. Save the file as `HelloWorld-app.xml` in the project directory you previously set up — `C:\Development\AIR\HelloWorld` or `/Development/AIR/HelloWorld`, Windows and Mac, respectively. Create a new document and enter the following:

```
<?xml version="1.0" encoding="utf-8"?>
<mx:WindowedApplication
    xmlns:mx="http://www.adobe.com/2006/mxml"
    layout="vertical"
    windowComplete="completeHandler();">

    <mx:Script>
        <![CDATA[

            // window has completed initial layout and is made visible.
            private function completeHandler():void
            {
            }

        ]]>
    </mx:Script>

    <mx:Label text="Hello World" />

</mx:WindowedApplication>
```

3. Save the file as `HelloWorld.mxml` in the project directory along with `HelloWorld-app.xml`.

The first snippet, saved as `HelloWorld-app.xml`, is the descriptor file for the *Hello World* application. Although the descriptor file is not needed to compile a SWF using the `amxmlc` compiler, it is necessary for debugging and previewing, as well as packaging the application for installation. The descriptor file specifies properties associated with the AIR application. It contains values that will be displayed during installation, and data to be displayed by the operating system after installation. The descriptor file also allows you to customize the appearance of the AIR application chrome — or visual display window — within the `<initialWindow>` element node. The properties defined in this example are only a subset of those available. Many are optional and have been left out. Subsequent chapters use them as they pertain to the specific applications you will be building.

The `application` tag is the root tag for the application descriptor file. The `xmlns` attribute is the URI reference for the AIR namespace. The last segment of the namespace (1.0) is the runtime version required to run the AIR application. The required child elements of the root application tag are `id`, `filename`, `version`, and parent `initialWindow`. The value of the `id` element must be unique — meaning no two AIR applications installed on your machine can share the same application ID. As such, best practice is to use a dot-delimited reverse-DNS-style string as an identifier. Supported characters for `id` include 0–9, a–z, A–Z, dot, and hyphen. Any special characters (aside from dot and hyphen), including spaces, will throw an Invalid Application error upon launch of the AIR application. For this example, the unique ID is given the value `com.aircmr.HelloWorld`, as it relates to the examples found in the code for this chapter on the accompanying website.

The `filename` element reflects the name given to the application and is displayed as the value for "Application name" within the installer window. With the optional `programMenuFolder` property set in the descriptor file, the filename will also be displayed within the subpath of the Windows Start ➪ Programs menu.

The `version` attribute is an application-defined designator and does not relate to the version of AIR. Its value is specified by the developer, and typically conforms to the standard `MajorVersion.MinorVersion` form. Within this example, the `version` value is `0.1`.

The `initialWindow` element has various optional child elements pertaining to the properties applied to the initial application window. Properties, such as positioning and size, are applied as children of the `initialWindow` node, but most have a default value and are considered optional. The `title`, `systemChrome`, `transparent`, and `visible` properties are all optional but are included in this example with their default values because they are frequently used to customize the visual aspects of your application. The only required property of `initialWindow` is the `content` element. The value for `content` is the URL of the SWF file generated when you compile your application.

The `name`, `description`, `installationFolder`, and `programMenuFolder` properties are all optional. The `description` value is displayed within the installation window. The `name` value appears in the title of the installation window; it is the application name available in the uninstall panel and is the name given to the installation folder. The `installFolder` element's value specifies the installation location of the application within the application directory of your operating system — `C:\Program Files` on Windows and `HD name/Applications` on Mac OS X. The `programMenuFolder` is the subpath displayed in the Windows Start ➪ Programs menu, where the application can be found under the value of `filename`. This setting is ignored by any operating system other than Windows. The `installFolder` and `programMenuFolder` property values follow the same character restrictions as the file and folder naming conventions of your operating system.

Many more properties can be set in the application descriptor file that are specific to the operating system (such as associated file types) and the look and feel of your AIR application (such as icons). These are optional and will be addressed in applications throughout this book.

The second snippet you saved as `HelloWorld.mxml` is your main application file. This book does not cover the Flex language and MXML markup, but it does describe additions and changes to the Application Program Interface (API) that pertains to AIR. A good first start is the `WindowedApplication` container:

```
<mx:WindowedApplication
    xmlns:mx="http://www.adobe.com/2006/mxml"
    layout="vertical"
    windowComplete="completeHandler();">
```

The `WindowedApplication` tag defines the container for the application. Those familiar with the Flex language are used to defining `Application` as their application container. In fact, `WindowedApplication` extends the `Application` component. It has extra attributes that can be set in the descriptor file and overridden within this tag, as well as specified events and styles unique to `WindowedApplication`. The `windowComplete` event is one such unique event, which is dispatched when the window's initial layout is completed and made visible. The `completeHandler()` method within the `<mx:Script>` tag is the handler for this event. Currently, no operations are performed in this method, but one will be added when the ADL tool is discussed in the next section.

To top off this mug of magic, a `Label` component is included, with the `text` property set to `"Hello World"`:

```
<mx:Label text="Hello World" />
```

With the `layout` attribute of the `WindowedApplication` tag set to `"vertical"`, this label appears centered at the top of the container in the launched application. So far, discussion has concerned what will happen once the application is installed and running. Now it's time to launch it.

Compiling, Debugging, and Packaging

In the previous section you created the necessary files for compiling and previewing your application. In this section you will use the command-line tools provided in the Flex 3 SDK to compile, preview, and package your first AIR application.

Compiling

To compile the AIR application, use the `amxmlc` compiler found in the `/bin` folder where you installed the Flex 3 SDK — for the purposes of this example, that is `C:\flex_sdk_3\bin` on Windows and `/Applications/flex_sdk_3/bin` on Mac OS X. The `amxmlc` compiler invokes the `mxmlc` compiler with an additional parameter pointing to the `air-config.xml` file found in the `/frameworks` folder of your installation directory. Compiling a Flex application using the `mxmlc` utility will load the `flex-config.xml` configuration file. The difference between the two configuration files is the addition of SWC files related to AIR, including `airframework.swc` and `airoglobal.swc`. Take a look at the `air_config.xml` file within the `/frameworks` folder of your SDK installation directory. The `amxmlc` compiler tool defaults to using `air-config.xml`, but you may also specify your own configuration file by using the `-load-config` compiler option.

To generate the application SWF file, begin by opening a command prompt. Change the directory to the `HelloWorld` project directory — for this example, that location is `C:\Development\AIR\HelloWorld` on Windows and `/Development/AIR/HelloWorld` on Mac. Enter the following.

On Windows:

```
> amxmlc -load-config "C:\flex_sdk_3\frameworks\air-config.xml" -output
  HelloWorld.swf HelloWorld.mxml
```

On Mac:

```
> amxmlc -load-config "/Applications/flex_sdk_3/frameworks/air-config.xml" -output
  HelloWorld.swf HelloWorld.mxml
```

The `air-config.xml` option points to the location where you have installed the Flex 3 SDK. Compiling the application with `amxlmc` produces a SWF file and does not launch the application on your system. If you click on the SWF file created, you won't see anything except the default background color. That's because it is running in the Flash Player, not the AIR runtime. You will launch the application using the ADL executable file later in this section, as well as package the application for installation using the ADT. To perform these operations, however, you first needed to generate the SWF file of the application using the `amxmlc`.

Basic options were purposely included in the entered command, and in fact you could have entered `> amxmlc HelloWorld.mxml` and achieved the same result. For the purposes of this example, the `-load-config` and `-output` options are included, as they are common settings you might override during compilation of your application.

The `-benchmark` option can be added to display not only the operations that take place when generating a SWF file from the `amxmlc` compiler, but also the amount of time for each operation.

The `-load-config` option points to the configuration file to be read by the `amxmlc` compiler. It is included here to show that you can specify a different configuration file for your project. You also have the opportunity to add a custom configuration to the `air-config.xml` file by specifying the following:

```
-load-config+=myConfig.xml
```

The `-output` option specifies the SWF file to which the application is compiled. When this option is left out, the compiler defaults to naming the SWF file whatever the main MXML or ActionScript file supplied as the file parameter. For the purposes of this example, the generated SWF is `HelloWorld.swf`. Note that the name of the generated SWF file must match the value given to the `content` element of the application descriptor file. Therefore, if you override the default output, make sure that the name matches the SWF that will be run within the AIR runtime for your application.

Also available are a handful of other options, which mainly involve adding SWC files to the library path and including Runtime Shared Library (RSL) files. These are discussed as they relate to projects later in this book but have been left out of this simple example.

Previewing and Debugging

The SWF file was generated using the `amxml` compiler, yet you have seen that the application does not launch upon completion of that command, and opening the SWF file in the Flash Player does not display anything other than the background color of the movie. To launch and preview the application, run the AIR Debug Launcher (ADL) tool found in the `/bin` folder of your installation directory. A single argument of the application descriptor file is needed to run the ADL. If you look at the descriptor file (`HelloWorld-app.xml`), you'll notice that the `content` value of the `initialWindow` element is set to the SWF you previously compiled.

Open a command prompt, change the directory to the project development directory, enter the following command, and press Enter:

```
> adl HelloWorld-app.xml
```

Your launched application is now running within the AIR runtime. Everything looks perfect and you can see the text "Hello World" rendered in your label. You can run the ADL alone to preview your application, but in developing a more complex application, you need some support for debugging. The ADL has not been utilized to the potential from which its acronym is derived — AIR Debug Launcher. To do so, first add a `trace` statement to the `HelloWorld.mxml` main file and recompile with the `-debug` option set for the `amxmlc`.

1. Open `HelloWorld.mxml` in a text editor and add the following shaded line:

```
<?xml version="1.0" encoding="utf-8"?>
<mx:WindowedApplication
```

```
    xmlns:mx="http://www.adobe.com/2006/mxml"
    layout="vertical"
    windowComplete="completeHandler();">

    <mx:Script>
        <![CDATA[

            // window has completed initial layout and is made visible.
            private function completeHandler():void
            {
                trace( "Hello World!" );
            }

        ]]>
    </mx:Script>

    <mx:Label text="Hello World" />

</mx:WindowedApplication>
```

2. Save the file as `HelloWorld.mxml`. Open a command prompt and change the directory to the project development directory — for this example, that would be `C:\Development\AIR\HelloWorld` on Windows and `/Development/AIR/HelloWorld` on Mac. Enter the following and press Enter:

```
> amxmlc -debug HelloWorld.mxml
```

   In comparison to the previous `amxmlc` command, the `-load-config` and `-ouput` options were omitted but generate the same result. Also added was the `-debug` option to generate a SWF file that has debugging enabled. A SWF file with debugging enabled allows communication between the application and the Flash Debugger tool.

3. Before running the ADL again, you need to run the Flash Debugger (FDB) in order to view the `trace` statement you added to the main file (`HelloWorld.mxml`). The FDB command-line tool can be found in the `/bin` directory where you installed the Flex 3 SDK. Since you added a path to the `/bin` folder of the installation to the system variables earlier in this chapter, you only need to enter > **fdb** into the command prompt to start the debugger.

4. Open a separate command prompt and start the Flash Debugger by entering the following and pressing Enter:

```
> fdb
```

   The printout will end with the FDB display prompt `<fdb>`, meaning you have started the Flash Debugger and it is ready to be run and connected with a launched debug SWF file. Running the debugger enables you to see any `trace` statements you have in your ActionScript code output in the console. Numerous other commands can be performed by the FDB, including setting breakpoints and handling faults; enter the **help** in the console after the command prompt to view these options.

If the preceding operation resulted in output on the console that states

```
Error: could not find a JVM
```

then you will have to manually enter the directory in which Java is installed on your machine. To do so, open the `jvm.config` *file located in the* `/bin` *folder of your Flex 3 SDK installation directory. The first variable listed,* `java.home`*, needs to point to the location of your installed Java Virtual Machine. Following the equals sign (=), enter that location. For example, the JRE directory might be* `C:/Program Files/Java/jre`.

Windows users must use forward slashes or double back-slashes for the location. If you don't, then the error will be thrown again when you try to start the FDB.

5. To run the debugger, enter the command **run** in the console and press Enter:

```
<fdb> run
```

If you are prompted with a security alert requesting assistance regarding running the FDB, select Unblock from the options. The console will display "Waiting for Player to Connect."

6. Open a separate command prompt and change the directory to the project development environment. For the purposes of this example, that is `C:\Development\AIR\HelloWorld` on Windows and `/Development/AIR/HelloWorld` on Mac. Enter the following command and press Enter:

```
> adl HelloWorld-app.xml
```

7. Switch to the console in which you started the Flash Debugger. You will see that the Flash Player has connected and the debugger is waiting for additional commands to perform. Enter the following and press Enter:

```
<fdb> continue
```

This will launch the Hello World application and display the following within the console in which the FDB running:

```
Additional ActionScript code has been loaded from a SWF or a frame.
Set additional breakpoints as desired, and then type 'continue'.
```

8. Enter the **continue** command again and press Enter. The console will print out the `trace` statement you added to `HelloWorld.mxml`:

```
[trace] Hello World!
```

By launching the debug version of the application using the ADL, you can do simple debugging with `trace` statements and have the opportunity to have a more robust debugging platform by setting breakpoints and fault handling if necessary. To stop the Flash Debugger, select the command prompt in which it is running and press Ctrl+C on Windows or Q on Mac.

Packaging

At this point, the SWF file has been compiled for your AIR application and you have your descriptor file. You also ran a debug version through the FDB to ensure that everything is working correctly. Before proceeding with packaging your application, if you have created a debug SWF, you may want to run the `amxmlc` compiler again without the debug option to generate the SWF file to be included with the installer file.

Now all that is left is packaging the application into an AIR file for installation using the AIR Developer Tool (ADT). The ADT batch file can be found in the `/bin` folder or the AIR installation directory, and has commands to create and sign certificates and create AIR application installer files.

Preparing an AIR installer file is a multi-step process, as each application must be signed using a digital certificate. As mentioned earlier, you can sign your AIR application by linking a certificate from a certificate authority, such as VeriSign or Thawte, or you can use the ADT to create a self-signed certificate. Using a certificate from a recognized provider assures users that they are not installing a fraudulent copy of your AIR application. Using a self-signed certificate does not provide information verifying the identity of the signer, but for the purposes of the examples used throughout this book, the applications you build will use a self-signed certificate.

To create a certificate to be signed when packaging your application into an AIR installer file, open a command prompt and change the directory to that of the development folder for the Hello World project. Enter the following command and press Enter:

```
>adt -certificate -cn HelloWorld 1024-RSA certificate.pfx password
```

Included in this command to generate a certificate and associated private key is the common name, the key type to use for the certificate (either 1024-RSA or 2048-RSA), the path of the generated certificate file (using either the `.pfx` or `.p12` extension) and the password used when signing the AIR file. To learn about additional operational parameters you can add when using the ADT `-certificate` command (such as your organization name), refer to the AIR documentation or enter > **adt -help** at the command prompt.

The certificate and private key are stored in a PKCS12-type keystore file, which is used to sign and package an AIR file using the `-package` command of the ADT tool.

With a command prompt open and pointing to the HelloWorld project development folder, enter the following command and press Enter:

```
> adt -package -storetype pkcs12 -keystore certificate.pfx HelloWorld.air
   HelloWorld-app.xml HelloWorld.swf
```

The `-storetype` parameter value is the version of the PKCS (Public Key Cryptography Standards) standard for storing private keys and certificates. The container, or keystore — created in the previous `-certificate` command and provided here as `certificate.pfx` for the `-keystore` parameter — is encrypted with a password. When you run the `-package` command, you will be prompted to enter the password you supplied when creating the certificate.

Following the signing options of the `-package` command is the name of the generated AIR file, the application descriptor file, and the application SWF file. Along with the application SWF file, you can specify additional space-delimited files and directories to be added to your build. Additional values (delimited by spaces) could include any icon files or embedded media you may need packaged with your application. The files and directories, however, need to reside in the current directory or any subdirectories in which the ADT is run. As such, you can use the `-C` option to change the directory for included files.

For example, you may have the following folder structure within the HelloWorld project:

```
/assets
   /images
      HelloWorld.png
/bin
   HelloWorld.swf
```

By running the following command using the -C option, you can include those files in your build:

```
>adt - package -storetype pkcs12 -keystore certificate.pfx HelloWorld.air
   HelloWorld-app.xml -C ./bin HelloWorld.swf -C ./assets/images HelloWorld.png
```

Relative paths between the current directory and the specified files in the directory paths using the -C option will keep their structure within the installation folder. For example, specifying `-C modules/module.swf` will place the `module.swf` file in a subdirectory titled `modules` within the application directory. All files not specified using a relative path will be included at the root of the package directory. If you prefer to have a specific directory structure within the application directory, then the -e command-line option is available, which enables you to place a file in a specified directory.

Whether you choose to specify the package file using the -C option or not, if all goes well, after running this command and entering your password, an AIR installer file named `HelloWorld.air` will be generated in your project directory.

Installing and Uninstalling

Installing an AIR application is as easy as double-clicking the AIR installer file. This section will show you how to install the Hello World application and explain what happens at the system level when an application is installed. You will also learn how to uninstall an AIR application, and the results of doing so.

Installing the Hello World Application

Double click on the `HelloWorld.air` file you generated previously, found in its usual location. Upon double-clicking the AIR file, the dialog shown in Figure 1-1 will be presented.

In the installer window shown in Figure 1-1, you will see the application name you specified in the `filename` element of your `HelloWorld-app.xml` descriptor file. You are also presented with the options to Install or Cancel. By clicking the Install button, the dialog shown in Figure 1-2 is displayed.

The title and description displayed in Figure 1-2 are the values specified for the `name` element and the `description` element in the application descriptor file, respectively.

You are presented with the option to cancel the installation again, but roll the dice and click Continue. The window will briefly display a progress bar, indicating the installation process. If you have chosen to start the application after installation, then when the installation has finished you will see the screen shown in Figure 1-3.

Amazing, right?

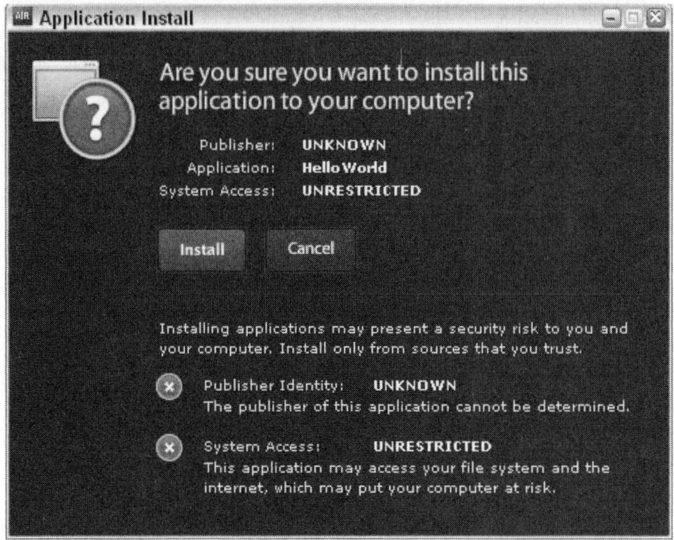

Figure 1-1

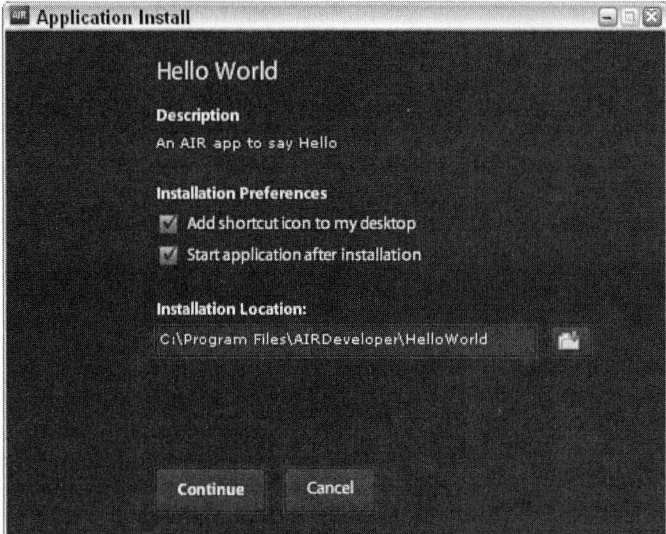

Figure 1-2

While waiting for the money to roll in, peruse the next sections, which cover what occurs during installation of an AIR application on your machine.

On Windows and Mac OS:

- Installs the application in the programs directory of your operating system. A directory is created using the path specified for the `installFolder`, and the application folder is titled after the `name` value specified in the application descriptor. This is known as the *application directory* and is accessed using the `File` class from the AIR API, as you will see in the examples throughout this book. For the example in this chapter, you will find the application installation at `C:\Program Files\AIRCMR\HelloWorld\Hello World` on Windows and `HD/Applications/AIRCMR/HelloWorld` on Mac OS X.

- Creates a directory for application storage titled after the value for the `id` element in the application descriptor file. Created within this directory is a folder titled `Local Store`. This is known as the *application storage directory* and is accessed using the `File` class from the AIR API. For the example in this chapter, you will find the storage directory at `C:\Documents and Settings\<user>\Application Data\com.aircmr. HelloWorld` on Windows and `Users/<user>/Library/Preferences/com.aircmr. HelloWorld` on Mac OS.
- Adds a shortcut on your Desktop named after the `filename` element in the descriptor file if you opted to create one from the installation window.

Figure 1-3

On Windows only:

- Adds the application to the Start menu under `AIRCMR/HelloWorld` — the values supplied for the `programMenuFolder` and `filename`, respectively.
- Adds the application titled Hello World — the value supplied as the `name` in the descriptor file — in the Add or Remove Programs list available in the Control Panel.

Navigate to the installation folder. On a Mac, Ctrl+click on the Hello World application and select Show Package Contents from the menu. In the root of this directory are the files specified in the parameters for the ADT when you packaged the AIR file. Also within this directory is the application's executable file and the application descriptor file, which has been renamed to `application.xml` and placed within the `META_INF/AIR` subdirectory.

The *application directory* and *application storage directory* can be referenced using the `File` class of the AIR API. These directories each serve their own purpose in creating and accessing resources for your applications at runtime, a topic discussed later in this book.

Uninstalling the Hello World Application

Why uninstall the Hello World application? Because you live on the edge, and you want to save that disk space for something grander. Fortunately enough, if you want to reinstall it, the AIR file is still available in the project's development directory.

To uninstall an AIR application on Windows, follow these steps:

1. Click Start ➪ Control Panel ➪ Add or Remove Programs.
2. Within the entry list, scroll to the AIR application you wish to uninstall and click once to select it.
3. Click the Remove button. Doing so will remove the installation directory from Program Files and remove the Desktop and Start Menu shortcuts you may have opted to create during the installation process.

To uninstall an AIR application on a Mac, all you have to do is drag the installation folder to the Trash and then empty the Trash.

Uninstalling the application removes the application directory and any ancillary files you opted to create through the installation window. Uninstalling with these processes does not, however, remove the application storage directory or any files created and associated with the application after installation.

Good-bye, Hello World! You are now armed with the tools and knowledge to start building and distributing AIR applications. You also have a structured development environment to make that process run smoothly.

The next section addresses adding improvements to the development process by introducing an Apache ANT build scheme and a simple debug panel available from the code examples for this chapter on the accompanying website.

Extra Tools

Some developers are just too busy to type multiple options into a command line. To automate the processes of deploying, debugging, and packaging discussed previously in this chapter, consider using Apache ANT, a popular tool for that purpose and a perfect fit for your build process, as it is cross-platform and requires Java, which is already on your machine. If you are more comfortable using another tool for automating the build process, you are encouraged to do so. However, if you are interested in setting up a build process through ANT, the following section will walk you through that process.

You may also find that running the Flash Debugger each time you launch an application to debug code can present a time-consuming obstacle within your development. As such, the concept of a simple debug panel that communicates to an AIR application using the `LocalConnection` class of the API is discussed. The code for the simple debug panel and the ANT build file can be found in the code examples for this chapter on the accompanying website.

ANT Build

A few chapters could easily be devoted to ANT alone, but in keeping with AIR application development, this section provides a brief overview of ANT build markup and not necessarily the intricate workings of the tool. Although this solution is presented to you for ease of development, this might not be your cup of tea. Thus, all examples within this book have been run using the command-line tools described previously in this chapter.

Apache ANT (from here on referred to as ANT) is a Java tool that uses XML markup to describe tasks and dependencies in automating the software build process. If you currently do not have ANT installed on your computer, then you will need to install it. Download the latest distribution from `http://ant.apache.org/bindownload.cgi`.

Install ANT in a directory that makes sense with your workflow — for example, `C:/ant-` on Windows. You will also need to add a path to your ANT installation within the Environment Variables.

> *If you work on a Mac, then you may already have ANT installed. Open a Terminal and type >* ***ant -version****. If you are presented with a "command not found" message, then either you don't have ANT installed on your machine or you don't have a path to the installation* `/bin` *directory set. If this is the case, then install ANT in the* `/usr/local` *directory and perform the following steps.*

To add a path to your ANT installation on Windows, follow these steps:

1. Click Start ➪ Control Panel ➪ System.
2. Select the Advanced tab from the menu.
3. Click on Environment Variables.
4. Within the System variables grid, navigate to and double-click on Path.
5. In the Variable Value field, add a semicolon (;) and then the path to the `/bin` folder within your ANT installation directory. For the purposes of this example, that is `;C:\ant\bin`.

Follow these steps to add a path to your ANT installation on Mac:

1. Open the terminal and type **open -e .profile**.
2. Add a colon (:) and the path to the `/bin` folder within your ANT installation directory. For the purposes of this example, that is `/usr/local/ant/bin`.

Running ANT from the command line requires a build file within the directory in which it is called. The ANT build file is an XML markup describing tasks and dependencies for the build process. Property values can also be set in the build file, enabling you to refer to the value of a property using the `${propertyname}` construct within tasks. A property file can also be set in the build file to separate out the property-value pairs from the build markup.

First create the build file as it relates to the Hello World application you built previously in this chapter:

1. Enter the following markup in any text editor:

```
<?xml version="1.0" encoding="utf-8"?>
<!-- ================================================================== -->
<!-- AIR Application Build File (Ant)                                   -->
<!-- ================================================================== -->

<project name="AIR Application" default="main" basedir=".">

    <property name="app.name" value="HelloWorld" />
    <property name="desc.name" value="HelloWorld-app" />
```

```
<property name="store.type" value="pkcs12" />
<property name="cert.type" value="1024-RSA" />
<property name="cert.name" value="certificate.pfx" />
<property name="cert.pass" value="password" />

<property name="src.dir" value="." />
<property name="deploy.dir" value="." />

<target name="main" depends="init,taskInput,compile,launch,package" />

<target name="init" description="Sets properties based on OS.">
    <condition property="amxmlc.exec" value="amxmlc.bat">
        <os family="windows" />
    </condition>
    <condition property="amxmlc.exec" value="amxmlc">
        <os family="mac" />
    </condition>
    <condition property="adt.jar" value="C:/flex_sdk_3/lib/adt.jar">
        <os family="windows" />
    </condition>
    <condition property="adt.jar" value="/Applications/flex_sdk_3/lib/adt.jar">
        <os family="mac" />
    </condition>
</target>

<target name="taskInput" description="Presents task options.">
    <input message="Please select a task..." validargs="compile,launch,package"
        addproperty="task.action" />
    <condition property="do.compile" value="true">
        <or>
            <equals arg1="${task.action}" arg2="compile" />
            <equals arg1="${task.action}" arg2="launch" />
            <equals arg1="${task.action}" arg2="package" />
        </or>
    </condition>
    <condition property="do.launch" value="true">
        <equals arg1="${task.action}" arg2="launch" />
    </condition>
    <condition property="do.package" value="true">
        <equals arg1="${task.action}" arg2="package" />
    </condition>
</target>

<target name="compile" depends="taskInput" description="Generates SWF.">
    <exec executable="${amxmlc.exec}">
        <arg line="-output ${deploy.dir}/${app.name}.swf" />
        <arg line="${src.dir}/${app.name}.mxml" />
    </exec>
</target>

<target name="launch" if="do.launch" depends="compile"
    description="Launmches application.">
    <exec executable="adl">
        <arg line="${deploy.dir}/${desc.name}.xml"/>
```

```
        </exec>
    </target>

    <target name="package" if="do.package" depends="compile"
        description="Packages AIR application.">
        <antcall target="create.certificate" />
        <java jar="${adt.jar}" fork="true" failonerror="true"
            inputstring="${cert.pass}">
            <arg value="-package" />
            <arg value="-storetype" />
            <arg value="${store.type}" />
            <arg value="-keystore" />
            <arg value="${cert.name}" />
            <arg value="${app.name}.air" />
            <arg value="${desc.name}.xml" />
            <arg value="${app.name}.swf" />
        </java>
    </target>

    <target name="create.certificate" if="do.package"
        description="Creates self signed certificate.">
        <java jar="${adt.jar}" fork="true" failonerror="true">
            <arg value="-certificate" />
            <arg value="-cn" />
            <arg value="${app.name}" />
            <arg value="${cert.type}" />
            <arg value="${cert.name}" />
            <arg value="${cert.pass}" />
        </java>
    </target>

</project>
```

2. Save the file as `build.xml` in the development directory of the Hello World project.

Three main execution tasks are associated with the ANT build file: `compile`, `launch`, and `package`. The type of task to run depends on the user input of the `taskInput` task. The `compile` task is always called, as the success of the `launch` and `package` tasks depends on the existence of a generated SWF file.

Along with these three main tasks that can be run based upon input is a task to create a self-signed certificate prior to packaging, and a task to set property values based on the operating system. The `init` task is run in order to set the OS-specific properties needed for running the command-line tools of the Flex 3 SDK. To run a `.bat` file within the `exec` ANT task on Windows, the extension needs to be included. On Mac OS X, the name of the file is sufficient. In order to run the ADT using the `java` directive, the path to the `.jar` file is needed. As such, a `condition` task is run to evaluate the correct path based on your operating system.

To run this build, open a command prompt, navigate to the development directory, and enter the following command:

```
>ant
```

After running this command, you will be prompted to input the task you wish to perform — `compile`, `launch`, or `package`. Each task will generate a SWF file. If you choose the `launch` task, the AIR application will then be run using the AIR Debug Launcher (ADL). If you choose to package your AIR application, then after the `package` task is complete, you will find a `certificat.pfx` file and a `HelloWorld.air` file within the development directory.

The property settings in this build file are pretty basic and may not suit larger projects. Play around with your own build file as it suits your needs per project. These files can be moved from one development directory to the next without affecting the automation process, though it is recommended that you change any application-specific property values.

Simple Debug Panel

If your debugging tasks are simply logging- or trace-related and don't rely on stepping through breakpoints or handling faults, then you may find it difficult to find the time to open a separate command prompt to launch the Flash Debugger. Creating a simple debug panel to handle all your `trace` statements would be an excellent example of an AIR application that is quick to create and extremely handy when it comes time to debug any of your other AIR applications.

Take what you have learned from this chapter and make your own simple debug panel — in fact, one is available in the code examples for this chapter on the accompanying website. The source is included and you may modify the code as you see fit. One possible addition is a write-to-log feature if you are feeling adventurous. The SimpleDebugPanel application does not employ anything specific to the AIR API and uses `LocalConnection` to pass logging statements from your application to the debug panel running under the AIR runtime. The `README` file included in the directory outlines correct usage in your applications, as you need to add some class files to your projects in order for the debug panel to receive log statements.

Summary

In this chapter you built your first AIR project, a simple Hello World application, and learned about the command-line tools provided in the AIR SDK installation. Also included in this chapter were some time-saving solutions for building and debugging applications. In the following chapters you will build applications that are practical in real-world scenarios — and, it is hoped, have some fun while doing so.

2

Simple Text Editor

With any new technology that has a file system API, you're probably wondering just how you would read and write files to your hard drive. There is probably no better way to learn this than to write the most versatile program of all time: The Almighty Text Editor. Granted, everyone has their own favorite text editing program that they've been using for years, especially if you're any sort of developer. The text editor you'll develop in this chapter is by no means a program that will replace your existing text editor, but perhaps it will be the start of your own customized text editor that you later extend with all the wonderful functionality that your current text editor is missing!

This program illustrates a few important things about the AIR file system API. First you're going to work with the `File` object to point to files on your hard drive. The chapter then covers how to use the `FileStream` and `FileMode` classes to read from and write to a file (in this case, text files). Lastly, you will learn how to use the `FileFilter` class to limit the types of files the user is allowed to open.

The Text Editor

A text editor is one of the simplest programs you could write, especially within the Flex and AIR frameworks. The reason it is so simple is that it essentially performs only two tasks: open or read a file and save or write a file. Aside from those tasks, you will dress it up with a light interface and a few accessory methods so you can perform actions such as New Document and Save As. The view, or display, of the program is simply a menu that enables you to perform these methods, and an area in which to edit the text. It really is that simple.

The View

Within your development directory create a folder titled "Simple Text Editor." This will be your working directory for this program. Because this application is so simple, start with the view just to get it out of the way:

1. Open your editor, create a new document, and enter the following:

```
<?xml version="1.0" encoding="UTF-8"?>
<application xmlns="http://ns.adobe.com/air/application/1.0">
    <id>com.aircmr.simpletexteditor</id>
    <name>SimpleTextEditor</name>
    <filename>SimpleTextEditor</filename>
    <version>v1</version>
    <initialWindow>
        <content>SimpleTextEditor.swf</content>
        <title>Text Editor</title>
    </initialWindow>
</application>
```

2. Save the file as `SimpleTextEditor-app.xml` in the working directory. Create another new document and enter the following:

```
<?xml version="1.0" encoding="utf-8"?>
<mx:WindowedApplication xmlns:mx="http://www.adobe.com/2006/mxml"
    layout="absolute" width="800" height="600" title="Text Editor"
    applicationComplete="onAppInit();" >

    <mx:Script><![CDATA[

    public function onAppInit():void
    {
        title = "Text Editor - Untitled.txt";
        defaultFile = File.documentsDirectory.resolvePath( "untitled.txt" );
        textChanged = false;

        application.addEventListener( KeyboardEvent.KEY_UP, onKeyUp );
    }

    ]]></mx:Script>
    <mx:MenuBar id="myMenuBar" labelField="@label"
                left="0" top="0" right="0" tabEnabled="false"
                itemClick="onItemClick(event);" >
        <mx:XMLList>
            <menuitem label="File" >
                <menuitem label="New"/>
                <menuitem label="Open"/>
                <menuitem label="Save"/>
                <menuitem label="Save As..."/>
            </menuitem>
        </mx:XMLList>
    </mx:MenuBar>
```

```
    <mx:TextArea id="fileTextArea"
        top="21" left="0" right="0" bottom="0"
        focusThickness="0" fontFamily="Arial"
        fontSize="14" tabEnabled="false"
        change="textChanged=true;" />
</mx:WindowedApplication>
```

3. Save the file as `SimpleTextEditor.mxml` in the working directory.

In the first step, you created `SimpleTextEditor-app.xml`, your application descriptor file. You should be familiar with what this file is for. If not, then you can refer to the Hello World example in Chapter 1.

You also created what is now the start of the main application file. This would, of course, be the file saved as `SimpleTextEditor.mxml`. Like the Hello World example, you started with the `Apollo-Application` component. The only difference here is that you set the `width` and `height` attributes so that the application window will initialize at a slightly larger size.

You also set up the visual part of the application by using two Flex components: `MenuBar` and `TextArea`. Specifically, you set up a `MenuBar` that sits at the top and stretches the width of the application window, similar to that of a Windows application. The `MenuBar` has also been populated with one menu set that contains text representations of basic commands needed for the text editor. Along with the menu, you also added a `TextArea` component, which sits below the menu and stretches the width and remaining height of the application window. This component enables you to populate it with the text, and input text so you can edit text files.

You can compile the code at this time to see just what the components look like and how they behave. To do this, open a command prompt and change to the application's working directory. Enter the following command and press Enter:

```
> amxmlc SimpleTextEditor.mxml
```

The application is now compiled as an `.swf` file. In order to run it, enter the following command and press Enter:

```
> adl SimpleTextEditor-app.xml
```

The application will launch and should look like Figure 2-1.

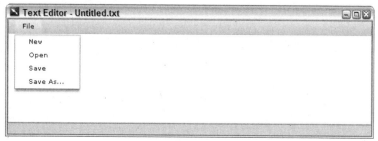

Figure 2-1

Some attributes of the components have been set to make the application behave less like a web application and more like a desktop application. You'll notice that the `tabEnabled` attribute of each component is set to `false`. This has been done so a user cannot gain focus of either of the components by pressing the Tab key. This would be detrimental, especially if someone wanted to insert a Tab character into their text file. Note also that the `focusThickness` of the `TextArea` component has been set to `0`. By default, the `TextArea` component will become highlighted with a slight outer glow. In this case, it doesn't make sense to have this appear, and you can't even see the entire glow when the component is stretched to the edges of the window.

The Logic

As mentioned earlier, the program should perform two basic tasks: saving and reading a text file. You might initially assume that you'll need a way to browse the hard drive for files to open, and browse it for a place to save a file. Luckily, AIR provides a very easy method for integrating with the user's operating system to perform such a task. Thus, you won't have to create any special components; everything can be handled in just one `.mxml` file.

The Basics

Open `SimpleTextEditor.mxml` in your editor if it is not open already. Make the following changes and additions to the markup:

```
<?xml version="1.0" encoding="utf-8"?>
<mx:WindowedApplication xmlns:mx="http://www.adobe.com/2006/mxml"
    layout="absolute" width="800" height="600" title="Text Editor"
    applicationComplete="onAppInit();" >

    <mx:Script><![CDATA[

    import flash.events.KeyboardEvent;
    import flash.filesystem.File;
    import flash.filesystem.FileMode;
    import flash.filesystem.FileStream;
    import flash.net.FileFilter;
    import mx.controls.Alert;
    import mx.events.CloseEvent;
    import mx.events.MenuEvent;

    private var browseHolder:File;
    private var currentFile:File;
    private var defaultFile:File;
    private var fileStream:FileStream;
    private var fileToOpen:File;
    private var fileToSave:File;
    private var textChanged:Boolean;
    public function onAppInit():void
    {
        title = "Text Editor - Untitled.txt";
        defaultFile = File.documentsDirectory.resolvePath( "untitled.txt" );
        textChanged = false;
```

```
        application.addEventListener( KeyboardEvent.KEY_UP, onKeyUp );     }
    private function onKeyUp( event:KeyboardEvent ):void
    {
        if( event.keyCode == Keyboard.TAB && !event.altKey &&
           !event.shiftKey && !event.ctrlKey )
        {
            var sb:Number = fileTextArea.selectionBeginIndex;
            var se:Number = fileTextArea.selectionEndIndex;

            var firstPart:String = fileTextArea.text.slice(0, sb);
            var secondPart:String = fileTextArea.text.slice( se );

            fileTextArea.text = firstPart + "\t" + secondPart;
        }
    }
    private function onItemClick( event:MenuEvent ):void
    {

    }

         ]]>
    </mx:Script>
    <mx:MenuBar id="myMenuBar" labelField="@label" left="0" top="0" right="0"
       tabEnabled="false" itemClick="onItemClick(event);" >
        <mx:XMLList>
            <menuitem label="File" >
                <menuitem label="New"/>
                <menuitem label="Open"/>
                <menuitem label="Save"/>
                <menuitem label="Save As..."/>
            </menuitem>
        </mx:XMLList>     <mx:TextArea id="fileTextArea"
        top="21" left="0" right="0" bottom="0"
        focusThickness="0" fontFamily="Arial"
        fontSize="14" tabEnabled="false"
        change="textChanged=true;" />

</mx:WindowedApplication>
```

This step does a few things to the application. First, it imports all the classes you'll need, most notably the `File`, `FileMode`, and `FileStream` classes from the AIR file system package. More important, and directly after that, a few variables for the application are set up:

```
import flash.events.KeyboardEvent;
import flash.filesystem.File;
import flash.filesystem.FileMode;
import flash.filesystem.FileStream;
import mx.controls.Alert;
import mx.events.CloseEvent;
```

```
import mx.events.FileEvent;
import mx.events.MenuEvent;

private var currentFile:File;
private var defaultFile:File;
private var fileStream:FileStream;
private var textChanged:Boolean;
```

First the variable named `currentFile`, which is of type `File`, is created. A `File` object represents a path to a file or folder. In this case, `currentFile` will represent a path to the current file the user has opened in the text editor. `File` objects are wonderful because they can also represent a path to a file or folder that does not exist yet. In other words, it can represent a file or folder you want to create at some later point. For instance, a variable named `defaultFile`, which is also of type `File`, is also created. This variable will represent the default file that a user is prompted to save if the user has not yet opened a text file.

You also need a `FileStream` object, which enables you to read and write data. Finally, in order to prevent a user from discarding changes, you created a simple `Boolean` variable named `textChanged`. Now that the application variables are set up, you can move on to the `onAppInit` function:

```
public function onAppInit():void
{
        title = "Text Editor - Untitled.txt";
        defaultFile = File.documentsDirectory.resolvePath( "untitled.txt" );
        textChanged = false;
        application.addEventListener( KeyboardEvent.KEY_UP, onKeyUp );
}
```

This snippet does something a little fun, at least in terms of using AIR for the first time. The `defaultFile` is set as a reference to a file named `untitled.txt` within the user's documents directory. The `File` class has a few static variables that come in very handy when developing AIR applications. In this case, you're using the static variable named `documentsDirectory`. This variable is of type `File` and holds a reference to a user's documents directory. On a Windows machine, it would most likely refer to the folder `C:\Documents and Settings\User_Name\My Documents`, and on an OS X machine it would refer to the folder `/Users/User_Name/Documents`. You've also taken advantage of the `resolvePath` method of a `File` object — specifically, `documentsDirectory`,. The `resolvePath` method creates a new `File` object with a path that is relative to its own. How handy (and thus fun) is that?

The next couple of lines are pretty simple. First, `textChanged` is set to `false` because no text has been changed yet. Second, an event listener was added to handle keyboard input. As mentioned earlier, the `tabEnabled` attribute of the Flex components is set to `false` to prevent the user from being able to tab out of the text area. It's an unfortunate thing to have to code around, but the text editor should behave like a text editor, not a web application. Thus, in the `onKeyUp()` event handler, there is some code that manually inserts a tab character into the text area whenever the user presses the Tab key.

The last bit of additions was made to the Flex components. An event listener was added to the `MenuBar` component to handle its `itemClick` event, and the `textChanged` variable is set to `false` when the `TextArea` component's text is changed. You could compile the code as it is now, but the following sections move on to the good stuff.

Reading and Writing Files

In your editor, make the following additions to `SimpleTextEditor.mxml`:

```
<?xml version="1.0" encoding="utf-8"?>
<mx:WindowedApplication xmlns:mx="http://www.adobe.com/2006/mxml"
    layout="absolute" width="800" height="600" title="Text Editor"
    applicationComplete="onAppInit();" >

    <mx:Script><![CDATA[

    import flash.events.KeyboardEvent;
    import flash.filesystem.File;
    import flash.filesystem.FileMode;
    import flash.filesystem.FileStream;
    import flash.net.FileFilter;
    import mx.controls.Alert;
    import mx.events.CloseEvent;
    import mx.events.MenuEvent;

    private var browseHolder:File;
    private var currentFile:File;
    private var defaultFile:File;
    private var fileStream:FileStream;
    private var fileToOpen:File;
    private var fileToSave:File;
    private var textChanged:Boolean;

    public function onAppInit():void
    {
        title = "Text Editor - Untitled.txt";
        defaultFile = File.documentsDirectory.resolvePath( "untitled.txt" );
        textChanged = false;
        application.addEventListener( KeyboardEvent.KEY_UP, onKeyUp );
    }

    private function onKeyUp( event:KeyboardEvent ):void
    {
        if( event.keyCode == Keyboard.TAB && !event.altKey && !event.shiftKey &&
            !event.ctrlKey )
        {
            var sb:Number = fileTextArea.selectionBeginIndex;
            var se:Number = fileTextArea.selectionEndIndex;

            var firstPart:String = fileTextArea.text.slice(0, sb);
            var secondPart:String = fileTextArea.text.slice( se );

            fileTextArea.text = firstPart + "\t" + secondPart;
        }
    }     private function onItemClick( event:MenuEvent ):void
    {

    }
```

```
s    private function onOpenComplete( event:Event ):void
     {
         var theText:String = fileStream.readUTFBytes( fileStream.
            bytesAvailable );
         var lineEndPattern:RegExp = new RegExp( File.lineEnding, "g" );

         fileTextArea.text = theText.replace( lineEndPattern, "\n" );
         textChanged = false;
         title = "Text Editor - " + currentFile.name;
         fileStream.close();
     }

     private function onReadIOError( event:IOErrorEvent ):void
     {
         Alert.show("The specified file cannot be opened.", "Error", Alert.OK,
            this);
     }

     private function onWriteIOError( event:IOErrorEvent ):void
     {
         Alert.show("The specified file cannot be saved.", "Error", Alert.OK,
            this);
     }
```

```
     private function openFile():void
     {
         if( fileStream != null )
         {
             fileStream.close();
         }

         fileStream = new FileStream();
         fileStream.addEventListener( Event.COMPLETE, onOpenComplete );
         fileStream.addEventListener( IOErrorEvent.IO_ERROR, onReadIOError );
         fileStream.openAsync( currentFile, FileMode.READ );
     }    private function saveFile():void
     {
         if( currentFile )
         {
             if( fileStream != null )
             {
                 fileStream.close();
             }

             var theText:String = fileTextArea.text;
             theText = theText.replace( /\r/g, "\n" );
             theText = theText.replace( /\n/g, File.lineEnding );

             fileStream = new FileStream();
             fileStream.openAsync( currentFile, FileMode.WRITE );
             fileStream.addEventListener( IOErrorEvent.IO_ERROR,
                onWriteIOError );
             fileStream.writeUTFBytes( theText );
```

```
                fileStream.close();

                textChanged = false;
            }
            else
            {
                promptUserToSaveFile();
            }
        }

        private function saveFile():void
        {
            if( currentFile )
            {
                if( fileStream != null )
                {
                    fileStream.close();
                }

                var theText:String = fileTextArea.text;
                theText = theText.replace( /\r/g, "\n" );
                theText = theText.replace( /\n/g, File.lineEnding );

                fileStream = new FileStream();
                fileStream.openAsync( currentFile, FileMode.WRITE );
                fileStream.addEventListener( IOErrorEvent.IO_ERROR,
                   onWriteIOError );
                fileStream.writeUTFBytes( theText );
                fileStream.close();
                textChanged = false;
            }
            else
            {
                promptUserToSaveFile();
            }
        }    ]]>
    </mx:Script>
        <mx:MenuBar id="myMenuBar" labelField="@label"
                    left="0" top="0" right="0" tabEnabled="false"
                    itemClick="onItemClick(event);" >
            <mx:XMLList>
                <menuitem label="File" >
                    <menuitem label="New"/>
                    <menuitem label="Open"/>
                    <menuitem label="Save"/>
                    <menuitem label="Save As..."/>
                </menuitem>
            </mx:XMLList>
        </mx:MenuBar>
        <mx:TextArea id="fileTextArea"
            top="21" left="0" right="0" bottom="0"
            focusThickness="0" fontFamily="Arial"
            fontSize="14" tabEnabled="false"
            change="textChanged=true;" />
    </mx:WindowedApplication>
```

This is where the real fun begins! Looking at what you just added, note that five new functions were included in the application. These functions are the meat and potatoes of the application because they perform all the hard stuff (and really, it isn't all that hard). Examine the first function, `openFile()`:

```
private function openFile():void
{
    if( fileStream != null )
    {
        fileStream.close();
    }

    fileStream = new FileStream();
    fileStream.addEventListener( Event.COMPLETE, onOpenComplete );
    fileStream.addEventListener( IOErrorEvent.IO_ERROR, onReadIOError );
    fileStream.openAsync( currentFile, FileMode.READ );
}
```

The `openFile()` function is where the `currentFile` will be opened. Before going anywhere, the first conditional statement checks whether the `fileStream` object is defined. If it is defined, then the `close()` method of the `fileStream` object is called to close the connection with the current file. This is merely a safeguard.

Once you pass this condition, the `fileStream` object is recreated. The new instance is then configured with two event listeners. The first event listener listens for a `COMPLETE` event of type `Event`. This event simply indicates when all the data from the file has been read into the input buffer. When this event is dispatched, the `onOpenComplete()` function is called. This function is examined very shortly. The second event listener listens for an `IO_ERROR` event of type `IOErrorEvent`. An `IOErrorEvent` is dispatched by the `fileStream` object whenever an error causes a read or write operation to fail. If and when this event is dispatched, the `onReadIOError()` function will be called. The `onReadIOError()` function simply alerts the user with a message that something has gone awry while reading the file.

After the event listeners are all set up, the `openAsync()` method of the `fileStream` object can be called. The `openAsync()` method requires two parameters: a `File` object and a string that specifies the mode in which you want the `fileStream` object to behave — in this case, passing the `currentFile` variable and using the public static variable `READ` from the `FileMode` class to specify the mode. The `openAsync()` method opens the specified file asynchronously, which means that the file's data is immediately read into the input buffer and the following code will continue to execute.

The `openFile()` function is now complete, so it is time to get at what you really want: the text. Take a look at the `onOpenComplete()` function that is called when all of the file's data has been received by the input buffer:

```
private function onOpenComplete( event:Event ):void
{
    var theText:String = fileStream.readUTFBytes( fileStream.bytesAvailable );
    var lineEndPattern:RegExp = new RegExp( File.lineEnding, "g" );

    fileTextArea.text = theText.replace( lineEndPattern, "\n" );
```

```
        textChanged = false;
        title = "Text Editor - " + currentFile.name;

        fileStream.close();
    }
```

The onOpenComplete() function is pretty simple. Immediately, the readUTFBytes() method of the fileStream object is called. This method will read the file's array of bytes and return a string of characters that adhere to UTF-8 (8-bit UCS/Unicode Transformation Format). The method requires just one parameter specifying how many bytes should be read; and because you know that the entire file has been buffered, you can use the bytesAvailable property of the fileStream object. Now the temporary variable named theText is full of all sorts of characters.

Now it's time to convert the line-ending characters of the file into characters that will display new lines properly in the TextArea component. As you may already know, line-ending characters vary depending on what operating system your application is running. Simple regular expressions are the best way to go about fixing this problem. When creating the new RegExp object, supply the first argument of the constructor with the public static variable lineEnding of the File class. This property will tell you the line-ending character sequence of the operating system your application is running on. What a lifesaver! Now that you have the pattern, you can call the replace method on theText and subsequently dump that text into the text property of the TextArea component.

Now that you have the text from the file displayed to the user, all that is left is some simple housekeeping. First, textChanged is set to false. Second, the title property of the application is updated with the name of the file that the user has opened. Third, the fileStream object is closed. The application is now set up to open text files, so you can move on to the other essential piece of functionality the application needs: the capability to save files. The saveFile() function is as follows:

```
private function saveFile():void
{
    if( currentFile )
    {
        if( fileStream != null )
        {
            fileStream.close();
        }

        fileStream = new FileStream();
        fileStream.openAsync( currentFile, FileMode.WRITE );
        fileStream.addEventListener( IOErrorEvent.IO_ERROR, onWriteIOError );
        var str:String = fileTextArea.text;
        str = str.replace( /\r/g, "\n" );
        str = str.replace( /\n/g, File.lineEnding );
        fileStream.writeUTFBytes(str);
        textChanged = false;
    }
    else
    {
        promptUserToSaveFile();
    }
}
```

The saveFile() function is where you'll be taking the text from the TextArea component and writing that data to a text file on the user's hard drive. The first item of business in this function is a conditional that deals with whether or not the user has already opened a file. This was determined by checking whether the currentFile variable is defined or not. If the variable is not null or undefined, then the file will be saved (thus replacing, or overwriting, the old file); and if the variable is null, then the promptUserToSaveFile() function (which will be added shortly) is called to prompt the user to save the file somewhere on their hard drive.

For example, suppose the user has opened a file and made some changes, and wants to save the file. First, as with the openFile() function, you need to check whether the fileStream variable is defined. If it is defined, then you call the FileStream object's close() method (again, this is just to be safe). After you are past this condition, you then create a new FileStream object; and, as in the openFile() function, call the openAsync() method, providing it with the currentFile and the mode in which you want the FileStream to work. In this case, use the static property WRITE of the FileMode class to specify that you'll be writing data to the file. The openAsync() method opens the FileStream object asynchronously.

Next, an event listener is added to fileStream to check for an I/O error during the file-writing process. Simply call the onWriteIOError() function when the IO_ERROR event is dispatched. It is hoped that this will never happen, but you can never tell whether a user will have a damaged disk sector! This function prompts the user with a message that something went wrong.

Note that this file will not be able to be compiled until a few more changes are made to it. However, the only thing left to do now is take the text from the TextArea component and dump it into the file. This is as easy as calling the FileStream object's writeUTFBytes() method and passing it the string of text. The writeUTFBytes() method writes the bytes that represent the characters of the string into the file. It really doesn't get much easier than that!

User Prompts

Now that the core functionality is in place, it's time to set up some prompts to give the user a pleasurable text-editing experience. Specifically, you need to enable users both to browse the hard drive for files to open and to browse for a location to save files. Aside from this, it would also be nice if users were able to create a new document. Add the following markup to SimpleTextEditor.mxml:

```
<?xml version="1.0" encoding="utf-8"?>
<mx:WindowedApplication xmlns:mx="http://www.adobe.com/2006/mxml"
    layout="absolute" width="800" height="600" title="Text Editor"
    applicationComplete="onAppInit();" >

    <mx:Script><![CDATA[

    import flash.events.KeyboardEvent;
    import flash.filesystem.File;
    import flash.filesystem.FileMode;
    import flash.filesystem.FileStream;
    import flash.net.FileFilter;
    import mx.controls.Alert;
    import mx.events.CloseEvent;
    import mx.events.MenuEvent;

    private var browseHolder:File;
    private var currentFile:File;
```

```
private var defaultFile:File;
private var fileStream:FileStream;
private var fileToOpen:File;
private var fileToSave:File;
private var textChanged:Boolean;

public function onAppInit():void
{
    title = "Text Editor - Untitled.txt";
    defaultFile = File.documentsDirectory.resolvePath( "untitled.txt" );
    textChanged = false;
    application.addEventListener( KeyboardEvent.KEY_UP, onKeyUp );
}

private function onKeyUp( event:KeyboardEvent ):void
{
    if( event.keyCode == Keyboard.TAB && !event.altKey && !event.shiftKey &&
       !event.ctrlKey )
    {
        var sb:Number = fileTextArea.selectionBeginIndex;
        var se:Number = fileTextArea.selectionEndIndex;

        var firstPart:String = fileTextArea.text.slice(0, sb);
        var secondPart:String = fileTextArea.text.slice( se );

        fileTextArea.text = firstPart + "\t" + secondPart;
    }
}    private function onItemClick( event:MenuEvent ):void
{
}

private function onAlertClose( event:CloseEvent ):void
{
    switch( event.detail )
    {
        case Alert.YES:
            saveFile();
            break;
        case Alert.NO:
            textChanged = false;
            newDocument();
            break;
    }
}


private function onFileOpenPanelSelect( event:FileEvent ):void
{
    currentFile = event.file as File;
    openFile();
}

private function onFileSavePanelSelect( event:FileEvent ):void
```

```
{
    currentFile = event.file as File;
    textChanged = false;
    title = "Text Editor - " + currentFile.name;
    saveFile();
}
```

```
private function onOpenComplete( event:Event ):void
{
    var theText:String = fileStream.readUTFBytes( fileStream
       .bytesAvailable );
    var lineEndPattern:RegExp = new RegExp( File.lineEnding, "g" );

    fileTextArea.text = theText.replace( lineEndPattern, "\n" );

    textChanged = false;
    title = "Text Editor - " + currentFile.name;

    fileStream.close();
}

private function onReadIOError( event:IOErrorEvent ):void
{
    Alert.show("The specified file cannot be opened.", "Error", Alert.OK,
       this);
}

private function onWriteIOError( event:IOErrorEvent ):void
{
    Alert.show("The specified file cannot be saved.", "Error", Alert.OK,
       this);
}

private function openFile():void
{
    if( fileStream != null )
    {
        fileStream.close();
    }

    fileStream = new FileStream();
    fileStream.addEventListener( Event.COMPLETE, onOpenComplete );
    fileStream.addEventListener( IOErrorEvent.IO_ERROR, onReadIOError );
    fileStream.openAsync( currentFile, FileMode.READ );
}

private function saveFile():void
{
    if( currentFile )
    {
        if( fileStream != null )
        {
```

```
                fileStream.close();
            }

            var theText:String = fileTextArea.text;
            theText = theText.replace( /\r/g, "\n" );
            theText = theText.replace( /\n/g, File.lineEnding );

            fileStream = new FileStream();
            fileStream.openAsync( currentFile, FileMode.WRITE );
            fileStream.addEventListener( IOErrorEvent.IO_ERROR, onWriteIOError );
            fileStream.writeUTFBytes( theText );
            fileStream.close();

            textChanged = false;
        }
        else
        {
            promptUserToSaveFile();
        }
    }
```

```
    private function promptUserToOpenFile():void
    {
        fileToOpen = ( currentFile != null ) ? currentFile.parent :
           File.documentsDirectory;
        fileToOpen.removeEventListener( Event.SELECT, onFileSaveSelect );

        var textFilter:FileFilter = new FileFilter( "Text",
           "*.as;*.css;*.html;*.txt;*.xml" );
        var allFilter:FileFilter = new FileFilter( "All Files", "*.*" );

        try
        {
            fileToOpen.browseForOpen( "Open", [textFilter, allFilter] );
            fileToOpen.addEventListener( Event.SELECT, onFileOpenSelect );
        }
        catch( error:Error )
        {
            trace("Failed:", error.message);
        }
    }

    private function promptUserToSaveFile():void
    {
        fileToSave = ( currentFile ) ? currentFile : defaultFile;
        fileToSave.removeEventListener( Event.SELECT, onFileOpenSelect );

        var typeFilter:FileFilter = new FileFilter( "Text",
           "*.as;*.css;*.html;*.txt;*.xml" );

        try
        {
            fileToSave.browseForSave("Save");
```

```
                fileToSave.addEventListener( Event.SELECT, onFileSaveSelect );
            }
            catch( error:Error )
            {
                trace("Failed:", error.message);
            }
        }

        private function newDocument():void
        {
            if( textChanged )
            {
                Alert.show("The text in your current document has changed.\nDo
                   you want to save your changes?", "Alert", (Alert.YES | Alert.NO
                   | Alert.CANCEL), this, onAlertClose);
            }
            else
            {
                currentFile = undefined;
                textChanged = false;
                fileTextArea.text = "";
            }
        }    ]]>
    </mx:Script>
        <mx:MenuBar id="myMenuBar" labelField="@label"
                    left="0" top="0" right="0" tabEnabled="false"
                    itemClick="onItemClick(event);" >
            <mx:XMLList>
                <menuitem label="File" >
                    <menuitem label="New"/>
                    <menuitem label="Open"/>
                    <menuitem label="Save"/>
                    <menuitem label="Save As..."/>
                </menuitem>
            </mx:XMLList>
        </mx:MenuBar>
        <mx:TextArea id="fileTextArea"
            top="21" left="0" right="0" bottom="0"
            focusThickness="0" fontFamily="Arial"
            fontSize="14" tabEnabled="false"
            change="textChanged=true;" />
</mx:WindowedApplication>
```

As you can see, six new functions were added. The first three functions are event handlers that will be used by the following three functions. Take a look at the function named `promptUserToOpenFile()`:

```
private function promptUserToOpenFile():void
{
    fileToOpen = ( currentFile != null ) ? currentFile.parent :
```

```
File.documentsDirectory;
    fileToOpen.removeEventListener( Event.SELECT, onFileSaveSelect );
    var textFilter:FileFilter = new FileFilter( "Text",
       "*.as;*.css;*.html;*.txt;*.xml" );
    var allFilter:FileFilter = new FileFilter( "All Files", "*.*" );

    try
    {
        fileToOpen.browseForOpen( "Open", [textFilter, allFilter] );
        fileToOpen.addEventListener( Event.SELECT, onFileOpenSelect );
    }
    catch( error:Error )
    {
        trace("Failed:", error.message);
    }
}
```

This function prompts the user with a dialog that enables them to choose a file to open (see Figure 2-2). Note that the dialog's appearance varies depending on the user's operating system. Figure 2-2 shows what the dialog looks like on Windows. Before the dialog appears, however, the function determines which directory on the user's computer to start browsing from. A simple conditional checks whether the user has a file open already. If so, it begins to browse from within the directory the file resides. Otherwise, the user will begin browsing from his or her documents directory.

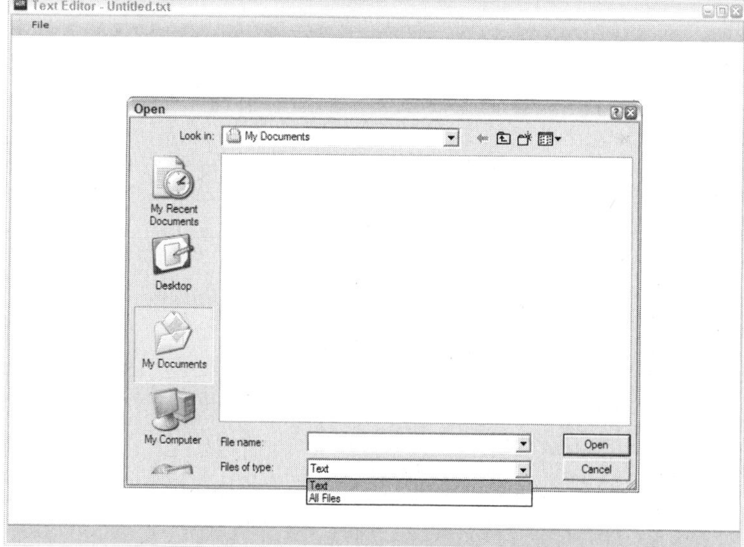

Figure 2-2

Following this procedure, notice the use of the `FileFilter` class. The `FileFilter` class is used to limit the types of files that the user is allowed to open from the dialog. Here, two instances of this class are created. The constructor of the `FileFilter` class accepts two parameters: The first is the description for the list of files, and the second is a semicolon-delimited string of file types. The file types must be represented by their file extension. After the `FileFilter` objects are created, the application attempts to present the dialog to the user by calling the `browserForOpen()` method of the `fileToOpen` object, which happens to be of type `File`. This method accepts two parameters: The first is the text that should appear in the title bar of the dialog, and the second is an array of `FileFilter` objects.

The last thing to do is add an event listener on the `fileToOpen` object so the application knows when the user has selected a file to open. This listens for the `SELECT` event of type `Event` and calls the `onFileOpen-PanelSelect()` function. This event is dispatched when the user clicks the Open button or double-clicks a file in the file list of the dialog. The following code shows the event handler:

```
private function onFileOpenPanelSelect( event:Event ):void
{
    currentFile = event.file as File;
    openFile();
}
```

Obviously, there's very little going on in this function, and that's because most of the work has been done already. All you need to do in this function is set the `currentFile` equal to the `file` property of the event object. This, of course, is the file that the user selected in the dialog. All you have to do now is call the `openFile()` function. As explained previously, the text from the selected file will then appear in the `TextArea` component. It's as simple as that!

Next, have a look at `promptUserToSaveFile()`:

```
private function promptUserToSaveFile():void
{
    fileToSave = ( currentFile ) ? currentFile : defaultFile;
    fileToSave.removeEventListener( Event.SELECT, onFileOpenSelect );

    var typeFilter:FileFilter = new FileFilter( "Text",
       "*.as;*.css;*.html;*.txt;*.xml" );

    try
    {
        fileToSave.browseForSave("Save");
        fileToSave.addEventListener( Event.SELECT, onFileSaveSelect );
    }
    catch( error:Error )
    {
        trace("Failed:", error.message);
    }
}
```

In this function, users are prompted with a dialog that enables them to choose a location to save the file they are working on (see Figure 2-3). This function is similar to that of the `promptUserToOpen()` function, with two slight differences. The first difference is the use of the `fileToSave` object and the conditional that determines its value. If the user is currently working on a file, then it is set equal to the `currentFile` object; otherwise, it is set equal to the `defaultFile` object. The second difference is the use of the `browse-ForSave()` method. Like the `browseForOpen()` method, this method presents the user with a dialog, but it is instead used for saving files.

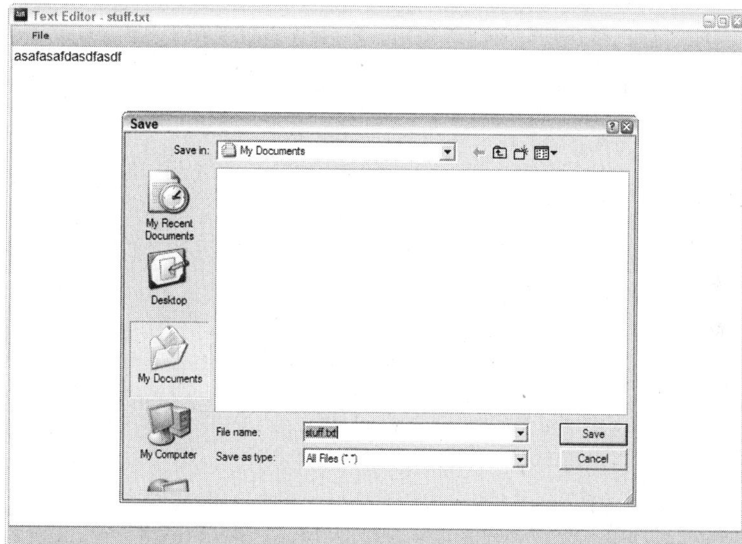

Figure 2-3

As with the Open dialog, you listen for the `SELECT` event of the `File` object you are using. When this event is dispatched, the `onFileSavePanelSelect()` function is called:

```
private function onFileSavePanelSelect( event:Event ):void
{
    currentFile = event.file as File;
    textChanged = false;
    title = "Text Editor - " + currentFile.name;
    saveFile();
}
```

Again, not too much is going on here, but that's because most of the work is done already. First, you set the `currentFile` equal to the file property of the event object (the file the user selected in the dialog). Next is some more housekeeping. The `textChanged` flag is reset to `false` and the `title` property of the application is updated to reflect the file the user is working on. Finally, the `saveFile()` function is called to save the file. You're almost done. Next up is the `newDocument()` function:

```
private function newDocument():void
{
    if( textChanged )
    {
        Alert.show("The text in your current document has changed.\nDo you want to
            save your changes?", "Alert", (Alert.YES | Alert.NO | Alert.CANCEL),
            this, onAlertClose);
    }
    else
    {
        currentFile = undefined;
    textChanged = false;
        fileTextArea.text = "";
    }
}
```

This function gives the user the option to create a new document — an option every text editor should have, right? First, check the `textChanged` flag to determine whether the user has made any changes to the current file. If the text has changed, then the user is prompted with a choice to either continue or save the file they are working on. Here, use an `Alert` component to handle this, and call the `onAlertClose()` function when the user makes a selection. Conversely, if the text has not changed, then you can assume the user does not need to save the file and you can reset the variables and clear the text from the `TextArea` component. Here is the `onAlertClose()` function:

```
private function onAlertClose( event:CloseEvent ):void
{
    switch( event.detail )
    {
        case Alert.YES:
            saveFile();
            break;
        case Alert.NO:
            textChanged = false;
            newDocument();
            break;
    }
}
```

This event handler merely checks the selection the user made in the preceding alert. If the user selected Yes, then save the file by calling the `saveFile()` function. If the user selected No, then set the `textChanged` flag to `false`. When the subsequent call of `newDocument()` is made, the user will not be prompted again.

Interface Activation

Last but not least, you need to active the interface. Since all the functionality is finished, this will be a total breeze. Add the following markup to the `onItemClick()` function within `SimpleTextEditor.mxml`:

```
private function onItemClick( event:MenuEvent ):void
{
    switch( event.label )
```

```
        {
            case "New":
                newDocument();
                break;

            case "Open":
                promptUserToOpenFile();
                break;
            case "Save":
                saveFile();
                break;
            case "Save As...":
                promptUserToSaveFile();
                break;
        }
    }
```

This event handler checks which item the user has selected from the `MenuBar` component. Since all the work is done, all that is necessary now is a call to the corresponding function. And guess what? Your simple text editor is now complete.

The entire markup of `SimpleTextEditor.mxml` should look something like this:

```
<?xml version="1.0" encoding="utf-8"?>
<mx:WindowedApplication xmlns:mx="http://www.adobe.com/2006/mxml"
    layout="absolute" width="800" height="600" title="Text Editor"
    applicationComplete="onAppInit();" >

    <mx:Script><![CDATA[

    import flash.events.KeyboardEvent;
    import flash.filesystem.File;
    import flash.filesystem.FileMode;
    import flash.filesystem.FileStream;
    import flash.net.FileFilter;
    import mx.controls.Alert;
    import mx.events.CloseEvent;
    import mx.events.MenuEvent;

    private var browseHolder:File;
    private var currentFile:File;
    private var defaultFile:File;
    private var fileStream:FileStream;
    private var fileToOpen:File;
    private var fileToSave:File;
    private var textChanged:Boolean;

    public function onAppInit():void
    {
        title = "Text Editor - Untitled.txt";
        defaultFile = File.documentsDirectory.resolvePath( "untitled.txt" );
        textChanged = false;
        application.addEventListener( KeyboardEvent.KEY_UP, onKeyUp );
    }
```

```
private function onKeyUp( event:KeyboardEvent ):void
{
    if( event.keyCode == Keyboard.TAB && !event.altKey && !event.shiftKey &&
       !event.ctrlKey )
    {
        var sb:Number = fileTextArea.selectionBeginIndex;
        var se:Number = fileTextArea.selectionEndIndex;

        var firstPart:String = fileTextArea.text.slice(0, sb);
        var secondPart:String = fileTextArea.text.slice( se );

        fileTextArea.text = firstPart + "\t" + secondPart;
    }
}

private function onItemClick( event:MenuEvent ):void
{
    switch( event.label )
    {
        case "New":
            newDocument();
            break;

        case "Open":
            promptUserToOpenFile();
            break;

        case "Save":
            saveFile();
            break;

        case "Save As...":
            promptUserToSaveFile();
            break;
    }
}

private function onAlertClose( event:CloseEvent ):void
{
    switch( event.detail )
    {
        case Alert.YES:
            saveFile();
            break;

        case Alert.NO:
            textChanged = false;
            newDocument();
            break;
    }
}

private function onFileOpenSelect( event:Event ):void
{
    currentFile = event.target as File;
```

```
        openFile();
    }

    private function onFileSaveSelect( event:Event ):void
    {
        currentFile = event.target as File;
        textChanged = false;
        title = "Text Editor - " + currentFile.name;
        saveFile();
    }

    private function onOpenComplete( event:Event ):void
    {
        var theText:String = fileStream.readUTFBytes( fileStream.bytesAvailable );
        var lineEndPattern:RegExp = new RegExp( File.lineEnding, "g" );

        fileTextArea.text = theText.replace( lineEndPattern, "\n" );

        textChanged = false;
        title = "Text Editor - " + currentFile.name;

        fileStream.close();
    }

    private function onReadIOError( event:IOErrorEvent ):void
    {
        Alert.show("The specified file cannot be opened.", "Error", Alert.OK, this);
    }

    private function onWriteIOError( event:IOErrorEvent ):void
    {
        Alert.show("The specified file cannot be saved.", "Error", Alert.OK, this);
    }

    private function openFile():void
    {
        if( fileStream != null )
        {
            fileStream.close();
        }
        fileStream = new FileStream();
        fileStream.addEventListener( Event.COMPLETE, onOpenComplete );
        fileStream.addEventListener( IOErrorEvent.IO_ERROR, onReadIOError );
        fileStream.openAsync( currentFile, FileMode.READ );
    }

    private function saveFile():void
    {
        if( currentFile )
        {
            if( fileStream != null )
            {
                fileStream.close();
            }
```

```
            var theText:String = fileTextArea.text;
            theText = theText.replace( /\r/g, "\n" );
            theText = theText.replace( /\n/g, File.lineEnding );

            fileStream = new FileStream();
            fileStream.openAsync( currentFile, FileMode.WRITE );
            fileStream.addEventListener( IOErrorEvent.IO_ERROR, onWriteIOError );
            fileStream.writeUTFBytes( theText );
            fileStream.close();

            textChanged = false;
        }
        else
        {
            promptUserToSaveFile();
        }
    }

    private function promptUserToOpenFile():void
    {
        fileToOpen = ( currentFile != null ) ? currentFile.parent :
           File.documentsDirectory;
        fileToOpen.removeEventListener( Event.SELECT, onFileSaveSelect );

        var textFilter:FileFilter = new FileFilter( "Text",
           "*.as;*.css;*.html;*.txt;*.xml" );
        var allFilter:FileFilter = new FileFilter( "All Files", "*.*" );

        try
        {
            fileToOpen.browseForOpen( "Open", [textFilter, allFilter] );
            fileToOpen.addEventListener( Event.SELECT, onFileOpenSelect );
        }
        catch( error:Error )
        {
            trace("Failed:", error.message);
        }
    }

    private function promptUserToSaveFile():void
    {
        fileToSave = ( currentFile ) ? currentFile : defaultFile;
        fileToSave.removeEventListener( Event.SELECT, onFileOpenSelect );

        var typeFilter:FileFilter = new FileFilter( "Text",
           "*.as;*.css;*.html;*.txt;*.xml" );

        try
        {
            fileToSave.browseForSave("Save");
            fileToSave.addEventListener( Event.SELECT, onFileSaveSelect );
        }
        catch( error:Error )
        {
            trace("Failed:", error.message);
```

```
        }
    }

    private function newDocument():void
    {
        if( textChanged )
        {
            Alert.show("The text in your current document has changed.\nDo you want
               to save your changes?", "Alert", (Alert.YES | Alert.NO
               | Alert.CANCEL), this, onAlertClose);
        }
        else
        {
            currentFile = undefined;
            textChanged = false;
            fileTextArea.text = "";
        }
    }
    ]]></mx:Script>
    <mx:MenuBar id="myMenuBar" labelField="@label"
                left="0" top="0" right="0" tabEnabled="false"
                itemClick="onItemClick(event);" >
        <mx:XMLList>
            <menuitem label="File" >
                <menuitem label="New"/>
                <menuitem label="Open"/>
                <menuitem label="Save"/>
                <menuitem label="Save As..."/>
            </menuitem>
        </mx:XMLList>
    </mx:MenuBar>
    <mx:TextArea id="fileTextArea"
        top="21" left="0" right="0" bottom="0"
        focusThickness="0" fontFamily="Arial"
        fontSize="14" tabEnabled="false"
        change="textChanged=true;" />
</mx:WindowedApplication>
```

Now that the code is complete, you can compile, deploy, and customize this application all you want. Jazz it up with your favorite icons or color scheme, or turn it into a component that could be part of a larger application. Nothing can stop you now!

There are many ways you could further improve upon a simple text editor. Think of the common menu items of your own favorite text editor, such as Find or Search and Replace. If you are really ambitious, you could perhaps add an Undo function or add rich text editing abilities. If your users are developers themselves, you could add a snippets manager that enables users to enter commonly used strings and access them through a simple menu. The possibilities are almost endless.

Summary

In this chapter you've seen just how easy it is to create a simple text editor, and all with just a little more than 200 lines of code (you could tighten it up a bit, too). It's safe to say you've made it through your first real AIR application and learned a little bit about the AIR file system API. Specifically, this chapter covered the `File` and `FileStream` objects, and described a few methods associated with each. You also learned how to use these objects when reading and writing files to a user's hard drive.

Along with learning these file system basics, you also discovered how to gain some basic information about your users' systems by accessing some static properties of the `File` class. This information included where the user's documents directory resides, and the line-ending character sequence of the user's operating system.

Lastly, you learned how to access the operating system's standard Open and Save dialog windows through the available methods of the `File` object. Not too shabby for your first AIR application. In the next chapter you will learn even more about the file system API, along with a few other great features of AIR, by creating a simple RSS reader.

3

Simple RSS Reader

Everyone tries to keep abreast of the latest news. As a newspaper is an aggregate of articles in print, a Really Simple Syndication (RSS) reader supplies you with information in a digital format. The RSS format is an XML markup delivering information about a *feed*, or collection of published articles, detailed through metadata elements. Online aggregators are notified of updates from multiple RSS feeds and facilitate staying up to date on what interests you from various sources.

In this chapter, you will build a simple RSS reader that displays posts from the Adobe XML News Aggregator (AXNA), an aggregate of various topics, including the lowdown about the latest information on the Flash Platform. While doing so, you'll uncover some more jewels in the AIR API as they pertain to network connectivity, the system tray, and windows.

Before you begin building the application, first consider what to expect from a desktop RSS reader. In general, the RSS reader should have the following qualities:

- Be aware of network resources and user presence, and handle polling the RSS feed accordingly.
- Unobtrusively display posts as they are received from the RSS feed.
- Present additional options pertaining to the application and RSS feed from the system tray.

The next section discusses how to achieve these goals.

Design

In the previous section, some primary goals were targeted for the RSS reader. Consuming an RSS feed and showing the lists of posts using the Flex framework is pretty straightforward, and you may have built an online feed reader already yourself. The RSS reader you will build in this chapter, however, will incorporate the capabilities of the AIR API, enabling you to bring that experience to the desktop. The following list expands on the goals considered for the application:

- **Be aware of network resource and user presence** — The main focus of the RSS Reader application is to present the user with the most recent posts of a feed. The application will continually poll an RSS feed to retrieve and present any new posts. When a user has lost connection to the Internet, the application must know to stop any requests until the connection is restored. The same understanding applies to a user's idleness while the application is running. In using the network monitoring classes and handling events of the AIR API, you can ensure an enjoyable reading experience.

- **Unobtrusively display posts as they are received from the RSS feed** — The RSS reader will present posts in a toaster window. The presentation of a toaster window varies between operating systems but generally refers to a display that appears above other native windows to show data pertaining to an application. While using the windowing API of AIR, the RSS reader will employ the same approach in presenting post in an unobtrusive manner and present controls to move through the digest of the RSS feed or close the window altogether.
- **Present additional options from the system tray** — Unlike most desktop applications, whereby a main window is present at all times within the z-order of native windows on your screen, the RSS reader runs within the system tray of your operating system and present new posts as they are received from the service. As such, in using the native menu API of AIR, the application will present system tray options that enable you to force a request, navigate to the feed in an Internet browser, or quit the application.

With these points in mind, you can start building the tools that address these requirements and create a desktop application that will keep you informed of what is happening in the Flash Platform world.

The next section covers the value object that is used as the model to display a single post within a toaster window from a list of posts received from the feed service.

Handling Data

As the result from an RSS feed is received by the application, data is parsed into a list of objects available for display within the RSS reader. The display of each post is dependent on properties assigned of a value object you will create in this section.

Within your development directory, create a folder titled `RSSReader`. This will be your working directory for the application. With that set, you can get to work.

Create a new document and enter the following ActionScript:

```
package com.aircmr.rssreader.data
{
    [Bindable]
    public class PostVO
    {
        public var author:String;
        public var title:String;
        public var description:String;
        public var link:String;
        public var date:String;
        public var id:String;
```

```
        public function PostVO( author:String, title:String,
                                description:String, link:String,
                                date:String, id:String )
        {
            this.author = author;
            this.title = title;
            this.description = description;
            this.link = link;
            this.date = date;
            this.id = id;
        }
    }
}
```

Save the file as `PostVO.as` in the directory `com/aircmr/rssreader/data` in your working directory.

The `PostVO` value object has public attributes pertinent to a post received from a feed service. The result of the service is a list of items in XML format. The properties of this value object are used to render text fields within the post display, aside from `link` and `id`, which are used to navigate to the original weblog post and retain the last read item, respectively.

To better understand how these objects are defined and handled by the application, the next section covers the classes for loading and parsing data from the feed service.

Parsing the RSS Feed

When the user is present and a network resource is available, the RSS reader will continually poll the subscribed feed service for XML data. As the data is received, the service classes you create in this section parse the XML into `PostVO` value objects used to display each post.

1. Create a new document and enter the following ActionScript:

```
package com.aircmr.rssreader.services
{
    import com.aircmr.rssreader.data.PostVO;

    import flash.events.Event;
    import flash.events.EventDispatcher;
    import flash.events.HTTPStatusEvent;
    import flash.events.IOErrorEvent;
    import flash.net.URLLoader;
    import flash.net.URLRequest;

    public class AbstractFeedService extends EventDispatcher
    {
        protected var _title:String;
        protected var _loader:URLLoader;
        [ArrayElementType("com.aircmr.rssreader.data.PostVO")]
        protected var _postItems:Array;
        protected var _lastReadId:String;
```

```
public function AbstractFeedService()
{
    _loader = new URLLoader();
    _loader.addEventListener( Event.COMPLETE, onFeedLoad );
    _loader.addEventListener( HTTPStatusEvent.HTTP_STATUS, onHTTPStatus );
    _loader.addEventListener( IOErrorEvent.IO_ERROR, onFeedLoadError );
}

protected function onHTTPStatus( evt:Event ):void
{
    // override
}

protected function onFeedLoad( evt:Event ):void
{
    // override ...
}

protected function onFeedLoadError( evt:IOErrorEvent ):void
{
    dispatchEvent( evt.clone() );
}

protected function updateLastRead():void
{
    _lastReadId = PostVO( _postItems[0] ).id;
}

protected function getItemsSince( id:String ):Array
{
    for( var i:int = 0; i < _postItems.length; i++ )
    {
        if( PostVO( _postItems[i] ).id == id ) break;
    }
    updateLastRead();
    return getItemsByAmount( i );
}

public function load( url:String ):void
{
    _postItems = new Array();
    _loader.load( new URLRequest( url ) );
}

public function getAllItems():Array
{
    updateLastRead();
    return _postItems;
}

public function getItemsByAmount( amt:int ):Array
{
    updateLastRead();
    return _postItems.slice( 0, Math.min( _postItems.length, amt ) );
```

```
        }

        public function getUnreadItems():Array
        {
            return getItemsSince( _lastReadId );
        }
        [Bindable]
        public function get title():String
        {
            return _title;
        }
        public function set title( str:String ):void
        {
            _title = str;
        }
    }
}
```

2. Save the file as `AbstractFeedService.as` in the directory `com/aircmr/rssreader/services` within your working directory.

3. Create a new document and enter the following ActionScript:

```
package com.aircmr.rssreader.services
{
    import com.aircmr.rssreader.data.PostVO;

    import flash.events.Event;

    [Event(name="complete", event="flash.events.Event" )]
    public class AXNAFeedService extends AbstractFeedService
    {
        private var _xml:XML;

        public static const LOAD_COMPLETE:String = "complete";
        private static const DC_NS:String =
                                    "http://purl.org/dc/elements/1.1/";
        private static const RSS_NS:String = "http://purl.org/rss/1.0/";

        private function parseData():void
        {
            var chan:XMLList = getElement( _xml, RSS_NS, "channel" );
            title = getElement( XML( chan ), RSS_NS, "title" )[0];

            var children:XMLList = getElement( _xml, RSS_NS, "item" );
            for( var i:Number = 0; i < children.length(); i++ )
            {
                var post:XML = XML( children[i] );
                var title:XMLList = getElement( post, RSS_NS, "title" );
                var description:XMLList = getElement(post, RSS_NS, "description");
                var link:XMLList = getElement( post, RSS_NS, "link" );
                var author:XMLList = getElement( post, DC_NS, "creator" );
                var date:XMLList = getElement( post, DC_NS, "date" );
                var id:XMLList = getElement( post, DC_NS, "identifier" );
```

```
                _postItems.push( new PostVO( author, title, description,
                                                        link, date, id ) );
            }
        }

        private function getElement( child:XML, ns:String,
                                        type:String ):XMLList
        {
            return child.descendants( new QName( ns, type ) );
        }

        override protected function onFeedLoad( evt:Event ):void
        {
            _xml = XML( _loader.data );
            parseData();
            dispatchEvent( new Event( AXNAFeedService.LOAD_COMPLETE ) );
        }
    }
}
```

4. Save the file as `AXNAFeedService.as` in the directory `com/aircmr/rssreader/services` within your working directory.

The first snippet, saved as `AbstractFeedService`, serves as a base class for any concrete feed services you may implement — such as the `AXNAFeedService`. The `AbstractFeedService` handles requesting data from the feed service and exposes methods for clients to access the data parsed into `PostVO` objects. Along with methods to return the full array or part of the array of posts, the `AbstractFeedService` class holds a reference to the last requested post using the `id` property of `PostVO`. After the initial load of returned data, the RSS Reader application continually polls the feed service and presents any items a user has not already been presented with. Items not already presented to the user can be accessed using the `getUnreadItems()` method.

With logic defining how to access post data, the `AbstractFeedService` acts as a base for a subclass that overrides the event handlers for the `Loader` instance and logically parses the returned data. The `AXNAFeedService` overrides the `onFeedLoad()` event handler and parses the returned data within the private `parseData()` method. The RSS Reader application will parse the RSS feed from the Adobe XML News Aggregator (AXNA). This feed is an XML serialization of a Resource Description Framework (RDF) and follows the RDF Site Summary (RSS) 1.0 specification. The parsing logic in the `AXNAFeedService` class knows how to handle this syntax, but you may prefer to read feeds in other syndicates, such as Atom. Feel free to create another subclass of `AbstractFeedService` that knows how to parse a different feed you may be interested in reading.

Adobe has publicly released code that can handle parsing various syndication formats. It can be downloaded from `http://code.google.com/p/as3corelib/` *and found in the* `xml.syndication` *package.*

In the `parseData()` method of `AXNAFeedService`, each post item is parsed in relation to the namespace URI of its child elements, and new `PostVO` value objects are added to an array:

```
private function parseData():void
{
    var chan:XMLList = getElement( _xml, RSS_NS, "channel" );
    title = getElement( XML( chan ), RSS_NS, "title" )[0];
```

```
        var children:XMLList = getElement( _xml, RSS_NS, "item" );
        for( var i:Number = 0; i < children.length(); i++ )
        {
            var post:XML = XML( children[i] );
            var title:XMLList = getElement( post, RSS_NS, "title" );
            var description:XMLList = getElement( post, RSS_NS, "description" );
            var link:XMLList = getElement( post, RSS_NS, "link" );
            var author:XMLList = getElement( post, DC_NS, "creator" );
            var date:XMLList = getElement( post, DC_NS, "date" );
            var id:XMLList = getElement( post, DC_NS, "identifier" );
            _postItems.push( new PostVO( author, title, description,
                                                  link, date, id ) );
        }
    }
```

The array of `PostVO` objects is assembled with properties received from the `getElement()` method by qualifying the XML elements using the ActionScript 3.0 `QName` class:

```
    private function getElement( child:XML, ns:String, type:String ):XMLList
    {
        return child.descendants( new QName( ns, type ) );
    }
```

The parameters of the `getElement()` method correspond to the parent node of a post item, the namespace in which the element resides, and the name of the element. The `descendants()` method of the ActionScript 3.0 `XML` object returns an `XMLList` of all descendants of the XML node. In this example, that return will be the node value of the qualified element supplied as the `child` argument.

Instances of the `PostVO` class represent a single post within a list of posts returned from a subscribed RSS feed. With the service classes to parse XML data and assemble the data object representing a single post created, it is time to start addressing how the application will present the post data to a user. In the next section you will create the view classes for posts as they are received from the Adobe XML News Aggregator.

Building the User Interface

The classes you created in the previous section are beneficial to the RSS Reader application because it continually polls an RSS feed for the latest posts. In this section, you will create both the display for those posts and the main MXML file that will handle communicating with the feed service and present system tray options pertinent to the application.

Recall that one of the original goals for the RSS reader was to present posts in an unobtrusive manner, meaning the application will display data without disrupting what users may currently be doing on their computer. Using the windowing API of AIR, in the next section you will create the view and window classes that will serve as toaster-style alerts.

Displaying Posts

Posts received from an RSS feed will be presented in a toaster-style alert. The toaster alert is a small window that resides at the depth of the z-order of native windows and takes up a small area in one quadrant of the user's screen. The classes you create in this section will make up the toaster alert window that is shown as data is received from the RSS feed service.

1. Create a new document and enter the following markup:

```
<?xml version="1.0" encoding="utf-8"?>
<mx:VBox
    xmlns:mx="http://www.adobe.com/2006/mxml"
    width="100%" height="100%"
    backgroundColor="0xF1F1F1"
    verticalGap="2" updateComplete="{this.measure()}"
    paddingLeft="10" paddingRight="10"
    paddingTop="10" paddingBottom="10">

    <mx:Style>
        .title {
            font: 'Arial';
            font-weight: 'bold';
            font-size: 12px;
            color: #336699;
        }
        .description {
            font: 'Arial';
            font-size: 11px;
            text-align: 'left';
            color: #333333;
        }
        .meta {
            font: 'Arial';
            font-size: 10px;
            color: #999999;
        }
    </mx:Style>

    <mx:Script>
        <![CDATA[
            import com.aircmr.rssreader.data.PostVO;
            private function onTitleClick():void
            {
                navigateToURL( new URLRequest( PostVO( data ).link ) );
            }
        ]]>
    </mx:Script>

    <mx:DateFormatter id="formatter" formatString="MM-DD-YYYY" />

    <mx:Text id="titleField" width="100%"
        styleName="title"
        htmlText="{data.title}" selectable="false"
        buttonMode="true" useHandCursor="true"
        click="onTitleClick();"
        />
    <mx:HBox width="100%" height="15"
        verticalAlign="middle">
        <mx:Text id="authorField"
```

```
            styleName="meta" maxWidth="170"
            htmlText="{data.author}"
            />
        <mx:VRule height="75%" />
        <mx:Text id="datField"
            styleName="meta"
            htmlText="{formatter.format( data.date )}"
            />
    </mx:HBox>
    <mx:Text id="description" width="100%" height="100%"
        styleName="description" truncateToFit="true"
        htmlText="{data.description}"
        />

</mx:VBox>
```

2. Save the file as `Post.mxml` in a directory named `com/aircmr/rssreader/ui` within your working directory.

3. Create a new document and enter the following markup:

```
<?xml version="1.0" encoding="utf-8"?>
<mx:Window
    xmlns:mx="http://www.adobe.com/2006/mxml"
    xmlns:ui="com.aircmr.rssreader.ui.*"
    systemChrome="none" showFlexChrome="false"
    transparent="true"
    alwaysInFront="true" type="lightweight"
    visible="false"
    width="300" height="200"
    closing="onClose(event);"
    creationComplete="onCreationComplete();">

    <mx:Script>
        <![CDATA[
            import mx.binding.utils.BindingUtils;
            import com.aircmr.rssreader.data.PostVO;

            [ArrayElementType("com.aircmr.rssreader.data.PostVO")]
            private var _posts:Array;
            private var _currentIndex:int = -1;
            private var _areaBounds:Rectangle;

            private var _cycleTimer:Timer;
            private static const CYCLE_DELAY:int = 5000;

            private function onCreationComplete():void
            {
                _cycleTimer = new Timer( CYCLE_DELAY );
                _cycleTimer.addEventListener( TimerEvent.TIMER, onTimer );

                var areaBounds:Rectangle = Screen.mainScreen.bounds;
                nativeWindow.x = areaBounds.width - width - 10;
                nativeWindow.y = areaBounds.height - height - 30;
            }
```

```
private function onClose( evt:Event ):void
{
    evt.preventDefault();
    stopDisplay();
}

private function onTimer( evt:TimerEvent ):void
{
    if( currentIndex < posts.length - 1 )
        currentIndex++;
    else
        stopDisplay();
}

private function stopDisplay():void
{
    _cycleTimer.reset();
    visible = false;
}

private function startDisplay():void
{
    currentIndex = 0;
    visible = true;
}

private function updatePost():void
{
    if( _posts == null ) return;
    post.data = _posts[_currentIndex];
    _cycleTimer.reset();
    _cycleTimer.start();
}

[Bindable]
public function get currentIndex():int
{
    return _currentIndex;
}
public function set currentIndex( num:int ):void
{
    _currentIndex = Math.max( 0, Math.min( num, posts.length - 1 ) );
    updatePost();
}

[Bindable]
public function get posts():Array
{
    return _posts;
}
public function set posts( arr:Array ):void
{
    _posts = arr;
    startDisplay();
```

```
            }

        ]]>
    </mx:Script>

    <mx:VBox width="100%" height="100%"
        borderStyle="solid" backgroundColor="0x336699" cornerRadius="5"
        paddingLeft="5" paddingRight="5" paddingTop="5" paddingBottom="5">

        <mx:Label text="{this.title}" color="0xFFFFFF" />
        <ui:Post id="post"
            width="100%" height="100%"
            mouseOver="{_cycleTimer.reset();}"
            mouseOut="{_cycleTimer.start();}"
             />
        <mx:HBox width="100%" height="20">
            <mx:Label text="&lt;&lt;"
                color="0xFFFFFF"
                click="{currentIndex--}"
                />
            <mx:Text text="{( currentIndex + 1 ) + '/' + posts.length}"
                color="0xFFFFFF"
                />
            <mx:Label text="&gt;&gt;"
                color="0xFFFFFF"
                click="{currentIndex++}"
                />
            <mx:Spacer width="100%" />
            <mx:Label text="close"
                color="0xFFFFFF"
                click="{stopDisplay();}"
                />
        </mx:HBox>

    </mx:VBox>

</mx:Window>
```

4. Save the file as `DigestToaster.mxml` in a directory named `com/aircmr/rssreader/windows` within your working directory.

The first snippet, saved as `Post.mxml`, is a simple component with fields that display data of a `PostVO` object. An instance of a `PostVO` object is supplied to the `Post` class using the inherited `data` property. Using the Flex data binding system, the text properties of the child fields are updated when the data is updated.

The `Post` class has a pretty straightforward layout and is used as the display for the second snippet — `DigestToaster.mxml`. The `DigestToaster` class extends the `mx.core.Window` class of the AIR windowing API and is the toaster-style alert window that is shown as new posts are returned from the RSS feed. The `Window` class acts as a container for native windows of an application on an operating system — specifically, an instance of `flash.display.NativeWindow`. While the `NativeWindow` class is an interface for native windows, components cannot be directly added to the display of `NativeWindow`.

Using the `Window` class, you can add components and control other properties of the native window through the `nativeWindow` property.

After initialization of the `NativeWindow` instance of the `Window` object, some properties become read-only. As such, attributes that pertain to the system chrome and window type are declared in the `<mx:Window>` tag:

```
<mx:Window
    xmlns:mx="http://www.adobe.com/2006/mxml"
    xmlns:ui="com.aircmr.rssreader.ui.*"
    systemChrome="none" showFlexChrome="false"
    transparent="true"
    alwaysInFront="true" type="lightweight"
    visible="false"
    width="300" height="200"
    closing="onClose(event);"
    creationComplete="onCreationComplete();">
```

Just as you may assign properties to the `<mx:WindowedApplication>` tag either within the declaration tag or in the descriptor file for an AIR application, you can assign properties to the native window in a `<mx:Window>` tag. To present the `DigestToaster` as a toaster window, the `systemChrome`, `showFlexChrome`, and `transparent` attributes are set to give the window its look and feel.

Along with the look of the window, `alwaysInFront` is set to `true` to have the window always appear at the top of the z-order on a user's screen, and the window `type` is set to `lightweight`. You can provide three main values for the type property of a Window: `normal`, `utility`, and `lightweight`. The `DigestToaster` is a `lightweight` window, which means that it will not show up within the Windows taskbar or Mac OS X menu, and will not be available in the System menu on Windows accessible through the Alt+Tab key command. Because the RSS Reader application is designed to be unobtrusive, the application will run within the system tray and present this `lightweight` window with posts as they become available.

Posts are given to the `DigestWindow` using the `posts` attribute. As posts are received, the `Post` display is updated based on the `currentIndex` property and a `Timer` instance is started:

```
private function updatePost():void
{
    if( _posts == null ) return;
    post.data = _posts[_currentIndex];
    _cycleTimer.reset();
    _cycleTimer.start();
}
```

Users can manually navigate through posts, or allow the `DigestToaster` to cycle through the array of `PostVO` objects using the timer. When all the posts have been shown or the user has explicitly decided to close the window, the window disappears from the screen. Note that the window is not entirely removed when this occurs, nor is it removed from the display list of the application. The appearance of the `DigestToaster` is driven by its `visible` property.

At this point, you have created the display for posts and the unobtrusive toaster-style window that appears as data is returned from the Adobe XML News Aggregator. In the next section, you will create the main application file, which will not only manage the `DigestWindow`, but also address the other usability goals of the RSS reader discussed earlier.

Bringing It All Together

The RSS Reader application will run in the background and present a toaster window when post data is received. As such, the main window of the application is the `DigestToaster`, which is not always present. To enable users to quit and perform other actions pertinent to the application, a menu needs to be accessible from either the Windows system tray or the Mac OS X dock. While the main application will address this issue, it will also have knowledge of network resources and user presence in order to effectively poll the RSS feed and present posts to read.

Create a new document and enter the following markup:

```
<?xml version="1.0" encoding="utf-8"?>
<mx:WindowedApplication
    xmlns:mx="http://www.adobe.com/2006/mxml"
    xmlns:ui="com.aircmr.rssreader.ui.*"
    layout="absolute" visible="false"
    backgroundColor="0xFFFFFF"
    applicationComplete="onAppComplete();"
    closing="onAppClosing();"
    networkChange="onNetworkChange();" >

    <mx:Script>
        <![CDATA[
            import com.aircmr.rssreader.windows.DigestToaster;
            import com.aircmr.rssreader.services.AbstractFeedService;
            import com.aircmr.rssreader.services.AXNAFeedService;

            import air.net.URLMonitor;
            import mx.binding.utils.BindingUtils;
            import mx.collections.ArrayCollection;
            import mx.events.FlexEvent;

            private var _feedTimer:Timer;
            private var _feedMonitor:URLMonitor;
            private var _feedService:AbstractFeedService;
            private var _isAvailable:Boolean = false;

            private var _toaster:DigestToaster;

            [Embed(source='/assets/AIRApp_16.png')]
            private var dockIcon:Class;

            private static const IDLE_THRESHOLD:int = 300; // 5 minutes
            private static const POLL_DELAY:int = 30000; // 30 seconds
            private static const MAX_AMOUNT:int = 10;
            private static const FEED:String =
                                    'http://weblogs.macromedia.com/mxna/xml/rss.cfm';

            private function onAppComplete():void
```

```
{
    this.includeInLayout = false;

    NativeApplication.nativeApplication.idleThreshold = IDLE_THRESHOLD;
    NativeApplication.nativeApplication.addEventListener(
                                Event.USER_IDLE , onUserIdle );
    NativeApplication.nativeApplication.addEventListener(
                                Event.USER_PRESENT, onUserPresent );

    BindingUtils.bindSetter( invalidateAvailability,
                                this, "isAvailable", true );

    _feedTimer = new Timer( POLL_DELAY, 1 );
    _feedTimer.addEventListener( TimerEvent.TIMER_COMPLETE,
                                              onFeedTimer );

    _feedService = new AXNAFeedService();
    _feedService.addEventListener( AXNAFeedService.LOAD_COMPLETE,
                                              onFeedLoad );

    _feedMonitor = new URLMonitor( new URLRequest( FEED ), [200,202] );
    _feedMonitor.addEventListener( StatusEvent.STATUS, onStatus );
    _feedMonitor.start();

    setToasterWindow();
}

private function onAppClosing():void
{
    NativeApplication.nativeApplication.exit();
}

private function setToasterWindow():void
{
    _toaster = new DigestToaster();
    _toaster.addEventListener( FlexEvent.HIDE, onToasterHide );
    _toaster.open();
}
private function setAvailableMenu():void
{
    var tip:String = "MXNA Reader - available";
    var shellMenu:NativeMenu = new NativeMenu();
    shellMenu.addItem( new NativeMenuItem( "Go to MXNA" ) );
    shellMenu.addItem( new NativeMenuItem( "Read Recent Posts" ) );
    shellMenu.addItem( new NativeMenuItem( "Quit MXNA Reader" ) );
    shellMenu.addEventListener( Event.SELECT, onShellMenuSelect );
    setMenu( shellMenu, tip );
}

private function setUnavailableMenu():void
{
    var tip:String = "MXNA Reader - unavailable";
    var shellMenu:NativeMenu = new NativeMenu();
    shellMenu.addItem( new NativeMenuItem( "Quit MXNA Reader" ) );
```

```
        shellMenu.addEventListener( Event.SELECT, onShellMenuSelect );
        setMenu( shellMenu, tip );
    }
    private function setMenu( menu:NativeMenu, tip:String ):void
    {
        var app:NativeApplication = NativeApplication.nativeApplication;
        if( NativeApplication.supportsDockIcon )
        {
            // Mac OSX
            ( app.icon as DockIcon ).menu = menu;
        }
        else
        {
            ( app.icon as SystemTrayIcon ).menu = menu;
            ( app.icon as SystemTrayIcon ).tooltip = tip;
        }
        app.icon.bitmaps = [( new dockIcon() ).bitmapData];
    }

    private function invalidateAvailability( args:* = null ):void
    {
        if( _isAvailable )
        {
            invokeService();
            setAvailableMenu();
        }
        else
        {
            setUnavailableMenu();
        }
    }

    private function invokeService( evt:Event = null ):void
    {
        _feedService.load( FEED );
    }

    private function onUserIdle( evt:Event ):void
    {
        _feedTimer.reset();
    }
    private function onUserPresent( evt:Event ):void
    {
        _feedTimer.start();
    }

    private function onFeedTimer( evt:TimerEvent ):void
    {
        invokeService();
    }

    private function onToasterHide( evt:FlexEvent ):void
    {
        _feedTimer.start();
```

```
        }
        private function onFeedLoad( evt:Event ):void
        {
            var items:Array = _feedService.getUnreadItems();
            if( items.length > 0 )
            {
                _toaster.title = _feedService.title;
                _toaster.posts = items;
            }
            else _feedTimer.start();
        }

        private function onStatus( evt:StatusEvent ):void
        {
            isAvailable = _feedMonitor.available;
        }

        private function onNetworkChange():void
        {
            _feedMonitor.start();
        }

        private function onShellMenuSelect( evt:Event ):void
        {
            var coll:ArrayCollection =
                                new ArrayCollection( evt.target.menu.items );
            var index:int = coll.getItemIndex( evt.target );
            switch( index )
            {
                case 0:
                    navigateToURL( new URLRequest(
                                "http://weblogs.macromedia.com/mxna/" ) );
                    break;
                case 1:
                    _toaster.title = _feedService.title;
                    _toaster.posts = _feedService.getItemsByAmount(MAX_AMOUNT);
                    _feedTimer.reset();
                    break;
                case 2:
                    _feedTimer.stop();
                    _feedMonitor.stop();
                    _toaster.close();
                    close();
                    break;
            }
        }

        [Bindable]
        public function get isAvailable():Boolean
        {
            return _isAvailable;
        }
        public function set isAvailable( bool:Boolean ):void
        {
```

```
                _isAvailable = bool;
            }
        ]]>
    </mx:Script>

</mx:WindowedApplication>
```

Save the file as RSSReader.mxml in the root of your working directory for the RSS Reader application.

There is quite a bit going on in the RSSReader class, and it utilizes some interesting parts of the AIR API that have not been introduced in the previous chapters. To begin, look at how the application monitors user presence in the applicationComplete event handler of the <mx:WindowApplicaiton>:

```
NativeApplication.nativeApplication.idleThreshold = IDLE_THRESHOLD;
NativeApplication.nativeApplication.addEventListener(
                                    Event.USER_IDLE , onUserIdle );
NativeApplication.nativeApplication.addEventListener(
                                    Event.USER_PRESENT, onUserPresent );
```

The applicationComplete event is dispatched after the application has been initialized and added to the display list. In the onAppComplete event handler, handlers for events related to user presence dispatched by the flash.desktop.NativeApplication Singleton are established. The NativeApplication instance represents the AIR application and is created upon startup. In the idleThreshold property of NativeApplication, you can set the amount of time, in seconds, allowed to elapse without user input. After that time has elapsed, the application will dispatch an idle event whose handler is set here as the onUserIdle() method. When presence is detected again by the application, the onUserPresent event handler is invoked. These methods simply control the Timer object used in polling the feed service. If a user is not present, then requests are stopped, resuming again when a user is detected by the application as being present.

Also within the onAppComplete() method, the application establishes a air.net.URLMonitor instance to handle status events related to the availability of a network resource:

```
_feedMonitor = new URLMonitor( new URLRequest( FEED ), [200,202] );
_feedMonitor.addEventListener( StatusEvent.STATUS, onStatus );
_feedMonitor.start();
```

The URLMonitor monitors the availability of a service. The first argument in the constructor for URLMonitor is the URL you wish to monitor. The RSS reader is requesting data from AXNA and the connection is considered available based on the HTTP status returned — the second argument in the constructor. The available property of the URLMonitor, which is checked in the onStatus() handler, changes the value of the isAvailable property of the RSSReader class. Through binding, when the isAvailable property has changed, the invalidateAvailability() method is invoked. The URLMonitor is instructed to begin monitoring the service in the onAppComplete() method, but also in the event handler for networkChange on the <mx:WindowedApplication>.

Depending on the value of the isAvailable property, the application is instructed to start or resume polling the RSS feed, and calls either of two methods that construct the native menu for display in the Windows system tray or Mac OSX dock:

```
private function setAvailableMenu():void
{
```

```
        var tip:String = "MXNA Reader - available";
        var shellMenu:NativeMenu = new NativeMenu();
        shellMenu.addItem( new NativeMenuItem( "Go to MXNA" ) );
        shellMenu.addItem( new NativeMenuItem( "Read Recent Posts" ) );
        shellMenu.addItem( new NativeMenuItem( "Quit MXNA Reader" ) );
        shellMenu.addEventListener( Event.SELECT, onShellMenuSelect );
        setMenu( shellMenu, tip );
    }

    private function setUnavailableMenu():void
    {
        var tip:String = "MXNA Reader - unavailable";
        var shellMenu:NativeMenu = new NativeMenu();
        shellMenu.addItem( new NativeMenuItem( "Quit MXNA Reader" ) );
        shellMenu.addEventListener( Event.SELECT, onShellMenuSelect );
        setMenu( shellMenu, tip );
    }
```

The `flash.display.NativeMenu` class enables you to construct a list of items that relate to any commands an application will run within the `select` event handlers. When a network resource is available, the RSS reader presents the options to navigate to the Adobe XML News Aggregator site, instruct the `DigestWindow` to open with the last received posts, or quit the application altogether — which is the sole option from the `NativeMenu` created when the availability of the network resource has been lost. Though the construction of a `NativeMenu` object is independent of the operating system, applying the menu to a system tray or dock icon differs between Windows and Mac OS X:

```
    private function setMenu( menu:NativeMenu, tip:String ):void
    {
        var app:NativeApplication = NativeApplication.nativeApplication;
        if( NativeApplication.supportsDockIcon )
        {
            // Mac OSX
            ( app.icon as DockIcon ).menu = menu;
        }
        else
        {
            ( app.icon as SystemTrayIcon ).menu = menu;
            ( app.icon as SystemTrayIcon ).tooltip = tip;
        }
        app.icon.bitmaps = [( new dockIcon() ).bitmapData];
    }
```

The `icon` property of the `NativeApplication` Singleton represents the application icon that appears in the Windows system tray and the Mac OS X dock. Depending on the operating system in which the AIR runtime is running, the type of icon differs — on Windows the `icon` property is of type `flash.desktop.SystemTrayIcon` and on Mac OS X it is `flash.desktop.DockIcon`. To determine what operating system the application is running in, you can check the `supportsDockIcon` property of `NativeApplication`. If the AIR application supports a dock icon, then the operating system is Mac OS X. Along with the different icon types are also properties vary between the systems. If the RSS reader is running in Windows, then a tooltip is displayed upon rollover of the icon in the system tray.

Image data is not inherently applied to an icon. On Mac OS X a default graphic is supplied to the icon when in the dock, whereas on Windows no icon will appear in the system tray unless explicitly set using the bitmaps property of the InteractiveIcon instance. This example uses an embedded graphic found in the /assets folder for the code for this chapter found on the CD-ROM included with this book, but you are free to use any graphic or array of graphics you wish.

When a user has chosen to quit the application from the native menu and the onShellMenuSelect() method is invoked, the application performs some cleanup to ensure that all processes of the application are properly stopped and any windows closed:

```
_feedTimer.stop();
_feedMonitor.stop();
_toaster.close();
close();
```

The Timer instance, which is used to continually poll the service, is stopped; the URLMonitor instance is instructed to stop polling for success; the DigestWindow is closed; and the application is closed explicitly. Because the main application window will not have a display while running, the command to close the application is presented from the system tray icon, rather than the typical chrome window button. The closing event handler of RSSReader then invokes the exit() method of the NativeApplication instance, which terminates the application.

Because the face of the application is the toaster-style alert presenting posts, properties of the main WindowedApplication need to be set in order to have it not appear in the system menu, and to enable it to perform the tasks you have defined in this section. In the next section you will create the application descriptor file and define the pertinent system chrome properties for the RSS reader.

Deploying the Application

It's time to deploy the RSS Reader application and start reading all the posts you may have missed from the Adobe XML News Reader while you were following along with the examples in this chapter. In this section you will create the descriptor file and deploy the application for installation. The system chrome attributes to set the main WindowedApplication as invisible and not available from the system menu will be declared within the descriptor file, along with properties related to the application as it appears on a user's computer.

The Descriptor File

Open your favorite text editor, create a new file, and enter the following markup:

```
<?xml version="1.0" encoding="UTF-8"?>
<application xmlns="http://ns.adobe.com/air/application/1.0">

    <id>com.aircmr.RSSReader</id>
    <filename>RSSReader</filename>
    <version>0.1</version>
    <name>RSS Reader</name>
    <description>A Reader for RSS feeds</description>
    <copyright>2007</copyright>

    <initialWindow>
```

```
        <content>RSSReader.swf</content>
        <systemChrome>none</systemChrome>
        <transparent>true</transparent>
        <visible>false</visible>
      </initialWindow>

      <installFolder>AIRCMR/RSSReader</installFolder>
      <programMenuFolder>AIRCMR</programMenuFolder>

  </application>
```

Save the file as `RSSReader-app.xml` in the root of your working directory along with the `RSSReader.mxml` file.

This file will serve as the application descriptor file. The element values declared within the `<initialWindow>` tag are important for hiding the main application window and allowing the system and dock icons to act as the access point for the RSS reader. The system chrome will not be drawn and made transparent and the `RSSReader` window will be made invisible on the display list.

Along with the attributes set for the chrome of the RSS reader, when the application is installed it will be named `RSSReader` and be available in the `AIRCMR` folder of the application directory of your operating system.

With the descriptor file in place, you are set to compile and package the RSS Reader AIR executable.

Compiling and Packaging

Two files are necessary to package an AIR application: the main SWF file and the XML application descriptor file. In this section you will produce the SWF file using the command-line tools and package the AIR application.

> *The graphic assets used for the dock and system tray icon in the examples can be found on the CD-ROM, or you can create your own. If you are following along with the examples in this chapter, those graphic assets reside in a folder named* `assets` *in the working directory.*

Open a command prompt, navigate to the working directory for the RSS reader, enter the following command, and press Enter:

```
> amxmlc RSSReader.mxml
```

If you have purchased a certificate from a certificate authority, such as VeriSign or Thawte, then you may use that certificate, rather than create the self-signed certificate, and skip the following operation. To create a self-signed certificate within the working directory, enter the following command:

```
> adt -cerificate -cn RSSReader 1024-RSA certificate.pfx password
```

With the command prompt still pointing to the working directory, enter the following command to package the RSS Reader application:

```
> adt -package -storetype pkcs12 -keystore certificate.pfx RSSReader.air RSSReader-
app.xml RSSReader.swf
```

You will be prompted to enter the password for the certificate. If you created a self-signed certificate from the second command, enter **password**. After running these commands, an `RSSReader.swf` file, a `certificate.pfx` file, and the `RSSReader.air` installer file are generated within your working directory.

Once the installer has been created successfully by running the last command, navigate to your working directory and double-click on the AIR installer to install and run RSS Reader. If all goes well, a toaster window will appear and present you with the most recent posts from the Adobe XML News Aggregator feed. While that toaster window is open, the state of the application will look something like what is shown in Figure 3-1.

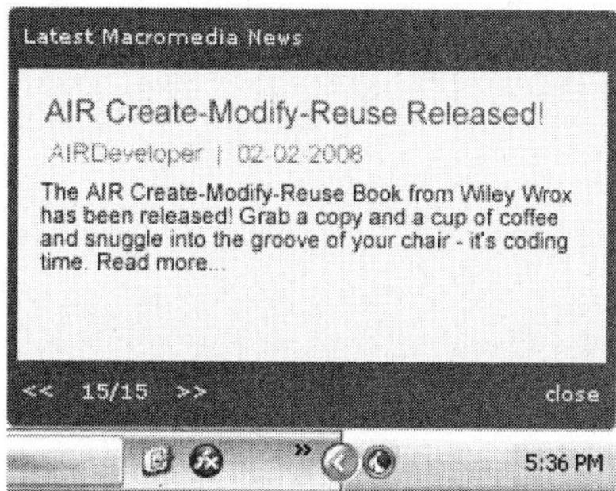

Figure 3-1

Start reading those posts you may have missed and let the application run in the background to present new posts received from the service in a toaster alert.

Summary

This chapter covered monitoring the availability of an online service and user presence,while developing an application that runs in the background and is accessed through the native menus of the system tray or dock icon. Detecting the operating system using the `supportsDockIcon` property of the `NativeApplication` class was introduced to determine the type of `InteractiveIcon` class available to the application. The `NativeMenu` class was introduced and applied to the application icon to enable access to commands while the main application window performs tasks in the background.

While incorporating these techniques into developing a desktop RSS reader, you were also introduced to some additional features of the windowing API as they relate to the system chrome properties and native window types. By using the `lightweight` `NativeWindowType`, an unobtrusive toaster-style alert is presented as new posts are received by the application, creating an enjoyable reading experience as you catch up on the latest news.

You can take what you have learned from building the RSS reader and target another feed or even multiple feeds. The concepts introduced in this chapter also apply to any number of other applications that are intended to run in the background and present users with application-specific windows.

Music Player

Let's face it: There are a lot of music players on the market. Programs such as Apple iTunes and Windows MediaPlayer control a large share of that market. Nevertheless, this does not mean there isn't room for another. Each existing player has features that make it stand out compared to others, but you might want a combination of features currently unavailable from any one player. This is your opportunity to create the next killer music app.

In this chapter, you will create a music player called airAMP, named after one of the first widely used MP3 programs. The intention of this exercise is to create one with the basic playback features, which you can use to build a more robust, full-featured music player. airAMP will utilize the AIR API to search a chosen directory for MP3 files that will populate a playlist. It will write the playlist back to the user's hard drive as an XML file. Additionally, it will leverage the AIR API's capability to create an application that is moderately styled and chromeless.

Through building this application, you will learn how to use several features within the Flex and AIR APIs, including the following:

- Utilizing the `File` class to select a directory
- Recursively searching a directory and its subdirectories for a file type (MP3)
- Utilizing the `FileStream` class to read and write to an XML file
- Creating an application that does not rely on the AIR chrome-window controls
- Loading, playing, and reading ID3 tags of MP3s using ActionScript

The next section discusses the design concepts behind developing airAMP.

Design

The features that you can build into a music player are seemingly endless. Although you could begin to write down everything that you think should be in the ideal music player, it is probably best to start with the basics, add a couple of minor thrills, and work up from there. However, don't abandon all of your great ideas — write them down and come back to them once the application is playing some tunes. Until then, begin considering how the airAMP music player will work.

The first thing to consider is where the music will come from. A traditional Flex music player for the Internet would be capable reading an XML file or receiving data containing MP3 file URLs through a dynamic feed. However, the AIR API enables you to play files off a hard drive. Furthermore, AIR enables you to recursively search through directories. This feature will be an ideal way to quickly populate airAMP with music. To do this, the application will use the `getDirectoryListingAsync()` method found in the `File` class. The result will be a listing of `File` objects representing MP3s.

When the search is complete and the results listing has been received, one way to prepare the data to be playback-ready would be to create a `Sound` object for every returned entry and use the `Sound` object's `load()` method by passing the `nativePath` property of the `File`. However, loading more than a couple of MP3s at once would slow the system down, if not crash the music player.

The solution to this would be to create a new value object for each entry returned. The value object would have information such as the file location, whether it has been loaded, and some basic track data such as music album title, song title, and artist title. Instead of loading all of the MP3s through the `Sound` object at once, only one MP3 will be executed at a time, and only when the object is referenced. To accomplish this, an application data model will store an `ArrayCollection` of value objects representing each MP3 location.

After the data has been populated, a sound manager class will be used to access any MP3 in the data model. The sound manager will manage all playback functionality such as play, pause, stop, next, previous, volume, and timeline position. When the user selects a track from the list, the sound manager will load the corresponding MP3 and begin to play it, dispatching events that affect the application's view.

The airAMP music player's view will have the following features:

- **Playback controls:** All playback controls will be grouped into a single component. This component will have buttons for previous, play, pause, stop, and next. It will also feature an area to display the artist's name and the song title. Lastly, it will have a timeline scrubber created from the `HSlider` component. The `HSlider` component's labels will be repurposed to show the running time for the sound file.
- **Playlist view:** All of the value objects representing each MP3 will be referenced in a modified `DataGrid` component. When the user selects an entry, the `DataGrid` will dispatch an event to the `SoundManager` class, which will get ready to play the selection.
- **Settings panel:** The settings panel gives users a way to select the music directory on their hard drive. In addition to this, the music player will give users the option of either using the same music database every time the application is opened, or refreshing the database by requerying the music directory.
- **Custom appearance:** The music player will look a little better than most out-of-the-box Flex apps. To accomplish this, it will have its own style sheet and custom button skins, and it will not use the native system window chrome. Although all of this is not necessary to the functionality of the application, a custom appearance always adds to the user experience.

Now that the basic design and functionality have been defined, you can begin building the airAMP music player. In the next section, you will learn how to set up the directory structure and gather the accompanying files.

Building the Directory Structure

Before discussing *how* the music player is built, it is important that the directory structure for this chapter is properly set up:

1. Begin by creating a new directory in your local development directory called "MusicPlayer." This directory will be your working directory for this application.
2. Create the package structure for this application by creating new directories — `com`, `aircmr`, and `musicplayer` — in your working directory. The music player package structure should look as follows: *working directory*`/com/aircmr/musicplayer`.
3. Download the corresponding `assets` directories from the `MusicPlayer` section on the accompanying web site and place them in the root of the working directory. These files will be used throughout the development of the music player.

Now that the directory structure has been set up, you can begin to build airAMP. The next section starts the development process with a discussion of where the data for the application is coming from and how the application will utilize it.

Handling Data

Most, if not all, software capable of playing MP3s has a playlist feature, and airAMP will be no exception. If you think about a playlist in terms of data, it is an array of references to music files on the user's hard drive. The music player searches a specified directory and returns an XML list of locations to MP3 files. This directory is specified in the user's settings. Both the settings and playlist data are read and written to corresponding XML files contained in the application's storage directory. The following sections describe these files.

External XML

Before the music player can query a directory for MP3s, it first has to load some basic settings information for the user to edit. All XML for this application is accessed through the `XMLFileService` class. Once loaded, it is parsed by the `XMLParserUtil` utility class. Both classes are discussed later in this section. For now, begin by building the XML.

settings.xml

Open a text editor and enter the following code:

```
<?xml version='1.0' encoding='utf-8'?>
<settings>
  <defaultMusicDirectory></defaultMusicDirectory>
  <refreshOnStartup>false</refreshOnStartup>
  <musicDataBaseLocation>xml/musicdatabase.xml</musicDataBaseLocation>
</settings>
```

Save the file as `settings.xml` in the root of your working directory.

The settings file is brief and to the point. The `<defaultMusicDirectory>` node will be the location of the user's chosen music directory. It will be assigned once the user has selected a directory. The `<refreshOnStartup>` node will be a toggle that informs the application whether it should query the `defaultMusicDirectory` for MP3s on startup, or just use the data provided in the `musicdatabase.xml` file. The `<musicDataBaseLocation>` node specifies the location and name of the music database. This XML is discussed in the next section.

musicdatabase.xml

The music database is not created by hand, meaning you don't have to create a new XML document called `musicdatabase.xml` within a text editor. When the music player first writes the file search XML to disk, this XML file will be created. However, it's helpful to see the data you are reading and writing beforehand:

```
<database>
    <fileItem>
        <name></name>
        <url></url>
        <songName></songName>
        <artist></artist>
        <album></album>
    </fileItem>
</database>
```

The music database is nothing more than a node tree of `<fileItem>` nodes. Each `<fileItem>` contains the saved properties for each track. The `XMLParserUtil` parses each node into a `TrackVO` value object, which represents a single track in the playlist. The `TrackVO` object and supporting classes are discussed in the following sections.

Data Objects

The application parses the data being read and managed as two separate types of objects: `SettingsVO` and `TrackVO`. Both objects are referenced and controlled by the `ApplicationDataModel`. The application's data model will be discussed momentarily. First, take a closer look at the data objects.

SettingsVO

The `SettingsVO` object is a basic value object containing getters and setters for four properties that you will access throughout the music player:

- `settingFileLocation (String)`: The location of the settings file (most likely `xml/settings.xml`)
- `musicDatabaseLocation (String)`: The name of the file to which you want to save the database. This is relative to the default AIR user resource directory.
- `defaultMusicDirectory (String)`: The location of the default music directory as specified by the user in the Settings panel.
- `refreshOnStartup (Boolean)`: A `true/false` variable specified by the user under the Settings panel that toggles the music player's capability to search for MP3s on application startup.

Create the `SettingVO` class by opening a document and inserting the following code:

```
package com.aircmr.musicplayer.data
{
    public class SettingsVO
    {
        private var _defaultMusicDirectory:String;
        private var _refreshOnStartup:Boolean;
        private var _musicDatabaseLocation:String;

        public function SettingsVO():void
        {
        }

        public function get defaultMusicDirectory():String
        {
            return _defaultMusicDirectory;
        }

        public function set defaultMusicDirectory( val:String ):void
        {
            _defaultMusicDirectory = val;
        }

        public function get refreshOnStartup():Boolean
        {
            return _refreshOnStartup;
        }

        public function set refreshOnStartup( val:Boolean ):void
        {
            _refreshOnStartup = val;
        }

        public function get musicDatabaseLocation():String
        {
            return _musicDatabaseLocation;
        }

        public function set musicDatabaseLocation( val:String ):void
        {
            _musicDatabaseLocation = val;
        }
    }
}
```

Save the file as `SettingsVO.as` in your working directory under the `com/aircmr/musicplayer/data/` directory.

TrackVO

The `TrackVO` object is a bit more involved, mainly because each `TrackVO` object represents an MP3 file on the user's hard drive. Therefore, each `TrackVO` object has to contain a `Sound` object that will represent the playable data.

Create a new document and insert the following code:

```
package com.aircmr.musicplayer.data
{
    import flash.events.Event;
    import flash.events.EventDispatcher;
    import flash.events.IOErrorEvent;
    import flash.filesystem.File;
    import flash.media.Sound;
    import flash.net.URLRequest;

    public class TrackVO extends EventDispatcher
    {
        public static const SONG_LOADED:String = "songLoaded";

        private var _file:File;
        private var _trackURL:String;
        private var _sound:Sound;
        private var _album:String;
        private var _trackTitle:String;
        private var _artist:String;
        private var _track:String;
        private var _loaded:Boolean = false;

        public function TrackVO( file:File=null , arg_trackURL:String = "" ,
            arg_album:String = "" , arg_artist:String = "" ,
            arg_trackTitle:String = "" , arg_track:String = "" ):void
        {
            _trackURL = arg_trackURL;
            _album = arg_album;
            _artist = arg_artist;
            _trackTitle = arg_trackTitle;
            _track = arg_track;

            _sound = new Sound();
            _sound.addEventListener( Event.COMPLETE, soundLoadCompleteHandler );
            _sound.addEventListener( Event.ID3, id3AvailableHandler );
            _sound.addEventListener( IOErrorEvent.IO_ERROR, songFileErrorHandler );
            if( file ) loadSong( file.nativePath );
        }

        public function loadSong( url:String = null ):void
        {
            if( !url ) url = _trackURL;

            var urlRequest:URLRequest = new URLRequest( url );
            _sound.load( urlRequest );
        }

        private function id3AvailableHandler( event:Event ):void
        {
            _album = _sound.id3.album;
            _artist = _sound.id3.artist;
            _trackTitle = _sound.id3.songName;
```

```
        _track = _sound.id3.track;
    }

    private function soundLoadCompleteHandler( event:Event ):void
    {
        dispatchEvent( new Event(TrackVO.SONG_LOADED) );
        _loaded = true;
    }

    private function songFileErrorHandler( event:IOErrorEvent ):void
    {
        trace( "error:"+event.errorID +" : file not found" );
    }

    public function get album():String
    {
        return _album;
    }

    public function set album(val:String):void
    {
        _album = val;
    }

    public function get artist():String
    {
        return _artist;
    }

    public function set artist(val:String):void
    {
        _artist = val;
    }

    public function get trackTitle():String
    {
        return _trackTitle;
    }

    public function set trackTitle(val:String):void
    {
        _trackTitle = val;
    }

    public function get track():String
    {
        return _track;
    }

    public function set trackURL( val:String ):void
    {
        _trackURL = val;
    }
```

```
        public function get trackURL():String
        {
            return _trackURL;
        }

        public function get sound():Sound
        {
            return _sound;
        }

        public function get loaded():Boolean
        {
            return _loaded;
        }
    }
}
```

Save the file as TrackVO.as in your working directory under the com/aircmr/musicplayer/data / directory.

When first instantiated, a TrackVO object will be assigned MP3 information such as the URL, album title, artist name, and song title. Therefore, this data object, like any value object, has mostly getters and setters. However, when the TrackVO object is called by the SoundManager, it will be used to store the Sound object information of the designated loaded MP3. The SoundManager class is explained in further detail later in this chapter.

A reference to a Sound object is declared in the TrackVO's constructor method, but nothing is loaded. Instead, the appropriate event handlers are added to the Sound object instance to check for load completion (Event.COMPLETE), ID3 information availability (Event.ID3), and load errors (IOErrorEvent .IO_ERROR).

In order to load an MP3 file, the SoundManager accesses the loadSong method of the TrackVO object. The loadSong method will accept an URL as a parameter, but if none exists, it will load the _trackURL property of the object. When called, a URLRequest object is instantiated with the URL of the MP3 file, and the load method is called on the Sound object. Once the Sound object has detected ID3 information, the id3AvailableHandler is called. When the Sound object has finished loading the MP3 file, the soundLoadCompleteHandler is called, which sets the public property, loaded, to true, and dispatches a Song.SONG_LOADED event.

The following list describes the available properties of the TrackVO object:

- album (String): The title of the album as defined in the ID3 information of the MP3
- artist (String): The name of the artist as defined in the ID3 information of the MP3
- trackTitle (String): The name of the song as defined in the ID3 information of the MP3
- track (Number): The track number as defined in the ID3 information of the MP3
- trackURL (String): The URL of the MP3 file
- sound (Sound): A reference to the Sound object pertaining to the TrackVO object
- loaded (Boolean): A Boolean indicating whether the Sound object has loaded an MP3

Now that you know what you're loading and to where you're loading it, it's time to take a look at how to load it. The next section discusses the `ApplicationDataModel` class.

ApplicationDataModel

The `ApplicationDataModel` class serves as a way to control all of the data being loaded into the application, and to ensure that you never have duplicate data. It is a Singleton, meaning that it can only be instantiated once. If you try to call `new ApplicationDataModel()`, the debugger throws an error. Therefore, you refer to the `ApplicationDataModel` by calling its `getInstance()` method. When you call `ApplicationDataModel.getInstance()`, it returns a reference to the class. If it's the first time the method has been called, a new instance of the class is created and returned, but this is the only time an instance is created.

What is the benefit of a Singleton in this situation? By only having one instance of the `ApplicationDataModel`, you can have complete access to the application data no matter where you are. Any data you change in one class will affect all other classes. This is especially useful if you are working with a team of developers and would like to ensure that everyone's pieces of the application are referring to the same data source.

The data in the music player is controlled almost exclusively through the main application class, but being a Singleton will be more convenient once you start adding your own functionality to the application.

Create a new document and insert the following code:

```
package com.aircmr.musicplayer.data
{
    import flash.events.Event;
    import flash.events.EventDispatcher;
    import mx.collections.ArrayCollection;

    public class ApplicationDataModel extends EventDispatcher
    {
        private static var _instance:ApplicationDataModel;

        public static const SETTINGS_CHANGE:String = "settingsChange";
        public static const TRACKLIST_CHANGE:String = "tracklistChange";

        private var _settingsFileLocation:String;
        private var _trackCollection:ArrayCollection;
        private var _settings:SettingsVO;

        public function ApplicationDataModel()
        {
            _trackCollection = new ArrayCollection();
            _settings = new SettingsVO();
        }

        public static function getInstance():ApplicationDataModel
        {
```

```
            if(_instance = null)
            {
                _instance = new ApplicationDataModel();
            }
            return _instance;
        }

        public function set trackCollection( val:ArrayCollection):void
        {
            _trackCollection = val;
            dispatchEvent( new Event( ApplicationDataModel.TRACKLIST_CHANGE ) );
        }

        public function get trackCollection():ArrayCollection
        {
            return _trackCollection;
        }

        public function set settings( val:SettingsVO ):void
        {
            _settings = val;
            dispatchEvent( new Event( ApplicationDataModel.SETTINGS_CHANGE ) );
        }

        public function get settings():SettingsVO
        {
            return _settings;
        }

        public function get settingsFileLocation():String
        {
            return _settingsFileLocation;
        }

        public function set settingsFileLocation( val:String ):void
        {
            _settingsFileLocation = val;
        }
    }
}
```

Save the file as `ApplicationDataModel.as` in your working directory under the `com/aircmr/musicplayer/data` directory.

The `ApplicationDataModel` stores three variables: `settings`, `trackCollection`, and `settingsLocation`. The `settingsLocation` string is hard-coded into the main application class. `settings` and `trackCollection` are assigned after the respective XML has been parsed. Here is an example:

```
ApplicationDataModel.getInstance().settings =
    XMLParserUtil.parseSettingsXML( event.xml );
```

Once the `settings.xml` file has been read by the `XMLFileService`, the `XMLParserUtil` parses the XML object and assigns it to the `settings` property on the `ApplicationDataModel`. Both `XMLFileService` and `XMLParserUtil` are discussed in the following section.

Accompanying Services and Utilities

The previous section covered the shared data model that will be populated with the settings and music track data for the music player. It touched upon the concept of querying the user's hard drive for MP3s in regard to building `TrackVO` objects. This section discusses how the application's data is accessed and parsed, and how it populates the `ApplicationDataModel` class. Begin with looking at the `XMLFileService` class.

XMLFileService

The `XMLFileService` service is a class that will aid in reading, writing, and copying XML from the user's computer. In particular, it is used to read and write the settings and music database XML files.

Create a new document and insert the following code:

```
package com.aircmr.musicplayer.services
{
    import com.aircmr.musicplayer.events.XMLFileServiceEvent;
    import flash.events.Event;
    import flash.events.EventDispatcher;
    import flash.events.IOErrorEvent;
    import flash.filesystem.File;
    import flash.filesystem.FileMode;
    import flash.filesystem.FileStream;
    import mx.controls.Alert;

    public class XMLFileService extends EventDispatcher
    {
        private var _file:File;
        private var _fileStream:FileStream;
        private var _fileName:String;

        public function XMLFileService():void {

        public function loadXMLFileFromStorage( fileName:String ):void
        {
            _file = File.applicationStorageDirectory.resolvePath( fileName );

            if( !_file.exists )
            {
                dispatchEvent( new XMLFileServiceEvent(
                    XMLFileServiceEvent.XML_FILE_NOT_FOUND ) );
                return;
            }

            _fileStream = new FileStream();
            _fileStream.addEventListener( Event.COMPLETE, onXMLFileLoadComplete );
            _fileStream.addEventListener( IOErrorEvent.IO_ERROR, errorHandler );
            _fileStream.openAsync( _file, FileMode.READ );
        }

        public function saveXMLFileToStorage( fileName:String , data:XML ):void
        {
```

```
        var xml_encoding:String = "<?xml version='1.0' encoding='utf-8'?>\n";
        var xml_toWrite:String = xml_encoding + data.toXMLString();

        _file = File.applicationStorageDirectory.resolvePath( fileName );

        _fileStream = new FileStream();
        _fileStream.addEventListener( Event.CLOSE, onXMLFileWriteComplete );
        _fileStream.openAsync( _file, FileMode.WRITE );
        _fileStream.writeUTFBytes( xml_toWrite );
        _fileStream.close();
    }

    public function copyXMLFileFromApplicationDirectoryToStorage(
        fileName:String ):void
    {
        var sourceFile:File =
            File.applicationDirectory.resolvePath( fileName );

        if( !sourceFile.exists )
        {
            dispatchEvent( new XMLFileServiceEvent(
                XMLFileServiceEvent.XML_FILE_NOT_FOUND ) );
            return;
        }

        var resultsFile:File =
            File.applicationStorageDirectory.resolvePath( fileName );

        sourceFile.addEventListener( IOErrorEvent.IO_ERROR , errorHandler );
        sourceFile.addEventListener( Event.COMPLETE , onXMLFileCopyComplete );
        sourceFile.copyToAsync( resultsFile , true );
    }

    private function onXMLFileCopyComplete( event:Event ):void
    {
        dispatchEvent(
            new XMLFileServiceEvent(XMLFileServiceEvent.XML_FILE_COPIED) );
    }

    private function onXMLFileLoadComplete( event:Event ):void
    {
        var xml:XML = XML(
            _fileStream.readUTFBytes( _fileStream.bytesAvailable ) );
        _fileStream.removeEventListener( Event.COMPLETE,
            onXMLFileLoadComplete );
        _fileStream.removeEventListener( IOErrorEvent.IO_ERROR, errorHandler );
        _fileStream.close();

        var xmlEvent:XMLFileServiceEvent =
            new XMLFileServiceEvent( XMLFileServiceEvent.XML_LOADED );
        xmlEvent.xml = xml;
        dispatchEvent( xmlEvent );
    }
```

```
        private function onXMLFileWriteComplete( event:Event ):void
        {
            dispatchEvent( new
               XMLFileServiceEvent(XMLFileServiceEvent.XML_FILE_WRITTEN) );
        }

        private function errorHandler( event:IOErrorEvent ):void
        {
            var errorMessage:String =
                "Error Loading File "+event.text+" FILE ERROR";
            var xmlEvent:XMLFileServiceEvent =
                new XMLFileServiceEvent( XMLFileServiceEvent.XML_ERROR );
            xmlEvent.message = errorMessage;
            dispatchEvent( xmlEvent );

            Alert.show( errorMessage );
        }

        public function get file():File
        {
            return _file;
        }

        public function set file( val:File ):void
        {
            _file = val;
        }
    }
}
```

Save the document as `XMLFileService.as` in the application's services package (*working directory*/com/aircmr/musicplayer/services).

The `XMLFileService` class is nothing more than a `File` instance and a `FileStream` instance, along with some event listeners that let the application know whether the open or save operation was successful. The following snippet demonstrates how the application first instantiates the `XMLFileService` and passes it a string representing the local URL:

```
var settingsXMLLoader:XMLFileService = new XMLFileService();
settingsXMLLoader.addEventListener( XMLFileServiceEvent.XML_FILE_NOT_FOUND,
    onSettingsNotFound );
settingsXMLLoader.addEventListener(XMLFileServiceEvent.XML_LOADED,
    settingsLoadedHandler );
settingsXMLLoader.loadXMLFileFromStorage(
    ApplicationDataModel.getInstance().settingFileLocation );
```

In this example, the `XMLFileService` is instantiated and immediately assigned event listeners. After the XML file is loaded, `settingsLoadedHandler()` is called. The `settingsLoadedHandler()` method receives an `XMLServiceEvent` object containing the unparsed `settings.xml` XML object. It populates the `settings` property in the data model by using the `XMLParserUtil` utility to parse the XML into a `SettingsVO` object. Both the `XMLServiceEvent` and `XMLParserUtil` classes will be discussed momentarily.

Copying Local Files

First, it is important to find out if and when the file exists. In the `XMLFileService` class, you are checking to see whether the `settings.xml` file resides in `applicationStorageDirectory` using `resolvePath()` and the `File` class' `exists` Boolean property:

```
var sourceFile:File = File.applicationStorageDirectory.resolvePath( fileName );
if( !sourceFile.exists )
{
    dispatchEvent( new Event( XMLFileService.FILE_NOT_FOUND ));
    return;
}
```

When users first run the music player, the `settings.xml` file won't exist in their application storage directory. The class instance will dispatch a `FILE_NOT_FOUND` event, and it is up to the controller, `MusicPlayer.MXML`, to make the next move. If the file does not exist in the storage directory, then it needs to be created.

There is a `settings.xml` file that contains some basic settings data located in the application directory. You can read the file from the application directory by referencing the `File` class' `applicationDirectory` property, instead of `applicationStorageDirectory`.

Because of the security features inside AIR, you will not be able to write back to the application directory. This directory is used only to store data and assets for which you want read-only access. Writing restrictions are quite a problem because the application needs to write the user's preferences back to `settings.xml`. Instead of trying to write back to the application directory, the `XMLFileService` should copy the file from this directory to the storage directory when it is not found in storage. The next time the application is instantiated, the `settings.xml` file will be found. This is accomplished in the `copyXMLFromApplicationDirectoryToStorage()` method using the `File` class' `copyToAsync()` method:

```
sourceFile.copyToAsync( resultsFile , true );
```

In this case, `sourceFile` is the `settings.xml` file contained in the application directory, and `resultsFile` is the path to the `settings.xml` file that will be written to the storage directory. Because this method is asynchronous, listeners will monitor whether the copy is successful or an error occurs. Should the copy be successful, the `XMLFileService` will then try to load the XML from the storage directory. After the XML has been loaded, an instance of the `XMLFileServiceEvent` is thrown.

Writing XML Data to Files

The music player application stores the `settings.xml` and `musicdatabase.xml` files in the storage directory. If the user has accepted new settings, or a new folder is queried for music, these files are rewritten. In terms of the `musicdatabase.xml` file, if one doesn't exist, then AIR will create one. In either situation, the first thing that needs to happen is the declaration of the encoding header:

```
var xml_encoding:String = "<?xml version='1.0' encoding='utf-8'?>\n";
```

This string ensures that the XML will be well formed. However, writing `encoding = 'utf-8'` does not mean anything if the file is not actually written as a UTF-encoded document. To write a UTF encoded document, open a new `FileStream` asynchronously and use the `writeUTFBytes()` method:

```
_fileStream.openAsync( _file, FileMode.WRITE );
_fileStream.writeUTFBytes( xml_toWrite );
_fileStream.close();
```

In this example, `_file` can be the path to either `settings.xml` or `musicdatabase.xml`. `xml_toWrite` is the XML with the `xml_encoding` string appended to the beginning of the XML object. Lastly, be sure to close the file after writing to it. If the file is not closed, then the `FileStream` object is not ready for garbage collection. Furthermore, you do not want additional data to be accidentally written to your file. Be sure to also close `FileStream` after reading from a file.

XMLFileServiceEvent

After the music application has read from, written to, or copied an XML file, a corresponding `XMLFileServiceEvent` is thrown. When reading data, the `XMLFileServiceEvent.XML_LOADED` event is dispatched and the `XMLFileServiceEvent` object is passed containing the loaded XML as the event object's `xml` property. This class is used exclusively with the `XMLFileService` class.

Create a new document and insert the following code:

```
package com.aircmr.musicplayer.events
{
    import flash.events.Event;

    public class XMLFileServiceEvent extends Event
    {
        public static const XML_FILE_COPIED:String = "xmlFileCopied";
        public static const XML_FILE_NOT_FOUND:String = "xmlFileNotFound";
        public static const XML_FILE_WRITTEN:String = "xmlFileWritten";
        public static const XML_LOADED:String = "xmlLoaded";
        public static const XML_ERROR:String = "xmlError";

        private var _xmlResults:XML;
        private var _message:String;

        public function XMLFileServiceEvent( type:String,
            bubbles:Boolean=false, cancelable:Boolean=false )
        {
            super( type, bubbles, cancelable );
        }

        public function get xml():XML
        {
            return _xmlResults;
        }

        public function set xml( val:XML ):void
        {
            _xmlResults = val;
        }

        public function get message():String
        {
```

```
            return _message;
        }

        public function set message( val:String ):void
        {
            _message = val;
        }
    }
}
```

Save the file as `XMLFileServiceEvent.as` in your working directory under the `com/aircmr/musicplayer/events` directory.

The next section explains how the music player's XML is parsed.

XMLParserUtil

After the XML has been loaded and the `XMLFileServiceEvent.XML_LOADED` event is dispatched, it needs to be parsed. Creating a utility to parse the XML will help keep your classes clean and organized. The `XMLParserUtil` class contains two public static methods: `parseSettingsXML()` and `parseSongDatabaseXML()`. `parseSettingsXML()` parses the XML into a `SettingsVO` object and returns the object to the caller. `parseSongDatabaseXML()` creates a new `TrackVO` object for every item in the XML, adds the `TrackVO` to an `ArrayCollection`, and returns the `ArrayCollection` to the caller. In both cases, the returned objects are added to the `ApplicationDataModel`.

Create a new document and insert the following code:

```
package com.aircmr.musicplayer.utils
{
    import com.aircmr.musicplayer.data.SettingsVO;
    import com.aircmr.musicplayer.data.TrackVO;
    import com.aircmr.musicplayer.events.XMLFileServiceEvent;
    import mx.collections.ArrayCollection;

    public class XMLParserUtil
    {
        public static function parseSettingsXML( xml:XML ):SettingsVO
        {
            var settingsVO:SettingsVO = new SettingsVO();
            settingsVO.refreshOnStartup = (xml.refreshOnStartup.toString());
            settingsVO.musicDatabaseLocation = xml.musicDatabaseLocation;
            settingsVO.defaultMusicDirectory = xml.defaultMusicDirectory;

            return settingsVO;
        }

        public static function parseSongDatabaseXML(
            musicDataBase:XML ):ArrayCollection
        {
            var trackCollection:ArrayCollection = new ArrayCollection();

            for(var i:Number = 0 ; i < musicDataBase.children().length(); i++)
            {
```

```
                var track:TrackVO = new TrackVO()
                track.trackURL = musicDataBase..url[i];
                track.album = musicDataBase..album[i];
                track.artist = musicDataBase..artist[i];
                track.trackTitle = musicDataBase..songName[i];

                trackCollection.addItem( track );
            }

            return trackCollection;
        }

    }
}
```

Save the file as `XMLParserUtil.as` in your working directory under the `com/aircmr/musicplayer/utils` directory.

The next section takes a look at a service that will help in querying the user's computer for music files.

FileSearch

One of the key features of the music player application is its ability to search through a specified directory and subdirectories for a particular file type. To add this behavior, you will create a search service that returns the data in an XML object.

Create a new document and insert the following code:

```
package com.aircmr.musicplayer.services
{
    import com.aircmr.musicplayer.events.FileSearchEvent;
    import flash.events.EventDispatcher;
    import flash.events.FileListEvent;
    import flash.events.IOErrorEvent;
    import flash.filesystem.File;

    public class FileSearch extends EventDispatcher
    {

        private var _file:File;
        private var _includeSubDirectories:Boolean = false;
        private var _fileTypeArray:Array;
        private var _xml:XML;
        private var _subDirectoryQueryList:Array;
        private var _returnValue:*;

        public function FileSearch(){}

        public function queryDirectoryListToXML( directoryName:String ,
            includeSubDirectories:Boolean = false, fileTypeArray:Array = null):void
        {
```

```
            _subDirectoryQueryList = new Array();

            _xml = new XML( "<database></database>" );
            _fileTypeArray = fileTypeArray;
            _includeSubDirectories = includeSubDirectories;

            _file = new File( directoryName );
            _file.addEventListener( IOErrorEvent.IO_ERROR , errorHandler );
            _file.addEventListener( FileListEvent.DIRECTORY_LISTING,
                queryDirectoryResults );
            _file.getDirectoryListingAsync();
        }

        private function queryDirectoryResults( event:FileListEvent ):void
        {
            var directoryList:Array = event.files;
            var subDirectoryList:Array = new Array();

            for ( var i:String in directoryList )
            {
                var file:File = directoryList[i];
                if ( file.isDirectory && _includeSubDirectories )
                {
                    _subDirectoryQueryList.push( file );
                }
                else
                {
                    if( _fileTypeArray.length > 0 )
                    {
                        if( checkFileType(file) )
                            _xml.appendChild( xmlNodeStructure(file) );
                    }
                    else
                    {
                        _xml.appendChild( xmlNodeStructure(file) );
                    }
                }
            }

            var searchDirectory:File = _subDirectoryQueryList.pop();
            if ( searchDirectory == null )
            {
                var searchEvent:FileSearchEvent =
                    new FileSearchEvent( FileSearchEvent.SEARCH_FINISHED );
                searchEvent.searchResults = _xml;
                dispatchEvent( searchEvent );
            }
            else
            {
                searchDirectory.addEventListener(
                    FileListEvent.DIRECTORY_LISTING, queryDirectoryResults );
                searchDirectory.getDirectoryListingAsync();
            }
        }
```

```
        private function checkFileType( file:File ):Boolean
        {
            for( var i:Number = 0 ; i < _fileTypeArray.length ; i++ )
            {
                if( file.extension == _fileTypeArray[i] )
                {
                    return true;
                    break;
                }
                else if ( i == _fileTypeArray.length - 1 )
                {
                    return false;
                    break;
                }
            }

            return false;
        }

        private function errorHandler( event:IOErrorEvent ):void
        {
            dispatchEvent( new FileSearchEvent( FileSearchEvent.SEARCH_FAILED ));
        }

        protected function xmlNodeStructure( file:File ):XML
        {
            var newNode:XML = new XML( "<fileItem></fileItem>" );
            newNode.name = file.name;
            newNode.url = file.url;

            return newNode;
        }
    }
}
```

Save the file as `FileSearch.as` in your working directory under the `com/aircmr/musicplayer/services` directory.

The intention of the `FileSearch` class is to create an abstract class that you can extend because you may want your retrieved data returned as a different data type. The music player application implements the `MP3FileSearch` class, which extends `FileSearch` and ensures that the returned data is parsed as an XML object that is later written to the `musicdatabase.xml` file. The `MP3FileSearch` class is discussed momentarily.

The `FileSearch` service has one public method: `queryDirectoryListToXML()`. This method accepts three arguments: the directory that you are searching, a Boolean representing whether you'd like to search subdirectories, and an array containing the extensions of the file type you are searching for. Please review the following example:

```
var fileSearch:FileSearch = new FileSearch();
fileSearch.addEventListener(FileSearchEvent.SEARCH_FINISHED,
    fileSearchResultHandler);
fileSearch.queryDirectoryListToXML( pathToDirectory , true, ["mp3"] );
```

After a new FileSearch is instantiated, a FileSearchEvent.SEARCH_FINISHED event is added to listen for the search results. The FileSearchEvent is discussed in the following section. Once the listener is added, queryDirectoryListToXML() is called and the arguments are passed.

In regard to the music player, once a search has been completed, fileSearchResultHandler() is called and the results (in XML) are parsed by the XMLParserUtil and then entered into the ApplicationDataModel.

How the Search Is Executed

When queryDirectoryListToXML() is called by the class that instantiated the FileSearch, a new File object is created with the path property defined as the directory to search. A listener is added to listen for the FileListEvent.DIRECTORY_LISTING event. Once the listener is assigned, the getDirectoryListingAsync() method is called:

```
_file = new File( directoryName );
_file.addEventListener( FileListEvent.DIRECTORY_LISTING, queryDirectoryResults );
_file.getDirectoryListingAsync();
```

getDirectoryListingAsync() returns an array of File objects that represent the contents of the directory. After the search has been executed, the FileListEvent object is passed to the queryDirectoryResults() method. The FileListEvent contains the result array of File objects, which are accessed through the event's files property.

The queryDirectoryResults() method loops through the results array, checking whether the File object represents a directory. If it does, and you have allowed subdirectory searching, the File object is added to the _subDirectoryQueryList array. If it doesn't, the method checks the extension property of the File object to determine whether it matches the desired query. If the search is a success, then the path to the file is added to an XML object.

After the File has been checked, the queryDirectoryResults() method checks whether _subDirectoryQueryList contains subdirectories. If it does, then getDirectoryListingAsync() is executed on the subdirectory File object, thus recursively searching each subdirectory. If _subDirectoryQueryList does not have any subdirectories, then a FileSearchEvent event is dispatched as FileSearchEvent.SEARCH_FINISHED. All search results are stored in the searchResults property of the dispatched FileSearchEvent object. The next section discusses this object.

FileSearchEvent

FileSearchEvent is exclusively dispatched by the FileSearch service. It extends the Event class and consists of the event type strings and the search results. The search results are assigned to the searchResults property and can be any class type, as denoted by the asterisk (*) wildcard.

Create a new document and insert the following code:

```
package com.aircmr.musicplayer.events
{
    import flash.events.Event;

    public class FileSearchEvent extends Event
    {
```

```
        static public const SEARCH_FINISHED:String = "searchFinished";
        static public const SEARCH_FAILED:String = "searchFailed";

        private var _searchResults:*;

        public function FileSearchEvent( type:String,
            bubbles:Boolean=false, cancelable:Boolean=false )
        {
            super( type, bubbles, cancelable );
        }

        public function get searchResults():*
        {
            return _searchResults;
        }

        public function set searchResults( val:* ):void
        {
            _searchResults = val;
        }
    }
}
```

Save the file as `FileSearchEvent.as` in your working directory under the `com/aircmr/musicplayer/events` directory.

With regard to the music player, the `FileSearchEvent` object is passed to the application controller's `fileSearchResultHandler()`method, which in turn passes the returned XML (contained in `FileSearchEvent.searchResults`) to the `XMLParserUtil` utility, which parses the results into `TrackVO` objects. In addition, the results are saved to the storage directory as `musicdatabase.xml`.

The next section discusses further customizations to the implementation of the `FileSearch` classes for the music player.

MP3FileSearch

As previously mentioned, the `FileSearch` class is meant to be extended. The purpose of this is to customize how you would like the results XML to be structured.

Create a new document and insert the following code:

```
package com.aircmr.musicplayer.services
{
    import flash.filesystem.File;
    import com.aircmr.musicplayer.utils.ID3Parser;

    public class MP3FileSearch extends FileSearch
    {

        public function MP3FileSearch():void
        {
            super();
        }
```

```
        override protected function xmlNodeStructure( file:File ):XML
        {
            var id3Information:Object = ID3Parser.returnID3Information( file );
            var newNode:XML = new XML( "<fileItem></fileItem>" );
            newNode.name = file.name;
            newNode.url = file.url;

            if( file.extension == "mp3" )
            {
                newNode.songName = id3Information.songName;
                newNode.artist = id3Information.artist;
                newNode.album = id3Information.album;
            }

            return newNode;
        }
    }
}
```

Save the file as `MP3FileSearch.as` in your working directory under the `com/aircmr/musicplayer/services` directory.

The only method that needs to be customized is `xmlNodeStructure()`. If you look back at the `xmlNodeStructure()` method of the `FileSearch` class, it only creates a `<fileItem>` node with the name of the file and its path. It would be nice if airAMP could retrieve additional file data such as the track's name, the artist, and an album title so that this information is displayed before the MP3 has been loaded. After all, up until the point where you play the MP3, you are just referencing the MP3 file on the hard drive, not actually loading it. This is done using the `ID3Parser` utility. The next section discusses this class in more detail.

After the XML node has been structured the way you want it, it is returned to the `queryDirectoryResults()`method of the `FileSearch` class and appended to the results XML object (`_xml`).

Currently, the `FileSearch` class and associated classes are set up to search for the returned MP3s. However, feel free to finagle the class into searching by filename versus by extension, and returning the results in different configurations. Regardless of how this class is used in airAMP, it is an excellent class to have in your code library.

ID3Parser

The `ID3Parser` utility is a small class containing one static function: `returnID3Information()`. It is used to retrieve the MP3 ID3v1 (version 1) track information at the time when the file has been located and referenced on the hard drive. Alternately, you can read a `Sound` object's ID3 information after the MP3 file has been loaded. However, in the case of airAMP, it would be nice to have a complete listing of the MP3's song, artists, and album titles. If you were to load every MP3 file into a `Sound` object at once, just to retrieve this information, the application would slow down to a crawl, if not crash. Using this parser utility will prevent that from happening while returning the track information.

This section does not cover ID3 information in detail or explain working with binary data in detail. To learn more about both topics, see Ben Stucki's "Working with Binary Data" on the Adobe Labs website (`http://labs.adobe.com/wiki/index.php/AIR:Articles:Working_with_Binary_Data`).

Create a new document and insert the following code:

```
package com.aircmr.musicplayer.utils
{
    import flash.filesystem.File;
    import flash.filesystem.FileMode;
    import flash.filesystem.FileStream;

    public class ID3Parser
    {
        public static function returnID3Information( file:File ):Object
        {
            var id3Info:Object = new Object();

            var fileStream:FileStream = new FileStream();
            fileStream.open( file, FileMode.READ );
            fileStream.position = file.size - 128;

            if( fileStream.readMultiByte(3, "iso-8859-1").match(/tag/i) )
            {
                id3Info.songName = fileStream.readMultiByte(30,"iso-8859-1");
                id3Info.artist = fileStream.readMultiByte(30,"iso-8859-1");
                id3Info.album = fileStream.readMultiByte(30,"iso-8859-1");
            }

            if( !id3Info.songName )
            {
                id3Info.songName = file.name;
            }

            if( !id3Info.artist )
            {
                id3Info.artist = "";
            }

            if( !id3Info.album )
            {
                id3Info.album = "";
            }

            fileStream.close();
            return id3Info;
        }
    }
}
```

Save the file as `ID3Parser.as` in your working directory under the `com/aircmr/musicplayer/utils` directory.

When `returnID3Information()` is called, a new `FileStream` instance is created and the referenced `File` object (passed in as an argument) is opened. Immediately, the read position within the file is set to 128 bytes in from the end of the file. This position sets the stream to read ID3v1 information.

The file is read using the `readMultiByte()` method of the `FileStream` class. The first three bytes are checked to determine whether they are the word "`tag`" If these bytes are indeed the word "`tag`," then the file contains ID3v1 information and the position continues to move through the file. From there, the bytes are read in increments of 30. The first 30 bytes represents the song name, and as such, the songName property of the id3info object is set. The next 30 bytes represent the artist's name. The last 30 bytes represent the album name. If you have been counting this out, there are still 35 bytes left in the file. There is optional information such as year, comments, and genre. However, for this application you only need the necessary information. After the ID3v1 information has been read, the FileStream is closed and the id3info object is returned to the caller, which in this case is the MP3FileSearch class.

There is more than one way to read ID3 information because there is more than one version of ID3 information. For instance, ID3v2 has more information, but it is more difficult to parse. Additionally, ID3v1 information is not necessarily defined — in this case, ID3Parser assigns the filename as the song name and leaves the artist's name and album title blank. To learn more about ID3 information, check out www.id3.org.

Now that the data has been defined and the MP3's file locations are known, the next step is to build a way to manage the audio files. In the next section, you will build a class to do just that.

Sound Manager

The ApplicationDataModel has been populated and the UI is just about ready to be built. One final step in ensuring that the data is being treated correctly is to build a SoundManager class that controls a selected Sound object and assures the player that only one MP3 file will play at a time. It will contain all functionality to interact with the MP3, such as play, pause, stop, volume, and playhead positioning. The UI will communicate directly with the SoundManager through public methods, and the manager will respond using custom events. Begin by building the class.

Create a new document and insert the following code:

```
package com.aircmr.musicplayer.managers
{
    import com.aircmr.musicplayer.data.TrackVO;

    import flash.events.Event;
    import flash.events.EventDispatcher;
    import flash.events.TimerEvent;
    import flash.media.Sound;
    import flash.media.SoundChannel;
    import flash.media.SoundTransform;
    import flash.utils.Timer;

    public class SoundManager extends EventDispatcher
    {
        public static const NO_SELECTED_TRACK:String = "noSelectedTrack";
        public static const TRACK_COMPLETE:String = "trackComplete";

        private var _volume:Number = 1;
        private var _channel:SoundChannel;
        private var _soundTransformer:SoundTransform;
        private var _durationTimer:Timer;
        private var _selectedTrack:TrackVO;
        private var _currentSound:Sound;
        private var _playing:Boolean = false;
```

```
private var _paused:Boolean = false;
private var _trackPosition:Number = 0;
private var _trackLength:Number = 0;
private var _artistTitle:String = "NO SONG CURRENTLY SELECTED";
private var _trackTitle:String = "----";
private var _albumTitle:String = "----";

public function SoundManager()
{
    _durationTimer = new Timer( 100 );
    _durationTimer.addEventListener( TimerEvent.TIMER, durationHandler );
    _soundTransformer = new SoundTransform();
    _channel = new SoundChannel();
}

public function selectTrack( track:TrackVO ):void
{
    _selectedTrack = track;
    _trackPosition = 0;
    if( playing ) playTrack( _selectedTrack );
}

public function play( event:Event=null ):void
{
    if( !_selectedTrack )
    {
        dispatchEvent( new Event( SoundManager.NO_SELECTED_TRACK ));
        return;
    }

    if( playing ) return;

    if( _paused )
    {
        pause();
        return;
    }

    playTrack( _selectedTrack );
}

public function stop( event:Event=null ):void
{
    _trackPosition = 0;
    _channel.stop();
    playing = false;
}

public function pause( event:Event=null ):void
{
    if( !_selectedTrack || (!playing && !_paused) ) return;

    if( playing )
    {
```

```
            _trackPosition = _channel.position;
            _channel.stop();
            playing = false;
            _paused = true;
        }
        else
        {
        playCurrentTrack( _trackPosition );
        }
    }

    public function playTrack( song:TrackVO ):void
    {
        stop();

        _selectedTrack = song;

        if( !song.loaded )
        {
            song.addEventListener( TrackVO.SONG_LOADED, songLoadEvent );
            song.loadSong();
        }
        else
        {
            currentSound = song.sound;
        }
    }

    public function setPlayheadPosition( val:Number ):void
    {
        playCurrentTrack( val );
    }

    private function songLoadEvent( event:Event ):void
    {
        if( _selectedTrack != event.target ) return;

        currentSound = event.target.sound as Sound;
    }

    private function durationHandler( event:TimerEvent ):void
    {
        trackPosition = _channel.position;
    }

    private function playCurrentTrack( position:Number = 0 ):void
    {
        _channel.stop();
        _channel = _currentSound.play( position );
        _channel.addEventListener( Event.SOUND_COMPLETE, onTrackComplete );
        _channel.soundTransform = _soundTransformer;

        _paused = false;
```

```
        playing = true;
    }

    private function onTrackComplete( event:Event ):void
    {
        dispatchEvent( new Event( SoundManager.TRACK_COMPLETE ));
    }

    public function set currentSound( sound:Sound ):void
    {
        _currentSound = sound;

        playCurrentTrack();

        trackTitle = _currentSound.id3.songName;
        artistTitle = _currentSound.id3.artist;
        trackLength = _currentSound.length;
    }

    public function get currentSound():Sound
    {
        return _currentSound;
    }

    [Bindable]
    public function set trackTitle( value:String ):void
    {
        if( value == null ) value = "UNKNOWN";
        _trackTitle = value;
    }

    public function get trackTitle():String
    {
        return _trackTitle;
    }

    [Bindable]
    public function set artistTitle( value:String ):void
    {
        if( value == null ) value = "UNKNOWN ARTIST";
        _artistTitle = value;
    }

    public function get artistTitle():String
    {
        return _artistTitle;
    }

    [Bindable]
    public function set albumTitle( value:String ):void
    {
        _albumTitle = value;
    }
```

```
        public function get albumTitle():String
        {
            return _albumTitle;
        }

        [Bindable]
        public function set trackLength( value:Number ):void
        {
            _trackLength = value;
        }

        public function get trackLength():Number
        {
            return _trackLength;
        }

        [Bindable]
        public function set trackPosition( value:Number ):void
        {
            _trackPosition = value;
        }

        public function get trackPosition():Number
        {
            return _trackPosition;
        }

        [Bindable]
        public function set playing( value:Boolean ):void
        {
            _playing = value;
            value ? _durationTimer.start() : _durationTimer.stop();
        }

        public function get playing():Boolean
        {
            return _playing;
        }

        [Bindable]
        public function set volume( val:Number ):void
        {
            _volume = val;

            _soundTransformer.volume = val;
            if( _channel ) _channel.soundTransform = _soundTransformer;
        }

        public function get volume():Number
        {
            return _volume;
        }
    }
}
```

Save the file as SoundManager.as in your working directory under the com/aircmr/musicplayer/managers directory.

The SoundManager is first instantiated by the music player's application controller class, MusicPlayer.mxml. It is accessed by the UI components through the controller class in order to keep each class as loosely coupled as possible. The following is a small snippet from the MusicPlayer.mxml file that you will create later in this chapter:

```
<ui:BottomControls id="bottomControls"
    volumeChange="{_soundManager.volume = bottomControls.volume}"
    volume="{_soundManager.volume}" />
```

In this example, the BottomControls component has a public property, volume, which is bound to the volume property of the SoundManager. Additionally, this particular component has an event, volumeChange, which is dispatched any time the volume is changed specifically by the component's interface controls. Any time volumeChange is dispatched, the inline code is accessed. During this process, the volume property of the SoundManager is set to the BottomControl's volume property.

Loading Songs

When the SoundManager is requested to play a song, it is passed a TrackVO object. Because the Sound object resides in the TrackVO object, the SoundManager only has to call the TrackVO's loadSong() method and listen for the SONG_LOADED event to be thrown:

```
_selectedTrack = song as TrackVO;
if( !song.loaded )
{
    song.addEventListener( TrackVO.SONG_LOADED, songLoadEvent );
    song.loadSong();
}
else
{
    currentSound = song.sound;
}
```

Once the Sound object has loaded, the TrackVO reference is assigned to _currentTrack, which in turn is assigned to the _channel SoundChannel object.

Monitoring Playhead Time

Unlike the VideoDisplay component, the SoundChannel does not have an event for monitoring the position of the playhead in the MP3. However, it is important that this application displays the time to the user. To monitor the time, the best solution is to use the Timer class.

In the SoundManager class' constructor method, a new Timer is instantiated and the durationHandler() method is assigned to the TimerEvent.TIMER event. The durationHandler() method updates the trackPosition property. The Timer class starts and stops when the playing property is changed:

```
public function set playing( value:Boolean ):void
{
    _playing = value;
    value ? _durationTimer.start() : _durationTimer.stop();
}
```

This ensures that the `trackPosition` is only updated whenever the song is playing. The `PlaybackControls` component uses the `trackPosition` property to updated its display. This is discussed further in the next section.

Building the User Interface

Now that the data for the airAMP music player is in place and the supporting classes are set up, the next step is to build the view. All interface elements for the music player are divided among four MXML components. They consist of the settings panel, playback controls, playlist view, and bottom controls. This section discusses how to build each element.

SettingsPanel

Because it is the first graphical element to be viewed by users, the `SettingsPanel` component is an excellent place to start. This component enables users to select their music directory and set their music player preferences.

Open a new document and insert the following ActionScript and MXML markup:

```
<?xml version="1.0" encoding="utf-8"?>
<mx:TitleWindow xmlns:mx="http://www.adobe.com/2006/mxml"
        width="400"
        title="Settings"
        showCloseButton="true"
        paddingLeft="10" paddingTop="10"
        paddingRight="10" paddingBottom="10"
        close="closeHandler( event )">

    <mx:Script>
    <![CDATA[
        import com.aircmr.musicplayer.events.XMLFileServiceEvent;
        import com.aircmr.musicplayer.services.XMLFileService;
        import com.aircmr.musicplayer.data.ApplicationDataModel;
        import mx.events.FlexEvent;
        import mx.controls.Alert;
        import mx.events.FileEvent;
        import flash.filesystem.File;
        import mx.managers.PopUpManager;

        public static const SETTINGS_UPDATED:String = "settingsUpdated";

        private var _file:File;

        [Bindable] private var _directoryPath:String = "";
        [Bindable] private var _refreshBoolean:Boolean;

        public static function show():SettingsPanel
        {
            var panel:SettingsPanel =
                SettingsPanel( PopUpManager.createPopUp(
                DisplayObject( mx.core.Application.application ),
                SettingsPanel, true ) );
```

```
            PopUpManager.centerPopUp(panel);
            panel.init();
            return panel;
        }

        private function init():void
        {
            _file = new File();
            _refreshBoolean =
                ApplicationDataModel.getInstance().settings.refreshOnStartup;
            _directoryPath =
      ApplicationDataModel.getInstance().settings.defaultMusicDirectory.toString();

            if( _directoryPath != "" ) _file.nativePath = _directoryPath;
            refreshButton.selected = _refreshBoolean;
            setWelcomeMessage();
        }

        private function closeHandler( event:Event ):void
        {
            dispatchEvent( new Event(Event.CANCEL) );
            PopUpManager.removePopUp( this );
        }

        private function browseHandler( event:Event ):void
        {
            _file.addEventListener( Event.SELECT , onDirectorySelect );
            _file.browseForDirectory( "SELECT YOUR MUSIC DIRECTORY ");
        }

        private function onDirectorySelect( event:Event ):void
        {
            var results:File = event.target as File;
            _directoryPath = results.nativePath;

            results.removeEventListener( Event.SELECT , onDirectorySelect );
        }

        private function applyHandler( event:Event ):void
        {
            _directoryPath = directoryInput.text;

              try
              {
              var _dirTest:File = new File();
              _dirTest.nativePath = _directoryPath;
            }
            catch( error:Error)
            {
                Alert.show( "Directory Path is Invalid.", "Oops..." );
                return;
            }

            if( _directoryPath != "" && _dirTest.exists )
```

```
        {
            ApplicationDataModel.getInstance().settings.defaultMusicDirectory =
                _directoryPath;
            ApplicationDataModel.getInstance().settings.refreshOnStartup =
                refreshButton.selected;

            var fileService:XMLFileService = new XMLFileService();
            fileService.addEventListener( XMLFileServiceEvent.XML_FILE_WRITTEN,
                fileWrittenHandler );
            fileService.saveXMLFileToStorage(
                ApplicationDataModel.getInstance().settingFileLocation,
                buildSettingsData() );
        }
        else
        {
            Alert.show( "Directory Path is Invalid.", "Oops..." );
        }
    }

    private function buildSettingsData():XML
    {
        var refreshData:String = (
            ApplicationDataModel.getInstance().settings.refreshOnStartup )
            ? "true" : "";

        var xml:XML = new XML("<settings></settings>");
        xml.defaultMusicDirectory =
            ApplicationDataModel.getInstance().settings.defaultMusicDirectory;
        xml.refreshOnStartup = refreshData;
        xml.musicDatabaseLocation =
            ApplicationDataModel.getInstance().settings.musicDatabaseLocation;

        return xml;
    }

    private function fileWrittenHandler( event:Event ):void
    {
        dispatchEvent( new Event(SettingsPanel.SETTINGS_UPDATED) );
        closeHandler( null );
    }

    private function setWelcomeMessage():void
    {
        if( _directoryPath != "" )
        {
            welcomeMessage.text = "Please select the directory where you store
            your mp3s. This may include subdirectories as well.";
        }
        else
        {
            welcomeMessage.text = "While looking through the settings, " +
                "we noticed that you've never selected your default MP3 "+
                "directory "+
```

```
                    "Please select the directory where you store your mp3s. " +
                    "This may include subdirectories as well.";
            }
        }
    ]]>
    </mx:Script>
    <mx:TextArea borderStyle="none" height="80"
        wordWrap="true" width="100%" id="welcomeMessage" />
    <mx:HBox width="100%">
        <mx:Label text="Directory:"/>
        <mx:TextInput id="directoryInput" width="100%" text="{_directoryPath}" />
    </mx:HBox>
    <mx:HBox horizontalAlign="right" width="100%">
        <mx:Button label="BROWSE" click="browseHandler(event);" />
    </mx:HBox>

    <mx:Spacer height="10" />
    <mx:HRule width="100%" />
    <mx:TextArea borderStyle="none" width="100%"
        text="Would you like the Music Player to search for new MP3s
            on start up? This will override any previous music databases." />
    <mx:HBox>
    <mx:Label text="Refresh on Startup:" />
    <mx:CheckBox id="refreshButton" />
    </mx:HBox>

    <mx:Spacer height="20" />
    <mx:HBox horizontalAlign="center" width="100%">
        <mx:Button label="APPLY SETTINGS" click="applyHandler(event);" />
        <mx:Button label="CANCEL" click="closeHandler(event);" />
    </mx:HBox>
</mx:TitleWindow>
```

Save the file as `SettingsPanel.mxml` in your working directory under the `com/aircmr/musicplayer/ui` directory.

Displaying the SettingsPanel

If you were to look back at the `openSettingsPopUp` method of the `MusicPlayer` application class, you would see that the `SettingsPanel` component is instantiated and `show()` is called. The `show` method is how this `<mx:TitleWindow>` component is added to the `DisplayList`. When called, this method in turn calls the `createPopUp()` method of the `PopUpManager` class, which is wrapped in a `SettingsPanel` object in order to refer to methods in the `SettingsPanel`, such as the `init` method.

The `PopUpManager` class' `createPopUp` method accepts three parameters. The first is the location where the pop-up is displayed; in this case you're passing it a reference to the parent application. The second is the object you want to display; this just so happens to be the `SettingsPanel`. The final parameter is a Boolean indicating whether the instance is a modal, meaning it receives all mouse focus until closed; set this to `true` because this is definitely the desired action, as you want to make sure that users can't click on anything else while they're in the Settings window.

After the `PopUpManager` creates the instance of the `SettingsPanel`, move the panel to the center of the application using the `centerPopUp` method of the `PopUpManager`. Lastly, run the `init` method of the `SettingsPanel` in order to set all of the default data, and return a reference to the pop-up `SettingsPanel` instance.

Closing the Settings Panel

This method dispatches an `Event.CANCEL` event and removes the `SettingsPanel` instance from the `PopUpManager` using the `removePopUp()` method.

Browsing for a Directory

This method is called when the user clicks the Browse button. It adds an event listener to the `File` object that was instantiated in the `init()` method, listening for the `Event.SELECT` event, which will call `onDirectorySelect`. Once a listener is added to the `File` object, you can call the `browseForDirectory` method of the `File` class. The `browseForDirectory` method opens a system directory selection window. When a user selects a directory and clicks OK, an `Event.SELECT` event is dispatched containing a reference to the `File` object that the method was called from.

onDirectorySelect()

The `DirectorySelect()` method accepts an `Event` object as a parameter. It immediately assigns the `target` of the event to the variable, `results`. Once results are declared, you can assign the `nativePath` property of it to the `_directoryPath`. In this instance, `nativePath` represents the directory path for the directory chosen by the user. `_directoryPath` is what is going to be written to the `settings` object in the data model. Lastly, remove the listener from the `File` object, as you're done browsing for the directory.

applyHandler

When the user clicks the Apply Settings button, `applyHandler()` is called. This method runs a try/catch and tests whether `_dirTest`, a `File` object, will accept the `_directoryPath` as its `nativePath`. Unfortunately, there is no way to check for malformed directory paths outside of this method. `nativePath` is assigned the `_directoryPath` if it successfully passes; if not, an error alert is shown and the `applyHandler` is aborted.

If `nativePath` is assigned, then you try to determine whether the directory exists in the system. If the data came from the `browseForDirectory()` method, then you shouldn't have a problem passing this test. If it fails, then you again alert the user.

If successful, assign the `defaultMusicDirectory` and `refreshOnStartup` properties of the `Settings` object in the data model. You then create a new `FileService` instance that has an event listener listening for the `FileService.FILE_WRITTEN` event, which will access the `fileWrittenHandler` method. After the event listener is set up, call the `saveXMLFileToResource` of the `FileService` class and pass it the location of the settings file and an XML object that is generated by `buildSettingsData`.

Saving the Settings

The `buildSettingsData` method returns an XML object containing the property values of the `Settings` object from the data model. This is passed to the `FileService` so it can be written to the `settings.xml` file in the user's resource directory.

fileWrittenHandler

The `fileWrittenHandler` dispatches a `SettingsPanel.SETTINGS_UPDATED` event and closes the pop-up after the file has been successfully written to the resource directory.

Because everything in this application relies on other components for events and data, it is difficult to see the `SettingsPanel` in action. However, Figure 4-1 illustrates what the finished product will look like.

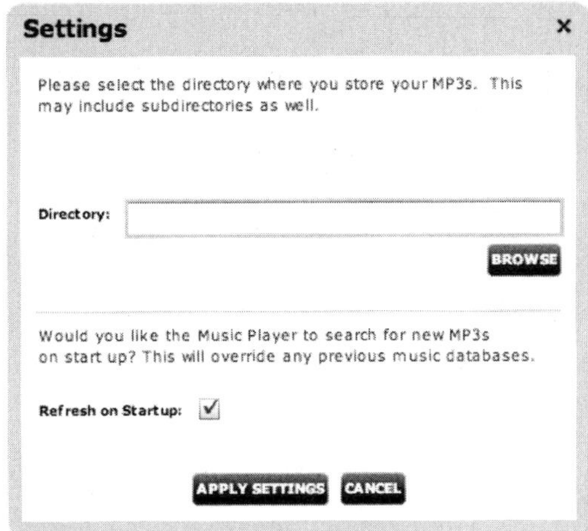

Figure 4-1

PlaybackControls

The `PlaybackControls` component will represent the entire user interface for playing, pausing, stopping, and advancing through a track. To preserve layout, it extends the `HBox` component. In addition to the playback buttons, it features an adjustable slider that represents the song's playback progress, as well as labels indicating play time, song title, and artist name.

Open a new document and insert the following ActionScript and MXML:

```
<?xml version="1.0" encoding="utf-8"?>
<mx:HBox xmlns:mx="http://www.adobe.com/2006/mxml"
    width="100%"
    height="60" verticalScrollPolicy="off" horizontalScrollPolicy="off"
    xmlns:ui="com.aircmr.musicplayer.ui.*" >

    <mx:Metadata>
        [Event(name="trackPositionUpdate", type="flash.events.Event")]
        [Event(name="playClick", type="flash.events.Event")]
        [Event(name="pauseClick", type="flash.events.Event")]
        [Event(name="stopClick", type="flash.events.Event")]
        [Event(name="previousClick", type="flash.events.Event")]
        [Event(name="nextClick", type="flash.events.Event")]
```

```
    </mx:Metadata>

    <mx:Script>
    <![CDATA[
        public static const TRACK_POSITION_UPDATE:String = "trackPositionUpdate";
        public static const PLAY_CLICK:String = "playClick";
        public static const PAUSE_CLICK:String = "pauseClick";
        public static const STOP_CLICK:String = "stopClick";
        public static const PREVIOUS_CLICK:String = "previousClick";
        public static const NEXT_CLICK:String = "nextClick";

        private var _artistTitle:String = "No track selected";
        private var _trackTitle:String = "---";
        private var _trackLength:Number;
        private var _trackPosition:Number;
        private var _newTrackPosition:Number;
        [Bindable] private var _labelArray:Array = ["00:00" , "00:00"];

        private function formatTimelineValue( num:Number ):String
        {
            return String( timeFormatter.format( new Date( num ) ));
        }

        private function handlePreviousClick( event:MouseEvent ):void
        {
            dispatchEvent( new Event( PlaybackControls.PREVIOUS_CLICK ) );
        }

        private function handlePlayClick( event:MouseEvent ):void
        {
            dispatchEvent( new Event( PlaybackControls.PLAY_CLICK ) );
        }

        private function handlePauseClick( event:MouseEvent ):void
        {
            dispatchEvent( new Event( PlaybackControls.PAUSE_CLICK ) );
        }

        private function handleStopClick( event:MouseEvent ):void
        {
            dispatchEvent( new Event( PlaybackControls.STOP_CLICK ) );
        }

        private function handleNextClick( event:MouseEvent ):void
        {
            dispatchEvent( new Event( PlaybackControls.NEXT_CLICK ) );
        }

      [Bindable]
       public function set artistTitle( val:String ):void
       {
           _artistTitle = val;
       }
```

```
public function get artistTitle():String
{
    return _artistTitle;
}

[Bindable]
public function set trackTitle( val:String ):void
{
    _trackTitle = val;
}

public function get trackTitle():String
{
    return _trackTitle;
}

[Bindable]
public function set trackLength( val:Number ):void
{
    _trackLength = val;
}

public function get trackLength():Number
{
    return _trackLength;
}

[Bindable]
public function set trackPosition( val:Number ):void
{
    _trackPosition = val;
    var timeLeft:String = String("-" +
        timeFormatter.format( new Date( trackLength - val ) ));
    var timeElapsed:String = String(
        timeFormatter.format( new Date( val ) ));
    _labelArray = [timeElapsed , timeLeft];

    if( _trackPosition == 0 && _trackLength == 0 )
        _labelArray = ["00:00" , "00:00"];
}

public function get trackPosition():Number
{
    return _trackPosition;
}

[Bindable("trackPositionUpdate")]
public function set newTrackPosition( val:Number ):void
{
    if( val == trackLength ) return;
    _newTrackPosition = val;
    dispatchEvent( new Event( PlaybackControls.TRACK_POSITION_UPDATE ) );
}
```

```
        public function get newTrackPosition():Number
        {
            return _newTrackPosition;
        }


    ]]>
    </mx:Script>

    <mx:DateFormatter id="timeFormatter" formatString="NN:SS" />

    <mx:HBox id="playControls" verticalAlign="middle"
        height="100%" horizontalGap="0" x="3" y="3">
        <mx:Button styleName="previousBtn" click="handlePreviousClick(event);" />
        <mx:Button styleName="playBtn" click="handlePlayClick( event );" />
        <mx:Button styleName="pauseBtn" click="handlePauseClick( event );" />
        <mx:Button styleName="stopBtn" click="handleStopClick( event );" />
        <mx:Button styleName="nextBtn" click="handleNextClick( event );" />
    </mx:HBox>
    <mx:Spacer width="100%" />
    <mx:VBox verticalGap="-2" y="-2" id="trackInfoDisplay"
        width="320" height="100%"
        styleName="trackInfoDisplayContainer" >
        <mx:Text width="100%" id="artistDisplay"
            textAlign="center" selectable="false"
            text="{artistTitle}" styleName="albumTextDisplay" />
        <mx:Text width="100%" id="trackDisplay"
            textAlign="center" selectable="false"
            text="{trackTitle}" styleName="albumTextDisplay" />
         <mx:HSlider id="scrubber"
            width="100%" height="20"
            dataTipFormatFunction="formatTimelineValue"
            allowTrackClick="true"
            liveDragging="true"
            tickInterval="0"
            labelOffset="0"
            labels="{_labelArray}"
            change="{newTrackPosition = scrubber.value}"
            value="{trackPosition}"
            minimum="0"
            maximum="{trackLength}"
        />
    </mx:VBox>
</mx:HBox>
```

Save the file as `PlaybackControls.mxml` in your working directory under the `com/aircmr/musicplayer/ui` directory.

Before discussing the features of the `PlaybackControls` component, take a moment to review what the finished component will look like. Figure 4-2 shows the displayed component.

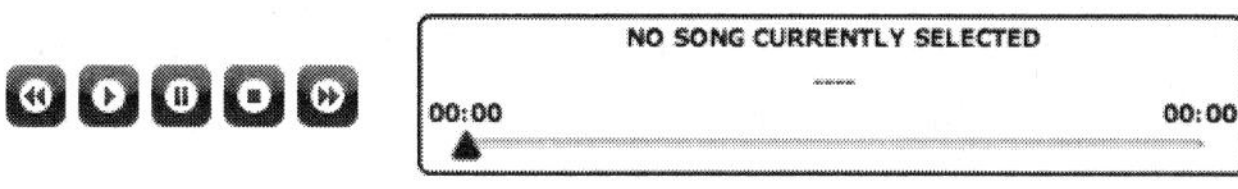

Figure 4-2

This application uses a stylesheet found in the `assets` *folder, along with some custom button skins. If you decide not to use these, comment out the* `styleName` *property of each button.*

Button Controls

The button controls for features such as play, pause, stop, forward, and next all perform in the same manner. When the user clicks one of the buttons, an event is dispatched that is listened to by the `SoundManager` in the application controller. For instance, pressing Play button dispatches the `PLAY_CLICK` event, which tells the `SoundManager` that a song needs to play. The responsibility is left to the `SoundManager` class to deal with that event effectively.

trackInfoDisplay

One of the nested component displays is the `trackInfoDisplay`. This group of components displays information such as playhead position, song duration, artist name, and song title.

Playhead Progress and Live Scrubbing

One feature that many music players have is some sort of progress bar that the user can drag (scrub) to change the playhead's position in the song. In airAMP, this is represented by an `HSlider` component.

The first challenge is to display the progress. This is accomplished by binding the `value` property of the `HSlider` component to the `trackPosition` property of `PlaybackControls`. The `trackPosition` property is updated by the `SoundManager` class. However, updating the `value` property alone will not make the `HSlider` move, unless it is aware of the total duration of the song. This is set by binding the `maximum` property of `HSlider` to the `trackLength` property of `PlaybackControls`. The `trackLength` property is updated by the `SoundManager` through the application controller when a new song is loaded. Now that the `HSlider`'s slider track represents the length of the song, the *thumb* (the black triangular button in Figure 4-2) will move along that track when the `HSlider`'s `value` is updated.

The next challenge is to enable *live scrubbing*. Live scrubbing enables the position in the song to be updated when the user drags the thumb along the track. Because the thumb represents the position in the song, when the user moves it, the component just needs to report the new time to the `SoundManager`. This is accomplished by utilizing the `CHANGE` event of `HSlider`. When the `CHANGE` event is dispatched, the `newTrackPosition` of the `PlaybackControl` is set to the thumb position. After the `newTrackPosition` is set, the `PlaybackControls` component dispatches the `TRACK_POSITION_UPDATE` event, which is received by the application controller. The application controller class in turn updates the playhead position in the `SoundManager` by calling the `setPlayheadPosition()`method and passing it the new played value from the `PlaybackControls`. Lastly, the `liveDragging` property of `HSlider` must be set to `true` in order to enable clicking and dragging the thumb.

Handling Time Stamps

Another feature that would be handy is the capability to display the `trackPosition` in terms of time elapsed versus total time. The `trackPosition` value is represented in seconds. Unfortunately, most video time stamps are represented as 01:30, meaning one minute and thirty seconds. In order to format the time in such a manner, use a Flex `DateFormatter`:

```
<mx:DateFormatter id="timeFormatter" formatString="NN:SS" />
```

This `DateFormatter` will format the `trackPosition` into `"NN:SS"`, which represents minute minute : second second. You access this formatter by calling the following:

```
timeFormatter.format( new Date( trackPosition ) )
```

The `DateFormatter` class looks for a `Date` object to be sent through the format method. By passing a new `Date` object with the `trackPosition` value to the `DateFormatter`, the result is a `String` that looks like 01:30.

The labels of `HSlider` are updated by setting the `labels` property to the `Bindable] _labelArray`. When the `trackPosition` property is updated by the application controller, the `_labelArray` is rewritten with two strings: `timeLeft` and `timeElapsed`. Both values are parsed in the NN:SS format using the `DateFormatter`. The effect is a display that is similar to the Apple iTunes progress display.

PlaylistView

The `PlaylistView` is used to display the track listing. It is a custom component that extends the `DataGrid` component.

Open a new document and insert the following ActionScript and MXML:

```
<?xml version="1.0" encoding="utf-8"?>
<mx:DataGrid xmlns:mx="http://www.adobe.com/2006/mxml"
    width="100%" height="90%" rowCount="5"
    doubleClickEnabled="true"
    change="onChangeSong(event);"
    doubleClick="playSelected(event);" >
    <mx:Metadata>
        [Event(name="playSelected", type="flash.events.Event")]
        [Event(name="selectedItemChange", type="flash.events.Event")]
    </mx:Metadata>
    <mx:Script>
        <![CDATA[
            import com.aircmr.musicplayer.data.TrackVO;

            public static const PLAY_SELECTED:String = "playSelected";
            public static const SELECTED_ITEM_CHANGE:String = "selectedItemChange";

            private var _selectedTrack:TrackVO;
```

```
public function playTrackAt( val:int = 0 ):void
{
    selectedIndex = val;
    playSelected();
}

public function next( event:Event=null ):void
{
    if( !_selectedTrack ) selectedIndex = 0;

    selectedIndex =
    ( selectedIndex == dataProvider.length - 1 ) ? 0 : selectedIndex+1;
    scrollToIndex( selectedIndex );

    selectedTrack = this.selectedItem as TrackVO;
    dispatchEvent( new Event( PlaylistView.SELECTED_ITEM_CHANGE ));
}

public function previous( event:Event=null ):void
{
    if( !_selectedTrack ) selectedIndex = 0;

    selectedIndex =
    ( selectedIndex == 0) ? dataProvider.length : selectedIndex - 1;

   scrollToIndex( selectedIndex );

    selectedTrack = this.selectedItem as TrackVO;
    dispatchEvent( new Event( PlaylistView.SELECTED_ITEM_CHANGE ));
}

private function playSelected( event:MouseEvent = null ):void
{
    selectedTrack = this.selectedItem as TrackVO;

    dispatchEvent( new Event( PlaylistView.PLAY_SELECTED ) );
}

private function onChangeSong( event:Event ):void
{
    selectedTrack = this.selectedItem as TrackVO;
}

public function get selectedTrack():TrackVO
{
    return _selectedTrack;
}

public function set selectedTrack( val:TrackVO ):void
{
```

```
                _selectedTrack = val;
            }
        ]]>
    </mx:Script>
    <mx:columns>
        <mx:DataGridColumn dataField="trackTitle"
            headerText="Song Name" width="200" />
        <mx:DataGridColumn dataField="artist" headerText="Artist" width="150" />
        <mx:DataGridColumn dataField="album" headerText="Album" width="150" />
    </mx:columns>
>/mx:DataGrid>
```

Save the file as PlaylistView.mxml in your working directory under the com/aircmr/musicplayer/ui directory.

DataProvider

The trackCollection property of the ApplicationDataModel is the PlaylistView's dataProvider. If you recall, the trackCollection ArrayCollection is populated with TrackVO objects representing the song data. The DataGrid display is populated by assigning each DataGridColumn's dataField a property that corresponds with a property in the TrackVO object. For example, dataField = "artist" would display the TrackVO.artist property. Each entry in the DataGrid then represents the supplied TrackVO. By calling the DataGrid's selectedItem, you are referencing a TrackVO object for the song.

Changing Tracks

The SoundManager relies on the PlaylistView for the selected track. This applies even when the user presses the Play button and the track isn't selected. For instance, when the user clicks the Play button, an event is sent through the controller to the SoundManager. If the SoundManager's selectedTrack property is null, then the NO_SELECTED_TRACK event is dispatched, which in turn calls the PlaylistView's playTrackAt() method. At this point, the playTrackAt() method sets the PlaylistView's selectedTrack property to the selectedItem at the supplied index. Lastly, the PlaylistView dispatches a PLAY_SELECTED event, telling the SoundManager that a song has been selected and needs to be played.

This may seem a little convoluted, but the components are still loosely coupled. In other words, you could replace the SoundManager with any class that you wish to control through the PlaylistView and you would only have to change the event listeners on the application controller level.

Later in this chapter, you will implement this component in the MusicPlayer.mxml file. Figure 4-3 shows the PlaylistView component as a playlist in the airAMP music player.

BottomControls

The last component set for the airAMP music player is the BottomControls component. This component extends the BottomBar component and is to be used with a Panel component. It consists of three components: the settings button, the volume controller HSlider, and a Spacer to separate the two. You can view this component at the bottom of Figure 4-3.

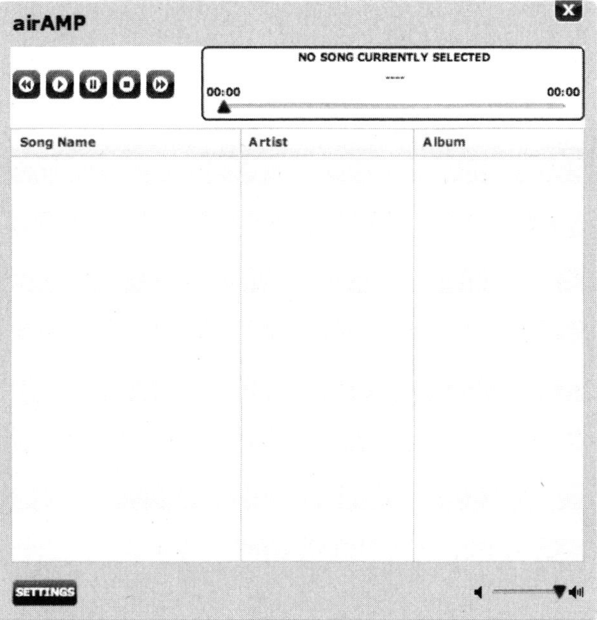

Figure 4-3

Open a new document and insert the following ActionScript and MXML:

```
<?xml version="1.0" encoding="utf-8"?>
<mx:ControlBar xmlns:mx="http://www.adobe.com/2006/mxml" width="100%" height="100%">
    <mx:Metadata>
        [Event(name="volumeChange", type="flash.events.Event")]
        [Event(name="settingsClick", type="flash.events.Event")]
    </mx:Metadata>
    <mx:Script>
        <![CDATA[
            import mx.events.SliderEvent;
            public static const VOLUME_CHANGE:String = "volumeChange";
            public static const SETTINGS_CLICK:String = "settingsClick";

            private var _volume:Number = 1;

            private function settingsButtonHandler( event:MouseEvent ):void
            {
                dispatchEvent( new Event( BottomControls.SETTINGS_CLICK ) );
            }

            private function formatVolume( num:Number ):String
            {
```

```
            return String( Math.round( num * 100 ));
        }

        private function onVolumeChangeHandler( event:SliderEvent ):void
        {
            volume = event.value;
        }

        [Bindable("volumeChange")]
        public function get volume():Number
        {
            return _volume;
        }

        public function set volume( val:Number ):void
        {
            _volume = val;
            dispatchEvent( new Event( BottomControls.VOLUME_CHANGE ));
        }

    ]]>
</mx:Script>
    <mx:Button id="settingBtn" label="SETTINGS" x="5"
        click="settingsButtonHandler( event );" />
    <mx:Spacer width="100%" />
    <mx:HBox horizontalGap="2" y="10">
        <mx:Image source="@Embed('/assets/images/volumeLow.png')" />
        <mx:HSlider id="volumeController"
            width="70" height="4"
            allowTrackClick="true"
            invertThumbDirection="true"
            dataTipFormatFunction="formatVolume"
            liveDragging="true"
            maximum="1"
            minimum="0"
            tickInterval="0"
            value="{volume}"
            change="onVolumeChangeHandler( event );"
            />
            <mx:Image source="@Embed('/assets/images/volumeHigh.png')" />
    </mx:HBox>
</mx:ControlBar>
```

Save the file as `BottomControls.mxml` in your working directory under the `com/aircmr/musicplayer/ui` directory.

The Volume Controls

The `BottomControls` component is fairly minimal, but the volume controls are a little complicated. If you have read the section "Playhead Progress and Live Scrubbing" for the `PlaybackControls` component, you should be familiar with how to move a thumb button along a `HSlider` track. The volume controls are no different.

The volumeController HSlider's value property is bound to the BottomControls public volume property. Likewise, when the thumb is moved, a CHANGE event is dispatched which in turn sets the volume property and dispatches an additional event, VOLUME_CHANGE, to the controller (or whatever class happens to be listening). The following snippet is the BottomControls instantiation in the application controller, the MusicPlayer.mxml file:

```
<ui:BottomControls id=''bottomControls''
volumeChange="{_soundManager.volume = bottomControls.volume}"
volume="{_soundManager.volume}"
settingsClick="openSettingsPopUp( event );" />
```

In this example, the volumeChange event is assigned the inline code that changes the SoundManager's volume property to the BottomControls' volume property. This sets the volume of the SoundManager to the volume of the slider any time the thumb is dragged. Likewise, the value of the HSlider is bound to the volume property of the BottomControls class, which is then bound to the volume property of the SoundManager, thus creating a bridge between the BottomControls' volume slider and the volume of the sound that is playing through the application controller and SoundManager.

Bringing It All Together

All of the components, data, and supporting classes have been built. The airAMP music player is just about done. The final step in developing the application is to set up the final MXML file and bring it all together.

Open a new document and insert the following ActionScript and MXML:

```
<?xml version="1.0" encoding="utf-8"?>
<mx:Application xmlns:mx="http://www.adobe.com/2006/mxml"
    layout="absolute"
    xmlns:local="*"
    xmlns:ui="com.aircmr.musicplayer.ui.*"
    usePreloader="false"
    horizontalScrollPolicy="off"
    verticalScrollPolicy="off"
    applicationComplete="onCreationCompleteHandler(event);"
    initialize="onInitHandler(event);">

    <mx:Style source="assets/style/app.css" />

    <mx:Script>
        <![CDATA[
        import mx.controls.Alert;
        import com.aircmr.musicplayer.utils.XMLParserUtil;
        import com.aircmr.musicplayer.managers.SoundManager;
        import com.aircmr.musicplayer.events.XMLFileServiceEvent;
        import com.aircmr.musicplayer.events.FileSearchEvent;
        import com.aircmr.musicplayer.services.FileSearch;
        import com.aircmr.musicplayer.services.XMLFileService;
        import com.aircmr.musicplayer.services.MP3FileSearch;
```

```
import com.aircmr.musicplayer.ui.SettingsPanel;
import com.aircmr.musicplayer.data.SettingsVO;
import com.aircmr.musicplayer.data.ApplicationDataModel;
import mx.events.FlexEvent;
import mx.core.IFlexDisplayObject;
import mx.managers.PopUpManager;
import flash.display.NativeWindow;

public static const TITLE:String = "airAMP";
private var _nativeWindow:NativeWindow;

[Bindable]
private var _soundManager:SoundManager;

private function onInitHandler( event:Event ):void
{
    _soundManager = new SoundManager();
    _soundManager.addEventListener( SoundManager.NO_SELECTED_TRACK,
        handleNoSelectedTrack );
    _soundManager.addEventListener( SoundManager.TRACK_COMPLETE,
        handleTrackPlayComplete );

    ApplicationDataModel.getInstance().settingFileLocation="settings.xml";
    ApplicationDataModel.getInstance().addEventListener(
        ApplicationDataModel.TRACKLIST_CHANGE , onTrackListChange );

    loadSettingsXMLFile();

    topMenu.addEventListener(MouseEvent.MOUSE_DOWN, onMouseDownHandler);
}

private function onCreationCompleteHandler( event:Event ):void
{
    _nativeWindow = stage.nativeWindow;
    _nativeWindow.title = TITLE;
    _nativeWindow.width = 505;
    _nativeWindow.height = 505;
    stage.quality = StageQuality.BEST;
}

private function onSettingsNotFound( event:Event ):void
{
    var xmlFileService:XMLFileService = new XMLFileService();
    xmlFileService.addEventListener( XMLFileServiceEvent.XML_FILE_COPIED,
        loadSettingsXMLFile );
    xmlFileService.copyXMLFileFromApplicationDirectoryToStorage(
        ApplicationDataModel.getInstance().settingFileLocation );
}

private function loadSettingsXMLFile( event:Event = null ):void
{
    var settingsXMLLoader:XMLFileService = new XMLFileService();
    settingsXMLLoader.addEventListener(
        XMLFileServiceEvent.XML_FILE_NOT_FOUND , onSettingsNotFound );
```

```
        settingsXMLLoader.addEventListener( XMLFileServiceEvent.XML_LOADED,
            settingsLoadedHandler );
        settingsXMLLoader.loadXMLFileFromStorage(
            ApplicationDataModel.getInstance().settingFileLocation );
    }

    private function settingsLoadedHandler( event:XMLFileServiceEvent ):void
    {
        ApplicationDataModel.getInstance().settings =
            XMLParserUtil.parseSettingsXML( event.xml );

        if( ApplicationDataModel.getInstance().settings.defaultMusicDirectory
            == "")
        {
            openSettingsPopUp();
        }
        else
        {
          (ApplicationDataModel.getInstance().settings.refreshOnStartup) ?
            searchDirectoriesForMp3s(null) :
            loadMp3sFromXML(null);
        }
    }

    private function onCloseClickHandler( event:MouseEvent ):void
    {
        _nativeWindow.close();
    }

    private function onMouseDownHandler( event:MouseEvent ):void
    {
        _nativeWindow.startMove()
    }

    private function openSettingsPopUp( event:Event = null ):void
    {
        var settingsPanel:SettingsPanel;
        settingsPanel = SettingsPanel.show();
        settingsPanel.addEventListener( SettingsPanel.SETTINGS_UPDATED,
           searchDirectoriesForMp3s );
    }

    private function searchDirectoriesForMp3s( event:Event ):void
    {
        var fileSearch:MP3FileSearch = new MP3FileSearch();
        fileSearch.addEventListener(FileSearchEvent.SEARCH_FINISHED,
            fileSearchResultHandler);
        fileSearch.addEventListener(FileSearchEvent.SEARCH_FAILED,
            fileSearchFailHandler);
        fileSearch.queryDirectoryListToXML(
            ApplicationDataModel.getInstance().settings.defaultMusicDirectory,
            true, ["mp3"] );
    }
```

```
private function fileSearchResultHandler( event:FileSearchEvent ):void
{
    var xmlToSave:XML = event.searchResults as XML;

    ApplicationDataModel.getInstance().trackCollection =
        XMLParserUtil.parseSongDatabaseXML( xmlToSave );

    var fsSaveResultsToXML:XMLFileService = new XMLFileService();
    fsSaveResultsToXML.addEventListener(
        XMLFileServiceEvent.XML_FILE_WRITTEN , databaseSavedHandler );
    fsSaveResultsToXML.saveXMLFileToStorage(
        ApplicationDataModel.getInstance().settings.musicDatabaseLocation,
        xmlToSave );
}

private function fileSearchFailHandler( event:FileSearchEvent ):void
{
    Alert.show( "Music search failed. Perhaps
        you moved the directory?", "Oops..." );
}

private function databaseSavedHandler( event:Event ):void {}

private function loadMp3sFromXML( event:Event ):void
{
    var mp3XMLLoader:XMLFileService = new XMLFileService();
    mp3XMLLoader.addEventListener(XMLFileServiceEvent.XML_LOADED,
        onMP3DatabaseLoaded );
    mp3XMLLoader.loadXMLFileFromStorage(
        ApplicationDataModel.getInstance().settings.musicDatabaseLocation);
}

private function onMP3DatabaseLoaded( event:XMLFileServiceEvent ):void
{
    ApplicationDataModel.getInstance().trackCollection =
        XMLParserUtil.parseSongDatabaseXML( event.xml );
}

private function onTrackListChange( event:Event ):void
{
    playlistView.dataProvider =
        ApplicationDataModel.getInstance().trackCollection;
}

private function handleNoSelectedTrack( event:Event ):void
{
    playlistView.playTrackAt( 0 );
}

private function handleTrackPlayComplete( event:Event ):void
{
```

```
            playlistView.next();
        }
        ]]>
    </mx:Script>

    <mx:Canvas id="mainContainer">
        <mx:Panel id="mainPanel" height="500" width="500" title="{TITLE}" >
            <ui:PlaybackControls x="0" y="4" id="playbackControls"
                trackPositionUpdate="{_soundManager.setPlayheadPosition(
                playbackControls.newTrackPosition);}"
                trackPosition="{_soundManager.trackPosition}"
                trackLength="{_soundManager.trackLength}"
                artistTitle="{_soundManager.artistTitle}"
                trackTitle="{_soundManager.trackTitle}"
                playClick="{_soundManager.play();}"
                pauseClick="{_soundManager.pause();}"
                stopClick="{_soundManager.stop();}"
                nextClick="{playlistView.next();}"
                previousClick="{playlistView.previous();}" />
            <ui:PlaylistView id="playlistView"
                selectedItemChange="{_soundManager.selectTrack(
                    playlistView.selectedTrack ); }"
                playSelected="{ _soundManager.playTrack(
                    playlistView.selectedTrack ); }" />
            <ui:BottomControls id="bottomControls"
                volumeChange="{_soundManager.volume = bottomControls.volume}"
                volume="{_soundManager.volume}"
                settingsClick="openSettingsPopUp( event );" />
        </mx:Panel>

        <mx:Canvas id="topMenu" width="100%" height="50">
            <mx:Button id="closeBtn" click="onCloseClickHandler(event);"
                styleName="closeBtn" x="460" />
        </mx:Canvas>
    </mx:Canvas>
</mx:Application>
```

Save the file as `MusicPlayer.mxml` in your working directory.

`MusicPlayer.mxml` is the basis of the airAMP music player. It acts as both a view and a controller for this application. Most of the functionality, at least in terms of how the accompanying classes perform with one another, has been explained throughout the chapter. The final bit of functionality for the music player is a customized, chromeless application. You will learn how to create that in the next section.

How Application and WindowedApplication Differ

Typically, in an AIR application, the main application MXML file extends the `<mx:WindowedApplication>` container. However, this application demonstrates how to create an AIR application without having to use this container, sticking with the fairly typical default Flex `<mx:Application>`.

With regard to an application built with the AIR API, the main consideration when choosing one over the other, is that `<mx:WindowedApplication>` allows you access to the default window's controls, such as `Close`, `Minimize`, and `Restore`. Having access to these controls also means that you can style the system chrome for both Macs and PCs. It enables you to click and drag the window around and listen for its move event; and you are able to listen to events thrown by the window's interface and add effects quickly to those events, such as minimize and close. Lastly, because `WindowedApplication` extends the `Application` container, you have access to all of the events, styles, and methods made available to you when building a Flex application for the Web.

This sounds pretty ideal, except that it also means you are confined to a basic look and feel that is pretty standard to most applications. This isn't such a big deal, but music players generally look different from the norm.

In such cases, when you think you want a little more control over the look and feel of your application, use `<mx:Application>`. It provides a bit more control over the physical shape of the application window (in this case, a rounded rectangle), you can adjust the opacity of your application, and you can place the controls for the window wherever you want. In addition to maximize, minimize, and close, you could create your own functionality; that's up to you.

However, all of the functionality mentioned in the previous paragraph must be implemented by hand, meaning you have to create your own Close buttons, and you have to listen for a `MouseEvent.MOUSE_DOWN` event so that users will be able to move the window around on their screen.

Implementing Close Application and Window Dragging Functionality

Start with the `<mx:Application>` constructor. Within the constructor, in addition to the namespace declarations and default style attributes, assign the method `onCreationCompleteHandler` to the `creationComplete` event and pass it the constructor's event variable. Once the `Application` has been created, and its children have been properly initialized and added to the Application's stage, it will fire the `creationComplete` event, accessing the following method, which is nested in the `< mx:Script / >` markup:

```
private function onCreationCompleteHandler( event:Event ):void
{
    _nativeWindow = stage.nativeWindow;
    _nativeWindow.title = TITLE;
    _nativeWindow.width = 505;
    _nativeWindow.height = 505;
    stage.quality = StageQuality.BEST;
}
```

When this method is invoked, you assign the private variable `_nativeWindow` a reference to the `stage.nativeWindow`. By assigning this to `_nativeWindow`, you are making this private variable a reference to the native desktop's window instance. Within the `onCreationCompleteHandler`, you're also assigning the title of the window, the width, and the height of the application.

Once `_nativeWindow` is assigned, you will be able to interact with the application window directly. Most of the window's interaction is in the nested canvas container entitled `topMenu`. For instance, the Close button entitled `closeBtn` has a handler named `onCloseClickHandler` assigned to the `click` event. The `onCloseClickHandler` is a private method defined in the application's `<mx:Script>` tags:

```
private function onCloseClickHandler( event:MouseEvent ):void
{
  _nativeWindow.close();
}
```

This is a fairly straightforward piece of code, but it works wonders. After the user clicks Close, the `onCloseClickHandler` will access the `close()` method of the `_nativeWindow` reference, causing the application to close.

Next, take a look at the `init()` method defined in the application's `<mx:Script>` tags. At first glance, there is a lot going on in this method. After all, this method is called after the application has been initialized, but before the `creationComplete` event is dispatched. Regardless, you're only interested in a snippet of code at this point. After the application is initialized, the `topMenu` container should be added to the Application's stage. You only need it as a reference at this point, so whether or not it has called a `creationComplete` event is irrelevant. You're going to add a listener to the `topMenu` method that will listen for the `MouseEvent.MOUSE_DOWN` event, at which point you'll call the private `onMouseDownHandler` method:

```
topMenu.addEventListener(MouseEvent.MOUSE_DOWN, onMouseDownHandler);
```

The `onMouseDownHandler` invokes the `startMove()` method of the `_nativeWindow` reference. This enables users to click and drag the window around their desktop. You could have applied this `MouseEvent` to the `<mx:Canvas>` container that wraps the whole application, except it would nullify all mouse events on nested components, rendering the application useless. However, enabling users to click on the top area is enough functionality for this application:

```
private function onMouseDownHandler( event:MouseEvent ):void
{
  _nativeWindow.startMove();
}
```

Users can now close the application, and they are able to move the application around on their desktop. If you wanted to, you could also add minimize, maximize, restore, and resize functionality to your application, just as you did in the prior code. Please keep in mind that you're using these methods as an alternative to using the default functionality that is available through the `<mx:WindowedApplication>` container, although this certainly does not restrict you from utilizing `close()`, `startMove()`, or any other methods available in the `NativeWindow` class in any Flex/AIR application.

At this point, if you were to compile the application, you should be able to browse your hard drive and play some music. Figures 4-4 and 4-5 show the final airAMP music player.

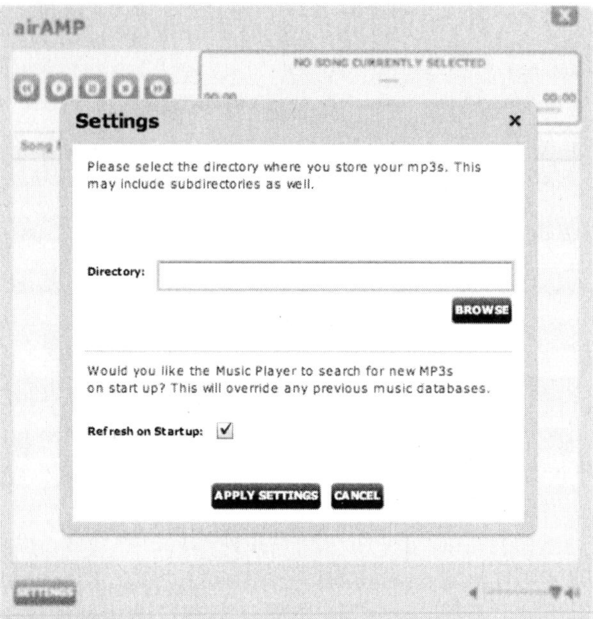

Figure 4-4

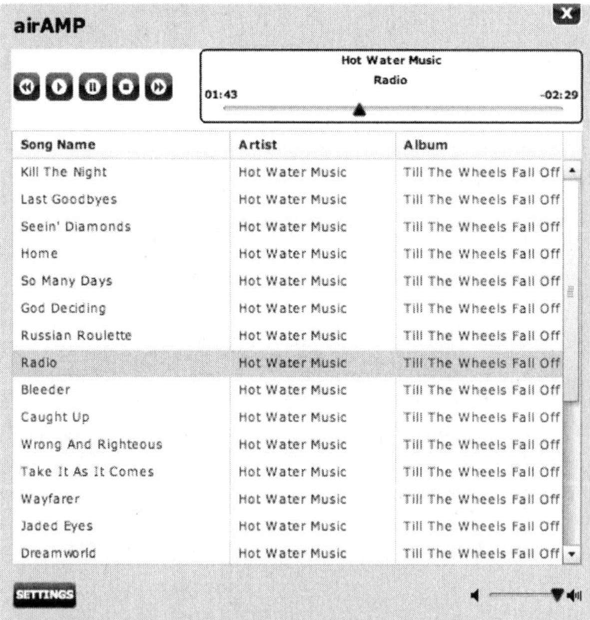

Figure 4-5

Deploying the Application

The airAMP music player is nearing completion. The last step is to create a descriptor file and package everything as a deployable AIR file.

The Descriptor File

The final file needed in the creation of the airAMP music player is the application descriptor file. This XML file contains properties for the application, such as for the initial window settings, copyright, title, and icon URLs. It is packaged and distributed with the final deployable file.

Create a new document and enter the following markup:

```
<?xml version="1.0" encoding="UTF-8"?>
<application xmlns="http://ns.adobe.com/air/application/1.0">
    <id>com.aircmr.MusicPlayer</id>
    <filename>MusicPlayer</filename>
    <version>0.1</version>
    <name>AIR Amp</name>
    <description></description>
    <copyright>2008</copyright>

    <initialWindow>
        <title/>
        <content>MusicPlayer.swf</content>
        <systemChrome>none</systemChrome>
        <transparent>true</transparent>
        <visible>true</visible>
    </initialWindow>

    <installFolder>AIRCMR/MusicPlayer</installFolder>
    <programMenuFolder>AIRCMR</programMenuFolder>
</application>
```

Save the file as `MusicPlayer-app.xml` in the root of your working directory along with the `MusicPlayer.mxml` and `settings.xml` files.

This file will be the descriptor file for the music player. Because the application will have its own window design and interface, the `<systemChrome>` property is set to `none`, and `<transparent>` is set to `true`.

Once the descriptor is created, move on to compiling and packaging the application.

Compiling and Packaging

The final step in creating the airAMP music player is to compile and package it. Once you have the `MusicPlayer.mxml`, `MusicPlayer -app.xml`, `settings.xml`, and the `assets` directory available in your working directory, begin packaging the application by first compiling the `MusicPlayer.mxml` into a SWF.

Open a command prompt, navigate to the working directory for the music player, enter the following command, and press Enter:

```
> amxmlc MusicPlayer.mxml
```

With the command prompt still pointing to the working directory, package the widget as an AIR installer by entering the following command and pressing Enter:

```
> adt -package MusicPlayer MusicPlayer-app.xml MusicPlayer.swf settings.xml
```

Now that the package is created, navigate to your working directory. If the widget packaged correctly, you should have a `MusicPlayer.air` file. Execute the `MusicPlayer.air` package in order to install the application on your hard drive. After it is installed, open it, select your MP3 directory, hit Play, and enjoy!

Summary

Now that you've created your very own music player, you will never go back to iTunes. Regardless of whether or not this application is worthy of the audiophiles on the Internet, it was an excellent way to jump into some terrific Flex and AIR concepts.

This chapter covered how to use < `mx:Application` > instead of < `mx:WindowedApplication` >. You looked at how to search a directory using the `File` object and how to read data using `FileStream.readMultiByte`. You were able to practice reading data from and writing data to the hard drive using `FileStream.writeUTFBytes`, and you took a brief look at how to manipulate and create custom components in both ActionScript 3 and MXML.

It is hoped that by this point, you're sitting in front of your computer rocking out to your favorite tunes. Of course, many features commonly found in music players weren't added due to space limitations. However, you're encouraged to use this application as a starting place and add some additional features. Here are some suggestions on where to go from here:

- Add the capability to search for any song within the player.
- Add audio visualization using the `SoundMixer.computeSpectrum` method to spice up the display.
- Add the capability to download the album art of the song you're playing.
- Add the capability to open just one file.
- Add the capability to drag and drop files into the player and have it automatically write them to the XML database.
- Add the capability to create in-player playlists.
- Add the capability to read and parse an iTunes music database XML file.

As you can see, there is an endless supply of ideas for enhancing and extending the basic music player you created in this chapter. Above all, take your time and enjoy working to make this your own AIR music player.

5

Mini CMS

Making a content management system (CMS) in AIR is a fantastic idea. What could be better than a cross-platform desktop application that enables you to manage remote content? OK, a lot of things are better, but in the context of AIR, the CMS is a pretty snazzy possibility. The application you will create in this chapter should give you a good start on creating a simple CMS application. You could approach the creation of a CMS in many different ways, but in this case the application is going to be kept rather simple, as it is hoped that it serves as a stepping-stone for creating a CMS of your own that is specific to your needs.

In this chapter, the application will enable you to manage a remote XML data set and its associated assets. The data set that the application manages is a hypothetical list of items that resembles a simple list of article or journal entries. Each item in the list also contains an associated image file. The application will enable you to edit, add, and delete items from the list. After you are done editing the content, the application uploads the new data set and any images that you selected from your local hard disk to the remote storage area.

The following section discusses the design of the application. This includes the logistics of managing the data and the components that are necessary for the user interface. After design, you'll get into the code and learn about the important classes and functions that will tie everything together.

Design

As always, it's a good idea to make a list of goals that your application should aim to fulfill. The Mini CMS application should enable users to do the following:

- ❑ Configure the remote gateway URL.
- ❑ Validate the remote gateway URL.
- ❑ Download the remote XML data set and save it on their hard drive.
- ❑ Display a selectable list of all the items in the data set.

- Display the fields of a selected item in an editable form.
- Add, edit, and delete items from the list.
- Edit the fields of a selected item.
- Browse their hard drive for an asset file (image).
- Save the changes of individual items.
- Revert back to the original data.
- Upload the edited XML data set and any local assets to the remote storage area.

The preceding list should give you a decent idea of what the application is going to need in terms of classes and the user interface. The first item on the list, concerning the gateway URL, may seem a bit vague to you right now, but the following section explains this component of the application.

The Remote Gateway

The remote gateway is a vital part of the application. It is a server-side script that handles communication between the application and the server. The script also stores the URL to the data file and the assets folder. The script can be written in a variety of scripting languages, including ASP, JSP, PHP, and Ruby, among others. In this chapter, the gateway script is written in PHP because it is widely available and often used in conjunction with Flash and Flex projects. More important, there are three actions that the gateway must handle:

- URL validation
- Data file upload
- Asset file upload

When users configure their application, especially when configuring the location of a remote item, it's a good idea to ensure that they have entered the correct URL. Enabling users to validate what they have entered also gives the application the chance to grab the path to the data set and assets folder. Without these variables, the application cannot function. After the user has validated the gateway URL, the application should be ready to download the data, enabling the user to edit to their heart's content. Keep in mind that this script file will not be packaged with the application. It is your responsibility to upload the script, along with the initial assets and data file, to a remote server in order for the application to function.

Settings Management

After the user has validated the gateway URL and received the remote settings, it's a good idea to store that information for later use. Not only should the settings be available throughout other parts of the application, but they should also be saved on the user's computer so that users don't have to reconfigure the application the next time they launch it.

To make the settings information available throughout the application, you will create a data model using the almighty Singleton class pattern. This class will be named `SettingsModel`. The singleton pattern ensures that only one instance of a `Settings` object can be created within the entire application, ensuring that all components and objects in the application will be reading from the one and only source of settings information.

To save the settings information so it will be available the next time the user uses the application, you will create a service class that loads and saves a simple XML file in the application's storage directory. This class will be named `SettingsService`.

Data Management

In addition to managing the settings data, you'll also have to manage the main data set. The main data set is an XML file that, once the settings have been validated, must be downloaded from the remote location and then saved into the application's storage directory. To make this process friendlier, you will create a service class named `XMLDataService`. A `Complete` event will be dispatched when the XML has been completely loaded, as well as an `Error` event if there is a problem loading the data.

When the data is available to the application, it needs be parsed into objects that will be friendly for the display components. The edited data also needs to be serialized back into XML so it can be saved to a local file before uploading. Two classes will be created to handle this requirement. The first class is another service class, this time named `ListDataService`, which will handle the conversion of the data. The second class, named `ItemData`, is a generic object that will describe each item in the data set.

Uploading Files

After the user has finished making changes to the data, the application needs to upload the data set and any local assets that the user has chosen to use for any edited items. This class will be yet another service class named `UploadService`. This class enables you to add local files into a queue to be uploaded. Events are dispatched when the upload process ends or encounters an error.

User Interface

The user interface is relatively simple for this application. First you will create a component that enables the user to edit and validate the gateway URL. This component will be named `SettingsPanel` and will behave as a pop-up. After the `SettingsPanel` component, you will create a component that enables users to edit the data of an item from the data set. This component will contain form fields that correspond to each property of an item from the data set. This component is named `ItemEditor`. Lastly, you will use a `List` component to present each item from the data set. Aside from a few buttons here and there, these are the major interface components for the application.

Code and Code Explanation

This section dives into the code defining the functionality of each class and component of the application. Throughout the remaining sections, you will create each class and component required by the application. At the end, you will bring it all together by creating the main application file. First, however, within your development directory create a folder named Mini CMS. This will be your working directory for this application.

The Remote Gateway

The remote gateway script is the cornerstone of this application. Fortunately, the script is extremely simple, and even if you don't understand PHP, you can probably get the gist of what's happening after a first glance.

Open your editor and create a new document. Enter the following markup:

```
<?php

// Configuration
$GLOBALS['xmlDataURL']        = 'http://yourdomain.com/minicms/dataset.xml';
$GLOBALS['xmlDataPath']       = '/serverpath/minicms/dataset.xml';
$GLOBALS['assetsFolderURL']   = 'http://yourdodmain.com/minicms/assets/';
$GLOBALS['assetsFolderPath'] = '/serverpath/minicms/assets/';

switch( $_GET['action'] )
{
    case 'validate':
        handleValidate();
        break;

    case 'uploadAsset':
        handleUploadAsset();
        break;

    case 'uploadData':
        handleUploadData();
        break;
}

function handleValidate()
{
    echo 'success=1&xmlDataURL='.$GLOBALS['xmlDataURL'].'&assetsFolderURL='.$GLOBALS
        ['assetsFolderURL'];
}

function handleUploadData()
{
    echo "\nReceiving upload...\n";
    echo "Filename: " . $_FILES['Filedata']['name']."\n";
    echo "File Size: " . $_FILES['Filedata']['size']."\n";
    move_uploaded_file($_FILES['Filedata']['tmp_name'], $GLOBALS['xmlDataPath']);
    echo "File moved to: ".$GLOBALS['xmlDataPath']."\n";
}

function handleUploadAsset()
{
    echo "\nReceiving upload...\n";
    echo "Filename: " . $_FILES['Filedata']['name']."\n";
    echo "File Size: " . $_FILES['Filedata']['size']."\n";
    move_uploaded_file($_FILES['Filedata']['tmp_name'], $GLOBALS
        ['assetsFolderPath'].$_FILES['Filedata']['name']);
    echo "File moved to: ".$GLOBALS['assetsFolderPath'].$_FILES
        ['Filedata']['name']."\n";
}

?>
```

Save the file as `gateway.php` within the working directory.

In order for the application to work properly within the context of your own server, modify the configuration variables at the beginning of the script:

```
// Configuration
$GLOBALS['xmlDataURL']        = 'http://yourdomain.com/minicms/dataset.xml';
$GLOBALS['xmlDataPath']       = '/serverpath/minicms/dataset.xml';
$GLOBALS['assetsFolderURL']   = 'http://yourdodmain.com/minicms/assets/';
$GLOBALS['assetsFolderPath'] = '/serverpath/minicms/assets/';
```

The previous snippet contains the configuration variables necessary for the gateway script. Of course, you'll have to change these to work within the context of your server. URLs should be configured to match that of your own domain name and internal folder structure. Paths should be configured using the physical path to the XML data file and assets folder. If you are unsure of the disk path, create a test script within the folder to which you plan to upload the gateway script. Then use the PHP function `getcwd()` within this script. This function outputs the physical path of the current working directory — in other words, the path to the directory in which the script resides. Keep in mind that when it is time to upload this file to your server, the server must have PHP installed and running on it. In addition, the server must have permission to write files to its hard drive.

The remote gateway script is programmed to handle three actions: validation, data upload, and asset upload. The application specifies which action to perform by setting a query string variable named `action`. For instance, when a user attempts to validate the gateway URL, the application will take the user's input and attach the validation query string. The URL that the application will attempt to load looks something like this: `http://www.yourdomain.com/minicms/gateway.php?action=validate`.

Regarding the validation process, note that the application relies on the gateway script to provide it with two setting variables:

```
function handleValidate()
{
    echo 'success=1&xmlDataURL='.$GLOBALS['xmlDataURL'].'&assetsFolderURL='.$GLOBALS
        ['assetsFolderURL'];
}
```

Here, the `handleValidate` function simply outputs a message that the application will be able to read if the user enters a valid URL for the gateway script. The message will be parsed by the application to extract the URL to the XML data file, and the URL to the assets folder.

In the next section, you learn how to create the necessary files to manage the settings data.

Settings Model

In order for all components of this application to function properly, crucial information must be available to all classes and components throughout the application. You will create two classes to accomplish this. First, the `SettingsModel` class will utilize a Singleton pattern to serve as a repository for the important settings variables. Second, the `SettingsService` class will aid in the loading and saving of the settings data, both into the application and to the user's hard drive for later use. The settings will be saved in a simple XML file.

Within your development directory, create a folder titled Mini CMS. This will be your working directory for this program.

1. Open your editor and create a new document. Enter the following markup:

```
<?xml version='1.0' encoding='utf-8'?>
<settings>
    <gatewayurl></gatewayurl>
    <xmldataurl></xmldataurl>
    <assetsfolderurl></assetsfolderurl>
</settings>
```

2. Save the file as `settings.xml` within the working directory.

3. Create a new document and enter the following markup:

```
package com.aircmr.minicms.data
{

    import flash.errors.IllegalOperationError;
    import flash.events.Event;
    import flash.events.EventDispatcher;
    import flash.filesystem.File;

    final public class SettingsModel extends EventDispatcher
    {
        /* Static Variables */
        private static var _instance:SettingsModel = new SettingsModel();

        /* Static Methods */
        public static function getInstance():SettingsModel
        {
            return _instance;
        }

        /* Private Variables */
        private var _assetsFolderURL:String;
        private var _data:XML;
        private var _localDataFile:File;
        private var _xmlDataURL:String;
        private var _gatewayURL:String;
        private var _uploadURL:String;
        private var _validateURL:String;

        /* Constructor & Init */
        public function SettingsModel()
        {
            if( _instance != null )
            {
                throw new IllegalOperationError( "Error at :: SettingsModel.
                   SettingsModel is a Singleton with access through
                   SettingsModel.getInstance()." );
            }
        }

        /* Private Methods */
        private function deserialize():void
        {
```

```
        this.gatewayURL = ( String( _data.gatewayurl ).length > 0 ) ?
            _data.gatewayurl : null;
        this.xmlDataURL = ( String( _data.xmldataurl ).length > 0 ) ?
            _data.xmldataurl : null;
        this.assetsFolderURL = ( String( _data.assetsfolderurl ).length > 0 ) ?
            _data.assetsfolderurl : null;

        dispatchEvent( new Event( Event.INIT ) );
    }

    public function serialize():XML
    {
        var xml:XML = new XML( "<settings></settings>" );
        xml.appendChild( <gatewayurl>{_gatewayURL}</gatewayurl> );
        xml.appendChild( <xmldataurl>{_xmlDataURL}</xmldataurl> );
        xml.appendChild( <assetsfolderurl>{_assetsFolderURL}
            </assetsfolderurl> );
        return xml;
    }

    /* Gets & Sets */
    public function set data( value:XML ):void
    {
        _data = value;
        deserialize();
    }

    public function set gatewayURL( value:String ):void
    {
        _gatewayURL = value;
    }

    public function get gatewayURL():String
    {
        return _gatewayURL;
    }

    public function set assetsFolderURL( value:String ):void
    {
        _assetsFolderURL = value;
    }

    public function get assetsFolderURL():String
    {
        return _assetsFolderURL;
    }

    public function set xmlDataURL( value:String ):void
    {
        _xmlDataURL = value;

        if( _xmlDataURL != null )
        {
            var fileName:String = _xmlDataURL.substring(
```

```
                _xmlDataURL.lastIndexOf("/") + 1, _xmlDataURL.length );
            _localDataFile = File.applicationStorageDirectory.resolve( fileName );
        }
    }

    public function get xmlDataURL():String
    {
        return _xmlDataURL;
    }

    public function get localDataFile():File
    {
        return _localDataFile;
    }

  }
}
```

4. Save the file as `SettingsModel.as` in the directory `com/aircmr/minicms/data/` within your working directory.
5. Create a new document and enter the following markup:

```
package com.aircmr.minicms.services
{
    import flash.events.Event;
    import flash.events.EventDispatcher;
    import flash.events.IOErrorEvent;
    import flash.filesystem.File;
    import flash.filesystem.FileMode;
    import flash.filesystem.FileStream;

    public class SettingsService extends EventDispatcher
    {
        /* Constants */
        private static const UTF_ENCODING:String = "<?xml version='1.0'
           encoding='utf-8'?>";

        /* Private Variables */
        private var _data:XML;
        private var _file:File;
        private var _fileStream:FileStream;

        /* Constructor & Init */
        public function SettingsService()
        {

        }

        /* Private Methods */
        private function onFileReadComplete( event:Event ):void
        {
            _data = XML( _fileStream.readUTFBytes( _fileStream.bytesAvailable ) );
            _fileStream.close();
            dispatchEvent( new Event( Event.COMPLETE ) );
```

```
        }

        private function onFileWriteComplete( evt:Event ):void
        {
            trace( "Settings saved." );
        }

        private function onFileOpenError( evt:IOErrorEvent ):void
        {
            trace( "Could not load: settings.xml :: Error - " + evt.errorID );
        }

        /* Public Methods */
        public function load():void
        {
            _file = File.applicationStorageDirectory.resolve( "settings.xml" );

            _fileStream = new FileStream();
            _fileStream.addEventListener( Event.COMPLETE, onFileReadComplete );
            _fileStream.addEventListener( IOErrorEvent.IO_ERROR, onFileOpenError );
            _fileStream.openAsync( _file, FileMode.READ );
        }

        public function save( xml:XML ):void
        {
            var output:String = UTF_ENCODING + "\n" + xml.toXMLString();
            output = output.replace( /\n/g, File.lineEnding );

            _fileStream = new FileStream();
            _fileStream.openAsync( _file, FileMode.WRITE );
            _fileStream.addEventListener( Event.CLOSE, onFileWriteComplete );
            _fileStream.writeUTFBytes( output );
            _fileStream.close();
        }

        /* Gets & Sets */
        public function get data():XML
        {
            return _data;
        }
    }
}
```

6. Save the file as `SettingsService.as` in the directory `com/aircmr/minicms/services/` within your working directory.

In the previous six steps, you created the necessary files and classes to manage the settings for the application, including `settings.xml`, `SettingsModel.as`, and `SettingsService.as`.

Steps 1 and 2 cover the `settings.xml` file — the file that will be stored within the application's storage folder to retain the user's settings. Three setting values are stored in this file. The first, and most important, is the gateway URL. This is the only setting that is set by the user. Values for the XML data URL and the assets folder URL will be retrieved when the user validates the gateway URL.

In steps 3 and 4 you created the SettingsModel class. This class uses a Singleton pattern to ensure that only one instance of the class exists throughout the application. Singleton patterns are great when you want to create a single place for holding a set of data or functions. In the case of this application, it's the prefect approach for storing the setting values from the XML.

Aside from some XML parsing methods, note that this class creates an extra setting value named _localDataFile. This variable, which is an instance of the AIR File class, stores a reference to where the XML data file is saved after it is downloaded to the user's hard drive.

The following snippet contains the setter function for the SettingsModel _xmlDataURL property:

```
public function set xmlDataURL( value:String ):void
{
    _xmlDataURL = value;

    if( _xmlDataURL != null )
    {
        var fileName:String = _xmlDataURL.substring( _xmlDataURL.lastIndexOf("/")
           + 1, _xmlDataURL.length );
        _localDataFile = File.applicationStorageDirectory.resolve( fileName );
    }
}
```

It is also in this function that the _localDataFile property is set. The data file will always be stored within the application's storage directory, so by parsing the XML data URL for the filename, you can create a new instance of a File object by accessing the File class's public static variable named applicationStorageDirectory and passing the filename into its resolve method. This method will return a new File object that refers to the data file within the application's storage directory.

In steps 5 and 6 you created the SettingsService class. This class is created to handle the loading and saving of the settings to the user's hard drive:

```
public function load():void
{
    _file = File.applicationStorageDirectory.resolve( "settings.xml" );

    _fileStream = new FileStream();
    _fileStream.addEventListener( Event.COMPLETE, onFileReadComplete );
    _fileStream.addEventListener( IOErrorEvent.IO_ERROR, onFileOpenError );
    _fileStream.openAsync( _file, FileMode.READ );
}

public function save( xml:XML ):void
{
    var output:String = UTF_ENCODING + "\n" + xml.toXMLString();
    output = output.replace( /\n/g, File.lineEnding );

    _fileStream = new FileStream();
    _fileStream.openAsync( _file, FileMode.WRITE );
    _fileStream.addEventListener( Event.CLOSE, onFileWriteComplete );
    _fileStream.writeUTFBytes( output );
    _fileStream.close();
}
```

The preceding snippet contains the `load` and `save` methods of the `SettingsService` class. When the `load` method is first called, the `_file` property of the class is set — again, by using the `resolve` method of the `File` class's static property named `applicationStorageDirectory` and passing it the filename of the settings file.

The file is then opened by creating an instance of a new `FileStream` object, configuring the appropriate listeners, and utilizing its `openAsync` method. When the file is finished being read, the onFileReadComplete method is called and the data from the `settings.xml` file is converted to a handy dandy XML object and stored in the `_data` property. The class then dispatches a `COMPLETE` event to notify anything listening that the `settings.xml` file has been loaded and the data is available to be accessed. The `save` method is essentially the same process but in reverse, except the `FileStream` object's `writeUTFBytes` method is used to write the XML data to the `settings.xml` file.

In the next section, you will create the classes necessary for managing the XML data.

Data Management

What would a content manager be without content? Now that you have the means of managing the settings for the application, it's time to move on to managing the content data.

The data for this application has a specific schema. This schema happens to look like a simple list of journal or blog entries. Each item in the list has five properties: a date, a title, a subtitle, body text, and an associated image. To represent and manage this data within the application, you will create three class files and one XML file.

1. Open your editor and create a new document. Enter the following markup:

```
<?xml version='1.0' encoding='utf-8'?>
<data>
  <item>
    <date>2007-08-01</date>
    <title>Lorem Ipsum</title>
    <subtitle>Lorem Ipsum Dolor Sit</subtitle>
    <body>Lorem Ipsum Dolor Sit</body>
    <image></image>
  </item>
  <item>
    <date>2007-07-25</date>
    <title>Lorem Ipsum</title>
    <subtitle>Lorem Ipsum Dolor Sit</subtitle>
    <body>Lorem Ipsum Dolor Sit</body>
    <image></image>
  </item>
</data>
```

2. Save the file as `dataset.xml` within the working directory.
3. Create a new document and enter the following markup:

```
package com.aircmr.minicms.data
{
    import mx.utils.StringUtil;
```

```
import flash.filesystem.File;

public class ItemData
{

    private static const NEW_ITEM:String = "<item><title>Untitled</title>
       <subtitle></subtitle><body></body><date></date><image></image></item>";

    private var _body:String;
    private var _date:String;
    private var _edited:Boolean;
    private var _image:String;
    private var _localImage:File;
    private var _originalData:XMLList;
    private var _subtitle:String;
    private var _title:String;

    public function ItemData( originalData:XMLList = null )
    {
        if( originalData == null )
        {
            originalData = new XMLList( NEW_ITEM );
        }

        _originalData = originalData;

        revert();
    }

    public function revert():void
    {
        var today:Date = new Date();
        var todayStr:String = today.getFullYear() + "-" + (today.getMonth()
           + 1 ) + "-" + today.getDate();

        _date = ( StringUtil.trim( _originalData.date ) != "" ) ?
           _originalData.date : todayStr;
        _body = ( StringUtil.trim( _originalData.body ) != "" ) ?
           _originalData.body : "";
        _image = ( StringUtil.trim( _originalData.image ) != "" ) ?
           _originalData.image : "";
        _subtitle = ( StringUtil.trim( _originalData.subtitle ) != "" ) ?
           _originalData.subtitle : "";
        _title = ( StringUtil.trim( _originalData.title ) != "" ) ?
           _originalData.title : "";

        _edited = false;
    }

    public function set body( value:String ):void
    {
        _body = value;
        _edited = true
    }
```

```
public function set date( value:String ):void
{
    _date = value;
    _edited = true
}

public function set image( value:String ):void
{
    _image = value;
    _edited = true
}

public function set localImage( value:File ):void
{
    _localImage = value;
    _edited = true;
}

public function set subtitle( value:String ):void
{
    _subtitle = value;
    _edited = true
}

public function set title( value:String ):void
{
    _title = value;
    _edited = true;
}

public function get body():String
{
    return _body;
}

public function get date():String
{
    return _date;
}

public function get edited():Boolean
{
    return _edited;
}

public function get image():String
{
    return _image;
}

public function get localImage():File
{
    return _localImage;
}
```

```
        public function get subtitle():String
        {
            return _subtitle;
        }

        public function get title():String
        {
            return _title;
        }
    }
}
```

4. Save the file as `ItemData.as` in the directory `com/aircmr/minicms/data/` within your working directory.

5. Create a new document and enter the following markup:

```
package com.aircmr.minicms.services
{

    import com.aircmr.minicms.data.ItemData;
    import com.aircmr.minicms.data.SettingsModel;

    public class ListDataService
    {
        /* Constants */
        private static const UTF_ENCODING:String = "<?xml version='1.0'
            encoding='utf-8'?>";

        public function ListDataService()
        {

        }

        public function serialize( listData:Array ):XML
        {
            var xmlString:String = UTF_ENCODING + "\n" + "<data>\n"

            for( var i:int = 0; i < listData.length; i++ )
            {
                xmlString += "\t<item>\n";

                var item:ItemData = listData[i].data;

                xmlString += "\t\t<date>" + item.date + "</date>\n";
                xmlString += "\t\t<title>" + item.title + "</title>\n";
                xmlString += "\t\t<subtitle>" + item.subtitle + "</subtitle>\n";
                xmlString += "\t\t<body>" + item.body + "</body>\n";

                if( item.localImage != null )
                {
                    xmlString += "\t\t<image>" + SettingsModel.getInstance().
                        assetsFolderURL + item.localImage.name + "</image>\n";
                }
                else
                {
```

```
                xmlString += "\t\t<image>" + item.image + "</image>\n";
            }

            xmlString += "\t</item>\n";
        }

        xmlString += "</data>";

        return new XML( xmlString );
    }

    public function deserialize( xml:XML ):Array
    {
        var result:Array = new Array();

        for( var i:int = 0; i < xml.children().length(); i++ )
        {
            var itemData:ItemData = new ItemData( XMLList(
               xml.children()[i] ) );
            var newListItem:Object = new Object();
            newListItem.data = itemData;
            newListItem.label = itemData.title;
            result.push( newListItem );
        }

        return result;
    }

    public function getLocalFiles( listData:Array ):Array
    {
        var result:Array = new Array();

        for( var i:int = 0; i < listData.length; i++ )
        {
            var item:ItemData = listData[i].data;

            if( item.localImage != null )
            {
                result.push( item.localImage );
            }
        }

        return result;
    }
  }
}
```

6. Save the file as `ListDataService.as` in the directory `com/aircmr/minicms/services/` within your working directory.

7. Create a new document and enter the following markup:

```
package com.aircmr.minicms.services
{
    import com.aircmr.minicms.data.SettingsModel;
    import flash.net.URLLoader;
```

```
    import flash.net.URLRequest;
    import flash.events.ErrorEvent;
    import flash.events.Event;
    import flash.events.EventDispatcher;
    import flash.events.IOErrorEvent;
    import flash.filesystem.File;
    import flash.filesystem.FileMode;
    import flash.filesystem.FileStream;
    import mx.controls.Alert;


    public class XMLDataService extends EventDispatcher
    {
        /* Constants */
        private static const UTF_ENCODING:String = "<?xml version='1.0'
            encoding='utf-8'?>";

        /* Private Variables */
        private var _dataLoader:URLLoader
        private var _filename:String;
        private var _fileStream:FileStream;
        private var _listData:Array;
        private var _xmlData:XML;

        public function XMLDataService()
        {

        }

        /* Event Handlers */
        private function onDataLoadComplete( event:Event ):void
        {
            _xmlData = XML( String( _dataLoader.data ) );
            save();
        }

        private function onDataLoadError( event:IOErrorEvent ):void
        {
            dispatchEvent( new ErrorEvent( ErrorEvent.ERROR ) );
        }

        private function onFileWriteComplete( event:Event ):void
        {
            dispatchEvent( new Event( Event.COMPLETE ) );
        }


        /* Private Methods */
        private function save():void
        {
            var output:String = UTF_ENCODING + "\n" + _xmlData.toXMLString();
            output = output.replace( /\n/g, File.lineEnding );

            _fileStream = new FileStream();
```

```
            _fileStream.openAsync( SettingsModel.getInstance().localDataFile,
               FileMode.WRITE );
            _fileStream.addEventListener( Event.CLOSE, onFileWriteComplete );
            _fileStream.writeUTFBytes( output );
            _fileStream.close();
        }


        /* Public Methods */
        public function load( url:String ):void
        {
            _dataLoader = new URLLoader();
            _dataLoader.addEventListener( Event.COMPLETE, onDataLoadComplete );
            _dataLoader.addEventListener( IOErrorEvent.IO_ERROR, onDataLoadError );
            _dataLoader.load( new URLRequest( url ) );
        }

        public function updateXMLData( xml:XML ):void
        {
            _xmlData = xml;
            save()
        }

        /* Gets & Sets */
        public function get xmlData():XML
        {
            return _xmlData;
        }
    }
}
```

8. Save the file as `XMLDataService.as` in the directory `com/aircmr/minicms/services/` within your working directory.

In the previous eight steps, you created all the files necessary for managing the content data: `dataset.xml`, `ItemData.as`, `ListDataService.as`, and `XMLDataService.as`.

In steps 1 and 2 you created the data set file. This file will hold all the content that the application manages. This file is not packaged with the application when you deploy it. Instead, it is uploaded to the remote server. The application will, when configured with a validated gateway URL, download the current data set to the user's hard drive.

In steps 3 and 4 you created the `ItemData` class. Instances of this class are used to represent an item from the XML data. As you might expect, there is a corresponding property for each item's date, title, subtitle, and so on. There are also a few properties you might not expect. First, the `_originalData` property is used to store a reference to the item's original data. This property is used when users would like to cancel the changes they have made and revert to the original data. Second, the `_edited` property simply stores a Boolean value indicating whether or not the data for the item has been edited. Lastly, the `_localImage` property is used to store a reference to a file on the user's hard drive when he or she browses for a new image to associate with an item.

Steps 5 and 6 cover the `ListDataService` class. This class is used to serialize and deserialize the XML data. In other words, the class will convert the XML data from an `XML` object into an array of `ItemData` objects; it will also convert an array of `ItemData` objects into an `XML` object:

```
public function deserialize( xml:XML ):Array
{
    var result:Array = new Array();

    for( var i:int = 0; i < xml.children().length(); i++ )
    {
        var itemData:ItemData = new ItemData( XMLList( xml.children()[i] ) );
        var newListItem:Object = new Object();
        newListItem.data = itemData;
        newListItem.label = itemData.title;
        result.push( newListItem );
    }

    return result;
}
```

The preceding snippet contains the `deserialize` method of the `ListDataService` class. This method simply parses the XML and creates the aforementioned array of `ItemData` objects. The resulting array will be used later when populating a Flex `List` component.

The following snippet contains the `getLocalFiles` method of the `ListDataService` class:

```
public function getLocalFiles( listData:Array ):Array
{
    var result:Array = new Array();

    for( var i:int = 0; i < listData.length; i++ )
    {
        var item:ItemData = listData[i].data;

        if( item.localImage != null )
        {
            result.push( item.localImage );
        }
    }

    return result;
}
```

As you will soon see, users can arbitrarily change the image of an item in the list to a file they browsed for on their hard drive. Rather than compile the local files into an array as they are chosen, this method simply loops through an array of `ItemData` objects and checks whether the `localImage` property is defined. The resulting array of `File` objects will then be used by the `UploadService` class, created shortly.

In steps 7 and 8, you created the `XMLDataService` class. This class, similar to the `SettingsService` class, handles the loading and saving of the content data. Unlike the settings XML file that is loaded from the user's hard drive, the content data XML is instead downloaded from the remote server:

```
public function load( url:String ):void
{
    _dataLoader = new URLLoader();
    _dataLoader.addEventListener( Event.COMPLETE, onDataLoadComplete );
```

```
        _dataLoader.addEventListener( IOErrorEvent.IO_ERROR, onDataLoadError );
        _dataLoader.load( new URLRequest( url ) );
    }
```

The preceding snippet contains the `load` method of the `XMLDataService` class. Using the supplied `url` parameter, the XML file is downloaded from the remote server via a `URLLoader` object. When the loading process is complete, the `onDataLoadComplete` function is called, which in turn makes the XML data available via the `_xmlData` property, and calls the `save` method of the `XMLDataService` class:

```
    private function save():void
    {
        var output:String = UTF_ENCODING + "\n" + _xmlData.toXMLString();
        output = output.replace( /\n/g, File.lineEnding );

        _fileStream = new FileStream();
        _fileStream.openAsync( SettingsModel.getInstance().localDataFile,
           FileMode.WRITE );
        _fileStream.addEventListener( Event.CLOSE, onFileWriteComplete );
        _fileStream.writeUTFBytes( output );
        _fileStream.close();
    }
```

This method simply saves the XML data to the user's hard drive. Notice here the first use of the `SettingsModel` class. In this case, the method refers to the `localDataFile` property in order to save the XML data to the correct location/file. After the file has been written to the user's hard drive, the `onFileWriteComplete` method is called, which then dispatches a `COMPLETE` event to notify any listeners that the service has been completed.

In the next section you will create the `UploadService` class, which will in effect upload the appropriate files to the remote server.

Uploading Files

A crucial aspect of this application is the need to upload files to a remote location. At the very least, the application will have to upload one XML file (the updated data) to the remote server. Beyond this, users may have chosen a few images from their hard drive that will also need to be uploaded. In addition, note that any file that is not the XML data is considered an asset and should be uploaded to the assets folder. To manage these requirements, you will create another service class.

Open your editor and create a new document. Enter the following markup:

```
package com.aircmr.minicms.services
{
    import com.aircmr.minicms.data.SettingsModel;
    import flash.events.DataEvent;
    import flash.events.ErrorEvent;
    import flash.events.Event;
    import flash.events.EventDispatcher;
    import flash.filesystem.File;
    import flash.net.URLRequest;
    import flash.events.IOErrorEvent;
```

```
public class UploadService extends EventDispatcher
{

    private var _currentIndex:int;
    private var _filesToUpload:Array;
    private var _uploading:Boolean;

    public function UploadService()
    {
        _currentIndex = -1;
        _filesToUpload = new Array();
        _uploading = false;
    }

    /* Event Handlers */
    private function onUploadCompleteData( event:DataEvent ):void
    {
        trace( "File Uploaded: " + File( event.target ).nativePath );
        trace( "Server Response: " + String( event.data ) );
        trace( "------------------------------------------");
        File( event.target ).removeEventListener( DataEvent.UPLOAD_COMPLETE
           _DATA, onUploadCompleteData );
        nextFile();
    }

    private function onUploadError( event:IOErrorEvent ):void
    {
        dispatchEvent( new ErrorEvent( ErrorEvent.ERROR ) );
    }

    /* Private Methods */
    private function nextFile():void
    {
        _currentIndex++;

        if( _currentIndex != _filesToUpload.length )
        {
            var fileToUpload:File = _filesToUpload[_currentIndex];
            fileToUpload.addEventListener( IOErrorEvent.IO_ERROR,
               onUploadError );
            fileToUpload.addEventListener( DataEvent.UPLOAD_COMPLETE_DATA,
               onUploadCompleteData );

            var uploadReqest:URLRequest = new URLRequest();
            uploadReqest.method = "POST";
            uploadReqest.url = ( _currentIndex == 0 ) ?
               SettingsModel.getInstance().gatewayURL + "?action=uploadData" :
               uploadReqest.url = SettingsModel.getInstance().gatewayURL
               + "?action=uploadAsset";

            try
            {
                fileToUpload.upload( uploadReqest );
            }
```

```
                catch( error:Error )
                {
                    dispatchEvent( new ErrorEvent( ErrorEvent.ERROR ) );
                }
            }
            else
            {
                _uploading = false;
                dispatchEvent( new Event( Event.COMPLETE ) );
            }
        }

        /* Public Methods */
        public function addFile( file:File ):void
        {
            _filesToUpload.push( file );
        }

        public function addFiles( files:Array ):void
        {
            _filesToUpload = _filesToUpload.concat( files );
        }

        public function startUpload():void
        {
            if( !_uploading )
            {
                _uploading = true;
                nextFile();
            }
        }

    }

}
```

Save the file as `UploadService.as` in the directory `com/aircmr/minicms/services/` within your working directory.

You just created the `UploadService` class. This class will handle all the uploading functionality. An instance of this class enables the application to create a queue of files that need to be uploaded. By calling the `addFile` or `addFiles` methods, the application will be able to add files into the queue. All files that need to be uploaded are stored in the class property array named `_filesToUpload`. When the files need to be uploaded, the `startUpload` method will be called, which essentially makes a first call to the `nextFile` method:

```
private function nextFile():void
{
    _currentIndex++;

    if( _currentIndex != _filesToUpload.length )
    {
        var fileToUpload:File = _filesToUpload[_currentIndex];
```

```
            fileToUpload.addEventListener( IOErrorEvent.IO_ERROR, onUploadError );
            fileToUpload.addEventListener( DataEvent.UPLOAD_COMPLETE_DATA,
               onUploadCompleteData );

            var uploadReqest:URLRequest = new URLRequest();
            uploadReqest.method = "POST";
            uploadReqest.url = ( _currentIndex == 0 ) ?
               SettingsModel.getInstance().gatewayURL + "?action=uploadData" :
               uploadReqest.url = SettingsModel.getInstance().gatewayURL
               + "?action=uploadAsset";

            try
            {
                fileToUpload.upload( uploadReqest );
            }
            catch( error:Error )
            {
                dispatchEvent( new ErrorEvent( ErrorEvent.ERROR ) );
            }
        }
        else
        {
            _uploading = false;
            dispatchEvent( new Event( Event.COMPLETE ) );
        }
    }
```

The preceding snippet contains the `nextFile` method of the `UploadService` class. It is in this method that each file is uploaded to the remote server. This is achieved by using the `File` object's `upload` method. This method requires but one parameter of type `URLRequest`. Naturally, the `URLRequest` must be configured properly in order for the upload to be successful. In this case, the `method` property must be set to `POST` and the `url` property must be set to the gateway URL and its appropriate action query string. With that in mind, it is assumed that the first item in the list of files to upload is going to be the data file, and subsequent files are considered assets. The gateway URL is then retrieved from the `SettingsModel` class and the appropriate query string is appended to the URL.

Creating the User Interface

In this section you will create the user interface for the application. This completes the application by tying together all the classes you created in the previous sections.

Open your editor and create a new document. Enter the following markup:

```
<?xml version="1.0" encoding="utf-8"?>
<mx:Panel xmlns:mx="http://www.adobe.com/2006/mxml"
          width="472"
          height="146"
          title="Settings"
          borderColor="#EAEAEA"
          borderAlpha="1"
          creationComplete="init()">
```

```
<mx:Script><![CDATA[

    import com.aircmr.minicms.data.SettingsModel;
    import flash.filesystem.File;
    import mx.controls.Alert;
    import mx.managers.PopUpManager;
    import mx.managers.CursorManager;
    import mx.utils.StringUtil;

    /* Static Methods */
    public static function show():SettingsPanel
    {
        var prompt:SettingsPanel =
            SettingsPanel( PopUpManager.createPopUp(
            DisplayObject( mx.core.Application.application ),
            SettingsPanel, true ) );

        PopUpManager.centerPopUp( prompt );
        return prompt;
    }

    /* Private Variables */
    private var _settings:SettingsModel;
    private var _testLoader:URLLoader;

    /* Init */
    private function init():void
    {
        _settings = SettingsModel.getInstance();

        gatewayURLInput.addEventListener( Event.CHANGE, onInputChange );
        saveBtn.addEventListener( MouseEvent.CLICK, onSaveBtnClick );
        cancelBtn.addEventListener( MouseEvent.CLICK, onCancelBtnClick );
        verifyBtn.addEventListener( MouseEvent.CLICK, onVerifyBtnClick );

        saveBtn.enabled = false;

        if( _settings.gatewayURL == null )
        {
            cancelBtn.enabled = false;
        }
        else
        {
            gatewayURLInput.text = _settings.gatewayURL;
        }
    }

    /* UI Event Handlers */
    private function onCancelBtnClick( event:MouseEvent ):void
    {
        close();
    }

    private function onSaveBtnClick( event:MouseEvent ):void
```

```
{
    _settings.gatewayURL = gatewayURLInput.text;
    close();
    dispatchEvent( new Event( Event.CHANGE ) );
}

private function onVerifyBtnClick( event:MouseEvent ):void
{
    this.enabled = false;
    CursorManager.setBusyCursor();

    _testLoader = new URLLoader();
    _testLoader.addEventListener( Event.COMPLETE, onTestResponse )
    _testLoader.addEventListener( IOErrorEvent.IO_ERROR, onTestError );
    _testLoader.load( new URLRequest( StringUtil.
       trim( gatewayURLInput.text ) + "?action=validate" ) );
}

private function onInputChange( event:Event ):void
{
    saveBtn.enabled = false;
}

/* Other Event Handlers */
private function onTestError( event:IOErrorEvent ):void
{
    Alert.show( "The gateway URL was unable to be verified.", "Error",
       (Alert.OK), this );
    this.enabled = true;
    CursorManager.removeBusyCursor();
}

private function onTestResponse( event:Event ):void
{
    var response:String = String( _testLoader.data );

    if( response.indexOf( "success=1" ) == 0 )
    {
        var responseVars:Array = response.split( "&" );

        for( var i:int = 0; i < responseVars.length; i++ )
        {
            var responseVar:Array = responseVars[i].split("=");

            switch( responseVar[0] )
            {
                case "xmlDataURL":
                    _settings.xmlDataURL = responseVar[1];
                    break;

                case "assetsFolderURL":
                    _settings.assetsFolderURL = responseVar[1];
                    break;
            }
```

```
            }

            saveBtn.enabled = true;
            this.enabled = true;
            CursorManager.removeBusyCursor();

            Alert.show( "Gateway URL verified.", "Success", (Alert.OK), this );
        }
        else
        {
            onTestError( null );
        }
    }

    /* Public Methods */
    public function close():void
    {
        PopUpManager.removePopUp( this );
    }

    ]]></mx:Script>

    <mx:VBox width="100%" paddingTop="10" paddingLeft="10" id="container">
        <mx:Text text="Gatway URL:"/>
        <mx:HBox width="100%">
            <mx:TextInput id="gatewayURLInput" width="367" />
            <mx:Button id="verifyBtn" label="Verify" />
        </mx:HBox>
        <mx:HBox width="100%" paddingTop="10" horizontalAlign="center">
            <mx:Button id="saveBtn" label="Save" />
            <mx:Button id="cancelBtn" label="Cancel" />
        </mx:HBox>
    </mx:VBox>
</mx:Panel>
```

Save the file as `SettingsPanel.mxml` in the directory `com/aircmr/minicms/ui/` within your working directory.

You just created the `SettingsPanel` interface component. This very simple component will act as a pop-up and enable users to input their gateway URL and attempt to verify it. Within the `onVerify-BtnClick` function, a `URLLoader` object is used to load a response from the gateway script by appending the user's input with the proper query string. When the `URLLoader` object receives the response from the gateway script, the `onTestResponse` function is called. Using the `data` property of the `URLLoader` object, the application parses the response to retrieve the settings that are stored within the gateway script. The `SettingsModel` is updated with the appropriate values.

Next, create the `ItemEditor` interface component. Open your editor and create a new document. Enter the following markup:

```
<?xml version="1.0" encoding="utf-8"?>
<mx:VBox xmlns:mx="http://www.adobe.com/2006/mxml"
```

```
        width="442"
        height="675"
        backgroundAlpha="1"
        backgroundColor="#ECECEC"
        creationComplete="init();">

    <mx:Script><![CDATA[

        import flash.filesystem.File;
        import com.aircmr.minicms.data.ItemData;

        private var _itemData:ItemData;
        private var _localImage:File;

        private function init():void
        {
            saveBtn.enabled = false;
            revertBtn.enabled = false;

            saveBtn.addEventListener( MouseEvent.CLICK, onSaveBtnClick );
            revertBtn.addEventListener( MouseEvent.CLICK, onRevertBtnClick );
            browseBtn.addEventListener( MouseEvent.CLICK, onBrowseBtnClick );
            dateField.addEventListener( Event.CHANGE, onItemEdited );
            titleInput.addEventListener( Event.CHANGE, onItemEdited );
            subtitleInput.addEventListener( Event.CHANGE, onItemEdited );
            bodyInput.addEventListener( Event.CHANGE, onItemEdited );
            imageInput.addEventListener( Event.CHANGE, onItemEdited );

            this.enabled = false;
        }

        /* Button Event Handlers */
        private function onSaveBtnClick( event:MouseEvent ):void
        {
            saveBtn.enabled = false;

            var year:String = String( dateField.selectedDate.getFullYear() );
            var month:String = String( dateField.selectedDate.getMonth() + 1 );
            var date:String = String( dateField.selectedDate.getDate() );

            month = ( month.length < 2 ) ? "0" + month : month;
            date = ( date.length < 2 ) ? "0" + date : date;

            _itemData.date = year + "-" + month + "-" + date;
            _itemData.body = bodyInput.text;
            _itemData.image = imageInput.text;
            _itemData.subtitle = subtitleInput.text;
            _itemData.title = titleInput.text;

            if( _localImage.nativePath != File.documentsDirectory.nativePath )
            {
                _itemData.localImage = _localImage;
            }
```

```
        dispatchEvent( new Event( Event.CHANGE ) );
    }

    private function onRevertBtnClick( event:MouseEvent ):void
    {
        _itemData.revert();
        updateUI();
        saveBtn.enabled = false;

        dispatchEvent( new Event( Event.CHANGE ) );
    }

    private function onBrowseBtnClick( event:MouseEvent ):void
    {
        var fileFilter:FileFilter = new FileFilter( "Images",
           "*.jpg;*.gif;*.png" );

        try
        {
            _localImage.browse( [fileFilter] );
            _localImage.addEventListener( Event.SELECT, onFileBrowseSelect );
        }
        catch( error:Error )
        {
            trace("Failed:", error.message);
        }
    }

    /* UI Event Handlers */
    private function onFileBrowseSelect( event:Event ):void
    {
        imageInput.text = _localImage.nativePath;
        imgLoader.load( "file:///" + _localImage.nativePath );
        saveBtn.enabled = revertBtn.enabled = true;
    }

    private function onItemEdited( event:Event ):void
    {
        revertBtn.enabled = saveBtn.enabled = true;
    }

    /* Private Methods */
    private function unloadImage():void
    {
        if( imgLoader.content != null )
        {
            imgLoader.content.loaderInfo.loader.unload();
        }
    }

    private function updateUI():void
    {
        revertBtn.enabled = _itemData.edited;
```

```
        var dateArr:Array = itemData.date.split("-");
        var year:Number = Number( dateArr[0] );
        var month:Number = Number( dateArr[1] ) - 1;
        var day:Number = Number( dateArr[2] );
        dateField.selectedDate = new Date( year, month, day );

        titleInput.text = _itemData.title;
        subtitleInput.text = _itemData.subtitle;
        bodyInput.text = _itemData.body;
        imageInput.text = _itemData.image;

       if( _itemData.image != null && _itemData.image != "" )
        {
            imgLoader.load( _itemData.image );
        }
        else
        {
            unloadImage();
        }
    }

    public function update( itemData:ItemData ):void
    {
        saveBtn.enabled = false;
        browseBtn.enabled = true;

        _localImage = File.documentsDirectory;
        _itemData = itemData;

        updateUI();

        this.enabled = true;
    }

    public function clear():void
    {
        _itemData = null;

        dateField.selectedDate = null;
        titleInput.text = "";
        subtitleInput.text = "";
        bodyInput.text = "";
        imageInput.text = "";

        saveBtn.enabled = false;
        revertBtn.enabled = false;
        browseBtn.enabled = false;
        this.enabled = false;

        unloadImage();
    }

    /* Gets & Sets */
    public function get itemData():ItemData
```

```
        {
            return _itemData;
        }

    ]]></mx:Script>

    <mx:HBox width="100%" paddingTop="10" paddingLeft="10">
        <mx:Button id="saveBtn" x="10" y="10" label="Save Changes"/>
        <mx:Button id="revertBtn" x="122" y="10" label="Revert"/>
    </mx:HBox>

    <mx:Canvas id="formContainer" width="100%" height="100%">
        <mx:Canvas id="formCanvas" width="{formContainer.width - 20}" height="100%">
            <mx:DateField id="dateField" x="10" y="8" formatString="YYYY-MM-DD" />
            <mx:Text x="10" y="36" text="Title" width="82" fontSize="12"
               fontWeight="bold"/>
            <mx:TextInput id="titleInput" y="55" minWidth="422" left="10"
               right="10"/>
            <mx:Text x="10" y="82" text="Subtitle" width="82" fontSize="12"
               fontWeight="bold"/>
            <mx:TextInput id="subtitleInput" y="101" minWidth="422" left="10"
               right="10"/>
            <mx:Text x="10" y="126" text="Body" width="82" fontSize="12"
               fontWeight="bold"/>
            <mx:TextArea id="bodyInput" y="147" height="187" borderStyle="inset"
               minWidth="422" left="10" right="10"/>
            <mx:Text x="10" y="339" text="Image" width="82" fontSize="12"
               fontWeight="bold"/>
            <mx:TextInput id="imageInput" minWidth="346" y="360" left="10"
               right="86" editable="false"/>
            <mx:Button id="browseBtn" y="359" label="Browse" left="{imageInput.x
               + imageInput.width + 8}"/>
            <mx:Canvas left="10" right="10" bottom="10" top="389">
                <mx:SWFLoader id="imgLoader"/>
            </mx:Canvas>
        </mx:Canvas>
    </mx:Canvas>

</mx:VBox>
```

Save the file as `ItemEditor.mxml` in the directory `com/aircmr/minicms/ui/` within your working directory.

The `ItemEditor` interface component will be used to edit the currently selected list item. This component should be, for the most part, self-explanatory. It is basically a form for editing the properties of an `ItemData` object.

Next, create the main application file. Open your editor and create a new document. Enter the following markup:

```
<?xml version="1.0" encoding="utf-8"?>
<mx:WindowedApplication xmlns:mx="http://www.adobe.com/2006/mxml"
                        xmlns:ui="com.aircmr.minicms.ui.*"
```

```
                        layout="absolute"
                        applicationComplete="onAppInit();"
                        closing="onAppClose();">

    <mx:Script><![CDATA[

        import com.aircmr.minicms.data.ItemData;
        import com.aircmr.minicms.data.SettingsModel;
        import com.aircmr.minicms.services.ListDataService;
        import com.aircmr.minicms.services.SettingsService;
        import com.aircmr.minicms.services.UploadService;
        import com.aircmr.minicms.services.XMLDataService;
        import com.aircmr.minicms.ui.SettingsPanel;
        import mx.controls.Alert;
        import mx.managers.CursorManager;

        private var _listDataService:ListDataService;
        private var _selectedIndex:Number;
        private var _settings:SettingsModel;
        private var _settingsPanel:SettingsPanel;
        private var _settingsService:SettingsService;
        private var _uploading:Boolean;
        private var _uploadService:UploadService;
        private var _xmlDataService:XMLDataService;

        [Bindable]
        private var _listData:Array;

        /* Application Event Handlers */
        public function onAppInit():void
        {
            this.systemManager.stage.window.width = 800;
            this.systemManager.stage.window.height = 600;

            _uploading = false;

            _settings = SettingsModel.getInstance();

            _listDataService = new ListDataService();

            _xmlDataService = new XMLDataService();
            _xmlDataService.addEventListener( Event.COMPLETE, onXMLDataLoaded );
            _xmlDataService.addEventListener( ErrorEvent.ERROR, onXMLDataError );

            _settingsService = new SettingsService();
            _settingsService.addEventListener( Event.COMPLETE, onSettingsLoaded );
            _settingsService.load();

            settingsBtn.addEventListener( MouseEvent.CLICK, onSettingsBtnClick );
            uploadBtn.addEventListener( MouseEvent.CLICK, onUploadBtnClick );
            addItemBtn.addEventListener( MouseEvent.CLICK, onAddItemBtnClick );
            deleteItemBtn.addEventListener( MouseEvent.CLICK, onDeleteBtnClick );
            revertBtn.addEventListener( MouseEvent.CLICK, onRevertBtnClick );
            dataList.addEventListener( Event.CHANGE, onDataListChange )
```

```
        itemEditor.addEventListener( Event.CHANGE, onItemEditorChange );
    }

    public function onAppClose():void
    {
        _settingsService.save( _settings.serialize() );
    }

    /* Button Event Handlers */
    private function onAddItemBtnClick( event:MouseEvent ):void
    {
        addItem();
    }

    private function onDeleteBtnClick( event:MouseEvent ):void
    {
        deleteSelectedItem();
    }

    private function onRevertBtnClick( event:MouseEvent ):void
    {
        revertAllChanges();
    }

    private function onSettingsBtnClick( event:MouseEvent ):void
    {
        openSettings();
    }

    private function onUploadBtnClick( event:MouseEvent ):void
    {
        uploadChanges();
    }

    /* UI Event Handlers */
    private function onDataListChange( event:Event ):void
    {
        if( dataList.selectedIndex > -1 )
        {
            _selectedIndex = dataList.selectedIndex;
            itemEditor.update( ItemData( dataList.selectedItem.data ) );
        }
        else
        {
            itemEditor.clear();
        }
    }

    private function onItemEditorChange( event:Event ):void
    {
        activateButtons();
        updateListItem();
    }
```

```
private function onSettingsPanelChange( event:Event ):void
{
    getData();
}

/* Service Event Handlers */
private function onSettingsLoaded( event:Event ):void
{
    _settings.data = _settingsService.data;

    if( _settings.gatewayURL == null || _settings.gatewayURL == "null" )
    {
        openSettings();
    }
    else
    {
        getData();
    }
}

private function onUploadComplete( event:Event ):void
{
    _uploading = false;
    this.enabled = true;
    CursorManager.removeBusyCursor();

    Alert.show( "Uploading complete", "Success", (Alert.OK), this,
       onSettingsPanelChange );
}

private function onUploadError( event:ErrorEvent ):void
{
    _uploading = false;
    this.enabled = true;
    CursorManager.removeBusyCursor();

    Alert.show( "There was an error during uploading. Please check your
       server settings.", "Error", (Alert.OK) );
}

private function onXMLDataError( event:ErrorEvent ):void
{
    Alert.show( "There was an error attempting to load the XML data. Please
       adjust your settings.", "Error", (Alert.OK) );
    CursorManager.removeBusyCursor();
}

private function onXMLDataLoaded( event:Event ):void
{
    if( _uploading )
    {
        _uploadService = null;
        _uploadService = new UploadService();
        _uploadService.addEventListener( Event.COMPLETE, onUploadComplete );
```

```
            _uploadService.addFile( _settings.localDataFile );
            _uploadService.addFiles( _listDataService.
               getLocalFiles( _listData ) );
            _uploadService.startUpload();
        }
        else
        {
            unselect();
            _listData = _listDataService.deserialize( _xmlDataService.xmlData );
            CursorManager.removeBusyCursor();
            this.enabled = true;
        }
    }


    /* Private Methods */
    private function activateButtons():void
    {
        uploadBtn.enabled = true;
        revertBtn.enabled = true;
    }

    private function addItem():void
    {
        var newItem:ItemData = new ItemData();

        var newListItem:Object = new Object();
        newListItem.label = newItem.title;
        newListItem.data = newItem;

        var tempList:Array = _listData;
        var toAdd:Array = [newListItem];

        _listData = null;
        _listData = toAdd.concat( tempList );

        unselect();

        activateButtons();
    }

    private function deleteSelectedItem():void
    {
        if( dataList.selectedIndex > -1 )
        {
            var selectedIndex:Number = dataList.selectedIndex;
            var deletedItem:ItemData = dataList.selectedItem.data;

            var tempList:Array = _listData;
            tempList.splice( selectedIndex, 1 );

            _listData = null;
            _listData = tempList;
```

```
                itemEditor.clear();

                activateButtons();
            }
        }

        private function openSettings():void
        {
            _settingsPanel = SettingsPanel.show();
            _settingsPanel.addEventListener( Event.CHANGE, onSettingsPanelChange );
        }

        private function getData():void
        {
            this.enabled = false;
            uploadBtn.enabled = false;
            revertBtn.enabled = false;
            CursorManager.setBusyCursor();
            _xmlDataService.load( _settings.xmlDataURL );
        }

        private function revertAllChanges():void
        {
            unselect();
            getData();
        }

        private function unselect():void
        {
            dataList.selectedIndex = -1;
            itemEditor.clear();
        }

        private function updateListItem():void
        {
            var temp:Array = _listData;

            temp[_selectedIndex].label = itemEditor.itemData.title;
            temp[_selectedIndex].data = itemEditor.itemData;

            _listData = null;
            _listData = temp;

            dataList.selectedIndex = _selectedIndex;
        }

        private function uploadChanges():void
        {
            if( !_uploading )
            {
                _uploading = true;
                this.enabled = false;
                CursorManager.setBusyCursor();
```

```
                _xmlDataService.updateXMLData( _listDataService.
                    serialize( _listData ) );
            }
        }

    ]]></mx:Script>

    <mx:VBox id="container" width="100%" height="100%">
        <mx:HBox width="100%" horizontalAlign="left" paddingTop="5"
            paddingLeft="10">
            <mx:Button id="settingsBtn" label="Settings"/>
            <mx:Button id="uploadBtn" label="Upload Changes" enabled="false" />
            <mx:Button id="revertBtn" label="Revert All Changes" enabled="false"/>
        </mx:HBox>
        <mx:HDividedBox width="100%" height="100%">
            <mx:Canvas width="40%" height="100%" backgroundAlpha="1"
                backgroundColor="#ECECEC">
                <mx:HBox x="10" y="10">
                    <mx:Button id="addItemBtn" label="Add Item" />
                    <mx:Button id="deleteItemBtn" label="Delete Item"
                        enabled="{dataList.selectedIndex > -1 }"/>
                </mx:HBox>
                <mx:List id="dataList"
                         top="40" bottom="0"
                         width="100%" height="100%"
                         alternatingItemColors="[#FFFFFF, #F6F6F6]"
                         dataProvider="{_listData}"/>
            </mx:Canvas>
            <ui:ItemEditor id="itemEditor" width="60%" height="100%" />
        </mx:HDividedBox>
    </mx:VBox>
</mx:WindowedApplication>
```

Save the file as `MiniCMS.mxml` within your working directory. This is the final piece of the application. It ties everything together to make this beauty sing. All the parts that you created previously can now talk to each other and respond according to their events.

When the application initializes, the `settings.xml` file is loaded into the application by creating an instance of the `SettingsService` class and calling the `load` method. After the settings are loaded, the application determines whether it should show the user the settings panel. It will only appear if the user has previously successfully validated his or her gateway script URL. It is only when the gateway script URL is validated that the application will retrieve the data from the remote server. This is performed in the `getData` method of this component by using an instance of the `XMLDataService` class.

When the data is loaded, an instance of the `ListDataService` class is used to create the `dataProvider` array that the `List` component, named `dataList`, will use. At this point, the user is free to edit the data as desired by selecting an item from the list and editing it within the instance of the `ItemEditor` component. Lastly, when the user has decided to upload their changes, the application saves the new XML data to the hard drive and begins the upload sequence by creating an instance of the `UploadService` class. At this point, the only thing left to do now is package and deploy the application.

Deploying the Application

Your application is now complete, but before it will work, you have to upload the gateway script (gateway.php) to a server on which PHP has been installed. You can upload the script anywhere on your server as long as the URL to it is available to the public. In addition to this, you may have to modify the permissions on the folders in which the data set and assets reside. If the permissions do not include the capability to write files within the folders, the uploading process will fail. Beyond this, the only step left is to deploy and install the application.

The Descriptor File

Open your editor, create a new document, and enter the following markup:

```
<?xml version="1.0" encoding="UTF-8"?>
<application xmlns="http://ns.adobe.com/air/application/1.0">
    <id>com.aircmr.minicms</id>
    <name>com.aircmr.MiniCMS</name>
    <filename>Mini CMS</filename>
    <version>v1</version>
    <initialWindow>
        <content>MiniCMS.swf</content>
        <title>Mini CMS</title>
    </initialWindow>
</application>
```

Save the file as MiniCMS-app.xml in your working directory.

This file will serve as the application descriptor file. The element values from this snippet are somewhat generic and should be changed as you see fit. With the descriptor file in place, you are set to compile and package the application's AIR executable.

Compiling and Packaging

Typically, two files are necessary to package an AIR application: the main SWF file and the XML application descriptor file. However, in the case of this application, you must also include the settings file. In this section, you will produce the SWF file using the command-line tools and package the AIR application.

Open a command prompt, navigate to the working directory for this application, enter the following command, and press Enter:

```
> amxmlc MiniCMS.mxml
```

If you have purchased a certificate from a certificate authority, such as VeriSign or Thawte, you may use that certificate, rather than create the self-signed certificate, and skip the following operation. To create a self-signed certificate within the working directory, enter the following command:

```
> adt -certificate -cn MiniCMS 1024-RSA certificate.pfx password
```

With the command prompt still pointing to the working directory, enter the following command and press Enter:

```
> adt -package -storetype pkcs12 -keystore certificate.pfx MiniCMS.air
   MiniCMS-app.xml MiniCMS.swf settings.xml
```

Once the installer has been successfully created by running the last command, navigate to your working directory and double-click on the `MiniCMS.air` file to install and run the application. If all goes well, the application will launch and look something like Figure 5-1. If you enter a valid gateway URL, the application should look something like Figure 5-2.

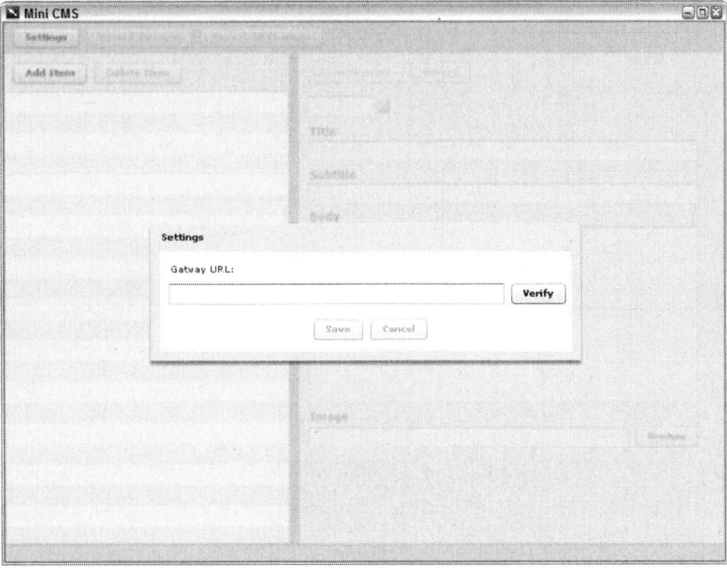

Figure 5-1

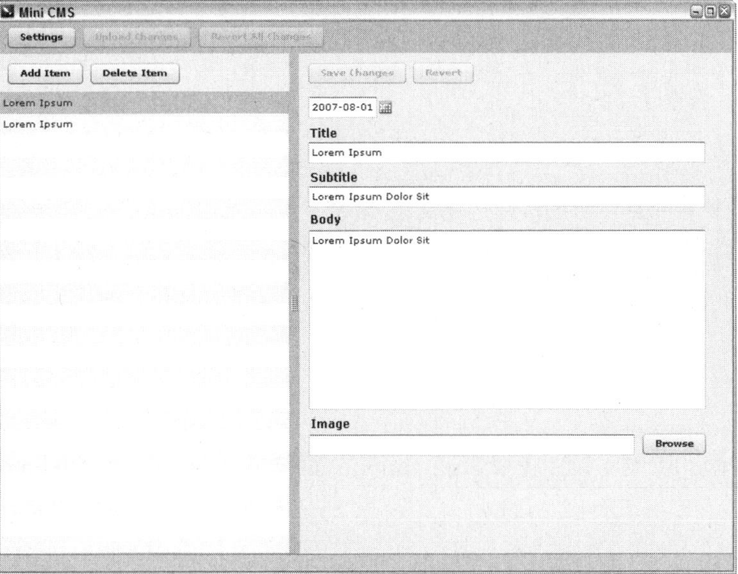

Figure 5-2

Summary

In this chapter you learned how to create a simple content management system application that manages an XML data set and its associated assets. More specifically, you learned how to upload files to a remote server using the `upload` method of the `File` class, and how to save XML files to the user's hard drive within the application's storage directory.

You might be thinking that the content this application manages is very specific and uses a schema that doesn't reflect the type of data you wish to manage. No problem — this application could be edited to accommodate your own situation. By making some simple changes to the `ItemEditor` and `ItemData` classes, you could easily change the schema for the data, and the application should, in theory, still work.

In the next chapter, you will continue to expand your knowledge of, and experience with, AIR by learning how to build an image viewer.

6

Image Viewer and Editor

If you're like most of us, you probably have dozens, if not hundreds of image files in various folders on your computer. You let these files freeload on your disk space because you know you will someday look at them again and maybe make a few adjustments. Looking at these images through a file browser can be an unrewarding experience. Perhaps if you had some type of photo displaying apparatus, you wouldn't forget about these works of art.

The image viewing application you build in this chapter will remind you of those precious moments and enable you to make adjustments to them. This program illustrates some important features of the AIR drag-and-drop API while continuing to delve into features available in the file system API discussed in the previous chapters.

In addition to displaying a single image, the application can display a bank of imported image files, enabling users to navigate through multiple images and select only what is wanted. With this capability in mind, the Image Viewer and Editor will handle multiple ways for adding to this preview bank, including the following:

- Importing all image files found in a chosen directory
- Importing multiple image files from a single directory
- Importing image files that have been dragged and dropped onto the application

The capability to save edited image files is a crucial part of the application as well, and includes the following:

- Overwriting an imported image file
- Saving an image to a chosen directory
- Saving an image by dragging it from the viewer into a directory

The next section discusses the plan to achieve these goals.

Design

In the previous chapters, you have already seen the power that the AIR file system API brings to a desktop Flash application. Reading from and writing to a file using the `FileStream` class is fairly straightforward, as is using a `File` object to browse for a file to buffer into the stream. From the previous examples in this book, you have opened and saved various text file formats for different purposes. The `File` class also makes available the opportunity to target multiple files to open — whether it is from a whole directory or multiple selected files from a spawned file browser.

The AIR API also offers another means through which you can bring files into and save files from your application. Of course, this refers to one the best features of the AIR API: drag-and-drop. Classes found in the `flash.desktop` package enable users to transfer data from a directory to your application and vice versa with the movement of the mouse.

Saving image files is relatively similar to the approach to saving text files. Specifically, a `ByteArray` object, rather than a `String`, is written to the file stream. The `FileStream` method `writeBytes` accepts a `ByteArray` and offset index and length integers. The classes found in the `mx.graphics.core` package (`PNGEncoder` and `JPEGEncoder`) encode `BitmapData` objects into `ByteArray` objects for different image file formats. In the underlying architecture, the Image Viewer and Editor will load in image files, store their bitmap data, and, when prompted, buffer that encoded data to a stream for saving image files.

This is all exciting stuff. The next section, "Handling Data," describes how to keep track of images and their data as you go through the process of opening, manipulating, and eventually saving files.

Handling Data

The Image Viewer and Editor will support viewing multiple image-file formats. The graphical data from each loaded file is presented in multiple views of the application. A thumbnail bank displays all previously opened files, and a view canvas shows the currently selected file to be viewed and edited.

That bitmap data from image files is received from requests to open multiple files from a single action — whether it is through a selection browser or dragging files onto the Image Viewer and Editor. Handling that data properly within the various processes of loading, manipulating, and saving will make for an enjoyable, speedy, and lightweight application.

The Data Object

At the heart of the Image Viewer and Editor is the ability to view images. In this section you will create the class that acts as a representation of a graphical asset. The application will have multiple views that work with properties held on this data object, whether textually or graphically, and this object will expose properties related to the original file and enable access to graphical data.

Within your development directory, create a folder titled `ImageViewer`. This will be your working directory for the application. With that set, you can get to work.

Create a new document and enter the following ActionScript:

```
package com.aircmr.imageviewer.data
{
    import flash.display.BitmapData;
    import flash.events.EventDispatcher;

    public class ImageData extends EventDispatcher
    {
        private var _name:String;
        private var _url:String;
        private var _bitmapData:BitmapData;
        private var _thumbnail:BitmapData;

        public function ImageData( sName:String, sUrl:String,
                            bBitmapData:BitmapData, bThumbnail:BitmapData = null )
        {
            _name = sName;
            _url = sUrl;
            _bitmapData = bBitmapData;
            _thumbnail = bThumbnail;
        }

         public function clean():void
         {
            if( _thumbnail != null ) _thumbnail.dispose();
            if( _bitmapData != null ) _bitmapData.dispose();
        }

        public function clone():ImageData
        {
            return new ImageData( _name, _url, _bitmapData.clone() );
        }

        public function get fileExtension():String
        {
            return _name.substr( _name.lastIndexOf( "." ),
                                        name.length ).toLowerCase();
        }

        [Bindable]
        public function set name( str:String ):void
        {
            _name = str;
        }
        public function get name():String
        {
            return _name;
        }

        [Bindable]
```

```
        public function set url( str:String ):void
        {
            _url = str;
        }
        public function get url():String
        {
            return _url;
        }

        [Bindable]
        public function set bitmapData( bmp:BitmapData ):void
        {
            _bitmapData = bmp;
        }
        public function get bitmapData():BitmapData
        {
            return _bitmapData;
        }

        [Bindable]
        public function set thumbnail( bmp:BitmapData ):void
        {
            _thumbnail = bmp;
        }
        public function get thumbnail():BitmapData
        {
            return _thumbnail;
        }
    }
}
```

Save the file as `ImageData.as` in the directory `com/aircmr/imageviewer/data` in your working directory.

The `ImageData` object has properties relative to a graphic file. The `name` and `url` properties — supplied in the constructor and through the getter/setter methods — relate to properties held on the original `File` object loaded by the application.

The `bitmapData` and `thumbnail` properties each allow access to graphical information buffered upon loading an image file. *Thumbnails*, smaller graphical representations of a larger image, are not received on load of an image file nor created by the `File` class. The application creates and sets these thumbnails while loading images to the thumbnail bank. The reason for this is twofold: First, re-rendering an image from a large size to a smaller size while scrolling through those images can prove to be an unenjoyable user experience. Second, thumbnail representations of image files come in very handy when enabling the dragging out of images to save.

A single instance of an `ImageData` object represents a single image file and its graphical information. The Image Viewer and Editor, however, enables the viewing, editing, and saving of multiple images. In the next section you will create a manager for the multiple `ImageData` objects that are used by multiple clients within the application.

Managing Data Objects

The ImageData class created in the previous section is a representation of a graphic file. When an image is loaded by the Image Viewer and Editor, it is presented for editing and added to a thumbnail bank, enabling a user to view any previously imported items. In this section you'll create a manager to keep track of all those data objects and dispatch events for any listening clients that pertain not only to the images available but also to the currently selected image to be viewed.

Create a new document and enter the following ActionScript:

```
package com.aircmr.imageviewer.data
{
    import flash.events.Event;
    import flash.events.EventDispatcher;
    import mx.collections.ArrayCollection;

    [Event(name="indexChange", type="flash.events.Event")]
    public class GalleryDataManager extends EventDispatcher
    {
        private static const _instance:GalleryDataManager =
                                                new GalleryDataManager();

        private var _currentIndex:int = 0;
        private var _list:ArrayCollection; //ImageData[]

        public static const INDEX_CHANGE:String = "indexChange";

        public static function getInstance():GalleryDataManager
        {
            return _instance;
        }

        public function GalleryDataManager():void
        {
            if( _instance == null )
            {
                init();
            }
            else
            {
                // throw error.
            }
        }

        private function init():void
        {
            _list = new ArrayCollection();
        }

        public function addImage( img:ImageData ):void
```

```
        {
            _list.addItem( img );
        }

        public function addMultipleImages( arr:Array ):void
        {
            list = new ArrayCollection( _list.toArray().concat( arr ) );
        }

        public function clean():void
        {
            for( var i:int = 0; i < _list.length; i++ )
            {
                 ( _list.getItemAt( i ) as ImageData ).clean();
            }
            _list = new ArrayCollection();
        }

        [Bindable]
        public function set list( arr:ArrayCollection ):void
        {
             _list = arr;
        }
        public function get list():ArrayCollection
        {
            return _list;
        }

        [Bindable("indexChange")]
        public function set currentIndex( index:int ):void
        {
            if( index < 0 || index > _list.length - 1 ) return;
            _currentIndex = index;
            dispatchEvent( new Event( INDEX_CHANGE ) );
        }
        public function get currentIndex():int
        {
            return _currentIndex;
        }
    }
}
```

Save the file as `GalleryDataManager.as` in a directory `com/aircmr/imageviewer/data` in your working directory.

The list of `ImageData` objects available for multiple clients is managed by the `GalleryDataManager`. The `GalleryDataManager` employs the Singleton pattern, which restricts the instantiation of the class to a single object and ensures that any layer of the application that is concerned with image data is working with the same information. Notification of changes to the list of images, available through the `list` property, is made through the inherent binding within the `ArrayCollection` class. Any change to the list or any item in the list will dispatch a `propertyChange` event — the default event for data binding.

Along with the list of images available within the application, an index within that list is managed by the `GalleryDataManager`. Changes to the `currentIndex` property dispatch an `indexChange` event.

By managing the current index within the list, you can ensure that multiple clients within the application are working with the same data.

As you begin to build the interface of the Image Viewer and Editor, views will subscribe to property changes of the `GalleryDataManager` and update accordingly. Before you begin building the displays for the data discussed in this section, however, it would be useful to look at how image files are loaded and how `ImageData` objects are created.

Queuing Image Files

Dealing with bitmap data can be quite intensive on your machine's processor, especially when asking the Flash Player to asynchronously load multiple image files in one fell swoop. A queue system to load multiple files is advantageous not only for passing along data as it is completely received, but also for checking for valid file formats along the way.

1. Open your favorite editor and enter the following ActionScript:

```
package com.aircmr.imageviewer.loaders
{
    import com.aircmr.imageviewer.data.ImageData;
    import com.aircmr.imageviewer.events.ImageLoadEvent;

    import flash.display.Bitmap;
    import flash.display.Loader;
    import flash.events.ErrorEvent;
    import flash.events.Event;
    import flash.events.EventDispatcher;
    import flash.events.IOErrorEvent;
    import flash.filesystem.File;
    import flash.net.URLRequest;

    [Event(name="load", type="flash.events.Event")]
    [Event(name="invalid", type="flash.events.Event")]
    [Event(name="complete", type="flash.events.Event")]
    public class ImageLoadQueue extends EventDispatcher
    {
        [ArrayElementType("flash.filesystem.File")]
        private var _queue:Array;
        private var _loader:Loader;
        private var _file:File;

        private var _filter:RegExp = /^\S+\.(jpg|jpeg|png)$/i;

        public static const INVALID:String = "invalid";
        public static const COMPLETE:String = "complete";

        public function ImageLoadQueue()
        {
            _queue = new Array();
            _loader = new Loader();
            _loader.contentLoaderInfo.addEventListener( Event.COMPLETE,
                                                        onLoadComplete );
            _loader.contentLoaderInfo.addEventListener( IOErrorEvent.IO_ERROR,
                                                        onLoadError );
```

```
        }

        private function validateFile( file:File ):Boolean
        {
            return _filter.exec( file.name ) != null;
        }

        private function onLoadError( evt:IOErrorEvent ):void
        {
            dispatchEvent( new ErrorEvent(ErrorEvent.ERROR,
                                    false, false, evt.text) );
        }

        private function onLoadComplete( evt:Event ):void
        {
            var data:ImageData = new ImageData( _file.name, _file.url,
                                ( _loader.content as Bitmap ).bitmapData );
            dispatchEvent( new ImageLoadEvent( ImageLoadEvent.LOAD, data ) );
            if( _queue.length <= 0 )
            {
                clear();
                dispatchEvent( new Event( COMPLETE ) );
            }
            else
            {
                loadNext();
            }
        }

        private function loadFile( file:File ):void
        {
            _file = file;
            if( validateFile( _file ) )
            {
                _loader.load( new URLRequest( _file.url ) );
            }
            else
            {
                dispatchEvent( new Event( INVALID ) );
                if( _queue.length > 0 ) loadNext();
                else dispatchEvent( new Event( COMPLETE ) );
            }
        }

        public function loadNext():void
        {
            if( _queue.length > 0 )
            {
                loadFile( _queue.shift() );
            }
        }

        public function loadAll():void
        {
```

```
            if( _queue.length <= 0 ) return;
             loadFile( _queue[0] );
            _queue.shift();
        }

        public function addFile( file:File ):void
        {
            _queue.push( file );
        }

        public function addFiles( arr:Array ):void
        {
            _queue = _queue.concat( arr );
        }

        public function clear():void
        {
            _queue = new Array();
        }
    }
}
```

2. Save the file as `ImageLoadQueue.as` in a directory `com/aircmr/imageviewer/loaders` within your working directory.
3. Create a new document and enter the following ActionScript:

```
package com.aircmr.imageviewer.events
{
    import com.aircmr.imageviewer.data.ImageData;

    import flash.events.Event;

    public class ImageLoadEvent extends Event
    {
        private var _imageData:ImageData;

        public static const LOAD:String = "load";

        public function ImageLoadEvent(type:String, imgData:ImageData)
        {
            super( type );
            _imageData = imgData;
        }

        public function get imageData():ImageData
        {
            return _imageData;
        }
    }
}
```

4. Save the file as `ImageLoadEvent.as` in the directory `com/aircmr/imageviewer/events` within your working directory.

The former snippet, saved as `ImageLoadQueue`, handles loading files sequentially. A client can add multiple `File` objects to the queue to be loaded and call the `loadAll()` method to begin the process. Alternatively, while the process is running, more files can be added if needed. Although the queue holds an array of `File` objects, the files themselves are not buffered into a `FileStream` for processing the data. Instead, the files are loaded using a `Loader` instance that makes a request based on the `url` property of the `File` instance:

```
_loader.load( new URLRequest( _file.url ) );
```

The `complete` event handler of the `Loader` instance creates a new `ImageData` object and dispatches an instance of the `ImageLoadEvent` class holding that data:

```
var data:ImageData = new ImageData( _file.name, _file.url,
   ( _loader.content as Bitmap ).bitmapData );
dispatchEvent( new ImageLoadEvent( ImageLoadEvent.LOAD, data ) );
```

As each file in the queue is loaded and the `load` event is fired, it is determined whether there are more files to be loaded or the queue has become empty. If the queue has no files left to load, then a "complete" event is dispatched from `ImageLoadQueue` to alert listening clients that the load process has finished.

You may note that some validating of file types is performed during this queue loading. Because a text file (at least in the context of this application) would seem out of place when viewing images, the `ImageLoadQueue` runs a check on the extension of the file it is requested to load. In doing so, a regular expression is used to ensure that the file is an image file in either JPG, JPEG, or PNG format:

```
private var _filter:RegExp = /^\S+\.(jpg|jpeg|png)$/i;
```

Discussing regular expressions requires a book in itself, but for the purposes of this example, it is enough to understand that this action matches any file with a name followed by a dot and either of the three image file extensions, without regard to letter case. If the `url` property of a `File` fails to meet this requirement, an `invalid` event is dispatched and the queue moves forward in loading.

At this point, you have a mechanism for loading image files, data objects to represent the file and its graphical data, and a manager for all images available for viewing and editing. It is time to start displaying this data and dive into more aspects of the AIR API.

Building the User Interface

At the beginning of this chapter was a brief discussion of the visual display of the Image Viewer and Editor and user interaction. (The main application class will handle most of the calls to load and save files, as well as the drag-and-drop capabilities in the AIR API, and is discussed later in the section "Bringing It All Together.") Before delving into getting the data in and saving the data out, how the data is displayed needs to be addressed. There will be three main interface views within the application:

- A thumbnail image browser will hold all previously opened image files and enable users to select a file to view.
- An image display will show the selected image and enable users to rotate and resize the image.
- An image editor panel will enable users to manipulate the currently viewed image file.

Combining what you have previously done in this chapter with regard to managing data, the following sections address displaying that data for browsing, viewing, and editing.

Browsing Opened Images

Along with displaying a list of available images to select for viewing, the thumbnail image browser also manages the load queue — `ImageLoadQueue` — adding files, instructing it to load, and listening for each completion. As such, the browser will also hold a control for importing all image files found in a targeted directory:

1. Open your favorite editor, create a new document, and enter the following markup:

```
<?xml version="1.0" encoding="utf-8"?>
<mx:Canvas
    xmlns:mx="http://www.adobe.com/2006/mxml"
    creationComplete="onCreationComplete();">

    <mx:Style>
        .browseControls {
            background-color: #EEEEEE;
        }
    </mx:Style>

    <mx:Metadata>
        [Event(name="select", type="flash.events.Event")]
    </mx:Metadata>

    <mx:Script>
        <![CDATA[
            import com.aircmr.imageviewer.data.ImageData;
            import com.aircmr.imageviewer.data.GalleryDataManager;
            import com.aircmr.imageviewer.events.ImageLoadEvent;
            import com.aircmr.imageviewer.loaders.ImageLoadQueue;

            import mx.collections.ArrayCollection;
            import mx.managers.CursorManager;
            import flash.filesystem.File;

            private var _queue:ImageLoadQueue;

            private var _browseFile:File;

            private var _heldSelectedIndex:int = 0;
            private var _selectLastFileOnComplete:Boolean = false;

            [Bindable]
            private var _columnCount:int;

            private function onCreationComplete():void
            {
                _queue = new ImageLoadQueue();
                _queue.addEventListener( ImageLoadEvent.LOAD, onImageFileLoad );
```

```
        _queue.addEventListener( ImageLoadQueue.COMPLETE,
                                 onFileQueueComplete );

        _browseFile = new File();
        _browseFile.addEventListener( Event.SELECT, onDirectorySelect );

        GalleryDataManager.getInstance().addEventListener(
                GalleryDataManager.INDEX_CHANGE, onGalleryIndexChange );

        onResize();
    }

    private function onDirectorySelect( evt:Event ):void
    {
        CursorManager.setBusyCursor();
        _queue.addFiles( _browseFile.getDirectoryListing() );
        _queue.loadAll();
    }

    private function onBrowse( evt:MouseEvent ):void
    {
        _browseFile.browseForDirectory( "Import files from directory..." );
    }

    private function onImageFileLoad( evt:ImageLoadEvent ):void
    {
        GalleryDataManager.getInstance().addImage( evt.imageData );
    }

    private function onFileQueueComplete( evt:Event ):void
    {
        if( _selectLastFileOnComplete )
        {
            GalleryDataManager.getInstance().currentIndex =
                            thumbGallery.dataProvider.length - 1;
            _selectLastFileOnComplete = false;
        }
        else
        {
            GalleryDataManager.getInstance().currentIndex =
                            Math.max( 0, _heldSelectedIndex );
        }
        CursorManager.removeBusyCursor();
    }

    private function onGalleryIndexChange( evt:Event ):void
    {
        var scrollPos:int = thumbGallery.horizontalScrollPosition;
        thumbGallery.horizontalScrollPosition = 0;
        var currIndex:int = thumbGallery.selectedIndex =
                        GalleryDataManager.getInstance().currentIndex;
        if( currIndex > scrollPos + _columnCount - 1 )
```

```
        {
            thumbGallery.horizontalScrollPosition =
                                        currIndex - _columnCount + 1;
        }
        else if( currIndex < scrollPos )
        {
            thumbGallery.horizontalScrollPosition = currIndex;
        }
        else
        {
            thumbGallery.horizontalScrollPosition = scrollPos;
        }
        enableControls();
        onThumbSelect();
    }

    private function onBrowseBack( evt:MouseEvent ):void
    {
        if( thumbGallery.horizontalScrollPosition > 0 )
        {
            try
            {
                thumbGallery.horizontalScrollPosition =
                            thumbGallery.horizontalScrollPosition - 1;
            }
            catch( e:Error )
            {
                thumbGallery.horizontalScrollPosition = 0;
                thumbGallery.horizontalScrollPosition =
                            thumbGallery.selectedIndex - _columnCount;
            }
        }
        enableControls();
    }
    private function onBrowseForward( evt:MouseEvent ):void
    {
        if( thumbGallery.horizontalScrollPosition <
             GalleryDataManager.getInstance().list.length - _columnCount )
            thumbGallery.horizontalScrollPosition += 1;

        enableControls();
    }

    private function onResize( evt:Event = null ):void
    {
        _columnCount = Math.ceil(thumbGallery.width/thumbGallery.height);
        thumbGallery.columnWidth = thumbGallery.rowHeight =
                Math.min( width / _columnCount, thumbGallery.height - 2 );
        thumbGallery.horizontalScrollPosition = 0;
        enableControls();
    }
```

```
        private function onThumbSelect( evt:Event = null ):void
        {
            dispatchEvent( new Event( Event.SELECT ) );
        }

        private function enableControls():void
        {
            var scrollPos:int = thumbGallery.horizontalScrollPosition;
            var len:int = GalleryDataManager.getInstance().list.length
            prevControl.enabled = scrollPos > 0;
            nextControl.enabled = scrollPos < len - _columnCount;
        }

        public function addFiles( files:Array, select:Boolean = false ):void
        {
            CursorManager.setBusyCursor();
            _selectLastFileOnComplete = select;
            _heldSelectedIndex = thumbGallery.selectedIndex;
            _queue.addFiles( files );
            _queue.loadAll();
        }

        public function get selectedImage():ImageData
        {
            return ( ( thumbGallery.dataProvider as ArrayCollection ).getItemAt
               ( GalleryDataManager.getInstance().currentIndex ) as ImageData );
        }

    ]]>
</mx:Script>

<mx:VBox width="100%" height="100%" verticalGap="0">

    <mx:HBox width="100%" height="26"
        verticalAlign="middle" horizontalAlign="right"
        paddingRight="5" paddingLeft="5"
        backgroundColor="0xEEEEEE">

        <mx:Label text="Import files from directory..." />
        <mx:Button id="browseButton"
            label="browse"
            click="onBrowse( event );"
            />

    </mx:HBox>

    <mx:HBox width="100%" height="100%"
        verticalAlign="middle" horizontalGap="2"
        paddingLeft="5" paddingRight="5" paddingTop="5" paddingBottom="5"
        backgroundColor="0xCCCCCC">

        <mx:Box id="prevControl" backgroundColor="0xCCCCCC">
            <mx:Image id="previousButton"
                source="@Embed(source='/assets/previous_up.png')"
```

```
                click="onBrowseBack( event );"
                />
        </mx:Box>

        <mx:HorizontalList id="thumbGallery"
            width="100%" height="100%"
            paddingLeft="5" paddingRight="5"
            horizontalScrollPolicy="off"
            itemRenderer="com.aircmr.imageviewer.ui.Thumbnail"
            dataProvider="{GalleryDataManager.getInstance().list}"
            resize="onResize( event );"
            change="{GalleryDataManager.getInstance().currentIndex =
               thumbGallery.selectedIndex}"
            />

        <mx:Box id="nextControl" backgroundColor="0xCCCCCC">
            <mx:Image id="nextButton"
                source="@Embed(source='/assets/next_up.png')"
                click="onBrowseForward( event );"
                />
        </mx:Box>

    </mx:HBox>

</mx:VBox>

</mx:Canvas>
```

2. Save the file as `ImageBrowser.mxml` in the directory `com/aircmr/imageviewer/ui` in your working directory.

3. Create a new document and enter the following ActionScript:

```
package com.aircmr.imageviewer.ui
{
    import com.aircmr.imageviewer.data.ImageData;
    import com.aircmr.imageviewer.utils.BitmapUtil;

    import flash.display.Bitmap;
    import flash.display.BitmapData;
    import flash.display.Shape;
    import flash.geom.Rectangle;

    import mx.controls.listClasses.IListItemRenderer;
    import mx.core.IDataRenderer;
    import mx.core.UIComponent;
    import mx.events.FlexEvent;

    [Style(name="borderColor", type="Number")]
    [Style(name="borderWeight", type="Number")]

    public class Thumbnail extends UIComponent
        implements IDataRenderer, IListItemRenderer
    {
        protected var _data:ImageData;
```

```
private var _holder:UIComponent;
private var _bitmap:Bitmap;
private var _border:Shape;
private var _useThumbnail:Boolean = false;

private static const PADDING:int = 4;

public function Thumbnail()
{
    super();
}

protected function doLayout():void
{
    var bounds:Rectangle = getBoundingArea();
    _border.graphics.clear();
    _border.graphics.lineStyle( getStyle( "borderWeight" ),
                                getStyle( "borderColor" ),
                                1, true, "normal", "miter" );
    _border.graphics.drawRect( bounds.x, bounds.y,
                                bounds.width, bounds.height );

    if( _data.thumbnail == null )
    {
        var bmd:BitmapData = BitmapUtil.generateThumbnail(
                                    _bitmap.bitmapData,
                                    bounds.width - ( PADDING * 2 ),
                                    bounds.height - ( PADDING * 2 ) );
        _data.thumbnail = bmd;
        _bitmap.bitmapData.dispose();
        _bitmap.bitmapData = bmd;
    }
    _bitmap.x = ( unscaledWidth / 2 ) - ( _bitmap.width / 2 );
    _bitmap.y = ( unscaledHeight / 2 ) - ( _bitmap.height / 2 );
}

private function getBoundingArea():Rectangle
{
    var bw:Number = getStyle( "borderWeight" );
    var px:Number = getStyle( "paddingLeft" ) + bw;
    var py:Number = bw;
    var pw:Number = unscaledWidth -
                ( getStyle( "paddingRight" ) + ( bw ) + px );
    var ph:Number = unscaledHeight - ( ( bw ) + py );
    return new Rectangle( px, py, pw, ph );
}

override protected function createChildren():void
{
    super.createChildren();
    if( _holder == null )
    {
        _holder = new UIComponent();
        addChild( _holder );
```

```
                _border = new Shape();
                _holder.addChild( _border );

                _bitmap = new Bitmap();
                _holder.addChild( _bitmap );
            }
        }

        override protected function commitProperties():void
        {
            if( _data != null )
            {
                if( _data.thumbnail != null )
                {
                    _bitmap.bitmapData = _data.thumbnail;
                }
                else _bitmap.bitmapData = _data.bitmapData.clone();
            }
        }

        override protected function updateDisplayList(unscaledWidth:Number,
                                                unscaledHeight:Number):void
        {
            super.updateDisplayList( unscaledWidth, unscaledHeight );
            doLayout();
        }

        [Bindable("dataChange")]
        public function set data( value:Object ):void
        {
            _data = ( value as ImageData );
            dispatchEvent( new FlexEvent( FlexEvent.DATA_CHANGE ) );
        }
        public function get data():Object
        {
            return _data;
        }
    }
}
```

4. Save the file as `Thumbnail.as` in the directory `com/aircmr/imageviewer/ui` in your working directory.

5. Create a new document and enter the following ActionScript:

```
package com.aircmr.imageviewer.utils
{
    import flash.display.BitmapData;
    import flash.geom.Matrix;

    public class BitmapUtil
    {
        public static function generateThumbnail( bmp:BitmapData, w:Number,
                                h:Number, crop:Boolean = false ):BitmapData
```

```
            {
                var scale:Number = 1.0;
                if( bmp.width > w || bmp.height > h )
                {
                    scale = Math.min( w / bmp.width, h / bmp.height );
                }

                var m:Matrix = new Matrix();
                m.scale( scale, scale );

                if( !crop )
                {
                    m.tx = ( w / 2 ) - ( ( bmp.width * scale ) / 2 );
                    m.ty = ( h / 2 ) - ( ( bmp.height * scale ) / 2 );
                }
                else
                {
                    w = bmp.width * scale;
                    h = bmp.height * scale;
                }

                var bmd:BitmapData = new BitmapData( w, h, true );
                bmd.draw( bmp, m );

                return bmd;
            }
        }
    }
```

6. Save the file as `BitmapUtil.as` in the directory `com/aircmr/imageviewer/utils` in your working directory.

The first snippet, saved as `ImageBrowser.mxml`, is the MXML component holding the thumbnail list control for browsing images. Along with controls to scroll through the thumbnail list, there is a `click` event handler assigned to a button to access a file browser for importing image files from a directory:

```
<mx:Button id="browseButton"
    label="browse"
    click="onBrowse( event );"
    />
private function onBrowse( evt:MouseEvent ):void
{
    _browseFile.browseForDirectory( "Import files from directory..." );
}
```

The `onBrowser()` event handler calls the `browseForDirectory()` method on the class-local `File` instance `_browseFile` instantiated within the `onCreationComplete()` method. The parameter for `browseForDirectory` is a string that will be shown in the title bar of the browser window. The event handler for the `select` event dispatched after selection of a directory from the opened browser window adds files to the `ImageLoadQueue` instance and instructs it to begin loading:

```
private function onDirectorySelect( evt:Event ):void
{
    CursorManager.setBusyCursor();
```

```
        _queue.addFiles( _browseFile.listDirectory() );
        _queue.loadAll();
    }
```

Upon load of an image file, the list property of the GalleryDataManager is updated through the public addImage() method, with the argument passed as the ImageData object held on the ImageLoadEvent instance:

```
    private function onImageFileLoad( evt:ImageLoadEvent ):void
    {
        GalleryDataManager.getInstance().addImage(evt.imageData);
    }
```

The visual thumbnail list itself is the mxml component HorizontalList. Through binding the HorizontalList instance's dataProvider property to the list property of GalleryDataManager, any change to the list of ImageData objects will be updated in the display:

```
    <mx:HorizontalList id="thumbGallery"
       width="100%" height="100%"
       paddingLeft="5" paddingRight="5"
       horizontalScrollPolicy="off"
       itemRenderer="com.apolloir.imageviewer.ui.Thumbnail"
       dataProvider="{GalleryDataManager.getInstance().list}"
       resize="onResize( event );"
       change="{GalleryDataManager.getInstance().currentIndex =
          thumbGallery.selectedIndex}"
       />
```

Likewise, any selection made from the display list — dispatching the change event — updates the bindable currentIndex property of GalleryDataManager. A change to the currentIndex is listened to by multiple views as you will see, but in the case of the ImageBrowser the handler for currentIndexChange updates the scroll position of the thumbnail display list.

> *There are some graphical assets used for the Back and Previous buttons in* ImageBrowser.mxml. *You are free to use your own, but those image files can be found in the /assets folder of the code examples for this chapter, on the accompanying website for this book.*

The second snippet, saved as Thumbnail.as, is the item renderer for the HorizontalList instance. When a change to the list's data provider is made, the list redraws itself, adding a new instance of the item renderer to its display list for each element in the data provider. As the HorizontalList iterates through elements in its data provider, each instance of a Thumbnail is provided that data through the data property:

```
    public function set data( value:Object ):void
    {
        _data = ( value as ImageData );
        invalidateProperties();
        dispatchEvent( new FlexEvent( FlexEvent.DATA_CHANGE ) );
    }
```

Upon supply of data, the value argument is recast as an ImageData object and a call to invalidate-Properties() is made. Without getting too in depth regarding the internal workings of the UIComponent within the Flex Framework, `invalidateProperties()` will lead to a call being made to the `commitProperties()` and `updateDisplayList()` methods — both of which are overridden in the `Thumbnail` class.

A `Thumbnail` instance displays a bitmap within a border. The `commitProperties()` override assigns the bitmap data to the bitmap, and the `updateDisplayList()` override makes a call to the `doLayout()` method:

```
protected function doLayout():void
{
        var bounds:Rectangle = getBoundingArea();
        _border.graphics.clear();
        _border.graphics.lineStyle( getStyle( "borderWeight" ),
                                    getStyle( "borderColor" ),
                                    1, true, "normal", "miter" );
        _border.graphics.drawRect( bounds.x, bounds.y,
                                    bounds.width, bounds.height );

        if( _data.thumbnail == null )
        {
            var bmd:BitmapData = BitmapUtil.generateThumbnail(
                                    _bitmap.bitmapData,
                                    bounds.width - ( PADDING * 2 ),
                                    bounds.height - ( PADDING * 2 ) );
            _data.thumbnail = bmd;
            _bitmap.bitmapData.dispose();
            _bitmap.bitmapData = bmd;
        }
        _bitmap.x = ( unscaledWidth / 2 ) - ( _bitmap.width / 2 );
        _bitmap.y = ( unscaledHeight / 2 ) - ( _bitmap.height / 2 );
    }
```

Within the `doLayout()` method, the border display is redrawn and the bitmap position is updated based on the size of the `Thumbnail` instance. A check for the availability of the thumbnail data on the `ImageData` instance is made as well in this method. If the thumbnail data is not available, then a thumbnail is created using the third snippet and saved as `BitmapUtil.as`, and a scaled `BitmapData` instance is assigned to that property.

To cut down on the processing required to continuously load, resize, and render any potentially large bitmaps as the thumbnail list grows, the `generateThumbnail()` method of `BitmapUtil` will return a scaled-down `BitmapData` instance based on the dimension parameters supplied:

```
var scale:Number = 1.0;
if( bmp.width > w || bmp.height > h )
{
    scale = Math.min( w / bmp.width, h / bmp.height );
}
var m:Matrix = new Matrix();
m.scale( scale, scale );
```

In looking at the `generateThumbnail()` method, the scale to apply to a bitmap is determined based on its current size. That scale value is then applied to a `Matrix` object which is used to transform a drawn copy of the supplied `BitmapData` instance:

```
var bmd:BitmapData = new BitmapData( w, h, true );
bmd.draw( bmp, m );
```

With the returned scaled-down version of the original bitmap data, you can save some redraw time and have a thumbnail to associate with the `ImageData` instance. This thumbnail will also play a part in another aspect of the application, as you will see in the following sections.

Viewing an Image

You can now browse through thumbnail-size images, but what's the fun of browsing if you can't see anything close up? In this section you'll create the display to view full-size images containing controls for viewing the images even bigger, or smaller, or sideways.

1. Create a new document and enter the following markup:

```
<?xml version="1.0" encoding="utf-8"?>
<mx:Canvas
    xmlns:mx="http://www.adobe.com/2006/mxml"
    xmlns:ui="com.aircmr.imageviewer.ui.*">

    <mx:Style>
        .controls {
            background-color: #EEEEEE;
        }
        .navControls {
         background-color: #CCCCCC;
        }
        .scaleCombo {
         background-color: #EEEEEE;
            focus-alpha: 0;
        }
    </mx:Style>

    <mx:Metadata>
         [Event( name="dragCopy", type="flash.events.Event" )]
    </mx:Metadata>

    <mx:Script>
        <![CDATA[
            import com.aircmr.imageviewer.data.ImageData;
            import com.aircmr.imageviewer.data.GalleryDataManager;

            [Bindable] private var _imageData:ImageData;
            private static const SCALE_MINIMUM:Number = 0.25;
            private static const SCALE_MAXIMUM:Number = 10;
            private static const COMBO_WIDTH:int = 80;

            private function onScaleChange( evt:Event ):void
            {
                stage.focus = this;
                var scale:Number = parseInt( sizeCombo.value.toString() ) / 100;
                var value:Number = Math.min( SCALE_MAXIMUM,
                                        Math.max( SCALE_MINIMUM, scale ) );
                imageDisplay.scale = value;
                // reset display text.
                sizeCombo.text = ( value * 100 ).toString() + "%";
            }
```

```
            private function onPrevious( evt:MouseEvent ):void
            {
                GalleryDataManager.getInstance().currentIndex -= 1;
            }

            private function onNext( evt:MouseEvent ):void
            {
                GalleryDataManager.getInstance().currentIndex += 1;
            }

            private function onRotateLeft( evt:MouseEvent ):void
            {
                imageDisplay.rotation -= 90;
            }

            private function onRotateRight( evt:MouseEvent ):void
            {
                imageDisplay.rotation += 90;
            }

            public function set imageData( img:ImageData ):void
            {
                _imageData = img;
            }

        ]]>
    </mx:Script>

    <mx:VBox width="100%" height="100%">

        <mx:HBox width="100%" height="30"
            paddingLeft="5" paddingRight="5"
            styleName="controls"
            horizontalAlign="right" horizontalGap="5"
            verticalAlign="middle"
            enabled="{_imageData != null}">
            <mx:Label id="imageName"
                truncateToFit="true"
                maxWidth="{width - COMBO_WIDTH - 15}"
                text="{_imageData.name}"
                />
            <mx:Image id="rotateLeft"
                source="@Embed(source='/assets/rotateLeft.png')"
                buttonMode="true" useHandCursor="true"
                click="onRotateLeft( event );"
                />
            <mx:Image id="rotateRight"
                source="@Embed(source='/assets/rotateRight.png')"
                buttonMode="true" useHandCursor="true"
                click="onRotateRight( event );"
                />

         <mx:ComboBox id="sizeCombo"
                width="{COMBO_WIDTH}"
                rowCount="6"
```

```
                styleName="scaleCombo"
                textAlign="left"
                editable="true"
                selectedIndex="2"
                enter="onScaleChange( event );"
                close="onScaleChange( event );">
                <mx:dataProvider>
                    <mx:Object label="25%" />
                    <mx:Object label="50%" />
                    <mx:Object label="100%" />
                    <mx:Object label="200%" />
                    <mx:Object label="500%" />
                    <mx:Object label="1000%" />
                </mx:dataProvider>
            </mx:ComboBox>

        </mx:HBox>

        <mx:HBox width="100%" height="100%"
            paddingLeft="5" paddingBottom="5" paddingRight="5">
            <ui:ImageDisplay id="imageDisplay" width="100%" height="100%"
                source="{_imageData.bitmapData}"
                />
        </mx:HBox>

        <mx:HBox width="100%" height="30"
            paddingLeft="5" paddingRight="5"
            styleName="navControls"
            horizontalAlign="center" horizontalGap="5"
            verticalAlign="middle">

            <mx:Box enabled="{GalleryDataManager.getInstance().currentIndex &gt; 0}"
                styleName="navControls">
                <mx:Image id="previousButon"
                    source="@Embed(source='/assets/previous_up.png')"
                    buttonMode="true" useHandCursor="true"
                    click="onPrevious( event );"
                    />
            </mx:Box>
            <mx:Box enabled="{GalleryDataManager.getInstance().currentIndex &lt;
               GalleryDataManager.getInstance().list.length - 1}"
                styleName="navControls">
                <mx:Image id="nextButton"
                    source="@Embed(source='/assets/next_up.png')"
                    buttonMode="true" useHandCursor="true"
                    click="onNext( event );"
                    />
            </mx:Box>

        </mx:HBox>

    </mx:VBox>

</mx:Canvas>
```

2. Save the file as `ImageCanvas.mxml` in the directory `com/aircmr/imageviewer/ui` in your working directory.

3. Create a new document and enter the following ActionScript:

```
package com.aircmr.imageviewer.ui
{
    import flash.display.Bitmap;
    import flash.display.BitmapData;
    import flash.events.Event;
    import flash.events.MouseEvent;
    import flash.geom.Rectangle;

    import mx.containers.Canvas;
    import mx.core.Container;
    import mx.core.UIComponent;

    [Event(name="dragCopy", type="flash.events.Event")]
    public class ImageDisplay extends UIComponent
    {
        private var _canvas:Container;
        private var _holder:UIComponent;
        private var _imgSource:BitmapData;
        private var _image:Bitmap;

        private var _scale:Number = 1.0;
        private var _rotation:Number = 0;

        public static const DRAG_COPY:String = "dragCopy";

        public function ImageDisplay()
        {
            addEventListener( Event.RESIZE, doLayout );
        }

        override protected function createChildren():void
        {
            super.createChildren();

            _canvas = new Canvas();
            addChild( _canvas );

            _holder = new UIComponent();
            _holder.addEventListener( MouseEvent.MOUSE_DOWN, onImageSelect );
            _canvas.addChild( _holder );

            _image = new Bitmap();
            _holder.addChild( _image );
        }

        private function doLayout( evt:Event = null ):void
        {
            if( _imgSource == null ) return;
            _image.rotation = _rotation;
            _image.scaleX = _image.scaleY = _scale;
```

```
        var bounds:Rectangle = getImageBounds();
        _image.x = bounds.x;
        _image.y = bounds.y;

        _holder.width = _image.width;
        _holder.height = _image.height;
        _holder.x = Math.max( 0, ( width - bounds.width ) / 2 );
        _holder.y = Math.max( 0, ( height -  bounds.height ) / 2 );

        _canvas.width = width;
        _canvas.height = height;
        _canvas.horizontalScrollPosition =
                Math.max( 0, ( bounds.width - _canvas.width ) / 2 );
        _canvas.verticalScrollPosition =
                Math.max( 0, ( bounds.height - _canvas.height ) / 2 );
    }

    private function getImageBounds():Rectangle
    {
        var x:Number = 0;
        var y:Number = 0;
        var w:Number = _imgSource.width * _scale;
         var h:Number = _imgSource.height * _scale;

        switch( _rotation )
        {
            case 90:
                x = h;
                w = h ^ w;
                h = h ^ w;
                w = h ^ w;
                break;
            case 180:
                x = w;
                y = h;
                break;
         case 270:
                y = w;
                w = h ^ w;
                h = h ^ w;
                w = h ^ w;
                break;
        }
        return new Rectangle( x, y, w, h );
    }

    private function onImageSelect( evt:MouseEvent ):void
    {
        dispatchEvent( new Event( ImageDisplay.DRAG_COPY, true ) );
    }

    public function get source():BitmapData
    {
```

```
            return _imgSource;
        }
        public function set source( bmp:BitmapData ):void
        {
            _imgSource = bmp;
            _rotation = 0;
            _image.bitmapData = _imgSource;
            doLayout();
        }

        public function get scale():Number
        {
            return _scale;
        }
        public function set scale( num:Number ):void
        {
            _scale = num;
            doLayout();
        }

        override public function get rotation():Number
        {
            return _rotation;
        }
        override public function set rotation( value:Number ):void
        {
            _rotation = ( value > 360 ) ? value - 360 : value;
            _rotation = ( _rotation < 0 ) ? _rotation + 360 : _rotation;
            doLayout();
        }
    }
}
```

4. Save the file as `ImageDisplay.as` in the directory `com/aircmr/imageviewer/ui` in your working directory.

The first snippet, saved as `ImageCanvas.mxml`, is the main display that will be added to the display list of the application. It holds the controls for resizing, rotation, and an alternative selection-navigation through the thumbnail browser. It also adds the second snippet, saved as `ImageDisplay.as`, to the display list, which simply shows the full-size selected image. Before addressing the `ImageDisplay`, some of the controls and properties of `ImageCanvas` need explaining.

There are some graphical assets used for the navigation and rotation buttons in `ImageCanvas.mxml`. *You are free to use your own, but those image files can be found in the /assets folder for the code examples of this chapter on the accompanying website.*

The `imageData` attribute of the `ImageCanvas` component is set as a bindable property that the controls and the `ImageDisplay` instance respond to upon update. The `HBox` container above the `ImageDisplay` component displays the name of the currently viewed image file and controls for size and rotation. Here are the declarations from the first `HBox`:

```
enabled="{_imageData != null}"
```

Binding to the availability of a supplied `ImageData` object enables and disables the contained controls and updates the `text` property of the label corresponding to the name property of the `ImageData` instance:

```
<mx:Label id="imageName"
    truncateToFit="true"
    maxWidth="{width - COMBO_WIDTH - 15}"
    text="{_imageData.name}"
    />
```

The rotation controls, named `rotateLeft` and `rotateRight`, have `click` event handlers that rotate the image display in increments of ninety degrees in either direction. Along with the rotation controls is an input-enabled `ComboBox` control that has fixed sizes to resize the image display in the view:

```
<mx:ComboBox id="sizeCombo"
    width="{COMBO_WIDTH}"
    rowCount="6"
    styleName="scaleCombo"
    textAlign="left"
    editable="true"
    selectedIndex="2"
    enter="onScaleChange( event );"
    close="onScaleChange( event );"
    >
    <mx:dataProvider>
        <mx:Object label="25%" />
        <mx:Object label="50%" />
        <mx:Object label="100%" />
        <mx:Object label="200%" />
        <mx:Object label="500%" />
        <mx:Object label="1000%" />
    </mx:dataProvider>
</mx:ComboBox>
```

The pre-fixed sizes increment in value from 25% to 1000%, with a defaulted selection of 100%; and with the `editable` property set to `true`, a user can input any size they choose within that range.

The `HBox` container declared below the `ImageDisplay` component in `ImageCanvas` holds controls for navigating through the thumbnail browser created in the previous section. Each control, named `previousButton` and `nextButton`, calla for an update to the `currentIndex` property of the `GalleryData-Manager` instance. Because a change to this property is listened for in the `ImageBrowser`, these controls allow you to navigate through thumbnails and select images for viewing without having to specifically click on a thumbnail.

Sandwiched between these two control boxes is the `ImageDisplay` component, the second snippet saved as `ImageDisplay.as`:

```
<mx:HBox width="100%" height="100%"
    paddingLeft="5" paddingBottom="5" paddingRight="5">
    <ui:ImageDisplay id="imageDisplay" width="100%" height="100%"
        source="{_imageData.bitmapData}"
        />
</mx:HBox>
```

The source of the ImageDisplay instance is updated by a change to the supplied ImageData object, which occurs when a new image is selected for viewing. Take a closer look into ImageDisplay to see how that data is rendered:

```
public function set source( bmp:BitmapData ):void
{
    _imgSource = bmp;
    _rotation = 0;
    _image.bitmapData = _imgSource;
    doLayout();
}
```

An update to the source property resets the internal rotation and bitmapData property of its Image child and makes a call to the doLayout() method. The doLayout() method handles rendering of the bitmap data with regard to the scale and rotation properties controlled from ImageCanvas discussed earlier in this section. In fact, the setter methods for those properties, scale and rotation, call doLayout() as well:

```
private function doLayout( evt:Event = null ):void
{
    if( _imgSource == null ) return;
    _image.rotation = _rotation;
    _image.scaleX = _image.scaleY = _scale;

    var bounds:Rectangle = getImageBounds();
    _image.x = bounds.x;
    _image.y = bounds.y;

    _holder.width = _image.width;
    _holder.height = _image.height;
    _holder.x = Math.max( 0, ( width - bounds.width ) / 2 );
    _holder.y = Math.max( 0, ( height -  bounds.height ) / 2 );

    _isViewSet = false;
    invalidateDisplayList();
}
```

The doLayout() method mainly handles the positioning of the scaled and rotated image within the display. The positioning of the image and its parent — the private member _holder — base their coordinate positions on a Rectangle object returned from the getImageBounds() method. The properties of that Rectangle itself are based on rotation and scale values. You may notice in the getImageBounds() method that the width and height values of a rotated image at 90 and 270 degrees are determined using the bitwise operation EXCUSIVE-OR (or XOR). This operation is an easy way to swap integer values of two variables without having to create a third value holder.

Aside from displaying the image in accordance with the bounds set by rotation and scale, ImageDisplay also dispatches a dragCopy event. The dragCopy event is fired from the mouseDown event handler on the image holder. This event is picked up from the main application and triggers the operation that enables a user to drag and save an image into a directory.

Using the Image Viewer and Editor to drag an image saved in one directory into another directory is neat and all, but it just results in having the same image file in two locations. The next section delves into manipulating that image so lost space on the hard drive is worth it.

Editing an Image

As images are loaded and viewed in the application, editing panels become available to apply transformations to that image. Using the bitmap data from an `ImageData` object and bitmap filters of the ActionScript API, you can build any type of image editing tools.

The subject of image processing requires a book, if not a library, in itself. It's up to you to build editors that will enable you to take out red-eye, squash faces, and add funny captions. Though it was tempting to include an editor for the last of those suggestions, the editor tool you will build in this section for the Image Viewer and Editor handles color transformations:

1. Create a new document and enter the following markup:

```
<?xml version="1.0" encoding="utf-8"?>
<mx:Panel
    xmlns:mx="http://www.adobe.com/2006/mxml"
    width="200" layout="vertical"
    paddingLeft="5" paddingRight="5" paddingBottom="5" paddingTop="5"
    creationComplete="onCreationComplete();">

    <mx:Script>
        <![CDATA[
            import com.aircmr.imageviewer.data.ImageData;

            protected var _src:ImageData;
            protected var _clone:BitmapData;

            protected function onCreationComplete():void
            {
                enabled = false;
            }

            protected function update():void
            {
                enabled = true;
                _clone = _src.bitmapData.clone();
                redChannel.value = 1;
                greenChannel.value = 1;
                blueChannel.value = 1;
                brightnessChannel.value = 0;
            }

            private function applyFilter():void
            {
                var mat:Array =
                [
                 redChannel.value, 0, 0, 0, 255*brightnessChannel.value,
                 0, greenChannel.value, 0, 0, 255*brightnessChannel.value,
                 0, 0, blueChannel.value, 0, 255*brightnessChannel.value,
                 0, 0, 0, 1, 0
                ];
                var transform:ColorMatrixFilter =
                                        new ColorMatrixFilter( mat );
```

```
                _src.bitmapData.applyFilter( _clone, _src.bitmapData.rect,
                                    new Point( 0, 0 ), transform );
            }

            public function clean():void
            {
                if( !enabled ) return;
                _clone.dispose();
            }

            public function set imageData( src:ImageData ):void
            {
                _src = src;
                update();
            }
        ]]>
    </mx:Script>

    <mx:VBox width="100%" verticalGap="-5">
        <mx:Label text="red" />
        <mx:HSlider  id="redChannel"
            width="100%"
            minimum="0" maximum="1"
            change="applyFilter();"/>
    </mx:VBox>
    <mx:VBox width="100%" verticalGap="-5">
        <mx:Label text="green" />
        <mx:HSlider id="greenChannel"
            width="100%"
            minimum="0" maximum="1"
            change="applyFilter();"/>
    </mx:VBox>
    <mx:VBox width="100%" verticalGap="-5">
        <mx:Label text="blue" />
        <mx:HSlider id="blueChannel"
            width="100%"
            minimum="0" maximum="1"
            change="applyFilter();"/>
    </mx:VBox>
    <mx:VBox width="100%" verticalGap="-5">
        <mx:Label text="brightness" />
        <mx:HSlider id="brightnessChannel"
            width="100%"
            minimum="-1" maximum="1"
            change="applyFilter();"/>
    </mx:VBox>

</mx:Panel>
```

2. Save the file as `ColorTransformPanel.mxml` in the directory `com/aircmr/imageviewer/ui/tools` in your working directory.

The `ColorTransformPanel` has slider controls to change the values relative to the red, green, and blue color channels of a displayed image. The fourth slider control that is declared and added to the display list pertains to the brightness of the displayed image. The slider controls are reset each time the `imageData` property is updated to display the original image unmanipulated.

The `change` event handler for all four slider controls is the `applyFliter()` method:

```
private function applyFilter():void
{
    var mat:Array =
            [
            redChannel.value, 0, 0, 0, 255*brightnessChannel.value,
            0, greenChannel.value, 0, 0, 255*brightnessChannel.value,
            0, 0, blueChannel.value, 0, 255*brightnessChannel.value,
            0, 0, 0, 1, 0
            ];
    var transform:ColorMatrixFilter = new ColorMatrixFilter( mat );
    _src.applyFilter( _clone, _src.bitmapData.rect, new Point( 0, 0 ), transform );
}
```

In the `applyFilter()` method, a `ColorMatrixFilter` is applied to the `bitmapData` property of the supplied `ImageData` object. By using a clone of the original bitmap data as the source image to produce the filtered image, the channel values are applied to the original bitmap data upon each `change` event from the controls, rather than an additive update to the values.

With the views for displaying and manipulating image files set, the next section explains how to bring all this functionality and data together to finish the Image Viewer and Editor.

Bringing It All Together

The main application file you build in this section will present the display views previously created and handle the loading in and saving out of image files, including the exciting drag-and-drop operations. Along with the drag-and-drop API, this section uncovers more features that pertain to the file system and introduces the graphics codecs that play a role in saving image files. Without further ado, bring it all together:

1. Create a new document and enter the following markup:

```
<?xml version="1.0" encoding="utf-8"?>
<mx:WindowedApplication
    xmlns:mx="http://www.adobe.com/2006/mxml"
    xmlns:ui="com.aircmr.imageviewer.ui.*"
    xmlns:tools="com.aircmr.imageviewer.ui.tools.*"
    layout="absolute"
    backgroundColor="0x666666"
    applicationComplete="onAppInit();"
    closing="onAppClosing();">

    <mx:Style>
        ImageCanvas {
            background-color: #FEFEFE;
         }

        Thumbnail {
```

```
            background-color: #EEEEEE;
            border-color: #DDDDDD;
            border-weight: 2;
        }
    </mx:Style>

    <mx:Script>
        <![CDATA[
            import com.aircmr.imageviewer.data.ImageData;
            import com.aircmr.imageviewer.data.GalleryDataManager
            import com.aircmr.imageviewer.utils.BitmapUtil;

            import flash.filesystem.FileMode;
            import flash.filesystem.FileStream;
            import flash.filesystem.File;

            import mx.events.MenuEvent;
            import mx.graphics.codec.IImageEncoder;
            import mx.graphics.codec.PNGEncoder;
            import mx.graphics.codec.JPEGEncoder;

            private var _currentImage:ImageData;
            private var _importFile:File;
            private var _exportFile:File;
            private var _tempDir:File;
            private var _tempFile:File;
            private var _dragCopy:Boolean = false;

            private static const DRAG_WIDTH:int = 100;
            private static const DRAG_HEIGHT:int = 100;
            private static const IMG_FILTER:FileFilter =
                            new FileFilter( "Images", "*.jpg;*.jpeg;*.png;" );

            private static const MENU_OPEN:String = "Open...";
            private static const MENU_SAVE:String = "Save";
            private static const MENU_SAVE_AS:String = "Save As...";

            private function onAppInit():void
            {
                _tempDir = File.createTempDirectory();

                _importFile = new File();
                _importFile.addEventListener( FileListEvent.SELECT_MULTIPLE,
                                                                onFilesSelect );

                _exportFile = new File();
                _exportFile.addEventListener( Event.SELECT, onExportSelect );

                addEventListener( NativeDragEvent.NATIVE_DRAG_ENTER, onDragEnter );
                addEventListener( NativeDragEvent.NATIVE_DRAG_DROP, onDragDrop );
                addEventListener( NativeDragEvent.NATIVE_DRAG_COMPLETE,
                                                                onDragComplete );
            }
```

```
        private function dragOverCanvas( px:Number, py:Number ):Boolean
        {
            return ( ( px > canvas.x && px < canvas.x + canvas.width ) &&
                  ( py > canvas.y && py < canvas.y + canvas.height ) );
        }

         private function getBitmapFile():File
        {
            _tempFile = _tempDir.resolvePath( _currentImage.name );

            var fileStream:FileStream = new FileStream();
            fileStream.open( _tempFile, FileMode.WRITE );
            fileStream.writeBytes(getEncodedBitmap(_currentImage.bitmapData));
            fileStream.close();
            return _tempFile;
        }

        private function getEncodedBitmap( bmp:BitmapData ):ByteArray
        {
            var encoder:IImageEncoder;
            switch( _currentImage.fileExtension )
            {
                case ".jpg":
                case ".jpeg":
                    encoder = new JPEGEncoder();
                    break;
                case ".png":
                    encoder = new PNGEncoder();
                    break;
            }
            return encoder.encode( bmp );
        }

        private function getDragPoint( bmp:BitmapData ):Point
        {
            return new Point( -bmp.width / 2, -bmp.height / 2 );
        }

        private function onDragEnter( evt:NativeDragEvent ):void
        {
            NativeDragManager.acceptDragDrop( this );
        }

        private function onDragComplete( evt:NativeDragEvent ):void
        {
            // copying to another location outside of application is
            // complete...
            _dragCopy = false;
            if( _tempFile.exists ) _tempFile.deleteFile();
        }

        private function onDragDrop( evt:NativeDragEvent ):void
        {
            if( _dragCopy ) return;
```

```
        NativeDragManager.dropAction = "copy";
        var files:Array = evt.clipboard.getData(
                            ClipboardFormats.FILE_LIST_FORMAT ) as Array;
        browser.addFiles(files, dragOverCanvas( evt.localX, evt.localY ));
    }

    private function onMenuItemClick( evt:MenuEvent ):void
    {
        switch( evt.label )
        {
            case MENU_OPEN:
                importItem();
                break;
            case MENU_SAVE:
                saveItem();
                break;
            case MENU_SAVE_AS:
                saveItemAs();
                break;
        }
    }

    private function onThumbnailSelect( evt:Event ):void
    {
        _currentImage = browser.selectedImage.clone();
        canvas.imageData = _currentImage;
        colorTool.imageData = _currentImage;
    }

    private function onFilesSelect( evt:FileListEvent ):void
    {
        browser.addFiles( evt.files, true );
    }

    private function onExportSelect( evt:Event ):void
    {
        var file:File = ( evt.target as File );
        _currentImage.name = file.name;
        _currentImage.url = file.url;
        saveItem( file.url );
    }

    private function onImageCanvasDragCopy( evt:Event ):void
    {
        _dragCopy = true;
        var transfer:Clipboard = new Clipboard();
        transfer.setData( ClipboardFormats.FILE_LIST_FORMAT,
                                    [getBitmapFile()], false );

        var thumb:BitmapData = BitmapUtil.generateThumbnail(
                                    _currentImage.bitmapData,
                                    DRAG_WIDTH, DRAG_HEIGHT,
                                    true );
        NativeDragManager.dropAction = "copy";
```

```
            NativeDragManager.doDrag( this, transfer, thumb,
                                            getDragPoint( thumb ) );
        }

        private function importItem():void
        {
            try
            {
                _importFile.browseForOpenMultiple("Select Files", [IMG_FILTER]);
            }
            catch( e:Error)
            {
                trace( "File:browseForOpenMultiple failed. :: " + e.message );
            }
        }

        private function saveItem( loc:String = null ):void
        {
            if( _currentImage == null ) return;
            _exportFile.url = loc == null ? _currentImage.url : loc;

            var fileStream:FileStream = new FileStream();
            fileStream.open( _exportFile, FileMode.WRITE );
            fileStream.writeBytes(getEncodedBitmap(_currentImage.bitmapData));
            fileStream.close();
        }

        private function saveItemAs():void
        {
            if( _currentImage == null ) return;
            _exportFile.url = _currentImage.url;
            _exportFile.browseForSave( "Save File As..." );
        }
        private function onAppClosing():void
        {
            GalleryDataManager.getInstance().clean();
            colorTool.clean();
            if( _currentImage != null ) _currentImage.clean();
            _tempDir.deleteDirectory( true );
        }
    ]]>
</mx:Script>

<mx:VBox width="100%" height="100%" paddingBottom="5">
    <mx:MenuBar id="menuBar"
        width="100%"
        labelField="@label"
        itemClick="onMenuItemClick( event );">
        <mx:XMLList>
            <menuitem label="File">
                <menuitem label="{MENU_OPEN}" />
                <menuitem label="{MENU_SAVE}" />
                <menuitem label="{MENU_SAVE_AS}" />
            </menuitem>
```

```
            </mx:XMLList>
        </mx:MenuBar>
        <mx:VBox width="100%" height="100%">

            <mx:HBox width="100%" height="100%"
                paddingLeft="5" paddingRight="5">
                <tools:ColorTransformPanel id="colorTool"
                    title="Color Transform"
                    />
                <ui:ImageCanvas id="canvas"
                    width="100%" height="100%"
                    dragCopy="onImageCanvasDragCopy( event );"
                    />
            </mx:HBox>

            <ui:ImageBrowser id="browser"
                width="100%" height="140"
                select="onThumbnailSelect( event );"
                />

        </mx:VBox>
    </mx:VBox>

</mx:WindowedApplication>
```

2. Save the file as `ImageViewer.mxml` in the root of your working directory for the Image Viewer and Editor.

There is a lot going on in the main application file, so the explanation begins with the view declaration and shows you how the displays are laid out and their events handled.

Opening and Saving through the Drag-and-Drop API

The nested `VBox` container within the parent vertical box of the layout is composed of the `ImageBrowser`, `ImageCanvas`, and `ColorTranformPanel` views created in the previous sections. The image browser dispatches a `select` event upon selection of a thumbnail to view:

```
<ui:ImageBrowser id="browser"
    width="100%" height="140"
    select="onThumbnailSelect( event );"
    />
```

The event handler for the `select` event dispatched from the `ImageBrowser` is the `onThumbnail-Select()` method, which updates the local `ImageData` instance by cloning the currently selected image. That clone is then passed on to the `ImageCanvas` and `ColorTransformPanel` instances through their respective `imageData` properties:

```
private function onThumbnailSelect( evt:Event ):void
{
    _currentImage = browser.selectedImage.clone();
    canvas.imageData = _currentImage;
    colorTool.imageData = _currentImage;
}
```

The ImageDisplay component of the ImageCanvas view dispatches a dragCopy event upon the click of a mouse. This event is bubbled up and captured by the ImageViewer using the onImageDragCanvas() event handler. This method is responsible for adding data to a Clipboard object and starting the native drag-and-drop gesture:

```
private function onImageCanvasDragCopy( evt:Event ):void
{
    _dragCopy = true;
    var transfer:Clipboard = new Clipboard();
    transfer.setData( ClipboardFormats.FILE_LIST_FORMAT,
                                            [getBitmapFile()], false );

    var thumb:BitmapData = BitmapUtil.generateThumbnail(
                                            _currentImage.bitmapData,
                                            DRAG_WIDTH, DRAG_HEIGHT,
                                            true );
    NativeDragManager.dropAction = "copy";
    NativeDragManager.doDrag( this, transfer, thumb, getDragPoint( thumb ) );
}
```

Similar to the mx.managers.DragManager, which enables you to drag data within a single Flex application, the flash.desktop.NativeDragManager enables you to drag data between AIR applications and the native operating system. The transferable data created during the initialization of the gesture is a flash.desktop.Clipboard object. A Clipboard instance acts as a container for data of a particular format. When starting a native drag-and-drop action, the clipboard data is passed into the static doDrag() method of the NativeDragManager.

The data set on the Clipboard instance is a representation of what is transferred on completion of the drag-and-drop operation. When applying data to the Clipboard object, you specify the data format, the data, and a Boolean flag indicating whether the data should be serialized. The Image Viewer and Editor enables you to drag edited images out of the application and save them as image files. As such, the transfer format is an array of files, though you will only be able to drag one image at a time. Serialization of the data will not happen and the data will not be available to be dropped on another AIR application.

Essentially, when a drag-and-drop gesture is made, the Image Viewer and Editor creates a temporary image file and adds it to the clipboard, enabling users to transfer that image as a file on their computer. Looking at the getBitmapFile() method, which is called when placing data on the Clipboard object, the ImageViewer is writing the bitmap data of the currently selected ImageData object to a file in a temporary directory created upon application initialization:

```
private function getBitmapFile():File
{
    _tempFile = _tempDir.resolvePath( _currentImage.name );

    var fileStream:FileStream = new FileStream();
    fileStream.open( _tempFile, FileMode.WRITE );
    fileStream.writeBytes( getEncodedBitmap( _currentImage.bitmapData ) );
    fileStream.close();
    return _tempFile;
}
```

The data given to the file stream buffer is a ByteArray created using the JPEGEncoder and PNGEncoder codecs available in the Flex 3 SDK. The getEncodedBitmap() method returns the appropriate encoded data based on the fileExtension property of the currently viewed ImageData object. That temporary image file will be saved to the directory to which the user has dragged it, and is removed from the temporary directory upon completion of the drop gesture. Upon completion of data being dragged from an AIR application to a directory, the dragComplete event is fired:

```
private function onDragComplete( evt:NativeDragEvent ):void
{
    // copying to another location outside of application is complete...
    _dragCopy = false;
    // remove temp file...
    if( _tempFile.exists ) _tempFile.deleteFile();
}
```

The onDragComplete() event handler resets the _dragCopy flag to false and instructs the temporary file to be removed using the deleteFile() method of the File class after first confirming its existence through the exists property. Along with being able to drag out and save image files, the Image Viewer and Editor is capable of opening image files that are dragged onto the application. Upon opening the application, listeners for events coming from the flash.desktop.NativeDragManager are created to respond to the drag-and-drop gestures. The dragEnter event handler specifies the application as the drop target to receive any transferable data held in the drag event:

```
private function onDragEnter( evt:NativeDragEvent ):void
{
    NativeDragManager.acceptDragDrop( this );
}
```

The dragDrop event handler receives the transferable data held on the flash.events.NativeDragEvent instance and supplies that data to the ImageBrowser:

```
private function onDragDrop( evt:NativeDragEvent ):void
{
    if( _dragCopy ) return;
    NativeDragManager.dropAction = "copy";
    var files:Array = evt.clipboard.getData(
                            ClipboardFormats.FILE_LIST_FORMAT ) as Array;
    browser.addFiles(files, dragOverCanvas( evt.localX, evt.localY ));
}
```

When files are dragged onto the Image Viewer and Editor, the transferable data from the NativeDragEvent is a list of File objects. A call to the addFiles() method of ImageBrowser is made, supplying that list of File objects and a flag indicating whether the files were dropped on the ImageCanvas or elsewhere in the application. A drop on the image canvas would initiate the selection of the last file in the list once all the files have been loaded.

This section has described how the drag-and-drop API is used by the Image Viewer and Editor, but what if a user doesn't want to drag files in and out? Opening and saving can be performed by selecting from the File menu as well.

Opening and Saving from the File API

The first item in the initial VBox container is a MenuBar component with menu items for opening and saving a file:

```
<mx:MenuBar id="menuBar"
    width="100%"
    labelField="@label"
    itemClick="onMenuItemClick( event );">
    <mx:XMLList>
        <menuitem label="File">
            <menuitem label="{MENU_OPEN}" />
            <menuitem label="{MENU_SAVE}" />
            <menuitem label="{MENU_SAVE_AS}" />
        </menuitem>
    </mx:XMLList>
</mx:MenuBar>
```

Upon selection of an item from the File menu drop-down, the appropriate action is taken in the itemClick event handler onMenuItemClick(). Two File instances are instantiated within the applicationComplete event handler of the ImageViewer. The _importFile instance handles importing operations, and the _exportFile instance handles saving operations. When the Open option is selected, the _importFile opens a file browser with multiple selection turned on by calling the browseForOpen-Multiple() method:

```
_importFile.browseForOpenMultiple( "Select Files", [IMG_FILTER] );
```

The first parameter of browseForOpenMultiple() is the title to be displayed in the file browser. The second parameter is an array of FileFilter objects that indicate the files to be displayed in the file browser dialog. Because the Image Viewer and Editor works only with image formats, only files with the extension of .jpg, .jpeg, or .png are allowed to be selected and shown within the file browser.

Along with the Open option, there are two options for saving images from the File menu. The first option saves the image data back out to the originally opened file, and the second opens a file browser to enable a user to save the image file into a desired directory with a different name:

```
private function saveItemAs():void
{
    if( _currentImage == null ) return;
    _exportFile.url = _currentImage.url;
    _exportFile.browseForSave( "Save File As..." );
}
```

Prior to calling browseForSave(), the url property on _exportFile is set to the url property of the currently displayed image. This action opens the file browser dialog to that directory and enables a user to choose a different directory and/or rename the image file. The parameter of browseForSave() on the File class is the same as the first parameter of browseForOpenMultiple() and relates to the title to be displayed in the file browser dialog.

When the application is instructed to save an image using the File menu options, the `saveItem()` method is invoked and data is written to the buffer of a `FileStream`:

```
private function saveItem( loc:String = null ):void
{
    if( _currentImage == null ) return;
    _exportFile.url = loc == null ? _currentImage.url : loc;

    var fileStream:FileStream = new FileStream();
    fileStream.open( _exportFile, FileMode.WRITE );
    fileStream.writeBytes( getEncodedBitmap(_currentImage.bitmapData) );
    fileStream.close();
}
```

You may recall that when dragging out an image, the image codecs are used to buffer data to a temporary file. The operations in the `saveItem()` method are no different and are written to the `File` instance allocated to saving image files.

With the Image Viewer and Editor all set to open, display, and save image files, it is time to deploy the application and start manipulating images.

Deploying the Application

Now that you have your application in place, it's time to deploy it, bring in some photos, and edit that image showing you wearing that goofy hat on your last vacation.

The Descriptor File

1. Open your favorite text editor and enter the following markup:

```
<?xml version="1.0" encoding="UTF-8"?>
<application xmlns="http://ns.adobe.com/air/application/1.0">

    <id>com.aircmr.ImageViewer</id>
    <filename>ImageViewer</filename>
    <name>Image Viewer</name>
    <version>v0.1</version>
    <description>An image viewer to view images</description>
    <copyright>2007</copyright>

    <initialWindow>
        <title>Image Viewer</title>
        <content>ImageViewer.swf</content>
        <systemChrome>standard</systemChrome>
        <transparent>false</transparent>
        <visible>true</visible>
        <width>680</width>
        <height>630</height>
    </initialWindow>
```

```
    <installFolder>AIRCMR/ImageViewer</installFolder>
    <programMenuFolder>AIRCMR</programMenuFolder>

</application>
```

2. Save the file as `ImageViewer-app.xml` in the root of your working directory along with the `ImageViewer.mxml file.`

This file will serve as the application descriptor file. The element values from this snippet are somewhat generic and should be changed as you see fit. When the application is installed, it will be named ImageViewer and be available in the `AIRCMR` folder of the application directory of your operating system.

With the descriptor file in place, you are set to compile and package the Image Viewer and Editor AIR executable.

Compiling and Packaging

Two files are needed to package an AIR application: the main SWF file and the XML application descriptor file. In this section you will produce the SWF file using the command-line tools and package the AIR application.

If you don't want to create your own, the graphic assets used in the examples can be found in the /assets folder of the code examples for this chapter on the accompanying website.

1. Open a command prompt, navigate to the *working directory* for the Image Viewer and Editor, enter the following command, and press Enter:

   ```
   > amxmlc ImageViewer.mxml
   ```

   If you have purchased a certificate from a certificate authority, such as VeriSign or Thawte, then you may use that certificate and skip the following operation, rather than create the self-signed certificate. To create a self-signed certificate within the working directory, enter the following command:

   ```
   > adt -cerificate -cn ImageViewer 1024-RSA certificate.pfx password
   ```

2. With the command prompt still pointing to the working directory, enter the following command to package the Image Viewer and Editor application:

   ```
   > adt -package -storetype pkcs12 -keystore certificate.pfx ImageViewer.air
     ImageViewer-app.xml ImageViewer.swf
   ```

   You will be prompted to enter the password for the certificate. If you created a self-signed certificate from the second command, then enter "**password**." After running these commands, an `ImageViewer.swf` file, a `certificate.pfx` file, and the `ImageViewer.air` installer file are generated within your working directory.

3. Once the installer has been created successfully by running the last command, navigate to your working directory and double-click on the AIR installer to install and run the Image Viewer and Editor. If all goes well, the application will launch and be ready to accept drag-and-drop image files — and, potentially, image files imported from the File menu. After you import an image file, the application should look something like Figure 6-1.

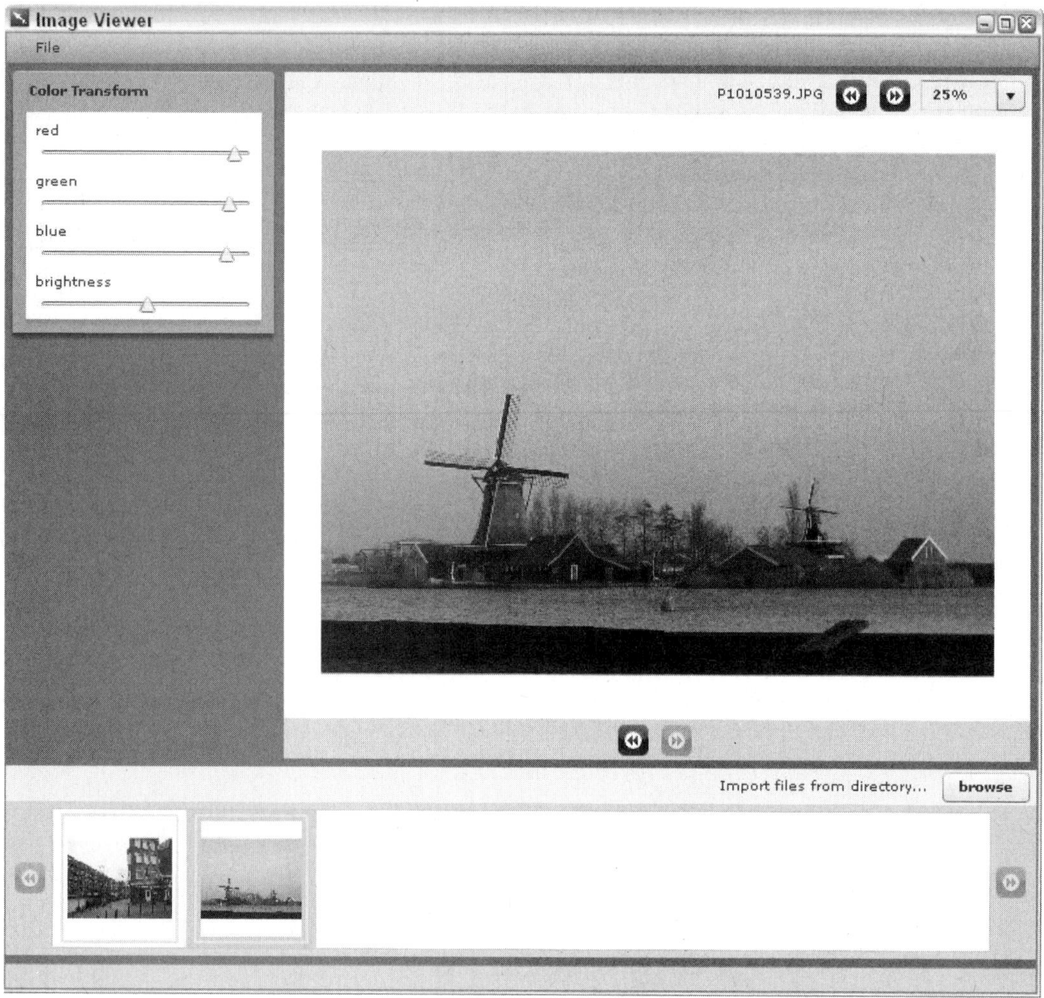

Figure 6-1

Play around with the color transformations, create your own image processing tools, and enjoy!

Summary

This chapter covered how to open and save files from the user's hard drive using both the file system API and the drag-and-drop API, all while creating an application to view and manipulate images. Your work with the file system API in the previous chapters has contributed to learning how to spawn a file browser dialog to select and open multiple files and to save files out based on file type.

After looking at the `NativeDataManager` class, you learned how to use static methods and properties to perform drag-and-drop operations as well as handle `NativeDragEvent` objects dispatched from a targeted display object. In the discussion of saving images, you were introduced to the codecs available in the Flex 3.0 SDK and learned how `ByteArray` data is added to the file stream buffer using the `File.writeBytes()` method.

In the next chapter you will continue to add to your understanding of AIR by learning about local databases as you create a Simple Calendar and Tracker.

7

HTML and CSS Editor

Now that you have a basic understanding of the HTML component, it's a good time to center an application around it, and a perfect program would be an HTML and CSS editor. As with the text editor from Chapter 2, it's probably safe to assume that everyone has their own favorite editor for both HTML and CSS. In an attempt to make this program unique, the application you will create in this chapter will allow the user to edit the HTML and CSS of any page, online or offline. Essentially, it will be a very basic web browser with the capability to edit the current page's HTML and CSS source. Just think of the possibilities you'll have with regard to editing the source of your favorite web page without having to save all the assets to your computer.

The main objective of this program is to illustrate just how easy it is to manipulate the JavaScript Document Object Model (DOM) of any HTML page that is loaded into the AIR HTML component. Do not fret if your JavaScript skills aren't up to snuff because all the code will look very familiar. Remember that ActionScript and JavaScript are both based on ECMAScript. The program will use the same techniques from Chapter 2 to enable users to export the edited HTML and CSS, which are just plain text files, to their hard drive.

Specifically, the application will need to perform the following tasks:

- Load and display an HTML page from a URL.
- Load and display an HTML page from the user's hard drive.
- Display the HTML source within the `<BODY>` tag of the loaded page.
- Display a selectable list of all the CSS styles from the loaded page.
- Display a selectable list of all the properties of a particular style.
- Enable users to edit the HTML source of the current page.
- Enable users to add and edit styles for the current page.
- Enable users to add, edit, and delete properties for a selected style.
- Enable users to save the HTML and CSS source to their hard drive.
- Enable users to revert back to the original source.

Now that you have a nice laundry list of actions the program should perform, it's time to assess what you have at your disposal to achieve this particular functionality.

Design

You've already learned a few things in previous chapters that should make following this chapter relatively easy. Specifically, you've learned how to save text files to a user's hard drive using the `File` and `FileStream` classes. You've also learned how to display HTML-formatted content using the AIR `HTML` component. In addition to these things, you will now learn how to use the `HTML` component's `domWindow` property. This property will act as your gateway into the world of JavaScript, which in turn will enable you to go wild with all the methods and properties it contains. In the end, this application will not only display the content and enable users to save it locally, it will enable users to dynamically edit the content and update the display by accessing the appropriate JavaScript methods and properties directly inline with the ActionScript.

Based on the functionality requirements listed previously, the application will require the following components:

- ❑ Application shell
- ❑ HTML preview
- ❑ HTML editor
- ❑ CSS editor
- ❑ Address bar

On an abstract level, the application shell is going to manage the changes made in all the other components and update the HTML preview accordingly. It will also manage the display by utilizing a tab navigation system so that users can easily switch between the preview, the HTML editor, and the CSS editor.

Before you do anything, create within your development directory a folder titled "HTML+CSS Editor." As in previous chapters, this will be your working directory for this application.

The Address Bar

The address bar is perhaps the simplest component of the application, and is thus a good place to start. This component will enable users to type in a website URL or browse their computer's hard drive for an HTML document. The path or URL will then be used by an instance of AIR's `HTML` component to update its `location` property.

Open your editor and create a new document. Enter the following markup:

```
<?xml version="1.0" encoding="utf-8"?>
<mx:Canvas xmlns:mx="http://www.adobe.com/2006/mxml"
    width="800" height="42">

    <mx:Script><![CDATA[
```

```
import flash.filesystem.File;
import flash.net.FileFilter;
import mx.events.FlexEvent;
import mx.utils.StringUtil;
import mx.utils.URLUtil;

private var _currentFile:File;
private var _fileToOpen:File;

private function onNewLocation( $event:Event ):void
{
    if( StringUtil.trim( locationInput.text ).length == 0 )
        return;

    if( locationInput.text.search(/^http/) == -1 &&
        locationInput.text.indexOf("file:///") == -1 )
    {
        locationInput.text = "http://" + locationInput.text;
    }

    dispatchEvent( new Event( Event.CHANGE ) );
}

private function onBrowseBtnClick( event:MouseEvent ):void
{
    _fileToOpen = ( _currentFile ) ? _currentFile : File.documentsDirectory;

    var fileFilter:FileFilter = new FileFilter( "HTML", "*.htm;*.html" );

    try
    {
        _fileToOpen.browseForOpen( "Open", [fileFilter] );
        _fileToOpen.addEventListener( Event.SELECT, onFileOpenSelect );
    }
    catch( error:Error )
    {
        trace("Failed:", error.message);
    }
}

private function onFileOpenSelect( event:Event ):void
{
    _currentFile = File( event.target );
    locationInput.text = "file:///";
    locationInput.text += _currentFile.nativePath.split( "\\" ).join( "/" );
    onNewLocation( null );
}

public function get location():String
{
    return locationInput.text;
}
public function set location( v:String ):void
{
```

```
            locationInput.text = v;
        }

        ]]></mx:Script>

        <mx:TextInput id="locationInput"
            left="10" top="10" right="136"
            enter="onNewLocation(event);"/>
        <mx:Button id="goBtn"
            width="42" y="10" right="86" label="Go"
            click="onNewLocation(event);"/>
        <mx:Button id="browseBtn"
            y="10" right="10" label="Browse"
            click="onBrowseBtnClick(event);"/>
    </mx:Canvas>
```

Save the file as `AddressBar.mxml` in the directory `com/aircmr/htmlcsseditor/ui/` within your working directory.

The address bar's interface is very simple. It utilizes just a `TextInput` component and two `Button` components. One of the buttons, labeled Browse, enables users to browse their hard drive for an HTML document:

```
private function onBrowseBtnClick( event:MouseEvent ):void
{
    _fileToOpen = ( _currentFile ) ? _currentFile : File.documentsDirectory;

    var fileFilter:FileFilter = new FileFilter( "HTML", "*.htm;*.html" );

    try
    {
        _fileToOpen.browseForOpen( "Open", [fileFilter] );
        _fileToOpen.addEventListener( Event.SELECT, onFileOpenSelect );
    }
    catch( error:Error )
    {
        trace("Failed:", error.message);
    }
}
```

The previous snippet contains the event handler for the Browse button's `CLICK` event. This code should look familiar if you have read some of the previous chapters. To summarize, users are presented with an Open dialog that enables them to browse and select an HTML file. Upon selecting a file, the `onFileOpenSelect` event handler function is called. Here, the `TextInput` component is updated with the native path of the selected file. Note that the backslashes of the native path are converted to forward slashes and the path is prefixed with `file:///` in order for the path to be friendly with AIR's `HTML` component.

The following snippet contains the `onNewLocation` function:

```
private function onNewLocation( $event:Event ):void
{
    if( StringUtil.trim( locationInput.text ).length == 0 )
```

```
            return;

        if( locationInput.text.search(/^http/) == -1 &&
            locationInput.text.indexOf("file:///") == -1 )
        {
            locationInput.text = "http://" + locationInput.text;
        }

        dispatchEvent( new Event( Event.CHANGE ) );
    }
```

This function is called whenever the user has specified a new URL or file path. Users can specify a new URL or file path in three ways: clicking the Go button, pressing the Enter key while the `TextInput` component has focus, or when selecting a file from their hard drive. After some quick and simple error checking, the component dispatches a `CHANGE` event. This event indicates to the application shell that the user wants to load a new URL or file.

That just about covers the important functionality of the address bar. This component is very simple and easily be reused or repurposed in another application that utilizes an HTML component. In the next section you learn how to create the HTML editor, another relatively simple component for this application.

The HTML Editor

Of the two editors, the HTML editor is by far the least complicated. Conceptually, it is a stripped-down text editor, but you're going to customize it a little bit for use within the context of this application. First, note that the HTML editor will only allow a user to edit the HTML source within the `<BODY>` tag in order to prevent the user from editing any inherent stylesheet code within the `<HEAD>` of the page. All stylesheet editing will be handled within the CSS editor component.

Not only should the editor do the obvious — enable the user to edit the HTML source — it should also do the following:

- Notify the application shell (or any other component, for that matter) when the HTML preview should be updated with the edited source.
- Notify the application shell when the user would like to revert back to the original source.
- Enable the user to save the full source to a local drive.
- Enable the user to turn word wrapping on and off.

Keeping all this in mind, it's time to create the HTML editor.

Open your editor and create a new document. Enter the following markup:

```
<?xml version="1.0" encoding="utf-8"?>
<mx:Canvas xmlns:mx="http://www.adobe.com/2006/mxml">

    <mx:Script><![CDATA[
```

```
import flash.filesystem.File;
import flash.filesystem.FileMode;
import flash.filesystem.FileStream;
import flash.net.FileFilter;
import mx.controls.Alert;
import mx.utils.StringUtil;

private var _fileToSave:File;
private var _fileStream:FileStream;
private var _fullSource:String;
private var _sourceLoader:URLLoader;

private function onFileSaveSelect( event:Event ):void
{
    var temp:String = _fullSource.substring( _fullSource.indexOf("<body") );
    var iStart:int = _fullSource.indexOf("<body") + temp.indexOf( ">" ) + 1;
    var iEnd:int = _fullSource.indexOf("</body");

    var firstPart:String = _fullSource.substring( 0, iStart );
    var endPart:String = _fullSource.substring( iEnd );

    var theSource:String = firstPart + sourceText.text + endPart;
    theSource = theSource.replace( /\r/g, "\n" );
    theSource = theSource.replace( /\n/g, File.lineEnding );

    _fileToSave = File( event.target );

    _fileStream = new FileStream();
    _fileStream.openAsync( _fileToSave, FileMode.WRITE );
    _fileStream.addEventListener( IOErrorEvent.IO_ERROR, onWriteIOError );
    _fileStream.writeUTFBytes( theSource );
    _fileStream.close();
}

private function onRevertBtnClick( event:MouseEvent ):void
{
    dispatchEvent( new Event( Event.CANCEL ) );
}

private function onSaveBtnClick( event:MouseEvent ):void
{
    _fileToSave = new File( File.documentsDirectory.nativePath + File.separator
        + "ExportedHTML.html" );

    try
    {
        _fileToSave.browseForSave("Save As...");
        _fileToSave.addEventListener( Event.SELECT, onFileSaveSelect );
    }
    catch( error:Error )
    {
        trace("Failed:", error.message);
    }
}
```

```
    private function onFullSourceLoaded( event:Event ):void
    {
        _fullSource = String( _sourceLoader.data );
        saveBtn.enabled = true;
    }

    private function onUpdateBtnClick( event:MouseEvent ):void
    {
        dispatchEvent( new Event( Event.CHANGE ) );
    }

    private function onWriteIOError( event:IOErrorEvent ):void
    {
        Alert.show("The specified file cannot be saved.", "Error", Alert.OK, this);
    }

    public function clear():void
    {
        sourceText.text = "";
        saveBtn.enabled = false;
        updateBtn.enabled = false;
        revertBtn.enabled = false;
        wrapBtn.enabled = false;
    }

    public function update( jsDoc:Object, url:String ):void
    {
        _sourceLoader = new URLLoader();
        _sourceLoader.addEventListener( Event.COMPLETE, onFullSourceLoaded )
        _sourceLoader.load( new URLRequest( url ) );

        sourceText.text = StringUtil.trim( jsDoc.body.innerHTML );

        updateBtn.enabled = true;
        revertBtn.enabled = true;
        wrapBtn.enabled = true;
    }

    public function get sourceCode():String
    {
        return sourceText.text;
    }

    ]]></mx:Script>

    <mx:VBox width="100%" height="100%" horizontalAlign="center">
        <mx:HBox width="100%" horizontalAlign="center">
            <mx:Button id="saveBtn"
                label="Save As..." enabled="false"
                click="onSaveBtnClick(event);" />
            <mx:Button id="updateBtn"
                label="Update" enabled="false"
                click="onUpdateBtnClick(event);" />
            <mx:Button id="revertBtn"
```

```
                    label="Revert" enabled="false"
                    click="onRevertBtnClick(event);" />
            </mx:HBox>
            <mx:CheckBox id="wrapBtn"
                label="Word Wrap" enabled="false"
                change="{sourceText.wordWrap = !sourceText.wordWrap}"/>
            <mx:TextArea id="sourceText"
                width="100%" height="100%" fontSize="14"
                fontFamily="Courier New" wordWrap="false"/>
        </mx:VBox>
    </mx:Canvas>
```

Save the file as HTMLEditor.mxml in the directory com/aircmr/htmlcsseditor/ui/ within your working directory.

It should be apparent that the previous two steps set up the HTML editor component in its entirety. Note some important functionality here that is specific to Adobe AIR within this component — first, the component's update function:

```
public function update( jsDoc:Object, url:String ):void
{
    _sourceLoader = new URLLoader();
    _sourceLoader.addEventListener( Event.COMPLETE, onFullSourceLoaded )
    _sourceLoader.load( new URLRequest( url ) );

    sourceText.text = StringUtil.trim( jsDoc.body.innerHTML );

    updateBtn.enabled = true;
    revertBtn.enabled = true;
    wrapBtn.enabled = true;
}
```

In this function the HTML source between the <BODY> tag is extracted and placed into the editable text field and the full source is retrieved from the original URL. The function requires two parameters. The first is a reference to an HTML page's JavaScript document object; the second is the URL of the page. Using the JavaScript document object, the function retrieves the body.innerHTML property of the DOM. This property is a string containing all the HTML code within the <BODY> tag of the current page and is used as the source code to display in the TextArea component. Finally, because you cannot access the full HTML source of a page via JavaScript, the URL of the current page is sent as a second parameter and a URLLoader is used to retrieve the full source.

Also within this component is some code that enables users to save the full source as an HTML file on their hard drive. This should look very familiar to you if you have built the simple text editor program from Chapter 2. The only difference here is that the text is prepared by replacing the original source with the edited source before being saved to the file.

Beyond the AIR-specific functionality of this component, which has been covered already, the remaining code should be somewhat self-explanatory. Notice that the component dispatches two generic events in order to notify what eventually will be the application shell when the user wants to update the HTML or revert back to the original source. That about covers the important parts of the HTML editor, so it's time to move on to the slightly more complicated CSS editor.

The CSS Editor

As mentioned previously, the CSS editor is a bit more complicated than the HTML editor, but this is purely by choice. Sure, the CSS editor could just be a plain editable text area like the HTML editor, but what fun would that be? Not to mention that it will be a lot easier to update the CSS on a per-style, per-property basis. In other words, rather than update all the CSS at once using a long string, the editor will notify the application shell when either a style or a style's property has been edited. In the end, the CSS editor should perform the following tasks:

- Enable users to view and edit all the styles of the current page.
- Enable users to view, edit, and delete the properties of any given style.
- Enable users to save the CSS source to their hard drive.
- Notify the application shell when a user has modified both a style and a style property.
- Notify the application shell when a user would like to revert back to the original source.

This is actually quite similar to the HTML editor, but the CSS data will be managed a little bit differently. Specifically, rather than a plain text area, a Flex `List` component will be used to display and manage the CSS styles, and a Flex `DataGrid` component will be used to display and manage the properties of a selected style.

Managing CSS Data

Because this component uses a more visual approach, it is necessary to abstract the CSS data into something manageable in ActionScript. In the following steps you will create two data classes that will help organize the CSS information:

1. Open your editor and create a new document. Enter the following markup:

```
package com.aircmr.htmlcsseditor.data
{

    public class CSSStyle
    {

        private var _styleSheetIndex:Number;
        private var _cssRuleIndex:Number;
        private var _selector:String;

        [Bindable]
        private var _properties:Array;

        public function CSSStyle( styleSheetID:Number, cssRuleID:Number,
                                  selector:String, properties:Array )
        {
            _styleSheetIndex = styleSheetID;
            _cssRuleIndex = cssRuleID;
            _selector = selector;
            _properties = properties;
        }
```

```
        public function addProperty( prop:CSSStyleProperty ):void
        {
            _properties.push( prop );
        }

        public function deleteProperty( prop:CSSStyleProperty ):void
        {
            _properties.splice( getPropertyIndex( prop ), 0 );
        }

        public function getPropertyIndex( prop:CSSStyleProperty ):Number
        {
            var result:Number = -1;
            for( var i:Number = 0; i < _properties.length; i++ )
            {
                if( prop == _properties[i] )
                {
                    result = i;
                    break;
                }
            }
            return result;
        }

        public function getStyleText( lineBreaks:Boolean = false,
                                      tabs:Boolean = false ):String
        {
            var buffer:String = _selector + " { ";
            if( lineBreaks ) buffer += "\n";

            for( var i:Number = 0; i < _properties.length; i++ )
            {
                if( tabs ) buffer +="\t";
                var prop:CSSStyleProperty = _properties[i];
                buffer += prop.name + ": " + prop.value + "; ";
                if( lineBreaks ) buffer += "\n";
            }

            buffer += "}";
            return buffer;
        }

        public function get styleSheetIndex():Number { return _styleSheetIndex; }
        public function get cssRuleIndex():Number { return _cssRuleIndex; }
        public function get selector():String { return _selector; }
        public function get properties():Array { return _properties; }

    }
}
```

2. Save the file as `CSSStyle.as` in the directory `com/aircmr/htmlcsseditor/data/` within your working directory.
3. Open your editor and create a new document. Enter the following markup:

```
package com.apolloir.htmlcsseditor.data
{
    public class CSSStyleProperty
    {

        private var _name:String;
        private var _value:String;

        public function CSSStyleProperty( name:String, value:String = "" )
        {
            _name = name;
            _value = value;
        }

        public function get name():String { return _name; }
        public function get value():String { return _value; }
        public function set value( v:String ):void { _value = v; }
    }
}
```

4. Save the file as `CSSStyleProperty.as` in the directory `com/aircmr/htmlcsseditor/data/` within your working directory.

In steps 1 and 2, you created the `CSSStyle` class. The purpose of this class is to abstract the relevant data of a CSS style for the application so it can be managed within ActionScript. If you are not familiar with JavaScript or how to access CSS information through the DOM, you might be wondering what the properties in this class are for. Briefly, `styleSheetIndex` and `cssRuleIndex` are references to the index of their respective arrays within the DOM. Saving this information will be especially handy when the user modifies or adds a style or its properties in any way. Also included in the class are some helpful methods for adding and deleting the properties of a style, and for just getting the raw text of the style property.

In steps 3 and 4, you created the `CSSStyleProperty` class. This class simply represents a property of a CSS style. Thus, a `CSSStyle` object also contains an array of `CSSStyleProperty` objects. This array will eventually become the data provider for the aforementioned `DataGrid` component.

Now, because it is necessary for the editor to notify the application shell when a user modifies or adds a style or property, a custom event object is needed. This event object must contain information about the modified style or property. Open your editor and create a new document. Enter the following markup:

```
package com.apolloir.htmlcsseditor.events
{

    import flash.events.Event;
    import com.apolloir.htmlcsseditor.data.CSSStyle;
    import com.apolloir.htmlcsseditor.data.CSSStyleProperty;

    public class CSSEditorEvent extends Event
    {

        public static const ADD_STYLE:String = "addStyle";
        public static const CHANGE_PROPERTY:String = "changeProperty";
```

```
        public var affectedStyle:CSSStyle;
        public var affectedProperty:CSSStyleProperty;

        public function CSSEditorEvent( type:String, style:CSSStyle,
                                        prop:CSSStyleProperty = null )
        {
            super( type );
            affectedStyle = style;
            affectedProperty = prop;
        }

    }
}
```

Save the file as `CSSEditorEvent.as` in the directory `com/a/htmlcsseditor/events/` within your working directory.

The `CSSEditorEvent` class will be used by the MXML component (which you will build shortly) whenever a user modifies or adds a style or property. The static properties of this class describe the three types of events that the CSS editor will dispatch. Each type of event will require a slightly different action by the application shell, but all three types of events need nothing more than a reference to the modified style and/or property, which can be accessed by the `affectedStyle` and `affectedProperty` properties of the event object.

With the data classes and custom event class completed, it's now time to move on to the MXML component and make good use of all this functionality.

User Interface and Logic

Again, in comparison to the HTML editor, the CSS editor is a bit more complicated, in terms of both its logic and its user interface (UI). The meat and potatoes of the UI in this case will be, as mentioned previously, a `List` component for the list of styles and a `DataGrid` component for the list of properties for the selected style. These are both paired with a set of buttons that enable users to modify the respective data. A few of these buttons will trigger a prompt, specifically when the user wants to add a style or property, or view the full CSS source.

In addition to the beefed-up UI, the logic is a bit lengthier as well. This is because instead of simply reading a property within the DOM, the component must parse the stylesheet data and convert it into the friendly data objects you created. As you will see, this component is a great example of how to integrate JavaScript with ActionScript.

1. Open your editor and create a new document. Enter the following markup:

```
<?xml version="1.0" encoding="utf-8"?>
<mx:Panel xmlns:mx="http://www.adobe.com/2006/mxml"
    width="300" height="120" title="Add Style"
    borderColor="#EAEAEA" borderAlpha="1">

    <mx:Script><![CDATA[

    import com.aircmr.htmlcsseditor.data.CSSStyle;
```

```
import mx.managers.PopUpManager;
import mx.utils.StringUtil;

private var _value:CSSStyle;
private var _styleSheetIndex:Number;
private var _cssRuleIndex:Number;

public static function show():AddStylePrompt
{
    var prompt:AddStylePrompt =
        AddStylePrompt( PopUpManager.createPopUp(
        DisplayObject( mx.core.Application.application ),
        AddStylePrompt, true ) );

    PopUpManager.centerPopUp( prompt );
    return prompt;
}

public function init( styleSheetIndex:Number, cssRuleIndex:Number ):void
{
    _styleSheetIndex = styleSheetIndex;
    _cssRuleIndex = cssRuleIndex;
}

private function onAddBtnClick( event:MouseEvent ):void
{
    _value = new CSSStyle( _styleSheetIndex, _cssRuleIndex,
                           selectorInput.text, [] );
    dispatchEvent( new Event( Event.SELECT ) );
    PopUpManager.removePopUp(this);
}

private function onCancelBtnClick( event:MouseEvent ):void
{
    dispatchEvent( new Event( Event.CANCEL ) );
    PopUpManager.removePopUp( this );
}

public function get value():CSSStyle
{
    return _value;
}

]]></mx:Script>

<mx:VBox horizontalAlign="center" width="100%" height="100%" paddingTop="10">
    <mx:HBox width="100%" horizontalAlign="left" verticalAlign="middle">
        <mx:Text fontWeight="bold" text="Selector:" paddingLeft="10"/>
        <mx:TextInput id="selectorInput" width="200" />
    </mx:HBox>
    <mx:HBox width="100%" horizontalAlign="center" paddingTop="10">
        <mx:Button id="addBtn" label="Add Style"
            enabled="{(selectorInput.text.length > 0)}"
            click="onAddBtnClick(event)" />
```

```
            <mx:Button id="cancelBtn" label="Cancel"
                click="onCancelBtnClick(event)" />
        </mx:HBox>
    </mx:VBox>
</mx:Panel>
```

2. Save the file as `AddStylePrompt.mxml` in the directory `com/aircmr/htmlcsseditor/prompts/` within your working directory.
3. Create another new document and enter the following markup:

```
<?xml version="1.0" encoding="utf-8"?>
<mx:Panel xmlns:mx="http://www.adobe.com/2006/mxml"
    width="300" height="150" title="Add Property"
    borderColor="#EAEAEA" borderAlpha="1">

    <mx:Script><![CDATA[

    import com.aircmr.htmlcsseditor.data.CSSStyleProperty;
    import mx.managers.PopUpManager;
    import mx.utils.StringUtil;

    private var _value:CSSStyleProperty;

    public static function show():AddPropertyPrompt
    {
        var prompt:AddPropertyPrompt =
            AddPropertyPrompt( PopUpManager.createPopUp(
            DisplayObject( mx.core.Application.application ),
            AddPropertyPrompt, true ) );

        PopUpManager.centerPopUp( prompt );
        return prompt;
    }

    private function onAddBtnClick( event:MouseEvent ):void
    {
        var name:String = StringUtil.trim( nameInput.text );
        var value:String = StringUtil.trim( valueInput.text );
        _value = new CSSStyleProperty( name, value );
        dispatchEvent( new Event( Event.SELECT ) );
        PopUpManager.removePopUp(this);
    }

    private function onCancelBtnClick( event:MouseEvent ):void
    {
        dispatchEvent( new Event( Event.CANCEL ) );
        PopUpManager.removePopUp( this );
    }

    public function get value():CSSStyleProperty
    {
        return _value;
    }
```

```
    ]]></mx:Script>

    <mx:VBox horizontalAlign="center" width="100%" height="100%" paddingTop="10">
        <mx:HBox width="100%" horizontalAlign="left" verticalAlign="middle">
            <mx:Text fontWeight="bold" text="Name:" paddingLeft="10"/>
            <mx:TextInput id="nameInput" width="200" />
        </mx:HBox>
        <mx:HBox width="100%" horizontalAlign="left" verticalAlign="middle">
            <mx:Text fontWeight="bold" text="Value:" paddingLeft="10"/>
            <mx:TextInput id="valueInput" width="200" />
        </mx:HBox>
        <mx:HBox width="100%" horizontalAlign="center" paddingTop="10">
            <mx:Button id="addBtn" label="Add Property"
                enabled="{(nameInput.text.length > 0)}"
                click="onAddBtnClick(event)" />
            <mx:Button id="cancelBtn" label="Cancel"
                click="onCancelBtnClick(event)" />
        </mx:HBox>
    </mx:VBox>
</mx:Panel>
```

4. Save the file as `AddPropertyPrompt.mxml` in the directory `com/aircmr/htmlcsseditor/prompts/` within your working directory.
5. Create another new document and enter the following markup:

```
<?xml version="1.0" encoding="utf-8"?>
<mx:TitleWindow xmlns:mx="http://www.adobe.com/2006/mxml"
    layout="absolute" width="800" height="600"
    title="CSS Source" showCloseButton="true"
    horizontalAlign="center" verticalAlign="middle"
    borderColor="#EAEAEA" borderAlpha="1"
    close="onClose(event)">

    <mx:Script><![CDATA[

    import flash.filesystem.File;
    import flash.filesystem.FileMode;
    import flash.filesystem.FileStream;
    import flash.net.FileFilter;
    import mx.controls.Alert;
    import mx.managers.PopUpManager;

    private var _fileToSave:File;
    private var _fileStream:FileStream;

    public static function show():CSSSourceWindow
    {
        var prompt:CSSSourceWindow =
            CSSSourceWindow( PopUpManager.createPopUp(
            DisplayObject( mx.core.Application.application ),
            CSSSourceWindow, true ) );

        PopUpManager.centerPopUp( prompt );
```

```
        return prompt;
    }

    private function onClose( event:Event ):void
    {
        PopUpManager.removePopUp(this);
    }

    private function onFileSaveSelect( event:Event ):void
    {
        var theText:String = cssSource.text;
        theText = theText.replace( /\r/g, "\n" );
        theText = theText.replace( /\n/g, File.lineEnding );

        _fileToSave = File( event.target );

        _fileStream = new FileStream();
        _fileStream.openAsync( _fileToSave, FileMode.WRITE );
        _fileStream.addEventListener( IOErrorEvent.IO_ERROR, onWriteIOError );
        _fileStream.writeUTFBytes( theText );
        _fileStream.close();
    }

    private function onSaveBtnClick( event:MouseEvent ):void
    {
        _fileToSave = new File( File.documentsDirectory.nativePath + File.separator
            + "ExportedCSS.css" );

        try
        {
            _fileToSave.browseForSave("Save As...");
            _fileToSave.addEventListener( Event.SELECT, onFileSaveSelect );
        }
        catch( error:Error )
        {
            trace("Failed:", error.message);
        }
    }

    private function onWriteIOError( event:IOErrorEvent ):void
    {
        Alert.show("The specified file cannot be saved.", "Error", Alert.OK, this);
    }

    public function set source( v:String ):void
    {
        cssSource.text = v;
    }

    ]]></mx:Script>
    <mx:VBox width="100%" height="100%" paddingTop="5" horizontalAlign="left">
        <mx:Button id="saveBtn" label="Save As..."
            click="onSaveBtnClick(event)" />
        <mx:TextArea id="cssSource"
```

```
            width="100%" height="100%"
            selectable="true" editable="false">
        </mx:TextArea>
    </mx:VBox>
</mx:TitleWindow>
```

6. Save the file as `CSSSourceWindow.mxml` in the directory `com/aircmr/htmlcsseditor/prompts/` within your working directory.

7. Create another new document and enter the following markup:

```
<?xml version="1.0" encoding="utf-8"?>
<mx:Canvas xmlns:mx="http://www.adobe.com/2006/mxml"
    width="400" height="600" creationComplete="init();">

    <mx:Script><![CDATA[

    import com.aircmr.htmlcsseditor.data.CSSStyle;
    import com.aircmr.htmlcsseditor.data.CSSStyleProperty;
    import com.aircmr.htmlcsseditor.events.CSSEditorEvent;
    import com.aircmr.htmlcsseditor.prompts.AddStylePrompt;
    import com.aircmr.htmlcsseditor.prompts.AddPropertyPrompt;
    import com.aircmr.htmlcsseditor.prompts.CSSSourceWindow;
    import mx.controls.TextInput;
    import mx.events.DataGridEvent;
    import mx.managers.PopUpManager;
    import mx.utils.StringUtil;

    private var _addStylePrompt:AddStylePrompt;
    private var _addPropertyPrompt:AddPropertyPrompt;
    private var _selectedStyle:CSSStyle;
    private var _selectedProperty:CSSStyleProperty;
    private var _nextCSSRuleIndex:Number;

    [Bindable]
    private var _listData:Array;

    [Bindable]
    private var _gridData:Array;

    private function init():void
    {
        clear();

        viewSourceBtn.addEventListener( MouseEvent.CLICK, onViewSourceBtnClick );
        addStyleBtn.addEventListener( MouseEvent.CLICK, onAddStyleBtnClick );
        revertBtn.addEventListener( MouseEvent.CLICK, onRevertBtnClick );
        addPropBtn.addEventListener( MouseEvent.CLICK, onAddPropBtnClick );
        delPropBtn.addEventListener( MouseEvent.CLICK, onDelPropBtnClick );
        styleList.addEventListener( Event.CHANGE, onListChange );
        propertyGrid.addEventListener( DataGridEvent.ITEM_EDIT_END, onItemEditEnd );
        propertyGrid.addEventListener( Event.CHANGE, onGridChange );
    }

    private function onAddStyleBtnClick( event:MouseEvent ):void
```

```
{
    _addStylePrompt = AddStylePrompt.show();
    _addStylePrompt.init( 0, this._nextCSSRuleIndex );
    _addStylePrompt.addEventListener( Event.SELECT, onAddStylePromptSelect );
}

private function onAddPropBtnClick( event:MouseEvent ):void
{
    _addPropertyPrompt = AddPropertyPrompt.show();
    _addPropertyPrompt.addEventListener( Event.SELECT, onAddPropPromptSelect );
}

private function onDelPropBtnClick( event:MouseEvent ):void
{
    var selectedIndex:Number = propertyGrid.selectedIndex;
    var deletedProperty:CSSStyleProperty = CSSStyleProperty(
       propertyGrid.selectedItem );
    deletedProperty.value = "";

    var tempList:Array = _gridData;
    tempList.splice( selectedIndex, 1 );

    clearPropertyGrid();
    _gridData = tempList;

    dispatchEvent( new CSSEditorEvent( CSSEditorEvent.CHANGE_PROPERTY,
                                   _selectedStyle, deletedProperty ) );
}

private function onViewSourceBtnClick( event:MouseEvent ):void
{
    var buffer:String = "";

    for( var i:Number = 0; i < _listData.length; i++ )
    {
        buffer +=  CSSStyle( _listData[i].data ).getStyleText( true, true )
           + "\n\n";
    }

    var prompt:CSSSourceWindow = CSSSourceWindow.show();
    prompt.source = buffer;
}

private function onRevertBtnClick( event:MouseEvent ):void
{
    dispatchEvent( new Event( Event.CANCEL ) );
}


private function onAddStylePromptSelect( event:Event ):void
{
    var newStyle:CSSStyle = _addStylePrompt.value;
    var newListItem:Object = new Object();
    var toAdd:Array = [newListItem];
```

```
        newListItem.label = newStyle.selector;
        newListItem.data = newStyle;

        _listData = toAdd.concat( _listData );
        clearPropertyGrid();
        _nextCSSRuleIndex++

        dispatchEvent( new CSSEditorEvent( CSSEditorEvent.ADD_STYLE, newStyle ) );
    }

    private function onAddPropPromptSelect( event:Event ):void
    {
        var newProp:CSSStyleProperty = _addPropertyPrompt.value;
        _selectedStyle.addProperty( newProp );
        _gridData = null;
        _gridData = _selectedStyle.properties;
        dispatchEvent( new CSSEditorEvent( CSSEditorEvent.CHANGE_PROPERTY,
                                           _selectedStyle, newProp ) );
    }

    private function onItemEditEnd( event:DataGridEvent ):void
    {
        var newValue:String = StringUtil.trim( TextInput(
           propertyGrid.itemEditorInstance ).text );

        if( newValue.length < 1 )
        {
            propertyGrid.destroyItemEditor()
            event.preventDefault();
        }
        else
        {
            _selectedProperty.value = newValue;
        }

        dispatchEvent( new CSSEditorEvent( CSSEditorEvent.CHANGE_PROPERTY,
                                           _selectedStyle, _selectedProperty ) );
    }

    private function onGridChange( event:Event ):void
    {
        _selectedProperty = CSSStyleProperty( propertyGrid.selectedItem );
    }

    private function onListChange( event:Event ):void
    {
        if( styleList.selectedItem )
        {
            _selectedStyle = styleList.selectedItem.data;
            _gridData = _selectedStyle.properties;
        }
        else
        {
            clearPropertyGrid();
```

```
        }
    }

    private function clearPropertyGrid():void
    {
        _gridData = null;
        _selectedProperty = null;
    }

    private function clearStyleList():void
    {
        _listData = null;
        _selectedStyle = null;

    }

    public function clear():void
    {
        _nextCSSRuleIndex = 0;
        clearStyleList();
        clearPropertyGrid();
    }

    public function update( jsDoc:Object ):void
    {
        clear();

        _listData = new Array();

        if( jsDoc.styleSheets.length > 0 )
        {
            _nextCSSRuleIndex = jsDoc.styleSheets[0].cssRules.length;

            for( var i:int = 0; i < jsDoc.styleSheets.length; i++ )
            {
                for( var j:int = 0; j < jsDoc.styleSheets[i].cssRules.length; j++ )
            {
                    try
                    {
                        var selector:String =
                            jsDoc.styleSheets[i].cssRules[j].selectorText;
                        var styleText:String =
                            jsDoc.styleSheets[i].cssRules[j].style.cssText;
                    }
                    catch( error:Error ) { }

                    if( styleText != null && selector != null )
                    {
                        var styleProperties:Array = new Array();
                        var styleItems:Array = styleText.split( ";" );

                        for ( var k:int = 0; k < styleItems.length; ++k)
                        {
                            var prop:Array = String( styleItems[k] ).split( ":" );
```

```
                        if( prop.length == 2 )
                        {
                            var propName:String = StringUtil.trim( prop[0] );
                            var propValue:String = StringUtil.trim( prop[1] );

                            var newCSSStyleProperty:CSSStyleProperty =
                                new CSSStyleProperty( propName, propValue );
                            styleProperties.push( newCSSStyleProperty );
                        }
                    }

                    var newCSSStyle:CSSStyle =
                        new CSSStyle( i, j, selector, styleProperties );

                    var newListItem:Object = new Object();
                    newListItem.label = selector;
                    newListItem.data = newCSSStyle;

                    _listData.push( newListItem );
                }
            }
        }
    }
}

public function get selectedProperty():CSSStyleProperty
{
    return _selectedProperty;
}

public function get selectedStyle():CSSStyle
{
    return _selectedStyle;
}

]]></mx:Script>

<mx:HDividedBox width="100%" height="100%">
    <mx:VBox width="100%" height="100%">
        <mx:HBox width="100%" horizontalAlign="center">
            <mx:Button id="viewSourceBtn" label="View Source"
                enabled="{(_listData != null)}" />
            <mx:Button id="addStyleBtn" label="Add Style"
                enabled="{(_listData != null)}" />
            <mx:Button id="revertBtn" label="Revert"
                enabled="{(_listData != null)}" />
        </mx:HBox>
        <mx:List id="styleList" width="100%" height="100%"
            alternatingItemColors="[#FFFFFF, #F6F6F6]"
            dataProvider="{_listData}">
        </mx:List>
    </mx:VBox>
    <mx:VBox width="100%" height="100%">
        <mx:HBox width="100%" horizontalAlign="center">
```

```
                <mx:Button id="addPropBtn" label="Add Property"
                    enabled="{(_gridData != null)}" />
                <mx:Button id="delPropBtn" label="Delete Property"
                    enabled="{(propertyGrid.selectedIndex > -1)}" />
            </mx:HBox>
            <mx:DataGrid id="propertyGrid"
                width="100%" height="100%" sortableColumns="false"
                editable="true" dataProvider="{_gridData}">
                <mx:columns>
                    <mx:DataGridColumn headerText="Property"
                        dataField="name" editable="false"/>
                    <mx:DataGridColumn headerText="Value"
                        dataField="value" editable="true"/>
                </mx:columns>
            </mx:DataGrid>
        </mx:VBox>
    </mx:HDividedBox>
</mx:Canvas>
```

8. Save the file as `CSSEditor.mxml` in the directory `com/aircmr/htmlcsseditor/ui/` within your working directory.

That's a good chunk of code. You will be glad to know, and it is hoped that you already realized, that you created the entire CSS editor and its supporting components in those last eight steps. This includes all the necessary logic and user interface elements. In steps 1 through 4, you created two important prompts that enable users to both add new styles and add properties to a selected style. These two prompts use a particular pop-up method to be displayed to the user:

```
public static function show():AddStylePrompt
{
    var prompt:AddStylePrompt =
        AddStylePrompt( PopUpManager.createPopUp(
        DisplayObject( mx.core.Application.application ),
        AddStylePrompt, true ) );

    PopUpManager.centerPopUp( prompt );

    return prompt;
}
```

The preceding snippet is the static `show` function from `AddStylePrompt.mxml`. In the context of the application, the prompt appears whenever needed so the user may enter new style information. In addition, when the prompt is displayed, anything underneath it will be disabled and slightly blurred so that the user's full attention is given to the (very simple) task at hand. This is achieved by using the Flex `PopUpManager` class. It's a pretty handy class that makes creating pop-ups, alerts, and so forth extremely easy. Upon perusing the code of the other two prompts, note that they both use the same technique for being displayed. Also notice that the first two prompts make use of your CSS data classes: `CSSStyle` and `CSSStyleProperty`.

The following snippet is again from `AddStylePrompt.mxml`:

```
public function init( styleSheetIndex:Number, cssRuleIndex:Number ):void
{
```

```
        _styleSheetIndex = styleSheetIndex;
        _cssRuleIndex = cssRuleIndex;
    }

    private function onAddBtnClick( event:MouseEvent ):void
    {
        _value = new CSSStyle( _styleSheetIndex, _cssRuleIndex,
                               selectorInput.text, [] );

        dispatchEvent( new Event( Event.SELECT ) );
        PopUpManager.removePopUp(this);
    }
```

Here you can see that an `init` function is in place. This function is needed so some data may be specified before the potentially new `CSSStyle` object is created in the `onAddBtnClick` event handler function. In this case, it's important to specify the index of the stylesheet to which the style should be added, as well as the index of the CSS rule because any new style the user creates isn't part of the DOM yet. It just so happens that in this application any new style is added to the first stylesheet on the DOM. However, it's necessary to manage the rule index by incrementing it each time a style is added. This happens in `CSSEditor.mxml`. More on this shortly.

The `CSSSourceWindow` prompt, although it may not look like your run-of-the-mill prompt, was created in steps 5 and 6. This prompt, or perhaps we should say pop-up window, enables users to view all the CSS source and, if they'd like, save it to their computer. As before, you should recognize the simple file-saving functionality. Now that the prompts are out of the way, you can focus on the AIR-specific functionality:

```
    public function update( jsDoc:Object ):void
    {
        clear();

        _listData = new Array();

        if( jsDoc.styleSheets.length > 0 )
        {
            _nextCSSRuleIndex = jsDoc.styleSheets[0].cssRules.length;

            for( var i:int = 0; i < jsDoc.styleSheets.length; i++ )
            {
                for( var j:int = 0; j < jsDoc.styleSheets[i].cssRules.length; j++ )
            {
                    try
                    {
                        var selector:String =
                            jsDoc.styleSheets[i].cssRules[j].selectorText;
                        var styleText:String =
                            jsDoc.styleSheets[i].cssRules[j].style.cssText;
                    }
                    catch( error:Error ) { }

                    if( styleText != null && selector != null )
                    {
                        var styleProperties:Array = new Array();
                        var styleItems:Array = styleText.split( ";" );
```

```
                        for ( var k:int = 0; k < styleItems.length; ++k)
                        {
                            var prop:Array = String( styleItems[k] ).split( ":" );

                            if( prop.length == 2 )
                            {
                                var propName:String = StringUtil.trim( prop[0] );
                                var propValue:String = StringUtil.trim( prop[1] );

                                var newCSSStyleProperty:CSSStyleProperty =
                                    new CSSStyleProperty( propName, propValue );

                                styleProperties.push( newCSSStyleProperty );
                            }
                        }

                        var newCSSStyle:CSSStyle =
                            new CSSStyle( i, j, selector, styleProperties );

                        var newListItem:Object = new Object();
                        newListItem.label = selector;
                        newListItem.data = newCSSStyle;

                        _listData.push( newListItem );
                    }
                }
            }
        }
    }
```

The previous snippet is from CSSEditor.mxml, which you created in steps 7 and 8. As with the HTML editor, the CSS editor also contains an update function. This function sets up all the data for the editor by parsing all the CSS data from the provided DOM. This function is complicated, so the following paragraphs break it down further.

Recall how the AddStylePrompt component needed to be initialized with a couple of parameters, One of them was used to specify the style's CSS rule index. Therefore, before any parsing is done, the beginning index is determined by the amount of CSS rules in the first stylesheet and stored in the component's _nextCSSRuleIndex variable:

```
_nextCSSRuleIndex = jsDoc.styleSheets[0].cssRules.length;
```

The initial for loop loops through the styleSheets array property of the DOM. Each item in this array refers to a different JavaScript styleSheet object. The following loop loops through the cssRules array property of each styleSheet object (remember you're working with JavaScript here). A cssRule object in JavaScript contains two properties that you will use to get the style data and property data. First, the selectorText property directly relates to the selector property of your CSSStyle object:

```
var selector:String = jsDoc.styleSheets[i].cssRules[j].selectorText;
```

Second, because there isn't an easily accessible array that contains all the properties of the style, you must dig a little further and use the cssText property of the style property of the CSS rule:

```
var styleText:String = jsDoc.styleSheets[i].cssRules[j].style.cssText;
```

Knowing that this string contains the style's properties delimited by semicolons (and assuming the string doesn't contain any syntax errors), it can converted into an array using the array's `split` method:

```
var styleItems:Array = styleText.split( ";" );
```

This array is then looped through and each string in this array is converted to an even smaller array by again using the array's `split` method, with the property name and value delimited by a colon:

```
var propName:String = StringUtil.trim( prop[0] );
var propValue:String = StringUtil.trim( prop[1] );

var newCSSStyleProperty:CSSStyleProperty =
    new CSSStyleProperty( propName, propValue );
styleProperties.push( newCSSStyleProperty );
```

The resulting array is then used to create a new `CSSStyleProperty` object, which is pushed into a temporary array. The resulting array, containing all the properties, is used when creating the `CSSStyle` objects:

```
var newCSSStyle:CSSStyle = new CSSStyle( i, j, selector, styleProperties );
```

Last but not least for this function, an array of generic objects is created to be used as the data provider for the `List` component:

```
var newListItem:Object = new Object();
newListItem.label = selector;
newListItem.data = newCSSStyle;

_listData.push( newListItem );
```

The `update` function is an important function in the CSS editor, but the event handlers are just as important. The event handlers interpret the interaction between the user and the interface and dispatch events when the user adds, modifies, or deletes CSS styles and properties. For example, when a user clicks the Add Style button (which is appropriately named `addStyleBtn`), the user is presented with the `AddStylePrompt` pop-up, they enter the new style information, and upon clicking the OK button, the new style is added to the display list and the component dispatches an event notifying any other components that a style has been added:

```
private function onAddStyleBtnClick( event:MouseEvent ):void
{
    _addStylePrompt = AddStylePrompt.show();
    _addStylePrompt.init( 0, this._nextCSSRuleIndex );
    _addStylePrompt.addEventListener( Event.SELECT, onAddStylePromptSelect );
}
```

The previous snippet from `CSSEditor.mxml` contains the event handler for the `click` event of `addStyleBtn`. Keep in mind that this, and almost all other event handlers, is set up in the `init` function of the component. In the event handler you can see the use of the `AddStylePrompt`'s static `show` method.

A reference to the prompt is saved in the _addStylePrompt variable so a few of its own methods may be called. Here, the init function is called to specify some initial style data, and an event handler is set up for when the user clicks the OK button:

```
private function onAddStylePromptSelect( event:Event ):void
{
    var newStyle:CSSStyle = _addStylePrompt.value;

    var newListItem:Object = new Object();
    newListItem.label = newStyle.selector;
    newListItem.data = newStyle;

    var toAdd:Array = [newListItem];
    _listData = toAdd.concat( _listData );

    clearPropertyGrid();

    _nextCSSRuleIndex++;

    dispatchEvent( new CSSEditorEvent( CSSEditorEvent.ADD_STYLE, newStyle ) );
}
```

The previous snippet contains the aforementioned event handler. The new CSSStyle object is retrieved from the prompt just before it is removed from the display list. After that, it is tossed into a new generic object and added to the beginning of the display list's data provider. Subsequently, the CSS rule index is incremented by one so that the next time a style is added, nothing is overwritten.

You're finally using that custom event class you created previously. For obvious reasons, the ADD_STYLE event is used. Thus, it requires you to specify the most recently affected style as its third parameter. Eventually, this event will notify the application shell when it should add the style to the DOM. Speaking of events, there are two other instances where the CSSEditorEvent class is used:

```
private function onAddPropPromptSelect( event:Event ):void
{
    var newProp:CSSStyleProperty = _addPropertyPrompt.value;

    _selectedStyle.addProperty( newProp );

    _gridData = null;
    _gridData = _selectedStyle.properties;

    dispatchEvent( new CSSEditorEvent( CSSEditorEvent.CHANGE_PROPERTY,
       _selectedStyle, newProp ) );
}
```

The previous snippet contains the event handler that is called when the user adds a new property via the AddPropertyPrompt component. The newly created CSSStyleProperty object is retrieved from the prompt before it is removed from the display list and is then added into the list of properties of the currently selected CSSStyle via its own addProperty method. The data provider for the DataGrid component is then updated with the new property object and the CHANGE_PROPERTY event is dispatched to notify any listeners that a property has changed.

If you browse through the rest of CSSEditor.mxml, you should notice the use of the CHANGE_PROPERTY event in two other event handlers: onItemEditEnd and onDelPropBtnClick. You might be wondering why the event is not more descriptive or specific to the action the user is taking, but rest assured, there's no problem. For this application, it's only necessary to use one type of event whenever modifying the properties of a style because one simple chunk of code can handle both cases (adding and editing). This will be more apparent shortly when you build the application shell.

That covers the most important functionality of the CSS editor. In the next section you will learn how to tie the two editors together and create the application shell.

Building the Application Shell

It's finally time to build the application shell. The application shell ties together the address bar, HTML editor, CSS editor, and an instance of AIR's HTML component into one handy application. Once complete, all your hard work will finally pay off.

Open your editor and create a new document. Enter the following markup:

```
<?xml version="1.0" encoding="utf-8"?>
<mx:WindowedApplication xmlns:mx="http://www.adobe.com/2006/mxml"
    xmlns:ui="com.aircmr.htmlcsseditor.ui.*"
    layout="absolute" applicationComplete="onAppInit();">

    <mx:Style>
    .myTabs {
         highlightAlphas: 0.34, 0;
         fillAlphas: 0.88, 0.2;
         fillColors: #cccccc, #ffffff;
         backgroundAlpha: 0.5;
    }
    </mx:Style>

    <mx:Script><![CDATA[

    import com.aircmr.htmlcsseditor.data.CSSStyleProperty;
    import com.aircmr.htmlcsseditor.data.CSSStyle;
    import com.aircmr.htmlcsseditor.events.CSSEditorEvent;

    private var _currentJSDoc:Object;

    private function onAppInit():void
    {
        this.systemManager.stage.nativeWindow.width = 800;
        this.systemManager.stage.nativeWindow.height = 600;

        addressBar.addEventListener( Event.CHANGE, onAddressBarChange );

        htmlEditor.addEventListener( Event.CHANGE, onHTMLEditorChange );
        htmlEditor.addEventListener( Event.CANCEL, onAddressBarChange );

        cssEditor.addEventListener( CSSEditorEvent.ADD_STYLE, onCSSEditorAddStyle );
        cssEditor.addEventListener( CSSEditorEvent.CHANGE_PROPERTY,
           onCSSEditorChangeProperty );
        cssEditor.addEventListener( Event.CANCEL, onAddressBarChange );
```

```
        html.addEventListener( Event.COMPLETE, onHTMLLoadComplete );
        html.addEventListener( Event.LOCATION_CHANGE, onHTMLLocationChange );
    }

    private function onAddressBarChange( event:Event ):void
    {
        html.location = addressBar.location;
    }

    private function onCSSEditorAddStyle( event:CSSEditorEvent ):void
    {
        var newStyle:CSSStyle = event.affectedStyle;

        if( _currentJSDoc.styleSheets[0] == undefined )
        {
            var newSS:Object = _currentJSDoc.createElement("style");
            newSS.type = "text/css";
            _currentJSDoc.getElementsByTagName( "head" )[0].appendChild( newSS );
        }

        _currentJSDoc.styleSheets[0].insertRule( newStyle.getStyleText(),
           newStyle.cssRuleIndex );
    }

    private function onCSSEditorChangeProperty( event:CSSEditorEvent ):void
    {
        var ssIndex:Number = event.affectedStyle.styleSheetIndex;
        var ruleIndex:Number = event.affectedStyle.cssRuleIndex;
        var prop:String = event.affectedProperty.name;
        var value:String = event.affectedProperty.value;
        _currentJSDoc.styleSheets[ssIndex].cssRules[ruleIndex].style.setProperty(
           prop, value );
    }

    private function onHTMLEditorChange( event:Event ):void
    {
        _currentJSDoc.body.innerHTML = htmlEditor.sourceCode;
    }

    private function onHTMLLoadComplete( event:Event ):void
    {
        _currentJSDoc = html.domWindow.document;
        htmlEditor.update( _currentJSDoc, html.location );
        cssEditor.update( _currentJSDoc );
    }

    private function onHTMLLocationChange( sevent:Event ):void
    {
        addressBar.location = html.location;
        htmlEditor.clear();
        cssEditor.clear()
    }

    ]]></mx:Script>
```

```
    <mx:VBox width="100%" height="100%">
        <ui:AddressBar id="addressBar" width="100%" />
        <mx:TabNavigator id="tabNav" width="100%" height="100%"
            backgroundAlpha="0.5" creationPolicy="all"
            horizontalAlign="center" horizontalGap="1"
            tabStyleName="myTabs" tabWidth="100">
            <mx:Canvas id="previewTab" label="Preview">
                <mx:HTML id="html" width="100%" height="100%" />
            </mx:Canvas>
            <mx:Canvas id="sourceTab" label="Source">
                <ui:HTMLEditor id="htmlEditor" width="100%" height="100%" />
            </mx:Canvas>
            <mx:Canvas label="CSS">
                <ui:CSSEditor id="cssEditor" width="100%" height="100%" />
            </mx:Canvas>
        </mx:TabNavigator>
    </mx:VBox>
</mx:WindowedApplication>
```

Save the file as `HTMLCSSEditor.mxml` in your working directory. The following sections explain what you just created.

Creating the User Interface

First, you need a way to display the components to users in a meaningful way. Lucky for you, Flex has a really great component, `TabNavigator`, that enables users to choose which component they want to use at any given time. Basically, a tab will be used for each of the three main components (`HTMLEditor`, `CSSEditor`, and `HTML`), and the address bar will remain above them:

```
<mx:VBox width="100%" height="100%">
    <ui:AddressBar id="addressBar" width="100%" />
    <mx:TabNavigator id="tabNav" width="100%" height="100%"
        backgroundAlpha="0.5" creationPolicy="all"
        horizontalAlign="center" horizontalGap="1"
        tabStyleName="myTabs" tabWidth="100">
        <mx:Canvas id="previewTab" label="Preview">
            <mx:HTML id="html" width="100%" height="100%" />
        </mx:Canvas>
        <mx:Canvas id="sourceTab" label="Source">
            <ui:HTMLEditor id="htmlEditor" width="100%" height="100%" />
        </mx:Canvas>
        <mx:Canvas label="CSS">
            <ui:CSSEditor id="cssEditor" width="100%" height="100%" />
        </mx:Canvas>
    </mx:TabNavigator>
</mx:VBox>
```

As you can see, an instance of the `HTMLEditor`, the `CSSEditor`, and AIR's `HTML` component are placed within an instance of the Flex `Canvas` component. Each `Canvas` component represents a tab that will appear when the application is finally compiled. The component handles all the mouse interaction for you and manages the display of each tab and its contents. It's really as simple as that. Next you will learn how to manage all the events for all the components.

Adding the Event Handlers

Essentially, the application shell just needs to respond to the events of all the components. The subsequent event handlers will not only make the components work in harmony, but some of them will, most importantly, make the necessary modifications to the DOM so that users can view their changes to the HTML and CSS. Take a look at all the events that the shell is concerned with:

```
private function onAppInit():void
{
    this.systemManager.stage.window.width = 1024;
    this.systemManager.stage.window.height = 768;

    addressBar.addEventListener( Event.CHANGE, onAddressBarChange );

    htmlEditor.addEventListener( Event.CHANGE, onHTMLEditorChange );
    htmlEditor.addEventListener( Event.CANCEL, onAddressBarChange );

    cssEditor.addEventListener( CSSEditorEvent.ADD_STYLE, onCSSEditorAddStyle );
    cssEditor.addEventListener( CSSEditorEvent.CHANGE_PROPERTY,
       onCSSEditorChangeProperty );

    cssEditor.addEventListener( Event.CANCEL, onAddressBarChange );

    html.addEventListener( Event.LOCATION_CHANGE, onHTMLLocationChange );
    html.addEventListener( Event.COMPLETE, onHTMLLoadComplete );
}
```

The `onAppInit` function handles the application's `APPLICATION_COMPLETE` event. In other words, it is called when the application has been completely created by the runtime. Aside from setting the width and height of the application's window, the event handlers of all the components are configured. You should first recognize the use of the `CSSEditorEvent` class that you created earlier in the chapter. In addition, note the event handlers configured for the `HTML` component. The `HTML` component's `LOCATION_CHANGE` event notifies the application when the `location` property of the `HTML` component has changed, essentially informing it to reset the editors in preparation for a new DOM. Additionally, the `HTML` component's `COMPLETE` event notifies the application when the last loading operation caused by setting the `location` property has completed. This event is important because it alerts the application to the fact that a new DOM is present and can be accessed by the editors. Now that you have an overview of all the events, it's time to go over each event handler:

```
private function onAddressBarChange( event:Event ):void
{
    html.location = addressBar.location;
}
```

The previous snippet contains the `onAddressBarChange` function, which handles the `AddressBar` component's `CHANGE` event. The only action necessary here is to update the `location` property of the `HTML` component:

```
private function onHTMLLocationChange( sevent:Event ):void
{
    addressBar.location = html.location;
    htmlEditor.clear();
    cssEditor.clear()
}
```

The preceding snippet contains the onHTMLLocationChange function, which handles the HTML component's LOCATION_CHANGE event. Very simply, the address bar is updated with the new location, and both the HTML and CSS editors are cleared of their data.

The following snippet contains the onHTMLLoadComplete function, which handles the HTML component's COMPLETE event:

```
private function onHTMLLoadComplete( event:Event ):void
{
    _currentJSDoc = html.domWindow.document;
    htmlEditor.update( _currentJSDoc, html.location );
    cssEditor.update( _currentJSDoc );
}
```

Again, very simply, a reference to the HTML component's JavaScript DOM is stored in the _currentJSDoc variable by directly referring to the domWindow.document property of the component. Also, each editor is updated by calling its respective update method, both of which require that the current DOM be passed as a parameter. The onHTMLEditorChange function handles the HTMLEditor component's CHANGE event:

```
private function onHTMLEditorChange( event:Event ):void
{
    _currentJSDoc.body.innerHTML = htmlEditor.sourceCode;
}
```

This event notifies the shell when the user would like to update the HTML source of the current HTML content with the changes they made to the HTML source. In order to do this, it is necessary to use some JavaScript to dynamically update the HTML source. This is done by reassigning the innerHTML property of the DOM's body property to the HTML editor's sourceCode property. Next, the onCSSEditorAddStyle function handles the CSSEditor component's ADD_STYLE event:

```
private function onCSSEditorAddStyle( event:CSSEditorEvent ):void
{
    var newStyle:CSSStyle = event.affectedStyle;

    if( _currentJSDoc.styleSheets[0] == undefined )
    {
        var newSS:Object = _currentJSDoc.createElement("style");
        newSS.type = "text/css";
        _currentJSDoc.getElementsByTagName( "head" )[0].appendChild( newSS );
    }

    _currentJSDoc.styleSheets[0].insertRule( newStyle.getStyleText(),
       newStyle.cssRuleIndex );
}
```

This event notifies the shell when the user has added a style in the CSS editor. First, the new style information is retrieved from the event object's affectedStyle property. This property is of type CSSStyle, which you defined earlier in this chapter. The CSSStyle object is saved in a temporary variable called newStyle. Next, the application checks whether there is an available stylesheet to add the new style to. If there is not, then one is created dynamically using some JavaScript. The new style information is then added to the first stylesheet of the current DOM by calling its insertRule method. This JavaScript function's first parameter is a string representing the style definition and in this case is provided by the new style's `getStyleText` method. The second parameter is a number representing the index of the rule to be added and is supplied by the new style's `cssRuleIndex` property.

The `onCSSEditorChangeProperty` function handles the `CSSEditor` component's `CHANGE_PROPERTY` event:

```
private function onCSSEditorChangeProperty( event:CSSEditorEvent ):void
{
    var ssIndex:Number = event.affectedStyle.styleSheetIndex;
    var ruleIndex:Number = event.affectedStyle.cssRuleIndex;
    var prop:String = event.affectedProperty.name;
    var value:String = event.affectedProperty.value;
    _currentJSDoc.styleSheets[ssIndex].cssRules[ruleIndex].style.setProperty(
       prop, value );
}
```

This event notifies the shell when the user has modified a CSS style's properties in any way. First, the stylesheet index and CSS rule index of the affected style are saved in a corresponding temporary variable. Second, unlike the previous event handlers, the name and value of the affected property are saved in corresponding temporary variables via the event's `affectedProperty` property. All four variables are then used to specify which stylesheet and which CSS rule to update while calling the `setProperty` method of the specified JavaScript style object.

Your application is now complete. The only step left is to deploy it and install it. Then you'll be on your way to editing all the HTML and CSS of your favorite websites!

Deploying the Application

Open your editor and create a new document — the application descriptor file. Enter the following markup:

```
<?xml version="1.0" encoding="UTF-8"?>
<application xmlns="http://ns.adobe.com/air/application/1.0">
    <id>com.aircmr.htmlcsseditor</id>
    <name>HTML CSS Editor</name>
    <filename>HTML CSS Editor</filename>
    <version>v1</version>
    <initialWindow>
        <content>HTMLCSSEditor.swf</content>
        <title>HTML CSS Editor</title>
    </initialWindow>
</application>
```

Save the file as `HTMLCSSEditor-app.xml` in your working directory. The element values from this snippet are somewhat generic and should be changed as you see fit. With the descriptor file in place, you are set to compile and package the application's AIR executable.

Recall that two files are necessary to package an AIR application: the main SWF file and the XML application descriptor file. In this section you will produce the SWF file using the command-line tools, and package the AIR application.

Open a command prompt, navigate to the working directory for this application, enter the following command, and press Enter:

```
> amxmlc HTMLCSSEditor.mxml
```

If you have purchased a certificate from a certificate authority, such as VeriSign or Thawte, then you may use that certificate, rather than create the self-signed certificate, and skip the following operation. To create a self-signed certificate within the working directory, enter the following command:

```
> adt -certificate -cn HTMLCSSEditor 1024-RSA certificate.pfx password
```

With the command prompt still pointing to the working directory, enter the following command and press Enter:

```
> adt -package -storetype pkcs12 -keystore certificate.pfx HTMLCSSEditor.air
  HTMLCSSEditor-app.xml HTMLCSSEditor.swf
```

Once the installer has been created successfully by running the last command, navigate to your working directory and double-click on the `HTMLCSSEditor.air` file to install and run the application. If all goes well, the application will launch and look something like Figure 7-1.

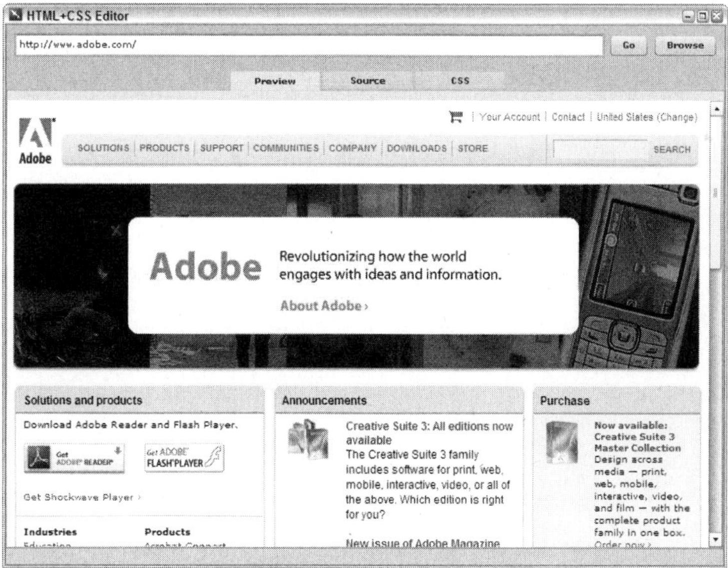

Figure 7-1

Summary

In this chapter you learned how to create an application that is essentially centered on AIR's `HTML` component. You learned about the component's native events, some of its properties, and, most importantly, its `domWindow` property. Through this property you learned how to access the JavaScript DOM of the loaded HTML content and thus integrate JavaScript and ActionScript. This integration enabled your application to perform its most important functionality: to dynamically modify HTML and CSS content. Finally, you utilized some of the techniques that you learned in previous chapters to save simple text files to the user's hard drive.

In the next chapter you will again expand your experience with AIR and learn how to build a weather widget.

8

Weather Widget

Widgets, or desktop applets you interact with, are everywhere. With programs such as Yahoo's Konfabulator, Google's Desktop Gadgets, Microsoft Vista's Sidebar, and Apple's Dashboard, widgets have grown in popularity. Every operating system has at least three different choices of widget engines. However, no one brand seems to be simple to develop and easy to distribute, especially across all platforms. Even if one particular widget is easy to program, you are still left wondering whether the end-user has the particular system installed on their computer. The best option is to create the same widget for at least Microsoft Vista's Sidebar and Apple's Dashboard, except you're still left wondering about everyone running Microsoft Windows XP. Given this conundrum, you might conclude that this niche market is a mess.

You *could* create a widget using the Adobe AIR API — after all, it's what this chapter is about. Why would you create a widget using AIR and not one of the other systems available for widgets? Because of the volume of AIR applications being developed by both large companies and independent developers, the probability of the end-user having the Adobe AIR installed on their computer is pretty high. This can be said for Windows, OS X, and Linux platforms. Therefore, AIR enables you to develop a widget using a familiar set of tools (Flex, ActionScript, and the AIR API) and reach a larger audience with minimal effort.

This chapter takes an in-depth look at creating a widget that retrieves the weather for a particular location. Although this is a fairly common type of widget, it serves as a basis from which you can develop future widgets in AIR. This chapter discusses the following Flex/AIR concepts for building a widget:

- ❑ Creating a "chromeless" application that is always in front of other applications
- ❑ Utilizing `minimize()` and `restore()` commands to hide and show the application
- ❑ Creating dynamic icons and menus for Microsoft Windows's System Tray and Mac OS X's dock

Design

A common problem in the computer industry is the perception that the viewable size of an application reflects its complexity. In other words, something such as a banner ad on the web is considered to be "simple" and therefore easy to create in a minimal amount of time. If you're talking about a program such as Adobe Photoshop, then this perception is moderately accurate. However, simplicity in design does not always mean it will be easy to build. Even a small application, such as a widget, can be complex.

The weather widget is an example of a small yet fairly involved application. Because it is supposed to be a functional ornament for the end user's desktop, the viewable size has to be small. However, it still needs to be able to store the user's information; and at a minimum, it has to show at least today's weather. Overall, the Weather Widget application will have the following features:

- **Multiple views:** In addition to the current and four-day forecast views, the widget will also have a loading screen that is displayed when the data is loading. There will also be a settings screen containing options such as zip code entry, refresh interval, a Celsius/Fahrenheit toggle, and an "always in front" toggle.
- **Native menu system:** In order to keep the widget's view small and compact, the menu system will be hidden, and accessible as either a contextual menu (right-click on the widget) or a system tray (dock) menu. It will have the options to exit the application, toggle between single and four-day forecasts, open the settings view state, and toggle between minimized and restored window views.
- **Dynamic system tray (dock) icon:** Users will be able to view the current temperature as an icon in either their system tray (Windows) or dock (OS X). As mentioned in the previous bullet point, when the user clicks on the dynamic icon, they will be presented with the menu for the widget. If the user minimizes the application in Microsoft Windows, the widget will be completely hidden, with the exception of the system tray icon, meaning the application instance will not be shown in the taskbar, but will be accessible through the system tray icon.

Lastly, the data needs to be pulled from an external weather system. There are a few different options for weather services. This application will use Google's publicly available weather feed, which was chosen because of its easily interpreted XML structure, multi-day forecast set, and icon images. Although this widget will be initially set up to use Google, the choice to continue to use it is up to you. The following are some alternatives:

- National Weather Service XML Web Service (`www.weather.gov/xml`
- Yahoo! Weather (`http://developer.yahoo.com/weather`)
- AccuWeather.comRSSFeed (`www.accuweather.com/rss-center.asp`)

Building the Directory Structure

Before discussing *how* the weather widget is built, it is important that the directory structure for this chapter is properly set up.

Begin by creating a new directory in your local development directory called `WeatherWidget`. This directory will be your working directory for this application.

Next, create the package structure for this application by creating three new directories — `com`, `aircmr`, and `weatherwidget` — in your working directory. The weather widget package structure should look as follows: `working directory/com/aircmr/weatherwidget`.

Lastly, download the corresponding `assets` and `icons` directories from the `WeatherWidget` section of the accompanying website and place them in the root of the working directory. These files will be used throughout the development of the weather widget.

Now that the directory structure has been set up, you can begin to build the Weather Widget application. The next section starts the development process by discussing where the data for the application is coming from and how the application will utilize it.

Handling Data

In terms of functionality, widgets are, for the most part, data driven. They reside on the user's desktop and display some sort of data in a condensed form, both physically and functionally. For instance, the weather widget will be used to display a single or four-day forecast. Therefore, it must be able to handle data for either situation. In addition to the weather data, the widget must also keep track of some basic user preferences such as zip code.

XML

All external data for the weather widget will be received as XML. This applies to both settings and weather information. The weather XML will be retrieved from Google through an HTTP request. The settings XML will be accessed through the `FileStream` class from the user's `applicationDirectory`. Once received, the XML will be parsed into `WeatherVO` and `SettingsVO` data objects by the `XMLParserUtil` class and added to the applications data model, `WidgetDataModel`. The following sections look at this process in detail.

Weather XML

First, review the XML data coming from Google. Begin by opening a web browser and browsing to `www.google.com/ig/api?weather=02139`.

More than likely, your web browser has parsed the text and image links from the XML. To view the raw XML, you may have to click View ➪ Source. The name of this option varies depending on your browser.

If all is well, you will be able to check the weather in Cambridge, Massachusetts. (It is probably raining and cold.) As previously mentioned, Google's weather XML data is straightforward. A `<weather>` node encapsulates the weather information. Location information resides in the `<forecast_information>` node. The current weather information (for the day) is located in the `<current_conditions>` node. Following the current weather data is the four-day forecast information, located in four corresponding `<forecast_conditions>` nodes. Look over this XML document and become familiar with it. The ways in which the weather widget utilizes this data is discussed in more detail throughout this chapter.

Settings XML

Now that the weather widget has weather data, it needs a way to store information such as the zip code and whether or not the temperature should be in degrees Fahrenheit or Celsius. The `settings.xml` file will store such data. Create a new document with the following markup:

```
<?xml version='1.0' encoding='utf-8'?>
<settings>
    <zipCode></zipCode>
    <refreshInterval>1800</refreshInterval>
    <useCelsius></useCelsius>
    <alwaysInFront>true</alwaysInFront>
</settings>
```

Save this document in the root of your working directory as `settings.xml`.

The settings file is brief and to the point. The `<zipCode>` node will store the user's zip code after they have entered it. `<refreshInterval>` will store the interval in which the application will ping Google's server for weather data and update the widget. `<useCelsius>` will store a Boolean value representing how the user would like the data displayed (either Fahrenheit or Celsius). Lastly, `<alwaysInFront>` will indicate whether the user prefers the widget to always remain in front of all opened windows.

Data Objects

Now that the format and structure of the data is known, the Weather Widget application needs a way to store that data internally. As previously mentioned, the XML will be loaded through either an HTTP request or through the `FileStream` class. Once the data has been loaded, it is parsed into specific objects and stored in the `WidgetDataModel` class. Begin building the data model by first creating the `WeatherVO` value object class.

WeatherVO

The `WeatherVO` class will store all weather data that is parsed from the response to the Google HTTP request. It needs to store the data for the name of the day of the week, current temperature, low temperature, high temperature, icon URL, weather condition, wind direction, and humidity.

Create a new document and insert the following code:

```
package com.aircmr.weatherwidget.data
{
    public class WeatherVO
    {
        private var _dayOfWeek:String;
        private var _currentTemp:Number;
        private var _lowTemp:Number;
        private var _highTemp:Number;
        private var _iconURL:String;
        private var _condition:String;
        private var _date:Date;
        private var _wind:String;
```

```
private var _humidity:String;

public function WeatherVO(){};

[Bindable]
public function get dayOfWeek():String
{
    return _dayOfWeek;
}

public function set dayOfWeek( val:String ):void
{
    _dayOfWeek = val;
}

[Bindable]
public function get currentTemp():Number
{
    return _currentTemp;
}

public function set currentTemp( val:Number ):void
{
    _currentTemp = val;
}

[Bindable]
public function get lowTemp():Number
{
    return _lowTemp;
}

public function set lowTemp( val:Number ):void
{
    _lowTemp = val;
}

[Bindable]
public function get highTemp():Number
{
    return _highTemp;
}

public function set highTemp( val:Number ):void
{
    _highTemp = val;
}

[Bindable]
public function get iconURL():String
{
    return _iconURL;
}
```

```
        public function set iconURL( val:String ):void
        {
            _iconURL = val;
        }

        [Bindable]
        public function get condition():String
        {
            return _condition;
        }

        public function set condition( val:String ):void
        {
            _condition = val;
        }

        [Bindable]
        public function get date():Date
        {
            return _date;
        }

        public function set date( val:Date ):void
        {
            _date = val;
        }

        [Bindable]
        public function get wind():String
        {
            return _wind;
        }

        public function set wind( val:String ):void
        {
            _wind = val;
        }

        [Bindable]
        public function get humidity():String
        {
            return _humidity;
        }

        public function set humidity( val:String ):void
        {
            _humidity = val;
        }
    }
}
```

Open a file browser and create a new directory called `data` under the weather widget package in your working directory (a path similar to `working directory/com/aircmr/weatherwidget/data`).

Save the document as `WeatherVO.as` under the `data` directory.

SettingsVO

Next, create the `SettingsVO` object. This object will store all the user's preferences during the session. If at any point the user changes a preference in the Settings window, the new data will be stored in this object and written to the `settings.xml` file as well. The `settings.xml` file is stored in the `SettingsVO` object as `_settingsXMLLocation`. The remainder of the data stored in this object corresponds directly with the data in the `settings.xml` file. You may also notice that there is a reference to a `TemperatureUtil` class. This class stores the constants for the temperature labels such as Fahrenheit and Celsius and is discussed in further detail in the section "TemperatureUtil." Until then, begin by creating the `SettingsVO` class:

```
package com.aircmr.weatherwidget.data
{
    import com.aircmr.weatherwidget.utils.TemperatureUtil;

    public class SettingsVO
    {

        private var _useCelsius:Boolean = false;
        private var _zipCode:String;
        private var _refreshInterval:Number = 300;
        private var _settingsXMLLocation:String;
        private var _cityLocation:String;
        private var _alwaysInFront:Boolean = true;

        public function Settings():void
        {
        }

        public function getDegreeType():String
        {
            if( _useCelsius )
            {
                return TemperatureUtil.CELSIUS;
            }

            return TemperatureUtil.FAHRENHEIT;
        }

        [Bindable]
        public function get zipCode():String
        {
            return _zipCode;
        }

        public function set zipCode( val:String ):void
        {
            _zipCode = val;
        }
```

```
        [Bindable]
        public function get refreshInterval():Number
        {
            return _refreshInterval;
        }

        public function set refreshInterval( val:Number ):void
        {
            _refreshInterval = val;
        }

        [Bindable]
        public function get settingsXMLLocation():String
        {
            return _settingsXMLLocation;
        }

        public function set settingsXMLLocation( val:String ):void
        {
            _settingsXMLLocation = val;
        }

        [Bindable]
        public function get useCelsius():Boolean
        {
            return _useCelsius;
        }

        public function set useCelsius( val:Boolean ):void
        {
            _useCelsius = val;
        }

        [Bindable]
        public function get alwaysInFront():Boolean
        {
            return _alwaysInFront;
        }

        public function set alwaysInFront( val:Boolean ):void
        {
            _alwaysInFront = val;
        }
    }
}
```

Save the document as `SettingsVO.as` in `working directory/com/aircmr/weatherwidget/data/`.

The structures of both data objects are simple in nature. There are private variables that store the data, and getters and setters that control access to those variables. Each variable is marked `[Bindable]` in order to allow access through Flex data binding. In the next section you will build the Singleton that stores these objects.

The Data Model

The data model class for the application, `WidgetDataModel`, will act as the center access point for all data. It will store references to the settings and weather data. It is a Singleton, meaning there can be only one instance of this class instantiated per session. All other classes throughout the weather widget will be able to reference the data in the data model by calling the public static function `getInstance()`:

```
WidgetDataModel.getInstance().settings
```

If you were to try to instantiate another instance of this class, it would fail. This is particularly useful in the context of the weather widget because there will be multiple view states for the application, but the data between views should never change. Once the data has changed in the data model, the change will be reflected throughout the entire widget.

Create a new document and enter the following code:

```
package com.aircmr.weatherwidget.data
{
    import flash.events.Event;
    import flash.events.EventDispatcher;
    import mx.collections.ArrayCollection;

    [Event(name="settingsChange", type="flash.events.Event")]
    [Event(name="currentWeatherChange", type="flash.events.Event")]

    public class WidgetDataModel extends EventDispatcher
    {
        private static var _instance:WidgetDataModel;

        public static const CITY_CHANGE:String = "cityChange";
        public static const SETTINGS_CHANGE:String = "settingsChange";
        public static const CURRENT_FORECAST_CHANGE:String =
            "currentForecastChange";
        public static const FOURDAY_FORECAST_CHANGE:String =
            "fourdayForecastChange";
        public static const RIGHT_NOW_STRING:String = "Currently";

        private var _settings:SettingsVO;
        private var _weatherCollection:ArrayCollection
        private var _currentWeather:WeatherVO;
        private var _cityLocation:String;

        public function WidgetDataModel()
        {
            _settings = new SettingsVO();
            _currentWeather = new WeatherVO();
            _weatherCollection = new ArrayCollection();
        }

        public static function getInstance():WidgetDataModel
        {
            if(_instance == null)
            {
```

```
            _instance = new WidgetDataModel();
        }
        return _instance;
    }

    [Bindable("fourdayForecastChange")]
    public function get weatherCollection():ArrayCollection
    {
        return _weatherCollection;
    }

    public function set weatherCollection(
        val:ArrayCollection ):void
    {
        _weatherCollection = val;
        dispatchEvent(
            new Event( WidgetDataModel.FOURDAY_FORECAST_CHANGE ));
    }

    [Bindable("currentForecastChange")]
    public function get currentWeather():WeatherVO
    {
        return _currentWeather;
    }

    public function set currentWeather( val:WeatherVO ):void
    {
        _currentWeather = val;
        dispatchEvent(
            new Event( WidgetDataModel.CURRENT_FORECAST_CHANGE ));
    }

    [Bindable("settingsChange")]
    public function get settings():SettingsVO
    {
        return _settings;
    }

    public function set settings( val:SettingsVO ):void
    {
        _settings = val;
        dispatchEvent(
            new Event( WidgetDataModel.SETTINGS_CHANGE ));
    }

    [Bindable("cityChange")]
    public function get cityLocation():String
    {
        return _cityLocation;
    }

    public function set cityLocation( val:String ):void
    {
        _cityLocation = val;
```

```
                dispatchEvent( new Event( WidgetDataModel.CITY_CHANGE ));
            }
        }
    }
```

Save the document as `WidgetDataModel.as` in `working directory/com/aircmr/weatherwidget/data/`.

The `WidgetDataModel` will allow access to four main variables: `settings`, `currentWeather`, `cityLocation`, and `weatherCollection`. Once data has been parsed, these variables are assigned. If any changes are made to the data in the data model, a corresponding event is thrown to let the application know that the change was made. All four variables are marked as `[Bindable]` in order to allow access through Flex component data binding. In the next section, how the data is parsed and what each property is assigned is discussed in detail.

Accompanying Services and Utilities

The previous section covered where the data that is being loaded comes from (XML from Google and the local system), and where it is being loaded to (the data model). Now it is time to consider *how* the data is both loaded and parsed into the correct data object formats. Starting with the `XMLFileService`, this section discusses four additional classes that aid in the data flow of the weather widget.

XMLFileService

The XML for the weather data is loaded using the `URLLoader` class, which is a part of the ActionScript 3 framework. The weather widget assigns listeners to the `URLLoader` and passes it a `URLRequest`, which loads the XML from Google. Once the data is received, a `COMPLETE` event is dispatched and the data is parsed. This is a mostly automated process; however, the same cannot be said for the settings data.

You could create a new instance of `FileStream` and pass it a `File` object containing the local address of the `settings.xml` file, right in the main MXML class for the application, but the process will become convoluted, especially because some critical procedures need to happen in order to both read and write to the `settings.xml` file. It would be helpful to have a service class that aids in all things XML related, at least when dealing with XML locally.

Create a new document and insert the following code:

```
package com.aircmr.weatherwidget.services
{
    import com.aircmr.weatherwidget.events.XMLServiceEvent;
    import flash.events.Event;
    import flash.events.EventDispatcher;
    import flash.events.IOErrorEvent;
    import flash.filesystem.File;
    import flash.filesystem.FileMode;
    import flash.filesystem.FileStream;
    import mx.controls.Alert;

    public class XMLFileService extends EventDispatcher
    {
        public static const FILE_NOT_FOUND:String = "fileNotFound";
```

```
        public static const FILE_COPIED:String = "fileCopied";
        public static const FILE_LOADED:String = "fileLoaded";
        public static const FILE_WRITTEN:String = "fileWritten";
        public static const FILE_ERROR:String = "fileError";

        private var _xml:XML;
        private var _file:File;
        private var _fileStream:FileStream;

        public function XMLFileService( ):void {}

        public function loadXMLFromStorageDirectory( fileName:String ):void
        {
            _file = File.applicationStorageDirectory.resolvePath( fileName );

            if( !_file.exists )
            {
                dispatchEvent( new Event( XMLFileService.FILE_NOT_FOUND ));
                return;
            }

            _fileStream = new FileStream();
            _fileStream.addEventListener( Event.COMPLETE, resultHandler );
            _fileStream.addEventListener( IOErrorEvent.IO_ERROR, errorHandler );
            _fileStream.openAsync( _file, FileMode.READ );
        }

        public function saveXMLToStorage( fileName:String , data:XML ):void
        {
            var xml_encoding:String = "<?xml version='1.0' encoding='utf-8'?>\n";
            var xml_toWrite:String = xml_encoding + data.toXMLString();

            _file = File.applicationStorageDirectory.resolvePath( fileName );

            _fileStream = new FileStream();
            _fileStream.addEventListener( Event.CLOSE, onFileWriteComplete );
            _fileStream.openAsync( _file, FileMode.WRITE );
            _fileStream.writeUTFBytes( xml_toWrite );
            _fileStream.close();
        }

        public function copyXMLFromApplicationDirectoryToStorage( fileName:String
):void
        {
            var sourceFile:File = File.applicationDirectory.resolvePath( fileName );
            if( !sourceFile.exists )
            {
                dispatchEvent( new Event( XMLFileService.FILE_NOT_FOUND ) );
                return;
            }

            var resultsFile:File =
                File.applicationStorageDirectory.resolvePath( fileName );
```

```
            sourceFile.addEventListener( IOErrorEvent.IO_ERROR , errorHandler );
            sourceFile.addEventListener( Event.COMPLETE , onFileCopyComplete );
            sourceFile.copyToAsync( resultsFile , true );
        }

        private function resultHandler( event:Event ):void
        {
            _xml = XML( _fileStream.readUTFBytes( _fileStream.bytesAvailable ) );
            _fileStream.removeEventListener( Event.COMPLETE, resultHandler );
            _fileStream.removeEventListener( IOErrorEvent.IO_ERROR, errorHandler );
            _fileStream.close();

            var xmlEvent:XMLServiceEvent =
                new XMLServiceEvent( XMLServiceEvent.XML_LOADED );
            xmlEvent.xml = _xml;
            dispatchEvent( xmlEvent );
        }

        private function errorHandler( event:IOErrorEvent ):void
        {
           var errorMessage:String = "Error Loading File "+event.text+" FILE ERROR";

            var xmlEvent:XMLServiceEvent =
                new XMLServiceEvent( XMLServiceEvent.XML_ERROR );
            xmlEvent.message = errorMessage;
            dispatchEvent( xmlEvent );

            Alert.show( errorMessage );
        }

        private function onFileWriteComplete( event:Event ):void
        {
            dispatchEvent( new Event(XMLFileService.FILE_WRITTEN) );
        }

        private function onFileCopyComplete( event:Event ):void
        {
            dispatchEvent( new Event(XMLFileService.FILE_COPIED) );
        }

        public function get xml():XML
        {
            return _xml;
        }
    }
}
```

Save the document as `XMLFileService.as` in `working directory/com/aircmr/weatherwidget/services/`.

The `XMLFileService` class is nothing more than a `File` instance and a `FileStream` instance, along with some event listeners that let the application know if the open or save was successful. The following snippet demonstrates how the application first instantiates the XMLFileService and passes it a string representing the local URL:

```
var _xmlService:XMLFileService = new XMLFileService();
_xmlService.addEventListener( XMLFileService.FILE_NOT_FOUND , onSettingsNotFound );
_xmlService.addEventListener( XMLServiceEvent.XML_LOADED, onSettingsXMLLoaded );
_xmlService.loadXMLFromStorageDirectory(
    WidgetDataModel.getInstance().settings.settingsXMLLocation );
```

In this example, the XMLFileService instance is instantiated and immediately assigned event listeners. Once the XML file is loaded, onSettingsXMLLoaded is called. The onSettingsXMLLoaded method receives an XMLServiceEvent object containing the settings.xml XML object. It populates the settings property in the data model by using the XMLParserUtil utility to parse the XML into a SettingVO object. Both the XMLServiceEvent and XMLParserUtil classes will be discussed momentarily.

Copying Local Files

First, it is important to point out if and when the file is not found. In the XMLFileService class, you are checking whether the settings.xml file exists in applicationStorageDirectory using resolvePath and the exists File method:

```
_file = File.applicationStorageDirectory.resolvePath( fileName );
if( !_file.exists )
{
    dispatchEvent( new Event( XMLFileService.FILE_NOT_FOUND ));
    return;
}
```

When users first run the weather widget, the settings.xml file will not exist in their application storage directory. The class instance will dispatch a FILE_NOT_FOUND event, and it is up to the controller, WeatherWidget.MXML, to make the next move. If the file does not exist, then it needs to be created. (Fortunately, though, you created settings.xml at the beginning of this chapter.)

Regardless, there is a settings.xml file that contains some basic data. However, this file is located in the application directory. You can read the file from the application directory by referencing the File class's applicationDirectory, instead of applicationStorageDirectory. Because of the security features inside AIR, you will not be able to write back to the application directory. This directory is only used to store data and assets that you wish to have read-only access to. Writing restrictions are quite a problem because the application needs to write the users' preferences back to the settings.xml. Instead of trying to write back to the application directory, the XMLFileService should copy the file from this directory to the storage directory when it is not found in storage. The next time the application is instantiated, the settings.xml file will be found. This is accomplished in the copyXMLFromApplicationDirectoryToStorage method using the File class's copyToAsync method:

```
fileToCopy.copyToAsync( resultFileFromCopy , true );
```

Because this method is asynchronous, listeners will monitor whether the copy is successful or an error occurs. Should the copy be successful, the XMLFileService will then try to load the XML from the storage directory. Once the XML has been loaded, an instance of the XMLServiceEvent is thrown.

XMLServiceEvent

The XMLServiceEvent class is used to transfer the loaded XML data from the XMLFileService instance to the parser that is accessed through the application class. Open a new document and insert the following code:

```
package com.aircmr.weatherwidget.events
{
    import flash.events.Event;

    public class XMLServiceEvent extends Event
    {

        static public const XML_LOADED:String = "xmlLoaded";
        static public const XML_ERROR:String = "xmlError";

        private var _xmlResults:XML;
        private var _message:String;

        public function XMLServiceEvent( type:String,
            bubbles:Boolean=false, cancelable:Boolean=false )
        {
            super( type, bubbles, cancelable );
        }

        public function get xml():XML
        {
            return _xmlResults;
        }

        public function set xml( val:XML ):void
        {
            _xmlResults = val;
        }

        public function get message():String
        {
            return _message;
        }

        public function set message( val:String ):void
        {
            _message = val;
        }
    }
}
```

Save the document as XMLServiceEvent.as in the application's events package (working directory /com/aircmr/weatherwidget/events).

Once the application class receives the XMLServiceEvent object, it passes the public xml property the XMLParserUtil utility class, which parses the data. The next section discusses how this is accomplished.

XMLParserUtil

After the weather and settings data has been received from either the `URLLoader` or `XMLFileService` instances, it needs to be parsed into `WeatherVO`, and `SettingsVO` objects are added to the `WidgetDataModel`. The `XMLParserUtil` class aids in this process.

Create a new document and insert the following code:

```
package com.aircmr.weatherwidget.utils
{
    import com.aircmr.weatherwidget.data.*;
    import mx.collections.ArrayCollection;

    public class XMLParserUtil
    {

        public static function parseWeatherXMLFeedCurrentDay(
            weatherFeed:XML ):WeatherVO
        {
            var currCondition:XMLList = weatherFeed.weather.current_conditions;

            var currentWeather:WeatherVO = new WeatherVO();
            currentWeather.dayOfWeek = WidgetDataModel.RIGHT_NOW_STRING;
            currentWeather.condition = currCondition.condition.@data;
            currentWeather.currentTemp = currCondition.temp_f.@data;
            currentWeather.humidity = currCondition.humidity.@data;
            currentWeather.iconURL = "http://www.google.com" +
                currCondition.icon.@data;
            currentWeather.wind = currCondition.wind_condition.@data;
            currentWeather.lowTemp = weatherFeed..forecast_conditions[0].low.@data;
            currentWeather.highTemp =
                weatherFeed..forecast_conditions[0].high.@data;
            currentWeather.date = new Date();

            return currentWeather;
        }

        public static function parseWeatherXMLFeedFourDay(
            weatherFeed:XML):ArrayCollection
        {
            var weatherCollection:ArrayCollection = new ArrayCollection();

            for( var i:String in weatherFeed..forecast_conditions )
            {
                var weatherObj:WeatherVO = new WeatherVO();
                weatherObj.dayOfWeek =
                    weatherFeed..forecast_conditions[i].day_of_week.@data;
                weatherObj.lowTemp = weatherFeed..forecast_conditions[i].low.@data;
                weatherObj.highTemp =
                   weatherFeed..forecast_conditions[i].high.@data;
                weatherObj.iconURL = "http://www.google.com" +
                    weatherFeed..forecast_conditions[i].icon.@data;
                weatherObj.condition =
                    weatherFeed..forecast_conditions[i].condition.@data;
```

```
                if( weatherObj.dayOfWeek.toLocaleLowerCase() == "today" )
                    weatherObj.currentTemp =
                        weatherFeed.weather.current_conditions.temp_f.@data;

                weatherCollection.addItem( weatherObj );
            }

            return weatherCollection;
        }

        public static function parseWeatherXMLFeedLocation(
            weatherFeed:XML ):String
        {
            return weatherFeed.weather.forecast_information.city.@data;
        }

        public static function parseSettingsXML( settingsXML:XML,
            currentSettings:SettingsVO = null ):SettingsVO
        {
            var settings:SettingsVO =
                currentSettings ? currentSettings : new SettingsVO();
            settings.refreshInterval = settingsXML..refreshInterval;
            settings.zipCode = settingsXML..zipCode;
            settings.useCelsius = (settingsXML..useCelsius != "") ? true : false;
            settings.alwaysInFront =
                (settingsXML..alwaysOnTop != "") ? true : false;

            return settings;
        }
    }
}
```

Save the document as `XMLParserUtil.as` in your working directory under `com/aircmr/weatherwidget/utils/`.

There are four static methods in this class: `parseWeatherXMLFeedCurrentDay`, `parseWeatherXMLFeedFourDay`, `parseWeatherXMLFeedLocation`, and `parseSettingsXML`. Each receives an argument containing the XML object that is to be parsed.

parseWeatherXMLFeedCurrentDay

`parseWeatherXMLFeedCurrentDay` parses the `<current_conditions>` data and assigns it to the corresponding properties of a new `WeatherVO` instance.

The `<current_conditions>` data is more in depth than the four-day forecast. However, it lacks the high and low for the day. Instead, you can parse the high and low from the first `<forecast_conditions>` node since it is for that particular day:

```
currentWeather.lowTemp = weatherFeed..forecast_conditions[0].low.@data;
currentWeather.highTemp = weatherFeed..forecast_conditions[0].high.@data
```

Once the XML is parsed, the `currentWeather` `WeatherVO` object is returned to the method accessing the `XMLParserUtil` class.

parseWeatherXMLFeedFourDay

parseWeatherXMLFeedFourDay first creates a new ArrayCollection called weatherCollection. It loops through the four sets of <forecast_conditions> nodes, creating a new WeatherVO instance through each iteration and adding that object to the weatherCollection. When all four nodes have been parsed and the four WeatherVO objects have been created and properly assigned data, the weatherCollection is returned to the method calling the XMLParserUtil and assigned to the WidgetDataModel. When the data model has received the populated weatherCollection ArrayCollection, it dispatches a FOURDAY_FORECAST_CHANGE event.

parseWeatherXMLFeedLocation

parseWeatherXMLFeedLocation parses the weather feed's <forecast_information> node for the city name. Because the location zip code is used to retrieve the data, it would be good to display the name of the location instead. This method, called from the application controller, updates the location property of the WidgetDataModel and is displayed throughout the widget.

parseSettingsXML

The parseSettings accepts XML data passed to the application's onSettingsXMLLoaded method through the XMLServiceEvent that was received from the XMLFileService instance.

In addition to the XML, this method also accepts an optional SettingsVO object. In this case, the application passes a reference to the settings property in the WidgetDataModel in order to preserve properties such as settingsXMLLocation. A new SettingsVO object is created if one is not passed when the method is called.

After a SettingsVO object is established, the XML is parsed and assigned to the respective properties. If a property is expecting a Boolean value, a simple ternary operator checks whether the node has a value. If it does, then the Boolean is set to true; if not, the Boolean is set to false.

Once the XML is parsed and the data has been assigned, the XMLParserUtil returns the SettingsVO object to the application controller class and assigns the newly created object to the WidgetDataModel.

TemperatureUtil

Redundant coding is annoying. Throughout this application, you will need to refer to the temperature in degrees Fahrenheit and Celsius. Likewise, you will also need to convert Fahrenheit to Celsius and vice versa. You could just search for the degree symbol keycode every time you would like to type it, and you could just write the math to convert one to another. However, this would be very redundant considering how many times, spread out through how many classes, you will have to write this. Therefore, a basic utility will prove useful in the battle against redundant coding.

Create a new document and insert the following code:

```
package com.aircmr.weatherwidget.utils
{
    public class TemperatureUtil
    {
        public static const FAHRENHEIT:String = "°F";
        public static const CELSIUS:String = "°C";
```

```
        public static function convertFahrenheitToCelsius( temp:Number ):Number
        {
            return ( temp - 32 ) / 1.8;
        }

        public static function convertCelsiusToFahrenheit( temp:Number ):Number
        {
            return ( temp + 32 ) * 1.8;
        }

        public static function returnTempAsFormedString( temp:Number,
            useCelsius:Boolean = false,
            isInFahrenheit:Boolean = true ):String
        {
            var tempInC:String = String(
                Math.round( ( isInFahrenheit ) ?
                convertFahrenheitToCelsius( temp ) :
                temp) + TemperatureUtil.CELSIUS );
            var tempInF:String = String(
                Math.round( ( isInFahrenheit ) ? temp :
                convertCelsiusToFahrenheit( temp ) ) +
                TemperatureUtil.FAHRENHEIT );

            return String( ( useCelsius ) ? tempInC : tempInF );
        }

    }
}
```

Save this document as `TemperatureUtil.as` in your working directory under the `com/aircmr/weatherwidget/utils/` package.

The `TemperatureUtil` class contains public constants for `Strings` representing the degrees Fahrenheit and Celsius labels. It also has public methods used to convert the temperature data. Lastly, it has a method, `returnTempAsFormedString`, which both converts the data and returns it with the addition of the degrees label (for example, 85°F). You will use this `TemperatureUtil` class extensively as you begin to piece this application together.

Building the User Interface

So far, you have looked at how the data is parsed and how the weather application populates its data model. Because one of the goals of a widget is to create something visual for the user's desktop, you may be more interested in how the user interface (UI) for this application is set up. This section looks at each of the UI elements and discusses how the data model affects each piece. By the end of this section, your weather widget should begin to take shape.

View States

The weather widget will have four view states, settings, loading, current weather forecast, and four-day forecast. With the exception of the loading view, each state is contained as a separate component. The

`SettingsWindow` component is the first thing the user will see if a zip code is not present in the `settings.xml` file; and as such, it is the first view state to discuss.

SettingsWindow

The `SettingsWindow` is an MXML component that will allow the user access to options like zip code entry, weather data refresh rate, and temperature unit type. The following steps will help you build this view state. Open a new document and enter the following code and markup:

```
<?xml version="1.0" encoding="utf-8"?>
<mx:Canvas xmlns:mx="http://www.adobe.com/2006/mxml"
    show="refreshWindow();"
    clipContent="false" width="320" height="210" >
    <mx:Metadata>
        [Event(name="comboOpen", type="flash.events.Event")]
        [Event(name="comboClose", type="flash.events.Event")]
        [Event(name="save", type="flash.events.Event")]
        [Event(name="cancel", type="flash.events.Event")]
    </mx:Metadata>
    <mx:Script>
        <![CDATA[
            import com.aircmr.weatherwidget.services.XMLFileService;
            import com.aircmr.weatherwidget.utils.TemperatureUtil;
            import com.aircmr.weatherwidget.data.WidgetDataModel;
            import mx.controls.Alert;

            [Bindable]
            private var _intervalArray:Array =
                [{data: 300 , label: '5 Mins' },
                {data: 900 , label: '15 Mins' },
                {data: 1800 , label: '30 Mins' },
                {data: 2700 , label: '45 Mins' }];
            public static const SAVE:String = "save";
            public static const COMBO_OPEN:String = "comboOpen";
            public static const COMBO_CLOSE:String = "comboClose";

            private function refreshWindow():void
            {
                intervalSelector.selectedIndex = getSelectedIndex();
                inFront.selected =
                  WidgetDataModel.getInstance().settings.alwaysInFront;
                toggleDegrees(
                  WidgetDataModel.getInstance().settings.useCelsius );
            }

            private function getSelectedIndex():int
            {
                var interval:Number =
                 WidgetDataModel.getInstance().settings.refreshInterval;
                for( var i:int = 0 ; i < _intervalArray.length ; i++ )
                {
                    if( interval == _intervalArray[i].data ) return i;
                }
```

```
        return 0;

    }

    private function toggleDegrees( inCelsius:Boolean ):void
    {
        if( inCelsius )
        {
            celsius.selected = true;
            fahrenheit.selected = false;
        }
        else
        {
            celsius.selected = false;
            fahrenheit.selected = true;
        }
    }


    private function saveSettingsLocally():void
    {
        WidgetDataModel.getInstance().settings.zipCode =
            zipCodeInput.text;
        WidgetDataModel.getInstance().settings.refreshInterval =
            intervalSelector.selectedItem.data;
        WidgetDataModel.getInstance().settings.useCelsius =
            celsius.selected;
        WidgetDataModel.getInstance().settings.alwaysInFront =
            inFront.selected;

        var xmlFileService:XMLFileService = new
            XMLFileService();
        xmlFileService.addEventListener(
            XMLFileService.FILE_WRITTEN , onSettingsSaved );
        xmlFileService.saveXMLToStorage(
            WidgetDataModel.getInstance()
              .settings.settingsXMLLocation ,
            buildSettingsData() );
    }

    private function onSettingsSaved( event:Event ):void
    {
        dispatchEvent( new Event( SettingsWindow.SAVE ));
    }

    private function buildSettingsData():XML
    {
        var xml:XML = new XML("<settings></settings>");
        xml.zipCode =
            WidgetDataModel.getInstance().settings.zipCode;
        xml.refreshInterval =
            WidgetDataModel.getInstance()
              .settings.refreshInterval;
        xml.useCelsius = ( celsius.selected ) ? true : "";
```

```
                xml.alwaysInFront = ( inFront.selected ) ? true : "";

                return xml;
            }

            private function onComboOpen(event:Event):void
            {
                dispatchEvent( new Event( SettingsWindow.COMBO_OPEN ) );
            }

            private function onComboClose(event:Event):void
            {
                dispatchEvent( new Event(SettingsWindow.COMBO_CLOSE) );
            }

        ]]>
    </mx:Script>
    <mx:ZipCodeValidator source="{zipCodeInput}" property="text"
        trigger="{saveBtn}" triggerEvent="click"
        valid="saveSettingsLocally()"/>

    <mx:Label text="AIR Weather Widget Settings"
        color="0xFFFFFF" fontSize="18" y="-35" />

    <mx:VBox width="100%" height="100%">
        <mx:HBox>
            <mx:Label text="Zip Code:" color="0xFFFFFF" fontSize="14" />
            <mx:TextInput id="zipCodeInput"
                 width="65" fontSize="12" maxChars="5"
                text="{WidgetDataModel.getInstance().settings.zipCode}"
                restrict="0-9" />
        </mx:HBox>
        <mx:HBox>
            <mx:Label text="Refresh Interval:"
                 color="0xFFFFFF" fontSize="14" />
            <mx:ComboBox id="intervalSelector" rowCount="4"
                dataProvider="{_intervalArray}"
                selectedIndex="{getSelectedIndex()}"
                open="onComboOpen(event)"
                close="onComboClose(event)"  />
        </mx:HBox>
        <mx:HBox>
            <mx:Label text="Temperature In:"
                color="0xFFFFFF" fontSize="14" />
            <mx:CheckBox id="fahrenheit"
                click="toggleDegrees(false)"
                label="{TemperatureUtil.FAHRENHEIT}"
                color="0xFFFFFF"
                textRollOverColor="0xFFFFFF"
                textSelectedColor="0xFFFFFF" />
            <mx:CheckBox id="celsius"
                click="toggleDegrees(true)"
                label="{TemperatureUtil.CELSIUS}"
                color="0xFFFFFF"
```

```
                    textRollOverColor="0xFFFFFF"
                    textSelectedColor="0xFFFFFF" />
            </mx:HBox>
            <mx:HBox>
                <mx:Label text="Always In Front:"
                    color="0xFFFFFF" fontSize="14" />
                <mx:CheckBox id="inFront"
                    color="0xFFFFFF"
                    textRollOverColor="0xFFFFFF"
                    textSelectedColor="0xFFFFFF" />
            </mx:HBox>
            <mx:Spacer height="10" />
            <mx:HBox width="95%" horizontalAlign="right">
                <mx:Button label="SAVE" id="saveBtn" />
                <mx:Button label="CANCEL"
                    click="dispatchEvent(new Event(Event.CANCEL))" />
            </mx:HBox>
        </mx:VBox>
    </mx:Canvas>
```

Save this document as `SettingsWindow.mxml` in your `working directory/com/aircmr/weatherwidget/ui/ directory`.

Now that you have created the MXML document, take a quick look at what it is you just coded. Figure 8-1 demonstrates how the settings window looks.

Figure 8-1

The `SettingsWindow` is a `Canvas` container component that has a nested `VBox` containing the options for Zip Code, Refresh Interval, Temperature Display, and Always in Front. When the component is displayed, a `show` event calls the private `refreshWindow` method, which updates the visual representations of the settings property values. Otherwise, procedures are controlled through the user's interactions.

Zip Code

The zip code `TextInput` component's text is bound to the zip code property of the `SettingsVO` object in the data model. When the user clicks the Save button, an instance of the Flex `ZipCodeValidator` component validates the zip code. If it is successful, then the method `saveSettingsLocally` is called. This method is discussed in more detail in the section "Saving the Settings."

Refresh Interval

The refresh interval `ComboBox` component is assigned an array of predetermined intervals so the user doesn't keep pinging Google's server every five seconds for weather information. When the user opens the `SettingsWindow`, the `ComboBox` instance is assigned a `selectedIndex` from the `getSelectedIndex()` method.

Temperature Toggle

The temperature toggle is a label followed by two check boxes. The `refreshWindow` method first calls the `toggleDegrees` method and passes it the `settings useCelcius` property. The `toggleDegrees` method is also called when the user selects or deselects one of the `CheckBox` components. It accepts a Boolean value that if true, sets the Celsius `CheckBox`'s `selected` property to true and the Fahrenheit `CheckBox`'s `selected` property to `false`. The opposite happens if a value of `false` is passed in. Alternatively, you could use Flex's `RadioButtonGroup` control instead of this dual `CheckBox` solution.

Always in Front

The toggle for "Always in Front" is initially set when the `refreshWindow` method is called. When the Save button is clicked and the zip code passes validation, the `selected` value of the `CheckBox` is passed to the `alwaysInFront` property of the `SettingsVO` object.

Saving the Settings

The final function of the `SettingsWindow` is to save the settings information to the `settings.xml` file when the Save button is clicked. This is accomplished by the `saveSettingsLocally` method, which instantiates a new instance of `XMLFileService`. Once instantiated, an `XMLFileService.FILE_WRITTEN` event listener is added and the `saveXMLToStorage` method is called on the `XMLFileService` instance.

The `saveXMLToStorage` method accepts two arguments. The first is the location of the file you wish to write to. In this case, the location of the `settings.xml` file is stored in `WidgetDataModel.getInstance().settings.settingsXMLLocation`. The second is the XML you wish to write. However, the application needs to parse the `SettingsVO` object into XML before sending it to the `XMLFileService`, and this is done by the `buildSettingsData` method.

The `buildSettingsData` method creates a new `XML` object with the parent node `<settings>`. Once the `XML` object has been created, it assigns the property value of the `SettingsVO` object to identical properties in the `XML` object. Boolean values are checked using a ternary operation. If true, then insert `true` into the XML; if false, then send an empty value to the `XML` object. Once the `XML` object has been created and properly assigned, the method returns it to the `XMLFileService`.

When the file has been written to storage, a `SettingsWindow.SAVE` event is dispatched, telling the application that the settings have been changed and to act accordingly.

Cancel

When the user clicks the Cancel button, an `Event.CANCEL` event is dispatched alerting the application to close the `SettingsWindow` with no changes made.

Once the settings have been configured for the weather widget, you can load the weather data from Google and display the information after it is parsed. The next section takes a quick look at the weather loader view before showing the `CurrentWeatherItem` view.

Loading View

The loading view isn't a component per se. It is an external embedded SWF that is included on the CD-ROM. It is loaded by a `SWFLoader` class instance in the `WeatherWidget.mxml` class file. Although the loading view is not a component, it is the next view that is presented to the user. It is displayed after the settings have been updated and the weather data is being loaded. Figure 8-2 illustrates the loading view.

Figure 8-2

CurrentWeatherView

After the settings have been set and the weather data has been loaded and parsed, the `Current WeatherView` view is updated. `CurrentWeatherView` is an MXML component that has a `Canvas` that nests an `<mx:HBox>`, which displays the current day's weather data.

To begin creating the view, open a new document and insert the following markup and code:

```
<?xml version="1.0" encoding="utf-8"?>
<mx:Canvas xmlns:mx="http://www.adobe.com/2006/mxml"
    height="130" width="215"
    verticalScrollPolicy="off"
    horizontalScrollPolicy="off">
        <mx:Script>
        <![CDATA[
            import com.aircmr.weatherwidget.utils.TemperatureUtil;
            import com.aircmr.weatherwidget.data.*;

            private function drawBox( event:Event ):void
            {
                var box:Sprite = new Sprite();
                box.graphics.lineStyle( 1, 0xFFFFFF , .5 );
                box.graphics.drawRect( -2 , -2 ,
                    weatherIcon.content.width + 3, weatherIcon.content.height + 3);
                weatherIcon.addChild( box );
            }

            [Bindable]
            private var _dataProvider:WeatherVO;

            public function get dataProvider():WeatherVO
            {
                return _dataProvider;
            }

            public function set dataProvider( val:WeatherVO ):void
            {
                _dataProvider = val;
```

```
            }

        ]]>
    </mx:Script>
    <mx:HBox paddingLeft="10">
        <mx:VBox verticalGap="0">
            <mx:Image id="weatherIcon" source="{_dataProvider.iconURL}"
                complete="drawBox( event )" />
            <mx:Label text="{ TemperatureUtil.returnTempAsFormedString(
                    _dataProvider.currentTemp ,
                    WidgetDataModel.getInstance().settings.useCelsius ) }"
                color="#FFFFFF" fontWeight="bold" fontSize="16" />
        </mx:VBox>
        <mx:VBox verticalGap="-5">
            <mx:Label text="{_dataProvider.condition}" color="#FFFFFF"
                fontSize="14" fontWeight="bold" />
            <mx:Label text="{_dataProvider.humidity}" color="#FFFFFF" />
            <mx:Label text="{_dataProvider.wind}" color="#FFFFFF" />
            <mx:Label text="{'High: '+ TemperatureUtil.returnTempAsFormedString(
                    _dataProvider.highTemp,
                    WidgetDataModel.getInstance().settings.useCelsius )}"
                color="#FFFFFF" />
            <mx:Label text="{'Low: '+ TemperatureUtil.returnTempAsFormedString(
                    _dataProvider.lowTemp,
                    WidgetDataModel.getInstance().settings.useCelsius )}"
                color="#FFFFFF" />
        </mx:VBox>
    </mx:HBox>
</mx:Canvas>
```

Save the document as `CurrentWeatherView.mxml` in your working directory under `com/aircmr/weatherwidget/ui/`.

Before looking at the markup and code in detail, take a look at how the finished view will look. Figure 8-3 illustrates the `CurrentWeatherView` component.

Figure 8-3

This view state component is moderately straightforward. Each child component, such as a `Label`, accepts data from the `WidgetDataModel`. Because this application uses data binding, if any value changes in the data model, that change is reflected in the view state. If the `text` property is expecting a temperature value, the application utilizes the `returnTempAsFormedString` method of the `TemperatureUtil` class. The result is the temperature data properly formatted in either Celsius of Fahrenheit (for example, High 74°F).

```
<mx:Label
    text="{ TemperatureUtil.returnTempAsFormedString(
        _dataProvider.currentTemp ,
        WidgetDataModel.getInstance().settings.useCelsius)}"
/>
```

Now that the current weather view has been coded, creating a four-day forecast view shouldn't be too difficult. As long as the data is formatted correctly, it should be as easy as creating one day's weather view and repeating it for each day's weather data. The next section looks at this in depth.

FourDayForecastView and WeatherItem

As mentioned in the previous section, the concept for the four-day forecast is minimal. A `weather Collection` property in the `WidgetDataModel` contains four days' worth of `WeatherVO` instances. The trick to creating four days' of worth of weather views is as easy as creating one day's worth of a weather view and setting up a `Repeater` class that will replicate the single day view four times. Figure 8-4 illustrates this concept.

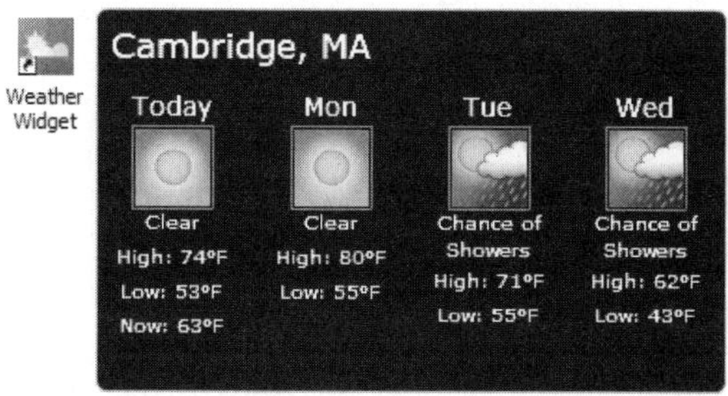

Figure 8-4

Begin to create the four-day view by first creating the single-day weather view.

Open a new document and insert the following code:

```
<?xml version="1.0" encoding="utf-8"?>
<mx:VBox xmlns:mx="http://www.adobe.com/2006/mxml"
    horizontalAlign="center"
    verticalGap="0">
    <mx:Script>
        <![CDATA[
            import com.aircmr.weatherwidget.utils.TemperatureUtil;
            import com.aircmr.weatherwidget.data.*;

            private function drawBox( event:Event ):void
            {
                var box:Sprite = new Sprite();
```

```
                box.graphics.lineStyle( 1, 0xFFFFFF , .5);
                box.graphics.drawRect( -2 , -2 , weatherIcon.content.width + 3,
                    weatherIcon.content.height + 3);
                weatherIcon.addChild( box );
            }

            [Bindable]
            private var _dataProvider:WeatherVO;

            public function get dataProvider():WeatherVO
            {
                return _dataProvider;
            }

            public function set dataProvider( val:WeatherVO ):void
            {
                _dataProvider = val;
                checkForCurrentWeather();
            }

            private function checkForCurrentWeather():void
            {
                if( !_dataProvider.currentTemp ) return;
                currentTemp.text = "Now: "+
                    TemperatureUtil.returnTempAsFormedString(
                        _dataProvider.currentTemp ,
                        WidgetDataModel.getInstance().settings.useCelsius )
                currentTemp.visible = true;
            }
        ]]>
    </mx:Script>

    <mx:Label text="{_dataProvider.dayOfWeek}" color="#FFFFFF" fontSize="14"  />
    <mx:Image id="weatherIcon" source="{_dataProvider.iconURL}" width="40"
        height="40" complete="drawBox( event );" />
    <mx:Text text="{_dataProvider.condition}" color="#FFFFFF" selectable="false"
        width="70" textAlign="center"/>
    <mx:Label text="{'High: '+ TemperatureUtil.returnTempAsFormedString(
            _dataProvider.highTemp ,
            WidgetDataModel.getInstance().settings.useCelsius )}"
        color="#FFFFFF" />
    <mx:Label text="{'Low: '+ TemperatureUtil.returnTempAsFormedString(
            _dataProvider.lowTemp ,
            WidgetDataModel.getInstance().settings.useCelsius )}"
        color="#FFFFFF" />
    <mx:Label id="currentTemp" color="#FFFFFF" visible="false"/>
</mx:VBox>
```

Save the document as `WeatherItem.mxml` in your working directory under `com/aircmr/weatherwidget/ui/`.

The `WeatherItem` view is similar to the `CurrentWeatherView` view; however, when the `dataProvider` is set, it accesses the `checkForCurrentWeather` method. This method checks to see whether the

WeatherItem is today's weather. If it is today's weather, it adds a "Now:" label and displays the current temperature. Each WeatherItem instance will be receiving data from the Repeater. The next block of code demonstrates this concept in more detail.

Create the FourDayForecastView by first opening a new document and inserting the following code:

```
<?xml version="1.0" encoding="utf-8"?>
<mx:HBox xmlns:mx="http://www.adobe.com/2006/mxml"
    verticalScrollPolicy="off" horizontalGap="15"
    horizontalScrollPolicy="off" height="200"
    xmlns:ui="com.aircmr.weatherwidget.ui.*">
        <mx:Script>
        <![CDATA[
            import mx.collections.ArrayCollection;

            [Bindable]
            private var _dataProvider:ArrayCollection;

            public function get dataProvider():ArrayCollection
            {
                return _dataProvider;
            }

            public function set dataProvider( val:ArrayCollection ):void
            {
                _dataProvider = val;
            }

        ]]>
    </mx:Script>
    <mx:Repeater dataProvider="{_dataProvider}" id="fourDayRepeater" >
        <ui:WeatherItem dataProvider="{fourDayRepeater.currentItem}" />
    </mx:Repeater>
</mx:HBox>
```

Save the document as FourDayForecastView.mxml in your working directory under com/aircmr/weatherwidget/ui/.

The FourDayForecastItem accepts an ArrayCollection as a dataProvider. This particular ArrayCollection will be the weatherCollection ArrayCollection in the data model. When the dataProvider is updated, it relays the data to the Repeater class. The Repeater will loop through the length of the weatherCollection and the appropriate numbers of WeatherItem instances, assigning each instance the corresponding WeatherVO from the collection:

```
<mx:Repeater dataProvider="{_dataProvider}" id="fourDayRepeater" >
    <ui:WeatherItem dataProvider="{fourDayRepeater.currentItem}" />
</mx:Repeater>
```

The four days' worth of WeatherItems appear in a row because they are nested in an <mx:HBox> container.

Bringing It All Together

The Weather Widget application is almost complete. Your current collection of parts includes the data for the application and the different view states. The last big step is to create the `WeatherWidget.mxml` file. However, before creating the main application markup and code, there is one last supporting UI component that needs to be discussed.

TrayIcon

The `TrayIcon` class is a UI element that is completely necessary for the success of the weather widget. It represents the icon that resides in the system tray on the Windows platform or in the dock on the OS X platform. You can assign the tray icon any bitmap by using the following code:

```
NativeApplication.nativeApplication.icon.bitmaps =
    [ my16x16icon.bitmapData , my128x128icon.bitmapData ];
```

Although in the example two icons are presented, both 16 and 128 pixel square icons, only one is necessary. In this application, the `TrayIcon` class will determine which size is necessary, as 16×16 is for Microsoft Windows and 128×128 is for Mac OS X. The `NativeApplication` class is a Singleton that represents the OS itself. You can reference the application by calling the `nativeApplication` instance of the `NativeApplication` Singleton.

Before getting into the code, take a look at how the system tray icon will appear on each OS. Figure 8-5 illustrates the weather widget's current temperature icon in the Microsoft Windows XP system tray. Figure 8-8 illustrates the weather widget's current temperature icon in the Mac OS X dock.

Figure 8-5

Open a new document and insert the following code:

```
package com.aircmr.weatherwidget.ui
{
    import com.aircmr.weatherwidget.utils.TemperatureUtil;
    import com.aircmr.weatherwidget.data.WidgetDataModel;
    import flash.display.BitmapData;
    import flash.display.DisplayObject;
    import flash.display.MovieClip;
    import flash.display.Sprite;
    import flash.text.AntiAliasType;
    import flash.text.TextField;
    import flash.text.TextFormat;

    public class TrayIcon extends Sprite
    {
        private var _sprite:Sprite;
```

```
    private var _currentTemperature:String;
    private var _height:Number = 16;
    private var _width:Number = 16;

    public function TrayIcon( supportsDockIcon:Boolean = false )
    {
        _currentTemperature =
            (
   !isNaN(WidgetDataModel.getInstance().currentWeather.currentTemp )
   || !WidgetDataModel.getInstance().currentWeather ) ?
   TemperatureUtil().returnTempAsFormedString(
       WidgetDataModel.getInstance().currentWeather.currentTemp ,
       WidgetDataModel.getInstance().settings.useCelsius ) : "--";

        addChild((supportsDockIcon)? OSXTrayIcon() : pcTrayIcon() );

    }

    public function getSpriteAsBitmapData():BitmapData
    {
        var bitmapData:BitmapData =
            new BitmapData( _width, _height, true, 0x00FFFFFF );
        bitmapData.draw( this );
        return bitmapData;
    }

    private function pcTrayIcon():Sprite
    {
        var pcIcon:Sprite = new Sprite();

        var textFormat:TextFormat = new TextFormat();
        textFormat.font = "Tahoma"
        textFormat.size = 11;
        textFormat.color = 0x333333;

        var textField:TextField = new TextField();

        textField.defaultTextFormat = textFormat;
        textField.antiAliasType = AntiAliasType.ADVANCED;
        textField.text = _currentTemperature;

        pcIcon.addChild( textField );

        return pcIcon;
    }

    private function OSXTrayIcon():Sprite
    {
        _height = 128;
        _width = 128;

        var OSXTrayIcon:Sprite = new Sprite();
        OSXTrayIcon.graphics.beginFill( 0x000000 , .9 );
        OSXTrayIcon.graphics
```

```
                .drawRoundRect(0, 0, _width, _height , 50 );

            var textFormat:TextFormat = new TextFormat();
            textFormat.font = "Tahoma"
            textFormat.size = 50;
            textFormat.color = 0xFFFFFF;

            var textField:TextField = new TextField();

            textField.defaultTextFormat = textFormat;
            textField.antiAliasType = AntiAliasType.ADVANCED;
            textField.text = _currentTemperature;
            textField.width = 128;
            textField.x = 10;
            textField.y = 30;

            OSXTrayIcon.addChild( textField );

            return OSXTrayIcon;
        }
    }
}
```

Save the document as `TrayIcon.as` in your working directory under `com/aircmr/weatherwidget/ui`.

The `TrayIcon` class is used by the main application class and is reassigned every time the weather data is queried. The following demonstrates how the `TrayIcon` class is used in this application:

```
NativeApplication.nativeApplication.icon.bitmaps =
    [ new TrayIcon( NativeApplication.supportsDockIcon ).getSpriteAsBitmapData() ];
```

On instantiation, the application passes the `NativeApplication` class's `supportsDockIcon` property value. The `supportsDockIcon` value is only true if the application is running in OS X. Once the `TrayIcon` class knows whether the icon is for Windows or OS X, it can call either the `pcTrayIcon` or `OSXTrayIcon` method, which returns the properly formatted `Sprite`.

The second part of the new `TrayIcon` instance instantiation calls the `getSpriteAsBitmapData` method. This method creates a new `BitmapData` instance, calls `BitmapData.draw`, which draws the `Sprite` data in that instance, and returns the `BitmapData` instance to the `Array` that is assigned to `NativeApplication.nativeApplication.icon.bitmaps`.

Finally, at the time of instantiation, the `TrayIcon` checks whether the current temperature has been assigned. If it has, then assign it to the private variable `_currentTemperature`; if it hasn't, then assign `_currentTemperature` two dashes (--).

Now that there is a system tray (or dock) icon to work with, the main application class can be built. Using this icon, the weather widget will be able to provide menus that manipulate the application from the tray icon. The next section discusses the menu system and the creation of the `WeatherWidget.mxml` file.

WeatherWidget.mxml Application Class

The `TrayIcon` class has been covered, and all the pieces of the puzzle are laid out and ready to be assembled. The data is ready to populate the `WidgetDataModel`, the states are ready to be instantiated, and the tray icon is ready to be added to the system tray or dock.

Create a new document and insert the following markup and code:

```
<?xml version="1.0" encoding="utf-8"?>
<mx:Application xmlns:mx="http://www.adobe.com/2006/mxml"
    layout="absolute"
    creationComplete="onCreationComplete(event)"
    horizontalScrollPolicy="off"
    verticalScrollPolicy="off"
    backgroundAlpha="0"
    xmlns:ui="com.aircmr.weatherwidget.ui.*">
    <mx:Script>
        <![CDATA[
            import com.aircmr.weatherwidget.services.*;
            import com.aircmr.weatherwidget.ui.*;
            import com.aircmr.weatherwidget.data.*;
            import com.aircmr.weatherwidget.events.XMLServiceEvent;
            import com.aircmr.weatherwidget.utils.XMLParserUtil;
            import mx.formatters.DateFormatter;
            import mx.managers.SystemManager;
            import mx.effects.easing.Quartic;

            public static const FOURDAY_FORECAST:String = "fourDayForecast";
            public static const CURRENT_FORECAST:String = "currentForecast";
            public static const LOADER:String = "loader";
            public static const SETTINGS:String = "settings";

            private var _timer:Timer;
            private var _lastUpdated:String = "N/A";
            private var _nativeWindow:NativeWindow;
            private var _lastSection:String;
            private var _xmlService:XMLFileService;
            private var _allowWindowMove:Boolean = true;

            private function onCreationComplete( event:Event ):void
            {
                WidgetDataModel.getInstance().settings.settingsXMLLocation =
                    "settings.xml";
                WidgetDataModel.getInstance().addEventListener(
                    WidgetDataModel.SETTINGS_CHANGE , onSettingsChange );
                WidgetDataModel.getInstance().addEventListener(
                    WidgetDataModel.CURRENT_FORECAST_CHANGE , onWeatherFeedLoad );

                _xmlService = new XMLFileService();
                _xmlService.addEventListener( XMLFileService.FILE_NOT_FOUND ,
                    onSettingsNotFound );
```

```
        _xmlService.addEventListener( XMLServiceEvent.XML_LOADED,
            onSettingsXMLLoaded );
        _xmlService.loadXMLFromStorageDirectory(
            WidgetDataModel.getInstance().settings.settingsXMLLocation );

        _timer = new Timer( 1000 );
        _timer.addEventListener( TimerEvent.TIMER , timeHandler );

        _nativeWindow =
            SystemManager.getSWFRoot( this ).stage.nativeWindow;
        _nativeWindow.addEventListener(
            NativeWindowDisplayStateEvent.DISPLAY_STATE_CHANGE,
            buildNativeMenu );
        _nativeWindow.alwaysInFront =
            WidgetDataModel.getInstance().settings.alwaysInFront;
        _nativeWindow.title = "AIR Weather Widget";

        buildNativeMenu();

        NativeApplication.nativeApplication.icon.bitmaps =
            [ new TrayIcon(
                NativeApplication.supportsDockIcon
                ).getSpriteAsBitmapData() ];
    }

    private function onSettingsXMLLoaded( event:XMLServiceEvent ):void
    {
        WidgetDataModel.getInstance().settings =
            XMLParserUtil.parseSettingsXML( event.xml,
            WidgetDataModel.getInstance().settings );
    }

    private function onSettingsNotFound( event:Event ):void
    {
        var xmlFileService:XMLFileService = new XMLFileService();
        xmlFileService.addEventListener(
            XMLFileService.FILE_COPIED , onSettingsFileCopiedSuccess );
        xmlFileService.copyXMLFromApplicationDirectoryToStorage(
            WidgetDataModel.getInstance().settings.settingsXMLLocation );
    }

    private function onSettingsFileCopiedSuccess( event:Event ):void
    {
        _xmlService.loadXMLFromStorageDirectory(
            WidgetDataModel.getInstance().settings.settingsXMLLocation );
    }

    private function timeHandler( event:TimerEvent ):void
    {
        if( _timer.currentCount ==
            WidgetDataModel.getInstance().settings.refreshInterval )
        {
            loadWeatherFeed();
            _timer.reset();
```

```
        }
    }

    private function onSettingsChange( event:Event ):void
    {
        if( WidgetDataModel.getInstance().settings.zipCode == "" )
        {
            currentState = WeatherWidget.SETTINGS;
        }
        else
        {
            _nativeWindow.alwaysInFront =
                WidgetDataModel.getInstance().settings.alwaysInFront;
            loadWeatherFeed();
        }
    }

    private function onSettingsCancel():void
    {
        currentState = ( _lastSection ) ?  _lastSection :
            WeatherWidget.LOADER;
    }

    private function loadWeatherFeed():void
    {
        currentState =  WeatherWidget.LOADER;

        var xmlLoader:URLLoader = new URLLoader();
        xmlLoader.addEventListener( Event.COMPLETE ,
            onWeatherFeedXMLLoaded );

        var xmlURLReq:URLRequest = new URLRequest(
            "http://www.google.com/ig/api?weather=" +
            WidgetDataModel.getInstance().settings.zipCode );
        xmlLoader.load( xmlURLReq );
    }

    private function onWeatherFeedXMLLoaded( event:Event ):void
    {
        var loadedXML:XML = XML( event.target.data );
        WidgetDataModel.getInstance().cityLocation =
            XMLParserUtil.parseWeatherXMLFeedLocation( loadedXML );
        WidgetDataModel.getInstance().weatherCollection =
            XMLParserUtil.parseWeatherXMLFeedFourDay( loadedXML );
        WidgetDataModel.getInstance().currentWeather =
            XMLParserUtil.parseWeatherXMLFeedCurrentDay( loadedXML );
    }

    private function onWeatherFeedLoad( event:Event ):void
    {
        _timer.start();

        currentState = ( _lastSection == WeatherWidget.LOADER ||
            !_lastSection )? WeatherWidget.CURRENT_FORECAST : _lastSection;
```

```
        NativeApplication.nativeApplication.icon.bitmaps = [ new TrayIcon(
            NativeApplication.supportsDockIcon ).getSpriteAsBitmapData() ];

         var dateFormat:DateFormatter = new DateFormatter();
        dateFormat.formatString = "L:NN:A";

        _lastUpdated = dateFormat.format( new Date() );

        buildNativeMenu();
    }

    private function onFourDayButtonClick( event:Event ):void
    {
        currentState = WeatherWidget.FOURDAY_FORECAST;
        buildNativeMenu();
    }

    private function onCurrentDayButtonClick( event:Event ):void
    {
        currentState = WeatherWidget.CURRENT_FORECAST;
        buildNativeMenu();
    }

    private function onSettingsClick( event:Event ):void
    {
        _lastSection = currentState;
        currentState = "settings";
        buildNativeMenu();
    }

    private function handleCloseButton( event:Event ):void
    {
        _nativeWindow.close();
    }

    private function handleMinimizeButton( event:Event ):void
    {
        _nativeWindow.minimize();
        _nativeWindow.visible = false;
    }

    private function handleRestoreButton( event:Event ):void
    {
        _nativeWindow.visible = true;
        _nativeWindow.restore();
    }

    private function checkWidgetLocation():void
    {
        if( _nativeWindow.x + backgroundContainer.width >=
            Screen.mainScreen.bounds.width )
        {
            _nativeWindow.x =
                Screen.mainScreen.bounds.width - backgroundContainer.width;
```

```
        }

        if( _nativeWindow.y + backgroundContainer.height >=
            Screen.mainScreen.bounds.height )
        {
            _nativeWindow.y =
                Screen.mainScreen.bounds.height-backgroundContainer.height;
        }

        if( _nativeWindow.y <= 0 ) _nativeWindow.y = 0;
        if( _nativeWindow.x <= 0 ) _nativeWindow.x = 0;
    }

    private function buildNativeMenu( event:Event = null ):void
    {
        var nativeMenu:NativeMenu = new NativeMenu();

        var title:NativeMenuItem = nativeMenu.addItem(
            new NativeMenuItem("AIR Weather Widget" ));
        var lastUpdated:NativeMenuItem = nativeMenu.addItem(
            new NativeMenuItem("Last Updated: "+ _lastUpdated ));
        nativeMenu.addItem( new NativeMenuItem("Seperator1", true ) );

        if( currentState == WeatherWidget.CURRENT_FORECAST ||
            currentState == null )
        {
            var fourDay:NativeMenuItem = nativeMenu.addItem(
                new NativeMenuItem("Show Four Day Forecast") );
            fourDay.addEventListener( Event.SELECT ,
                onFourDayButtonClick );
        }
        else
        {
            var currentDay:NativeMenuItem = nativeMenu.addItem(
                new NativeMenuItem("Show Todays Forecast") );
            currentDay.addEventListener( Event.SELECT ,
                onCurrentDayButtonClick );
        }

        nativeMenu.addItem( new NativeMenuItem("Seperator2", true ) );
        var settingsBtn:NativeMenuItem = nativeMenu.addItem(
            new NativeMenuItem("Settings") );
        settingsBtn.addEventListener( Event.SELECT , onSettingsClick );

        if( _nativeWindow.displayState ==
            NativeWindowDisplayState.MINIMIZED )
        {
            var restoreBtn:NativeMenuItem = nativeMenu.addItem(
                new NativeMenuItem("Show Widget") );
            restoreBtn.addEventListener(Event.SELECT, handleRestoreButton);
        }
        else
        {
            var hideBtn:NativeMenuItem = nativeMenu.addItem(
```

```
                new NativeMenuItem("Hide Widget to Tray") );
            hideBtn.addEventListener(Event.SELECT, handleMinimizeButton);
        }

        var closeBtn:NativeMenuItem = nativeMenu.addItem(
            new NativeMenuItem("Exit") );
        closeBtn.addEventListener(Event.SELECT, handleCloseButton );

        if( NativeApplication.supportsSystemTrayIcon )
        {
            SystemTrayIcon(
                NativeApplication.nativeApplication.icon).menu= nativeMenu;
        }
        else
        {
            DockIcon(
                NativeApplication.nativeApplication.icon).menu= nativeMenu;
        }

        backgroundContainer.contextMenu = nativeMenu;
    }
  ]]>
</mx:Script>

<mx:Box id="backgroundContainer"
    horizontalScrollPolicy="off" verticalScrollPolicy="off"
    backgroundColor="0x000000" backgroundAlpha=".9"
    borderStyle="solid" cornerRadius="6"
    paddingBottom="5" paddingLeft="5" paddingRight="5" paddingTop="5"
    height="100" width="150" mouseDown="_nativeWindow.startMove();"
    mouseUp="checkWidgetLocation();" >
    <mx:Canvas id="holder" width="100%" height="100%"
        horizontalScrollPolicy="off" verticalScrollPolicy="off" >
        <mx:SWFLoader id="loader"
            source="@Embed(source='assets/weatherLoader.swf')"
            x="{holder.width / 2 - loader.width /2 - 10}" />
        <mx:VBox>
            <mx:Label text="{WidgetDataModel.getInstance().cityLocation}"
                color="0xFFFFFF"
                fontSize="18"
                visible="false"
                id="cityLabel" />
            <mx:Canvas>
                <ui:CurrentWeatherView
                id="currentWeatherReport" visible="false"
                dataProvider="{WidgetDataModel.getInstance().currentWeather}"/>
                <ui:FourDayForecastView id="fullWeatherReport" visible="false"
                  dataProvider="
                    {WidgetDataModel.getInstance().weatherCollection}"/>
                <ui:SettingsWindow id="settingsWindow" visible="false"
                    save="onSettingsChange(event);"
                    cancel="onSettingsCancel();"
                    comboOpen="{ backgroundContainer.mouseEnabled = false }"
                    comboClose="{ backgroundContainer.mouseEnabled = true }" />
```

```
                </mx:Canvas>
            </mx:VBox>
        </mx:Canvas>
    </mx:Box>
    <mx:states>
        <mx:State name="{WeatherWidget.FOURDAY_FORECAST}">
            <mx:SetProperty target="{loader}" name="visible" value="false" />
            <mx:SetProperty target="{cityLabel}" name="visible" value="true" />
            <mx:SetProperty target="{currentWeatherReport}"
                name="visible" value="false" />
            <mx:SetProperty target="{fullWeatherReport}"
                name="visible" value="true" />
            <mx:SetProperty target="{settingsWindow}"
                name="visible" value="false" />
            <mx:SetProperty target="{backgroundContainer}" name="width"
                value="{fullWeatherReport.width + 15}" />
            <mx:SetProperty target="{backgroundContainer}" name="height"
                value="{fullWeatherReport.height}" />
        </mx:State>
        <mx:State name="{WeatherWidget.LOADER}">
            <mx:SetProperty target="{cityLabel}" name="visible" value="false" />
            <mx:SetProperty target="{fullWeatherReport}"
                name="visible" value="false" />
            <mx:SetProperty target="{currentWeatherReport}"
                name="visible" value="false" />
            <mx:SetProperty target="{settingsWindow}"
                name="visible" value="false" />
            <mx:SetProperty target="{loader}" name="visible" value="true" />
        </mx:State>
        <mx:State name="{WeatherWidget.CURRENT_FORECAST}">
            <mx:SetProperty target="{loader}" name="visible" value="false" />
            <mx:SetProperty target="{cityLabel}" name="visible" value="true" />
            <mx:SetProperty target="{currentWeatherReport}"
                name="visible" value="true" />
            <mx:SetProperty target="{fullWeatherReport}"
                name="visible" value="false" />
            <mx:SetProperty target="{settingsWindow}"
                name="visible" value="false" />
            <mx:SetProperty target="{backgroundContainer}"
                name="width" value="{currentWeatherReport.width}" />
            <mx:SetProperty target="{backgroundContainer}"
                name="height" value="{currentWeatherReport.height}" />
        </mx:State>
        <mx:State name="{WeatherWidget.SETTINGS}">
            <mx:SetProperty target="{loader}" name="visible" value="false" />
            <mx:SetProperty target="{cityLabel}" name="visible" value="false" />
            <mx:SetProperty target="{currentWeatherReport}"
                name="visible" value="false" />
            <mx:SetProperty target="{fullWeatherReport}"
                name="visible" value="false" />
            <mx:SetProperty target="{settingsWindow}"
                name="visible" value="true" />
            <mx:SetProperty target="{backgroundContainer}"
                name="width" value="{settingsWindow.width}" />
```

```
            <mx:SetProperty target="{backgroundContainer}"
                name="height" value="{settingsWindow.height}" />
        </mx:State>
    </mx:states>

    <mx:transitions>
        <mx:Transition fromState="*" toState="*">
            <mx:Resize target="{backgroundContainer}" duration="350"
                easingFunction="{Quartic.easeOut}"
                effectEnd="checkWidgetLocation();" />
        </mx:Transition>
    </mx:transitions>

</mx:Application>
```

Save this document as `WeatherWidget.mxml` in your working directory.

The `WeatherWidget` is an `<mx:Application>` container that acts as both a controller and a view manager for the widget. It contains a `<mx:Box>` component called `backgroundContainer` that wraps the UI elements, an `<mx:Script>` tag wrapping the ActionScript, an `<mx:states>` array containing the different view states, and an `<mx:transitions>` array containing the transition definition for the widget.

Going Chromeless

An AIR application, by default, is nested in a `<mx:WindowedApplication>` container. The `<mx:WindowedApplication>` class is a subclass of the `<mx:Application>` class that contains methods, properties, events, and styles that are pertinent in creating an application that matches the operating system's chrome. The key difference between using `<mx:WindowedApplication>` and `<mx:Application>` in an AIR application is that, with `<mx:Application>`, it is up to the developer to add and define the listeners that enable system commands such as close, minimize, or maximize, or that enable you to drag a window. These events are predefined with default values in `<mx:WindowedApplication>`. Given that the weather widget will have a look and feel of its own, the `<mx:Application>` class is used instead. In order to have a completely chromeless application, some additional properties need to be set in the application's descriptor file.

The `backgroundContainer` `<mx:Box>` acts as the window UI for the weather widget. It has a black, semi-transparent background, rounded corners, and a white one-pixel border. It includes a nested `<mx:Canvas>` container, which encloses the UI elements such as the `loader`, `<ui:CurrentWeatherView>`, `<ui:FourDayForecastView>`, and `<ui:SettingsWindow>`. All user interaction events are added to `backgroundContainer`. For instance, `mouseUp` and `mouseDown` events need to be defined in order to enable users to move the widget around their desktop. Therefore, you add the events as follows:

```
<mx:Box id="backgroundContainer"
    mouseDown="_nativeWindow.startMove();"
    mouseUp="checkWidgetLocation();" >
```

Note that the rest of the properties for the `<mx:Box>` instance are excluded from this example. On `mouseDown`, `startMove` instantiates the mouse movement handle for a `NativeWindow` instance. In this case, `_nativeWindow` is defined as `SystemManager.getSWFRoot( this ).stage.nativeWindow` in `onCreationCompleteHandler`. When the user releases the mouse after the window move, the `checkWidgetLocation` method verifies whether the weather widget remains on the desktop and moves it to the desktop if it is not.

The user can now move the widget around the desktop without having the system chrome. However, they still cannot exit or minimize the widget. If this were left like it is, users would ultimately shut their computer down in frustration (although there are other ways to close an application). Either way, there should be a menu system that enables users to close the widget. The next section discusses adding a menu to the weather widget.

Adding Menus and More Window Interaction

This widget will be pretty useless without some way for users to minimize, restore, or even exit the application. You could add buttons to the widget to access the aforementioned functionality, but adding a honking button to the facade of the widget will just clutter the elegance of a minimal display. Early versions of the weather widget had a sliding tray containing the buttons, though it was decided that even a tray felt clunky. The solution to the menu problem was to create a `NativeMenu` instance and apply it to the `contextMenu` property of the widget and to the system tray icon (dock icon on OS X). Figures 8-6, 8-7, and 8-8 show the `NativeMenu` applied to the widget.

Figure 8-6

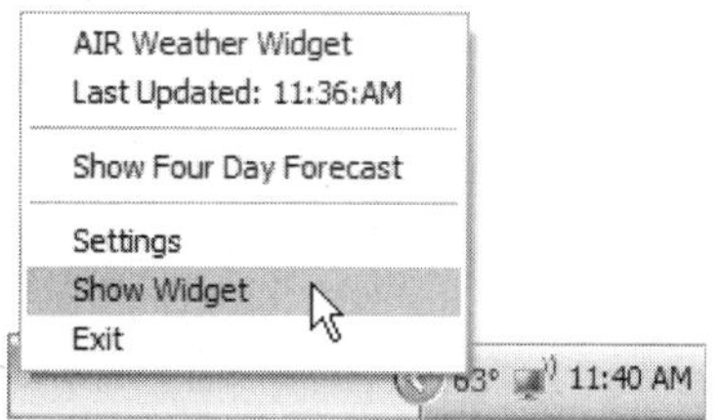

Figure 8-7

Looking through Figures 8-6, 8-7, and 8-8, all three menus are nearly identical. This is because there is only one instance of the `NativeMenu` class created and applied to the widget. Once the application has been created, `onCreationComplete` is accessed. The `onCreationComplete` in turn activates the `buildNativeMenus` method. This method is also called whenever new weather data has been loaded, or the widget's current state has changed.

Figure 8-8

The buildNativeMenu method first creates a new instance of NativeMenu. It then adds a new NativeMenuItem with the label "AIR Weather Widget". This is for aesthetics and nothing more. It adds another NativeMenuItem instance to the NativeMenu that displays a time code of the last time the weather feed was updated. Next, it runs through some conditional statements that detect the display states:

```
if( currentState == WeatherWidget.CURRENT_FORECAST
    || currentState == null )
{
    var fourDay:NativeMenuItem = nativeMenu.addItem( new
        NativeMenuItem("Show Four Day Forecast") );
    fourDay.addEventListener( Event.SELECT , onFourDayButtonClick );
}
else
{
    var currentDay:NativeMenuItem = nativeMenu.addItem( new
        NativeMenuItem("Show Todays Forecast") );
    currentDay.addEventListener(Event.SELECT , onCurrentDayButtonClick);
}
```

This example looks at the currentState property of the <mx:Application>. If currentState is the current forecast view, as opposed to the four-day forecast view, create a new NativeMenuItem titled fourDay and add an event listener for Event.SELECT. When the user clicks Show Four Day Forecast in the menu, onFourDayButtonClick will be accessed, which changes the view state to WeatherWidget.FOURDAY_FORECAST. Likewise, if currentState is equal to WeatherWidget.FOURDAY_FORECAST, the menu should display another NativeMenuItem entitled Show Today's Forecast in its place and assign an event listener that accesses the onCurrentDayButtonClick method.

The buildNativeMenu method then checks the displayState of the NativeWindow instance:

```
if( _nativeWindow.displayState == NativeWindowDisplayState.MINIMIZED )
{
    var restoreBtn:NativeMenuItem = nativeMenu.addItem( new
        NativeMenuItem("Show Widget") );
    restoreBtn.addEventListener( Event.SELECT , handleRestoreButton );
}
else
{
```

```
        var hideBtn:NativeMenuItem = nativeMenu.addItem( new
            NativeMenuItem("Hide Widget to Tray") );
        hideBtn.addEventListener( Event.SELECT , handleMinimizeButton );
    }
```

_nativeWindow is defined in the <mx:Application>'s onCreationCompleteHandler method. If _nativeWindow.displayState is equal to the MINIMIZED constant, create a new NativeMenuItem labeled Show Widget, which accesses the handleRestoreButton method. If the displayState property is MAXIMIZED or NORMAL, create a NativeMenuItem instance labeled Hide Widget to Tray that will instead access the handleMinimizeButton method. Minimizing and restoring is discussed in the next section.

The final NativeMenuItem instance is labeled Exit and accesses the handleCloseButton method. When called, the handleCloseButton method accesses the close() method on the _nativeWindow instance, exiting the application.

Finally, the buildNativeMenu method checks NativeApplication.supportsSystemTrayIcon. If the weather widget is running in Microsoft Windows, this will be true. If true, then assign the NativeMenu instance to the menu of the SystemTrayIcon. If false, then instead assign the NativeMenu to the DockIcon menu. Once the NativeMenu has been assigned to the dock or system tray, assign it to the contextMenu of the backgroundContainer instance. The contextMenu is the menu that is accessed when the user right-clicks on the widget.

Minimizing, Restoring, and Setting AlwaysInFront

Minimizing and restoring the window is as easy as calling the minimize and restore methods of the NativeWindow instance. However, in Microsoft Windows, this will only minimize the application to the system's taskbar. It would be helpful to have the application fully disappear, leaving only the system tray icon. You can make the system taskbar instance disappear by setting the visible property of the NativeWindow to false. Just be sure to set it to true when the widget is restored; otherwise, the user will not be able to see the widget.

The NativeWindow instance also has an alwaysInFront property that accepts a Boolean. This is assigned anytime the settings have been changed. The value comes from WidgetDataModel.getInstance().settings.alwaysInFront. This property controls whether or not the widget resides in front of all open windows.

The widget now has a menu system and the ability to minimize, restore, and change view states. The next section discusses adding animation when changing view states.

Animating the Views

With the exception of the loader view instance, when the view states are added to the stage, their visible property is set to false. Each view state is defined in the <mx:states> view array. When the currentState property of the <mx:Application> class is changed, the specified <mx:SetProperty> tags are accessed, changing the visibility of the view states and the height and width of the backgroundContainer. For example, setting currentState equal to WeatherWidget.FOURDAY_FORECAST will execute the following set of <mx:SetProperty> instances:

```
<mx:State name="{WeatherWidget.FOURDAY_FORECAST}">
    <mx:SetProperty target="{loader}" name="visible" value="false" />
```

```
        <mx:SetProperty target="{cityLabel}" name="visible" value="true" />
        <mx:SetProperty target="{currentWeatherReport}"
            name="visible" value="false" />
        <mx:SetProperty target="{fullWeatherReport}"
            name="visible" value="true" />
        <mx:SetProperty target="{settingsWindow}"
            name="visible" value="false" />
        <mx:SetProperty target="{backgroundContainer}"
            name="width" value="{fullWeatherReport.width + 15}" />
        <mx:SetProperty target="{backgroundContainer}"
            name="height" value="{fullWeatherReport.height}" />
    </mx:State>
```

If you were to run the application with *just* the state changes, the window would immediately resize and the four-day forecast would be displayed. It would be nice to add a little animation to it. Creating a `<mx:Transition>` instance will do just that.

The `<mx:Transition>` is assigned a `fromState` and a `toState` value. In this case, if the widget changes states, it should be animated. The nested `<mx:Resize>` instance sets the action that will be executed during the transition. It is assigned the `backgroundContainer` as a `target` with a `duration` of 350 milliseconds and a `Quartic.easeOut` `easingFunction`. Once the transition is run, the `backgroundContainer` will animate to the new size as specified in the `<mx:SetProperty>` instance of the called `<mx:State>`. When the transition is finished, it accesses the `effectEnd` method, which in turn calls the `checkWidgetLocation` method, which checks to ensure that the weather widget is on the desktop. The result is a wonderfully animated state change.

Accessing the Data

The weather widget now has all four states set up with animations and menus. The last development step is loading the data in. The data model classes are set up and ready to go, you just have to access them. The ideal place to do this is in the `onCreationCompleteHandler` method that is called once the `<mx:Application>` has completed the instantiation.

First, create a reference to the `WidgetDataModel` instance and assign event listeners for the data change events:

```
    _dataModelInstance = WidgetDataModel.getInstance();
    _dataModelInstance.settings.settingsXMLLocation = "settings.xml";
    _dataModelInstance.addEventListener(
        WidgetDataModel.SETTINGS_CHANGE , onSettingsChange );
    _dataModelInstance.addEventListener(
        WidgetDataModel.CURRENT_FORECAST_CHANGE , onWeatherFeedLoad );
```

The `onSettingsChange` method checks whether a zip code is specified. If there isn't, it changes the view state to `WeatherWidget.SETTINGS`. If a zip code is specified, then `onSettingsChange` accesses the `loadWeatherFeed()` method. The settings methods are discussed in more detail earlier in this chapter.

The `onWeatherFeedLoad` method begins the interval timer, setting the `currentState` to the last state or to the default `WeatherWidget.CURRENT_FORECAST` state. It also sets up the `TrayIcon` with the latest current temperature and sets the private `_lastUpdated` string to the current time stamp. Last, it calls `buildNativeMenu`, which changes the `NativeMenu` to reflect the latest state and time stamp changes.

The final step is to instantiate the data loading process by creating a new `XMLFileService` instance that will load the `settings.xml` file. This was discussed earlier in the chapter when the `XMLFileService` was introduced.

Deploying the Application

If you tested the application at this point, it should execute, load in the data, and animate to the current day's weather view. The menus should be assigned and the tray icon should display. You are just about finished with your weather widget. The last step is to package the application so it can be deployed. The next section discusses creating the descriptor file and packaging the AIR application for distribution.

The Descriptor File

The final file needed in the creation of your weather widget is the application descriptor file. This XML file contains properties for the application, such as for the initial window settings, copyright, title, and icon URLs. It is packaged and distributed with the final deployable file.

Create a new document and enter the following markup:

```
<application xmlns="http://ns.adobe.com/air/application/1.0">
    <id>com.aircmr.WeatherWidget</id>
    <filename>WeatherWidget</filename>
    <version>0.1</version>
    <name>AIR WeatherWidget</name>
    <description></description>
    <copyright>2008</copyright>

    <initialWindow>
        <title/>
        <content>WeatherWidget.swf</content>
        <systemChrome>none</systemChrome>
        <transparent>true</transparent>
        <visible>true</visible>
    </initialWindow>

   <icon>
       <image16x16>icons/16x16.png</image16x16>
       <image32x32>icons/32x32.png</image32x32>
       <image48x48>icons/48x48.png</image48x48>
       <image128x128>icons/128x128.png</image128x128>
   </icon>

     <installFolder>AIRCMR/WeatherWidget</installFolder>
     <programMenuFolder>AIRCMR</programMenuFolder>
</application></application>
```

Save the file as `WeatherWidget-app.xml` in the root of your working directory along with the `WeatherWidget.mxml` and `settings.xml` files.

This file will be the descriptor file for the weather widget. Because the widget will have its own window design and interface, the `<systemChrome>` property is set to `none`, and `<transparent>` is set to `true`.

No widget is complete without a custom icon. Included on the CD-ROM in this chapter's directory are four icon files for the widget: 16×16, 32×32, 48×48, and 128×128 pixel icon sizes. If you do not have these icon images, remove the icon URLs from the `<icon>` node set; otherwise, an error will be thrown when you package the AIR application.

Compiling and Packaging

The final step in creating the weather widget is to compile and package it. If you are planning to add the icon files and haven't yet, make sure that you copy them to your working directory's `/icons` folder before proceeding. You should also be sure to clear out the `<zipCode>` data in the `settings.xml` file if you have edited the original file in your working directory. Once you have the icons (optional), `WeatherWidget.mxml`, `WeatherWidget-app.xml`, `settings.xml`, and the `assets/` directory available in your working directory, begin packaging the application by first compiling the `WeatherWidget.mxml` into a SWF.

Open a command prompt, navigate to the working directory for the weather widget, enter the following command, and press Enter:

```
> amxmlc WeatherWidget.mxml
```

With the command prompt still pointing to the working directory, package the widget as an AIR installer by entering the following command and pressing Enter:

```
> adt -package WeatherWidget WeatherWidget-app.xml WeatherWidget.swf
settings.xml /icons/
```

Once the package is created, navigate to your working directory. If the widget packaged correctly, you should have a `WeatherWidget.air` file. Execute the `WeatherWidget.air` package in order to install the application on your hard drive. Once it is installed, open it, enter your zip code, and enjoy the weather. In case you're having a rainy day, or a blizzard, quickly switch to the four-day view to see if your week will look up. If all else fails, type in a zip code that starts with 90 and see how the weather is in sunny California.

Summary

In this chapter, you learned how to create a fully functional, full-featured weather widget. The widget requests the user's zip code, queries Google's XML weather feed, and displays either the current forecast or the four-day forecast. It features a minimal, chromeless design with multiple view states and dynamic interaction with the system tray (or dock). Although this widget performs a very specific function, and has a specific look and feel, the concepts that went into building it can be applied to building an even better widget.

You can use this application as a stepping-stone to develop different widgets, or add to the existing set of features. For instance, it might be handy to be able to create multiple instances of the weather widget for someone who would like to monitor the weather in more than one location. The widget could query the National Weather Service and display weather warnings in the specified area. The branding of the weather widget can be changed so that it doesn't display the weather at all; instead it might have an illustration that changes based on the weather data. Overall, you can use this application to leverage your ideas to create simplified, multi-platform, killer widgets.

9

Map Application

Map applications are prevalent in today's online location-based activity. Whether you are looking for directions, locating the nearest hotels to your destination, or just seeing what it looks like to be a bird flying over your town, you are requesting information from one of the various services online that can tell you what turn to make, where to stay, and where to land. Many of these services have a public API that application developers can use to integrate into their own applications.

The map application you will build in this chapter will enable you to search for locations using one such online map API, add destination markers to locations, and view and edit saved destinations without regard to an available network resource. This program will continue to delve into the database API discussed in previous chapters and introduce you to bridging code between ActionScript and JavaScript in communicating with an online service.

Before you begin building the application, you should consider what you expect from a desktop map application. In order to utilize an online service to retrieve map information, the following goals should be addressed:

- Communication with an online API through JavaScript to search for locations and add destinations
- Communication with a local database to save, view, and edit destination information

The next section discusses how to achieve these goals.

Design

The map application you will build deals primarily in communication — how you communicate with an online API to gather and manipulate data, and how you communicate with a local database to save and edit that data. How that data is presented plays as vital a role as the data itself in retrieving and saving locations. This chapter's introduction targeted some primary goals to consider prior to building the map application. The following list expands on those goals:

- Communication with an online API through JavaScript to search for locations and add destinations — The online map API that you will use in this chapter is the Yahoo! Maps AJAX API. In utilizing this service, you will be introduced to working with the HTML control and learn how to bridge code between your AIR application and JavaScript. Since this service relies on an Internet connection, communication to the Yahoo! Maps AJAX API will be limited to the availability of a network resource.
- Communication with a local database to save, view and edit destination information — The map application will make use of the AIR database API to insert new entries as well as retrieve and update previously saved entries from a local database. Because saved entries are available from a local database, communication is not limited to a network resource and data can be accessed without an Internet connection.

Outlining these two goals brings to light the need for two distinct view modes within the map application. When a network resource is available, the option to switch between each view mode will be made available, enabling you to interface with an online map API and a local database — touching on both communication points discussed above. When no Internet connection is available, you will be limited to interaction with the database only, enabling you to edit and add to any saved locations.

The next section covers the value objects and overlying data model that will be used by the map application to display and save destinations-based locations.

Handling Data

The map application will handle data going to and coming from two separate sources — an HTML document interfacing with an online API and a local database. It is important to consider that while the data interpreted by these two services may be different, the map application itself will operate with a single type of model. With this in mind, your view classes won't have to fuss over how to deal with a certain type of data based on where it is being retrieved from or being sent to.

Interfacing with the Yahoo! Maps AJAX API and the local database will involve different controllers, but those controllers should know how to handle the same type of data to be interpreted between those services and the map application. The next section addresses generalizing that data.

Value Objects

There are two specific types of data the map application will display: locations and destinations. As discussed previously, this data will be going to and coming from different sources. It is important that the application can handle abstracting that data so that users, when viewing destination-based locations, can find "that place" without specifically knowing its coordinates on a map. As with most online map applications, visual markers are used to denote destinations on a specified location. As such, the AIR application handles two major types of data between both the online service and the database: locations and destination markers.

Within your development directory, create a folder titled "Locator." This will be your *working directory* for the application. With that set, create the following classes:

1. Open your favorite text editor, create a new document and enter the following ActionScript:

```
package com.aircmr.locator.data
{
    public interface IDBEntry
    {
        function serialize():void;
        function deserialize():void;
    }
}
```

2. Save the file as `IDBEntry.as` in a directory `com/aircmr/locator/data` within your working directory.
   You will see that the `serialize()` and `deserialize()` methods that are implemented by the following two value objects will escape and unescape string attributes, respectively. In order to process a statement to the database correctly, it is important to present that information without special characters, such as a space or quotation mark. Serializing data prepares its attribute values to be entered into a database properly. Deserializing data coming from the database presents the value object as it was originally entered by the user. With that in mind, any data held by the application that will be entered into a database will implement `IDBEntry`.

3. Create a new document and enter the following ActionScript:

```
package com.aircmr.locator.data
{
    import flash.events.EventDispatcher;

    [Bindable]
    public class LocationVO extends EventDispatcher
        implements IDBEntry
    {
        public var id:int;
        public var name:String;
        public var content:String;

        public function LocationVO( id:int = -1,
                                    name:String = "",
                                    content:String = "" )
        {
            this.id = id;
            this.name = name;
            this.content = content;
        }

        public function serialize():void
        {
            name = escape( name );
            content = escape( content );
        }
```

```
        public function deserialize():void
        {
            name = unescape( name );
            content = unescape( content );
        }
    }
}
```

4. Save the file as `LocationVO.as` in the directory `com/aircmr/locator/data` along with `IDBEntry.as`.

5. Create a new document and enter the following ActionScript:

```
package com.aircmr.locator.data
{
    public class MarkerVO implements IDBEntry
    {
        public var id:int;
        public var locationId:int;
        public var jsId:String;
        public var caption:String;
        public var x:Number;
        public var y:Number;

        public function MarkerVO( id:int = -1,
                                    locationId:int = -1,
                                    jsId:String = "",
                                    caption:String = "",
                                    xpos:Number = 0, ypos:Number = 0 )
        {
            this.id = id;
            this.locationId = locationId;
            this.jsId = jsId;
            this.caption = caption;
            this.x = xpos;
            this.y = ypos;
        }

        public function serialize():void
        {
            caption = escape( caption );
        }
        public function deserialize():void
        {
            caption = unescape( caption );
        }
    }
}
```

6. Save the file as `MarkerVO.as` in the directory `com/aircmr/locator/data` in your working directory.

The `LocationVO` and `MarkerVO` classes you have just created will serve as value objects to be interpreted while interfacing between the map application and the Yahoo! Maps AJAX API and the local database.

Each object implements the IDBEntry interface to encode and decode their string attributes to and from a URL-encoded format.

The LocationVO class holds information related to a location. The name property relates to the information entered by a user, and the content property represents the graphical content displayed.

The MarkerVO class holds information related to a destination. The x and y properties represent the coordinates of the destination on the screen. The jsId property pertains to the ID given to a marker added through the Yahoo! Maps AJAX API and the caption attribute is the user-inputted caption relating to that destination.

The id property on each of these value objects is the unique ID given to an object when it has been entered into a database. Notice that the ID on both these data objects is defaulted to a value of -1 during instantiation. The map application will use this value to determine whether the information is a new entry to the database or an existing entry to update.

The locationId attribute on MarkerVO is important. This value relates to the ID value given to a location held in the database. Thinking in terms of database structure that will be addressed later in this chapter, each of these value objects — LocationVO and MarkerVO — relates to two separate tables of data. By assigning a field in a destination relative to the unique ID given to a location, you can link destinations to locations using a relational database.

In the next section you will create the overlying model that clients will interact with to edit and update these location and destination data objects.

The Data Model

In the previous section, you created the information objects used to represent destinations-based locations. In this section, you will create the model to access and update that information. Since the map application enables you to work without an Internet connection, multiple views are needed to present information based on the availability of a network resource. By registering event listeners in multiple display classes to property updates from a common model, you can ensure that the data being displayed is consistant. The display views used by the Map Application are covered shortly, but first you can get to work on the model.

Create a new document and enter the following ActionScript:

```
package com.aircmr.locator.data
{
    import flash.events.EventDispatcher;

    import mx.collections.ArrayCollection;

    [Bindable]
    public class LocatorDataManager extends EventDispatcher
    {
        private static var _instance:LocatorDataManager = new LocatorDataManager();
        public var currentAddress:String;
        public var location:LocationVO;
        public var markers:ArrayCollection;    // MarkerVO[]
```

```
        public static function getInstance():LocatorDataManager
        {
            return _instance;
        }

        public function LocatorDataManager()
        {
            if( _instance != null )
            {
                // singleton warning...
            }
        }

        public function refresh():void
        {
            currentAddress = "";
            location = new LocationVO();
            markers = new ArrayCollection();
        }

        public function addMarker( marker:MarkerVO ):void
        {
            markers.addItem( marker );
        }
    }
}
```

Save the file as `LocatorDataManager.as` in the directory `com/aircmr/locator/data` in your working directory along with the value objects previously created.

The `LocationVO` and `MarkerVO` objects reflect table entries, with their respective attributes relating to specified fields in a database table. The `LocatorDataManager` acts as manager for this data, while employing the Singleton pattern to ensure that all clients are working with the same data at any given time. Also relative to the current location and destination data is the actual address — meaning that the name of a location, such as "my house," is different from the actual address that is used in geocoding. The `currentAddress` property will be updated based on user input, and used to locate maps from either the online service or the database.

With the value objects created and managed, it's time to build the logic for this data to be passed back and forth from a database. In the next section you create the classes that will send and retrieve location and destination data from the local database.

Querying the Database

The SQL relational database engine included in Adobe AIR enables you to store data locally in a database file. The service you create in this section will create that database file and the necessary tables, as well as run queries to store and retrieve location and destination information.

1. Create a new document and enter the following ActionScript:

```
package com.aircmr.locator.services
{
    import com.aircmr.locator.data.LocationVO;
    import com.aircmr.locator.data.MarkerVO;
    import com.aircmr.locator.data.QueryVO;
    import com.aircmr.locator.events.DBResultEvent;

    import flash.data.SQLConnection;
    import flash.data.SQLResult;
    import flash.data.SQLStatement;
    import flash.events.Event;
    import flash.events.EventDispatcher;
    import flash.events.SQLErrorEvent;
    import flash.events.SQLEvent;
    import flash.filesystem.File;

    [Event(name="creationComplete", type="flash.events.Event")]
    [Event(name="creationError", type="flash.events.Event")]
    final public class DBService extends EventDispatcher
    {
        private var _connection:SQLConnection;
        private var _statement:SQLStatement;
        private var _dbFile:File;

        private var _isOpen:Boolean;
        private var _queryQueue:Array;
        private var _currentQuery:QueryVO;
        private var _isRunningQuery:Boolean;

        private static const FALL_THROUGH:String = "";
        private static const CREATE_TABLE_LOC:String = "createLocations";
        private static const CREATE_TABLE_MARK:String = "createMarkers";

        public static const CREATION_COMPLETE:String = "creationComplete";
        public static const CREATION_ERROR:String = "creationError";

        private static const DB:String = "Locator.db";

        public function DBService()
        {
            _connection = new SQLConnection();
            _connection.addEventListener( SQLEvent.OPEN, onConnectionOpen );
            _connection.addEventListener( SQLEvent.CLOSE, onConnectionClose );
            _connection.addEventListener( SQLErrorEvent.ERROR, onConnectionError );

            _queryQueue = new Array();
            _dbFile = File.applicationStorageDirectory.resolvePath( DB );
            invalidate();
        }
```

```
private function invalidate():void
{
    _statement = new SQLStatement();
    _statement.sqlConnection = _connection;
    _statement.addEventListener(SQLEvent.RESULT, onCreationQueryResult);
    _statement.addEventListener(SQLErrorEvent.ERROR, onCreationQueryError);

    var sqlCreateLoc:String = "CREATE TABLE IF NOT EXISTS locations (" +
                              "id     INTEGER     PRIMARY KEY," +
                              "name     TEXT     NOT NULL," +
                              "content     TEXT     NOT NULL);";

    var sqlCreateMark:String = "CREATE TABLE IF NOT EXISTS markers (" +
                              "id     INTEGER PRIMARY KEY," +
                              "jsId     TEXT     NOT NULL," +
                              "locationId     TEXT     NOT NULL," +
                              "caption     TEXT     NOT NULL," +
                              "x     FLOAT     NOT NULL," +
                              "y     FLOAT     NOT NULL);";

    addQuery( new QueryVO( CREATE_TABLE_LOC, sqlCreateLoc ), false );
    addQuery( new QueryVO( CREATE_TABLE_MARK, sqlCreateMark ), true );
}

private function open():void
{
    if( _isOpen ) return;
    _connection.open( _dbFile );
}

private function executeNextQuery():void
{
    if( !_isOpen ) open();
    else
    {
        if( _queryQueue.length > 0 )
        {
            if( !_isRunningQuery ) _isRunningQuery = true;
            _currentQuery = _queryQueue.shift();
            _statement.text = _currentQuery.query;
            _statement.itemClass = _currentQuery.itemClass;
            _statement.execute();
        }
        else
        {
            _isRunningQuery = false;
            _currentQuery = null;
            _connection.close();
        }
    }
}

private function onConnectionOpen( evt:SQLEvent ):void
{
```

```
        _isOpen = true;
        if( _queryQueue.length > 0 ) executeNextQuery();
    }
    private function onConnectionClose( evt:SQLEvent ):void
    {
        _isOpen = false;
        if( _queryQueue.length > 0 )
        {
            _queryQueue.splice( 0, 0, _currentQuery );
            _currentQuery = null;
            _isRunningQuery = false;
        }
    }
    private function onConnectionError( evt:SQLErrorEvent ):void
    {
        trace( "Database connection error!" );
    }

    private function onCreationQueryResult( evt:SQLEvent ):void
    {
        if( _queryQueue.length > 0 )
        {
            executeNextQuery();
        }
        else
        {
            _statement = new SQLStatement();
            _statement.sqlConnection = _connection;
            _statement.addEventListener( SQLEvent.RESULT, onQueryResult );
            _statement.addEventListener( SQLErrorEvent.ERROR, onQueryError );
            dispatchEvent( new Event( CREATION_COMPLETE ) );
            _isRunningQuery = false;
        }
    }

    private function onCreationQueryError( evt:SQLErrorEvent ):void
    {
        dispatchEvent( new Event( CREATION_ERROR ) );
        _isRunningQuery = false;
    }

    private function onQueryResult( evt:SQLEvent ):void
    {
        var result:SQLResult = _statement.getResult();
        if( _currentQuery.type != FALL_THROUGH )
            dispatchEvent( new DBResultEvent( _currentQuery.type, result ) );

        executeNextQuery();
    }
    private function onQueryError( evt:SQLErrorEvent ):void
    {
        dispatchEvent( evt );
        _isRunningQuery = false;
    }
```

```
public function saveLocation( location:LocationVO ):void
{
    location.serialize();
    var sqlSave:String;
    var sqlSelect:String;
    if( location.id == -1 )
    {
        // add new location...
        sqlSave = "INSERT INTO locations VALUES (" +
                              "null," +
                              "'" + location.name + "'," +
                              "'" + location.content + "');";
        sqlSelect = "SELECT * FROM locations ORDER BY id DESC LIMIT 1;";
    }
    else
    {
        // update saved location...
        sqlSave = "UPDATE locations SET " +
                  "name='" + location.name + "'," +
                  "content='" + location.content + "' " +
                  "WHERE id='" + location.id + "';";
        sqlSelect = "SELECT * FROM locations WHERE id='" +
                      location.id + "';";
    }
    addQuery( new QueryVO( FALL_THROUGH, sqlSave ), false );
    addQuery( new QueryVO(DBResultEvent.LOCATION_SAVED, sqlSelect), true );
    location.deserialize();
}

public function saveMarker( marker:MarkerVO ):void
{
    marker.serialize();
    var sqlSave:String;
    var sqlSelect:String;
    if( marker.id == -1 )
    {
        // add new marker...
        sqlSave = "INSERT INTO markers VALUES (" +
                              "null," +
                              "'" + marker.jsId + "'," +
                              "'" + marker.locationId + "'," +
                              "'" + marker.caption + "'," +
                              "'" + marker.x + "'," +
                              "'" + marker.y + "');";
        sqlSelect = "SELECT * FROM markers ORDER BY id DESC LIMIT 1;";
    }
    else
    {
        // update saved marker...
        sqlSave = "UPDATE markers SET " +
                  "locationId='" + marker.locationId + "'," +
                  "caption='" + marker.caption + "'," +
                  "x='" + marker.x + "'," +
```

```
                    "y='" + marker.y + "' " +
                    "WHERE id='" + marker.id + "';";
            sqlSelect = "SELECT * FROM markers WHERE id='" + marker.id + "';";
        }
        addQuery( new QueryVO( FALL_THROUGH, sqlSave ), false );
        addQuery( new QueryVO( DBResultEvent.MARKER_SAVED, sqlSelect ),true );
        marker.deserialize();
    }

    public function retrieveLocation( location:String ):void
    {
        var sqlSelect:String = "SELECT * FROM locations WHERE " +
                               "name='" + escape( location ) + "' " +
                               "LIMIT 1;";
        addQuery( new QueryVO( DBResultEvent.LOCATION_RETRIEVED, sqlSelect,
                                                          LocationVO ) );
    }

    public function retrieveAllLocations():void
    {
        var sqlSelect:String = "SELECT DISTINCT name FROM locations;";
        addQuery( new QueryVO(DBResultEvent.LOCATION_RETRIEVED_ALL,
                              sqlSelect, LocationVO ) );
    }

    public function retrieveMarkersFromLocation( id:int ):void
    {
        var sqlSelect:String = "SELECT * FROM markers WHERE " +
                               "locationId='" + id + "';"
        addQuery( new QueryVO( DBResultEvent.MARKER_RETRIEVED_ALL, sqlSelect,
                                                          MarkerVO ) );
    }

    public function addQuery( query:QueryVO, run:Boolean = true ):void
    {
        _queryQueue.push( query );
        if( !_isRunningQuery && run ) runQuery();
    }

    public function runQuery():void
    {
        if( _queryQueue.length > 0 ) executeNextQuery();
    }

    public function shutDown():void
    {
        if( _isRunningQuery )
        {
            _statement.removeEventListener(SQLEvent.RESULT, onQueryResult);
            _statement.removeEventListener(SQLErrorEvent.ERROR, onQueryError);
        }
        close();
    }
```

```
        public function close():void
        {
            if( _isOpen ) _connection.close();
        }
    }
}
```

2. Save the file as `DBService.as` in `com/aircmr/locator/services` within your working directory.

3. Create a new document and enter the following ActionScript:

```
package com.aircmr.locator.events
{
    import flash.data.SQLResult;
    import flash.events.Event;

    public class DBResultEvent extends Event
    {
        private var _result:SQLResult;

        public static const LOCATION_SAVED:String = "locationSaved";
        public static const LOCATION_RETRIEVED:String = "locationRetrieved";
        public static const LOCATION_RETRIEVED_ALL:String = "locationRetrievedAll";
        public static const MARKER_SAVED:String = "markerSaved";
        public static const MARKER_RETRIEVED:String = "markerRetrieved";
        public static const MARKER_RETRIEVED_ALL:String = "markerRetrievedAll";

        public function DBResultEvent( type:String, sqlResult:SQLResult )
        {
            super( type );
            _result = sqlResult;
        }

        public function get result():SQLResult
        {
            return _result;
        }
    }
}
```

4. Save the file as `DBResultEvent.as` in a directory `com/aircmr/locator/events` within your working directory.

5. Create a new document and enter the following ActionScript:

```
package com.aircmr.locator.data
{
    public class QueryVO
    {
        public var type:String;
        public var query:String;
        public var itemClass:Class;

        public function QueryVO( type:String, query:String,
                                        itemClass:Class = null )
```

```
        {
            this.type = type;
            this.query = query;
            this.itemClass = itemClass;
        }
    }
}
```

6. Save the file as `QueryVO.as` in the directory `com/aircmr/locator/data` in your working directory.

The first snippet, saved as `DBService.as`, is the service class that will interact with the database by running SQL query statements. This service will be instantiated from the main application class, which acts as an access point for views requesting specified data from the database. Upon creation of the `DBService` instance, an instance of `flash.data.SQLConnection` is created. The `SQLConnection` instance manages the connection to local database files and is supplied as the `sqlConnection` property of a `flash.data.SQLStatement` object:

```
public function DBService()
{
    _connection = new SQLConnection();
    _connection.addEventListener( SQLEvent.OPEN, onConnectionOpen );
    _connection.addEventListener( SQLEvent.CLOSE, onConnectionClose );
    _connection.addEventListener( SQLErrorEvent.ERROR, onConnectionError );

    _queryQueue = new Array();
    _dbFile = File.applicationStorageDirectory.resolvePath( DB );
    invalidate();
}
```

Along with the creation of a `SQLConnection`, the database file named `Locator.db` is created, if not already available, in the application storage directory. Unlike the application directory, which allows only read access to applications, you can read and write to the application storage directory, which is accessed from the static `applicationStorageDirectory` property of the `flash.filesystem.File` class.

In Windows, you can find the application storage directory in `C:\Documents and Settings\<username>\Application Data\<application name>\Local Store`. *On a Mac, the application storage directory is found in* `/Users/<username>/Library/Preferences/<application name>/Local Store`.

With an open connection to a database, SQL queries can be run using a `flash.data.SQLStatement` object. The `DBService` class manages queries through a queue, which can be added using the public `addQuery()` method:

```
public function addQuery( query:QueryVO, run:Boolean = true ):void
{
    _queryQueue.push( query );
    if( !_isRunningQuery && run ) runQuery();
}

public function runQuery():void
{
    if( _queryQueue.length > 0 ) executeNextQuery();
}
```

The third snippet, saved as QueryVO and supplied as the first argument for the addQuery() method, represents the query objects added to this managed queue. The three attributes held on QueryVO are type, query and itemClass which relate to the kind of query being made, the query statement string to execute, and the class to map the result data to, respectively. The SQLStatement class has the capability to map result data from a database query to a specified class, allowing you to work seamlessly with data retrieved from the database without having to parse and replace the property data manually. To map data to a specified class, you use the itemClass property of the SQLStatement class. A reference to this class is passed into the QueryVO object which is used for each new query.

All query types to be run and broadcast that are related to destination-based locations are listed in the DBResultEvent class — saved as the second snippet. As SQL statements are completed, the DBService dispatches DBResultEvent instances with an event type matching that of the type property of the QueryVO instance. The result property of a DBResultEvent is the data returned from the SQL query.

Take a look at one of the public methods that adds a query to the queue to be run:

```
public function retrieveAllLocations():void
{
    var sqlSelect:String = "SELECT DISTINCT name FROM locations;";
    addQuery(new QueryVO(DBResultEvent.LOCATION_RETRIEVED_ALL, sqlSelect));
}
```

The retrieveAllLocations() method calls to add a new QueryVO object to the queue, with the type value set to the LOCATION_RETRIEVED_ALL constant on DBResultEvent, and the query value set to a SQL statement that will select each name from all records held in the table titled locations in the local database Locator.db created upon initialization of the DBService. Upon receiving a result from the executed SQL statement, a new DBResultEvent is dispatched, with the type given to the QueryVO and the result of the query:

```
private function onQueryResult( evt:SQLEvent ):void
{
    var result:SQLResult = _statement.getResult();
    if( _currentQuery.type != FALL_THROUGH )
        dispatchEvent( new DBResultEvent( _currentQuery.type, result ) );
    executeNextQuery();
}
```

Unfortunately, all the possible statements and column types and constraints available in SQLite, the SQL engine included in Adobe AIR, is too much to cover in this chapter, and you're encouraged to read the documentation available from Adobe. However, short of covering all the statements run by DBService relating to storage and retrieval of location and destination data, the invalidate() method is of note.

Within the invalidate() method called from the constructor, two tables are created, if not previously existent, in the local database using the CREATE IF NOT EXISTS clause. These tables — titled locations and markers — will store the location and destination data available to the application and used in executing any subsequent queries on the database. Updates to the database are performed in the public saveLocation() and saveMarker() methods using the respective id properties of the LocationVO and MarkerVO objects to either insert a new entry or update an existing one.

Now that you have data objects to represent locations and destinations, and a means to store data locally, it's time to get to work on visually presenting this data. The next section discusses building the user interface that will enable you to access, manipulate, and save destination-based locations.

Building the User Interface

The user interface controls available from the map application are based on the availability of a network resource. You have the capability to work with online data, which is dependent on an Internet connection, and the capability to work with saved data, which doesn't require an Internet connection. As such, the map application has three primary views:

- **Mode control view** — The mode control view responds to the loss or gain of an Internet connection and enables a user to choose whether to work with data stored locally or data coming from an online map API.
- **Display view** — The display view updates its view based on the mode control. When a user opts or is forced to work offline, the display will render any saved graphics and markers upon selection of a location. While working online, the user can navigate and download graphics from the API presented in the display view.
- **Location control view** — The location control view updates its interface controls based on the mode control and enables a user to add, search, and edit locations.

The next section addresses the mode control from this list of primary views that affects the display states of the location control and map graphic views.

Handling View Modes

The map application enables a user to navigate locations and place markers. If an Internet connection is available, locations can be accessed through an online service or from saved data. If an Internet connection is not present, then only the stored data is available. The main application class you will create later in this chapter recognizes the option to connect to an online service, so the classes you will create in this section reflect that and present the option to work with either stored (offline) data or online data:

1. Open your favorite editor, create a new document and enter in the following ActionScript:

```
package com.aircmr.locator.ui
{
    public class ModeType
    {
        public static const ONLINE:String = "online";
        public static const OFFLINE:String = "offline";
    }
}
```

2. Save the file as `ModeType.as` in the directory `com/aircmr/locator/ui` in your working directory.

3. Create a new document and enter the following markup:

```
<?xml version="1.0" encoding="utf-8"?>
<mx:HBox xmlns:mx="http://www.adobe.com/2006/mxml"
    width="100%" height="100%"
    verticalAlign="middle"
    enabled="{isAvailable}"
    creationComplete="onCreationComplete();">

    <mx:Metadata>
        [Event(name="modeChanged", type="flash.events.Event")]
    </mx:Metadata>

    <mx:Script>
        <![CDATA[
            import mx.binding.utils.BindingUtils;

            private var _mode:String;
            private var _isAvailable:Boolean;

            public static const MODE_CHANGE:String = "modeChanged";

            private function onCreationComplete():void
            {
                BindingUtils.bindSetter( invalidateAvailability,
                                            this, "isAvailable" );
            }

            private function invalidateAvailability( args:* ):void
            {
                if( !_isAvailable && _mode == ModeType.ONLINE )
                {
                    mode = ModeType.OFFLINE;
                }
                else if( !(_mode != ModeType.OFFLINE && _isAvailable ) )
                {
                    mode = _isAvailable ? ModeType.ONLINE : ModeType.OFFLINE;
                }
            }

            private function onModeSelection():void
            {
                mode = modeGroup.selectedValue.toString();
            }

            private function getModeLabel( available:Boolean ):String
            {
                var str:String = "Network resource ";
                str += available ? "available." : "unavailable.";
                return str;
            }

            [Bindable]
            public function get isAvailable():Boolean
```

```
            {
                return _isAvailable;
            }
            public function set isAvailable( bool:Boolean ):void
            {
                _isAvailable = bool;
            }

            [Bindable("modeChanged")]
            public function get mode():String
            {
                return _mode;
            }
            public function set mode( str:String ):void
            {
                _mode = str;
                dispatchEvent( new Event( ModeControls.MODE_CHANGE ) );
            }

        ]]>
    </mx:Script>

    <mx:Label id="availableField" text="{getModeLabel(isAvailable)}" />
    <mx:VRule height="100%" />
    <mx:Label text="Search Mode:" />
    <mx:RadioButtonGroup id="modeGroup"
        change="onModeSelection();"
        selectedValue="{isAvailable ? ModeType.ONLINE : ModeType.OFFLINE}"
        />
    <mx:RadioButton id="onlineRB"
        groupName="modeGroup"
        value="{ModeType.ONLINE}"
        label="{ModeType.ONLINE}"
        />
    <mx:RadioButton id="offlineRB"
        groupName="modeGroup"
        value="{ModeType.OFFLINE}"
        label="{ModeType.OFFLINE}"
        />

</mx:HBox>
```

4. Save the file as `ModeControls.mxml` in the directory `com/aircmr/locator/ui` in your working directory along with the `ModeTypes.as` class previously created.

The first snippet, saved as `ModeTypes.as`, holds a list of possible modes for the map application. Since the application is only concerned with knowing whether the user would like to work with stored data or communicate with an online service, the available types are `offline` and `online`. This should not be misconstrued as the availability of a network resource, however, as a user has the option to work with saved (offline) data while connected to the Internet. The types listed in the `ModeTypes` class will be used to determine the current `mode` property updated and controlled by the second snippet — saved as `ModeControls.mxml`.

The ModeControls component displays RadioButton controls to select the mode that the map application is working under. As the mode property is updated, an event is dispatched for any clients that need to know of a change. While connected to the Internet, the user has a choice of mode and is dependent on the isAvailable property value being true. Within the creationComplete event handler, the invalidateAvailability() function is bound to the isAvailable property. Upon update of the isAvailable property, the invlidateAvailability()method is invoked, which determines the mode based on network resource availability and the current mode:

```
private function invalidateAvailability( args:* ):void
{
      if( !_isAvailable && _mode == ModeType.ONLINE )
      {
         mode = ModeType.OFFLINE;
      }
      else if( !(_mode != ModeType.OFFLINE && _isAvailable ) )
      {
         mode = _isAvailable ? ModeType.ONLINE : ModeType.OFFLINE;
      }
}
```

The status of connectivity to the online service is monitored by another client that informs the ModeControls component of any changes. The enablement of the component is determined by the value of the isAvailable property as well as the view based on the current state. The invalidateAvailability ()method ensures that if a user was working offline previously and any change to the network resource is made, listening clients are not notified from the update of the mode property.

With the control that the ModeControls component provides for selection of user mode, you can begin working on the view controls that respond to the selected mode type.

Displaying Locations

As opposed to looking at a list of geographical points, the map application graphically presents locations and enables users to mark destinations. Depending on the mode that is determined from user interaction and a network resource, there are two separate map displays. While working online, an HTML control is available to communicate with an online map API and renders graphics sent over HTTP. When working offline, an Image component displays graphics loaded from saved data.

1. Create a new document and enter the following markup:

```
<?xml version="1.0" encoding="utf-8"?>
<mx:Box xmlns:mx="http://www.adobe.com/2006/mxml"
    width="100%" height="100%"
    verticalAlign="middle" horizontalAlign="center"
    dragEnter="onDragEnter(event);"
    creationComplete="onCreationComplete();">

    <mx:Metadata>
        [Event(name="change", type="flash.events.Event")]
        [Event(name="complete", type="flash.events.Event")]
        [Event(name="prepared", type="flash.events.Event")]
        [Event(name="requestLocation", type="flash.events.Event")]
```

```
</mx:Metadata>

<mx:Script>
    <![CDATA[
        import com.aircmr.locator.data.LocatorDataManager;
        import com.aircmr.locator.data.MarkerVO;
        import com.aircmr.locator.util.ImageFileBuffer;
        import mx.binding.utils.BindingUtils;
        import mx.collections.ArrayCollection;
        import mx.events.DragEvent;
        import mx.managers.DragManager;
        import mx.managers.PopUpManager;

        [Bindable]
        private var _data:LocatorDataManager;
        private var _mode:String;
        private var _htmlLocation:String;
        private var _isMapAvailable:Boolean;

        private var _tempMarker:MarkerVO;
        private var _markerForm:MarkerForm;

        public static const MAP_HEIGHT:int = 424;
        public static const MAP_WIDTH:int = 424;
        public static const CHANGE:String = "change";
        public static const COMPLETE:String = "complete";
        public static const PREPARED:String = "prepared";
        public static const REQUEST_LOCATION:String = "requestLocation";

        private function onCreationComplete():void
        {
            _data = LocatorDataManager.getInstance();
            BindingUtils.bindSetter(invalidateAddress,_data,"currentAddress");
            BindingUtils.bindSetter(invalidateMode,this,"mode");
        }

        private function invalidateMode( arg:* ):void
        {
            switch( _mode )
            {
                case ModeType.ONLINE:
                    if( _isMapAvailable )
                        map.domWindow.showDefault();
                    displayCtrl.selectedChild = onlineCtrl;
                    break;
                case ModeType.OFFLINE:
                    displayCtrl.selectedChild = offlineCtrl;
                    if( image == null ) return;
                    image.source = null;
                    markerLayer.removeAllChildren();
                    break;
            }
        }
```

```
private function invalidateAddress( arg:* ):void
{
    switch( _mode )
    {
        case ModeType.ONLINE:
               map.domWindow.locateAddress( unescape(
                                               _data.currentAddress ) );
               map.domWindow.returnMarkers = onHTMLMarkers;
               map.domWindow.returnClean = onMapPrepared;
            break;
        case ModeType.OFFLINE:
            markerLayer.removeAllChildren();
            dispatchEvent(new Event(LocationDisplay.REQUEST_LOCATION));
            break;
    }
}

private function onMapLoadComplete():void
{
    _isMapAvailable = true;
    dispatchEvent( new Event( LocationDisplay.COMPLETE ) );
}
private function onMapLocationChange():void
{
    dispatchEvent( new Event( LocationDisplay.CHANGE ) );
}

private function onHTMLMarkers( value:Object, ...args ):void
{
    if( value == null ) return;
    var jsMarkers:* = value;
    var markers:ArrayCollection = _data.markers;
    for( var i:int = 0; i < jsMarkers.length; i++ )
    {
        var jsMarker:Object = jsMarkers[i];
        var marker:MarkerVO;
        var xyPt:Object = jsMarker._xy;
        for( var j:int = 0; j < markers.length; j++ )
        {
            marker = markers.getItemAt(j) as MarkerVO;
            if( marker.jsId == jsMarker.id )
            {
                marker.locationId = _data.location.id;
                marker.x = xyPt.x;
                marker.y = xyPt.y;
            }
        }
    }
    map.domWindow.clean();
}

private function onMapPrepared():void
{
    if( _data.location.content != "" )
```

```
        {
            // overwrite image file...
            ImageFileBuffer.bufferImage( map,
                            _data.location.content.replace( /.png/, '' ) );
        }
        else
        {
            // create new image file...
            _data.location.content = ImageFileBuffer.bufferImage( map,
                                    ( new Date().getTime() ).toString() );
        }
        map.domWindow.reset();
        dispatchEvent( new Event( LocationDisplay.PREPARED ) );
    }

    private function onDragEnter( evt:DragEvent ):void
    {
        dropCanvas.mouseEnabled = true;
        if( mode == ModeType.ONLINE )
        {
            map.domWindow.disableDrag();
        }
          DragManager.acceptDragDrop( dropCanvas );
    }

    private function onDragExit( evt:DragEvent ):void
    {
        dropCanvas.mouseEnabled = false;
        if( mode == ModeType.ONLINE )
        {
            map.domWindow.enableDrag();
        }
    }

    private function onDragDrop( evt:DragEvent ):void
    {
        dropCanvas.mouseEnabled = false;
        switch( mode )
        {
            case ModeType.ONLINE:
                var jsMarker:Object =
                  map.domWindow.addTempMarkerAt( evt.localX, evt.localY );
                _tempMarker = new MarkerVO( -1, -1, jsMarker.id );
                map.domWindow.enableDrag();
                break;
            case ModeType.OFFLINE:
                _tempMarker = evt.dragSource.dataForFormat("marker")
                                                        as MarkerVO;
                _tempMarker.x = evt.localX;
                _tempMarker.y = evt.localY;
                addMarker( _tempMarker, true );
                break;
        }
        openMarkerForm();
```

```
        }

        private function openMarkerForm():void
        {
            _markerForm = ( PopUpManager.createPopUp( this, MarkerForm, true )
                                                            as MarkerForm );
            _markerForm.x = x + ( width - _markerForm.width ) / 2;
            _markerForm.y = y + ( height - _markerForm.height ) / 2;
            _markerForm.data = _tempMarker;
            _markerForm.addEventListener( MarkerForm.CANCEL, onMarkerCancel );
            _markerForm.addEventListener( MarkerForm.SAVE, onMarkerSave );
        }
        private function closeMarkerForm():void
        {
            _tempMarker = null;
            PopUpManager.removePopUp( _markerForm );
        }

        private function onMarkerCancel( evt:Event ):void
        {
            if( mode == ModeType.ONLINE )
            {
                map.domWindow.removeMarker( _tempMarker.jsId );
            }
            else
            {
                markerLayer.removeChildAt( markerLayer.numChildren - 1 );
            }
            closeMarkerForm();
        }
        private function onMarkerSave( evt:Event ):void
        {
            _tempMarker.caption = unescape(
                escape(_tempMarker.caption).split( "%0D" ).join( "<br/>" ) );
            _data.addMarker( _tempMarker );
            if( mode == ModeType.ONLINE )
            {
                map.domWindow.saveMessageToMarker( _tempMarker.caption );
            }
            closeMarkerForm();
        }

        public function addMarker(value:MarkerVO, isTemp:Boolean = false):void
        {
            var marker:Marker = new Marker();
            marker.data = value;
            marker.x = value.x;
            marker.y = value.y - marker.height;
            markerLayer.addChild( marker );
            if( !isTemp ) _data.addMarker( value );
        }

        public function prepareForSave():void
        {
```

```
            if( mode == ModeType.ONLINE )
            {
                map.domWindow.getAllVisibleMarkers();
            }
              else dispatchEvent( new Event( LocationDisplay.PREPARED ) );
        }

        [Bindable]
        public function get mode():String
        {
            return _mode;
        }
        public function set mode( str:String ):void
        {
            _mode = str;
        }

        [Bindable]
        public function get htmlLocation():String
        {
            return _htmlLocation;
        }
        public function set htmlLocation( str:String ):void
        {
            _htmlLocation = str;
            map.location = _htmlLocation;
        }

    ]]>
</mx:Script>

<mx:Canvas width="{MAP_WIDTH}" height="{MAP_HEIGHT}">
    <mx:ViewStack id="displayCtrl"
        width="100%" height="100%">
        <mx:Canvas id="onlineCtrl"
            width="100%" height="100%">
            <mx:HTML id="map"
                width="{MAP_WIDTH}" height="{MAP_HEIGHT}"
                complete="onMapLoadComplete();"
                locationChange="onMapLocationChange();"
                />
        </mx:Canvas>
        <mx:Canvas id="offlineCtrl"
            width="100%" height="100%"
            borderStyle="solid" borderColor="0x999999">
            <mx:Image id="image"
                width="100%" height="100%"
                source="{_data.location.content}"
                />
            <mx:Canvas id="markerLayer"
                width="100%" height="100%"
                />
        </mx:Canvas>
    </mx:ViewStack>
```

```
        <mx:Canvas id="dropCanvas"
            width="100%" height="100%"
            alpha="0" backgroundColor="0x000000"
            dragEnter="onDragEnter(event);"
            dragDrop="onDragDrop(event);"
            dragExit="onDragExit(event);"
            mouseEnabled="false"
            />
    </mx:Canvas>

</mx:Box>
```

2. Save the file as `LocationDisplay.mxml` in the directory `com/aircmr/locator/ui` within your working directory.

3. Create a new document and enter the following ActionScript:

```
package com.aircmr.locator.util
{
    import flash.display.BitmapData;
    import flash.display.DisplayObject;
    import flash.filesystem.File;
    import flash.filesystem.FileMode;
    import flash.filesystem.FileStream;
    import flash.utils.ByteArray;

    import mx.graphics.codec.PNGEncoder;

    public class ImageFileBuffer
    {
        private static const STORAGE_DIR:String = "app-storage:/";
        public static const FILE_EXTENSION:String = ".png";

        public static function bufferImage( target:DisplayObject, name:String,
                                            w:Number = 0, h:Number = 0 ):String
        {
            var width:Number = ( w == 0 ) ? target.width : w;
            var height:Number = ( h == 0 ) ? target.height : h;
            var file:File = new File();
            file.url = STORAGE_DIR;
            file = file.resolvePath( name + FILE_EXTENSION );
            var bmp:BitmapData = new BitmapData( width, height );
            bmp.draw( target );
            var bytes:ByteArray = new PNGEncoder().encode( bmp );
            var stream:FileStream = new FileStream();
            stream.open( file, FileMode.WRITE );
            stream.writeBytes( bytes );
            stream.close();

            return STORAGE_DIR + file.name;
        }
    }
}
```

4. Save the file as `ImageFileBuffer.as` in the directory `com/aircmr/locator/util` within your working directory.

The first snippet, saved as LocationDisplay.mxml, is the main view class for displaying graphical locations and interfacing with DOM objects and methods of the HTML control. Based on the mode property bound to the invalidateMode() method, whether to display the HTML or Image controls within the ViewStack container is determined.

When a user chooses to save the current location, snapshots of the current map graphics rendered in the HTML control are made and saved to the application storage directory using the static bufferImage() method of the ImageFileBuffer class. The path returned is stored as the content value for a location, available on the LocationVO object, which is bound to the source property of the Image control.

To set destination markers on locations, the drag-and-drop API of the Flex framework is used by the dropCanvas container to recognize and respond to mouse gestures occurring over the graphic display. The LocationDisplay component handles adding those markers to the display, as well as their data to the LocatorDataManager Singleton.

Within the htmlLocation property setter, the location property of the HTML control is updated. When working in offline mode, the selected view displays any saved graphics related to a location. When working online, the map graphics are returned from the Yahoo! Maps AJAX API. Communication to that API is made from JavaScript methods within an HTML document loaded by the HTML control. Dot-notation syntax is used to access the JavaScript properties and methods available on an HTML control through the domWindow property. When the currentAddress property of the LocatorDataManager is updated, the invalidateAddress() method of the LocationDisplay instance is invoked, and, based on the selected mode, communication with the HTML Document Object Model (DOM) is made.

```
map.domWindow.locateAddress( unescape( _data.currentAddress ) );
map.domWindow.returnMarkers = onHTMLMarkers;
map.domWindow.returnClean = onMapPrepared;
```

Being able to bridge communication between ActionScript and JavaScript is an incredible asset to the AIR API, and this snippet demonstrates that you can call JavaScript methods directly and even assign ActionScript methods to method calls from JavaScript. With this type of interaction, you can perform AJAX operations rendered directly in the Flash Player! To fully grasp how the map application uses the Yahoo! Maps AJAX API to display graphics and markers, create the HTML document that will be loaded into the LocationDisplay component.

The HTML Document

The mx.controls.HTML control renders HTML content in an AIR application. The location property can be a URL of an HTML document available on a server or a path found on your file system. The map application will be packaged with the HTML document, which will be copied over and loaded from the application storage directory, and used to communicate with the Yahoo! Maps AJAX API.

Create a new document and enter the following markup:

```
<html>
    <head>
        <style type="text/css">
            #mapContainer {
              height: 424px;
              width: 424px;
            }
        </style>
```

```
        <script type="text/javascript"
    src="http://api.maps.yahoo.com/ajaxymap?v=3.7&appid=YOUR_ID_HERE"></script>
      </head>
      <body>
          <div id="mapContainer" />
          <script type="text/javascript">

              var tempMarker;
              var markers = new Array();
              var map = new YMap( document.getElementById( 'mapContainer' ),
                                                               YAHOO_MAP_REG );
              map.addZoomLong();
              YEvent.Capture( map, EventsList.onEndGeoCode, onGeoCodeResult );
              showDefault();

              function showDefault()
              {
                  map.removeMarkersAll();
                  map.drawZoomAndCenter(new YGeoPoint( 42.358028, -71.060417 ), 16);
              }

              function locateAddress( address )
              {
                  map.geoCodeAddress( address );
              }

              function onGeoCodeResult( result )
              {
                  map.drawZoomAndCenter( result.GeoPoint, 5 );
              }

              // update xy position of visible marker in latlon - called from
              // getAllVisibleMarkers
              function updateMarker( marker )
              {
                  marker._xy = map.convertLatLonXY( new YGeoPoint(
                                                    marker.YGeoPoint.Lat,
                                                    marker.YGeoPoint.Lon ) );
              }

              function clean()
              {
                  map.removeZoomControl();
                  hideMarkers();
                  setTimeout("returnClean()", 1000 );
              }

              function reset()
              {
                  map.addZoomLong();
                  showMarkers();
              }

              function disableDrag()
```

```
{
    map.disableDragMap();
}
function enableDrag()
{
    map.enableDragMap();
}

function hideMarkers()
{
    for( var i = 0; i < markers.length; i++ )
    {
        removeMarker( markers[i].id );
    }
}

function showMarkers()
{
    var marker;
    for( var i = 0; i < markers.length; i++ )
    {
        marker = markers.shift();
        updateMarker( marker );
        addTempMarkerAt( marker._xy.x, marker._xy.y, marker.id );
        saveMessageToMarker( marker.message );
    }
}

function convertLatLonXY( pt )
{
    return map.convertLatLonXT( pt );
}

function inBounds( marker, bounds )
{
    var pt = marker.YGeoPoint;
    return ( pt.Lat > bounds.LatMin &&
                pt.Lat < bounds.LatMax &&
                pt.Lon > bounds.LonMin &&
                pt.Lon < bounds.LonMax );
}

function getAllVisibleMarkers()
{
    var bounds = map.getBoundsLatLon();
    var arr = new Array();
    for( i = 0; i < markers.length; i++ )
    {
        updateMarker( markers[i] );
        if( inBounds( markers[i], bounds ) ) arr.push( markers[i] );
    }
    returnMarkers( arr );
}
```

```
            // arr = MarkerVO[] array from AS
            function addMarkers( arr )
            {
                for( var i = 0; i < arr.length; i++ )
                {
                    map.addOverlay( new YMarker( new YGeoPoint( arr[i].latitude,
                                                                arr[i].longitude ),
                                                                arr[i].jsId ) );
                }
            }

            function addTempMarkerAt( x, y, id )
            {
                var pt = map.convertXYLatLon( new YCoordPoint( x, y ) );
                tempMarker = new YMarker( pt, id );
                map.addOverlay( tempMarker );
                return tempMarker;
            }

            function saveMessageToMarker( msg )
            {
                tempMarker.message = msg;
                markers.push( tempMarker );
                var addMarker = markers[markers.length -1];
                YEvent.Capture( addMarker, EventsList.MouseClick,
                                function() { addMarker.openSmartWindow( msg ) } );
                tempMarker = null;
            }

            function removeMarker( id )
            {
                map.removeMarker( id );
            }
        </script>
    </body>
</html>
```

Save the file as `ymap.html` in the root of your working directory.

> *You need to register for an application ID in order to use the Yahoo! Maps AJAX API. To do so, go to* `https://developer.yahoo.com/wsregapp/index.php`*. Once you have an application ID, replace the "*`YOUR_ID_HERE`*" placeholder in the* `<script>` *tag of* `ymap.html` *with the ID you have obtained.*

When this file is loaded into the `HTML` control of the `LocationDisplay` component, a new `YMap` object from the Yahoo! Maps AJAX API is created and a default location set is fully zoomed out. The map application will interface with this `YMap` control in displaying locations and destinations markers while working online.

The JavaScript methods available on the `ymap.html` file produce numerous access points to communicate with the Yahoo! Map AJAX API. For the purposes of the map application you are building, the capabilities to drag and download map graphics, as well as add and remove markers, are available. Access to all these methods and properties is available from the `domWindow` property of the `HTML` control. As discussed previously, you can assign ActionScript methods as handlers for JavaScript method calls, as shown when the application is requesting all the visible markers:

```
function getAllVisibleMarkers()
{
    var bounds = map.getBoundsLatLon();
    var arr = new Array();
    for( i = 0; i < markers.length; i++ )
    {
        updateMarker( markers[i] );
        if( inBounds( markers[i], bounds ) ) arr.push( markers[i] );
    }
    returnMarkers( arr );
}
```

The `returnMarkers()` method is invoked in JavaScript and handled by the `onHTMLMarkers()` method of the `LocationDisplay` component:

```
private function onHTMLMarkers( value:Object, ...args ):void
{
    if( value == null ) return;
    var jsMarkers:* = value;
    var markers:ArrayCollection = _data.markers;
    for( var i:int = 0; i < jsMarkers.length; i++ )
    {
        var jsMarker:Object = jsMarkers[i];
        var marker:MarkerVO;
        var xyPt:Object = jsMarker._xy;
        var coord:* = jsMarker.getCoordPoint();
        for( var j:int = 0; j < markers.length; j++ )
        {
            marker = markers.getItemAt(j) as MarkerVO;
            if( marker.jsId == jsMarker.id )
            {
                marker.locationId = _data.location.id;
                marker.x = xyPt.x;
                marker.y = xyPt.y;
            }
        }
    }
    map.domWindow.clean();
}
```

The JavaScript `Array` object is passed as the value argument for the `onHTMLMarkers()` method. Within this method, any `MarkerVO` objects held on the `LocatorDataManager` instance are updated with the properties held on the JavaScript objects of the supplied array.

The Yahoo! Maps AJAX API has a lot to offer and is too much to cover in this chapter. Visit the online documentation for Yahoo! Maps AJAX API version 3.7 at `http://developer.yahoo.com/maps/ajax/V3.7/reference.html` if you are interested in discovering more.

In using the concept of adding markers to denote destinations on locations for Yahoo! Maps, the map application provides the capability to add markers to locations when working in offline mode as well.

Displaying Destinations

The MarkerVO class you created previously holds properties related to the position on the screen, not geographical coordinates. Though those points can be stored in the value object if you choose, they are graphical representations of a destination that you can add notes to, and they can be displayed when retrieving saved location data. In this section you will create the marker display and the form to add corresponding captions that is launched from the LocationDisplay object.

1. Create a new document and enter the following markup:

```
<?xml version="1.0" encoding="utf-8"?>
<mx:Canvas
    xmlns:mx="http://www.adobe.com/2006/mxml"
    width="27" height="28">

    <mx:Script>
        <![CDATA[
            import com.aircmr.locator.data.MarkerVO;

            import mx.core.IToolTip;
            import mx.managers.ToolTipManager;

            private var _tooltip:IToolTip;
            private var _data:MarkerVO;

            private function showCaption( evt:MouseEvent ):void
            {
                if( _data == null ) return;
                marker.addEventListener( MouseEvent.MOUSE_MOVE, updateTooltip );
                var pt:Point = localToGlobal(new Point( evt.localX, evt.localY ));
                _tooltip = ToolTipManager.createToolTip(
                            _data.caption.split("<br/>").join("\r"), pt.x, pt.y );
                _tooltip.y -= _tooltip.height;
            }

            private function hideCaption( evt:MouseEvent ):void
            {
                if( _tooltip == null ) return;
                ToolTipManager.destroyToolTip( _tooltip );
                marker.removeEventListener( MouseEvent.MOUSE_MOVE, updateTooltip );
            }

            private function updateTooltip( evt:MouseEvent ):void
            {
                var pt:Point = localToGlobal(new Point( evt.localX, evt.localY ));
                _tooltip.x = pt.x;
                _tooltip.y = pt.y - _tooltip.height;
            }

            override public function get data():Object
            {
                return _data;
            }
            override public function set data( value:Object ):void
```

```
            {
                _data = ( value as MarkerVO );
                super.data = value;
            }

        ]]>
    </mx:Script>

    <mx:Image id="marker"
        source="@Embed(source='/assets/marker_red.png')"
        mouseOver="showCaption(event);"
        mouseOut="hideCaption(event);"
        />

</mx:Canvas>
```

2. Save the file as `Marker.mxml` in the directory `com/aircmr/locator/ui`, along with the previously created `LocationDisplay.mxml` file, within your working directory.

3. Create a new document and enter the following markup:

```
<?xml version="1.0" encoding="utf-8"?>
<mx:Panel
    xmlns:mx="http://www.adobe.com/2006/mxml"
    width="300" height="300"
    title="Marker"
    creationComplete="onCreationComplete();">

    <mx:Metadata>
        [Event(name="save", type="flash.events.Event")]
        [Event(name="cancel", type="flash.events.Event")]
    </mx:Metadata>

    <mx:Script>
        <![CDATA[
            import com.aircmr.locator.data.MarkerVO;

            [Bindable]
            private var _markerData:MarkerVO;

            public static const SAVE:String = "save";
            public static const CANCEL:String = "cancel";

            private function onCreationComplete():void
            {
                stage.focus = captionField;
            }

            override public function get data():Object
            {
                return _markerData;
            }
            override public function set data(value:Object):void
            {
```

```
                _markerData = ( value as MarkerVO );
                super.data = value;
            }
        ]]>
    </mx:Script>

    <mx:VBox width="100%" height="100%"
        paddingLeft="5" paddingRight="5" paddingTop="5" paddingBottom="5">
        <mx:Label text="Add Caption:" />
        <mx:TextArea id="captionField"
            width="100%" height="100%"
            change="{_markerData.caption = captionField.text}"
            />
        <mx:HBox width="100%" height="30" horizontalAlign="center">
            <mx:Button id="saveButton"
                label="save" click="dispatchEvent( new Event( SAVE ) );"
                />
            <mx:Button id="cancelButton"
                label="cancel" click="dispatchEvent( new Event( CANCEL ) );"
                />
        </mx:HBox>
    </mx:VBox>
</mx:Panel>
```

4. Save the file as `MarkerForm.mxml` in the directory `com/aircmr/locator/ui` within your working directory.

`Marker.mxml` is the marker display for destinations. You may notice that it embeds the graphics file `marker_red.png` from an `assets` folder in your working directory. Feel free to make your own graphic or grab that file from the `/assets` folder of the code examples for this chapter on the accompanying website.

A `Marker` object takes a data type of `MarkerVO` and displays the associated `caption` property of that value object in a tooltip upon rollover. Assigning that caption value occurs within the `MarkerForm` container, which is presented in a pop-up upon the addition of a new marker to the display of `LocationDisplay`. The `MarkerForm` presents two options when adding a caption to a marker. If you choose to save the caption to the marker, the value object is updated and the `Marker` instance is kept on the display. If you choose to cancel, then the `Marker` is removed from the display.

You have created the display classes to view locations and destinations, and in the next section you will create the control view that enables you to navigate to locations and add destination markers.

Going Places

In the previous sections you have created the models and view classes to display destinations-based locations. What is missing from the map application thus far are user controls for navigating to and saving out those locations and destinations. Keeping in mind that available controls are also based on the current mode of the application — online or offline — get to work on the classes that will help you find where you want to go.

1. Create a new document and enter the following markup:

```
<?xml version="1.0" encoding="utf-8"?>
<mx:VBox xmlns:mx="http://www.adobe.com/2006/mxml"
    xmlns:ui="com.aircmr.locator.ui.*"
    width="100%"
    verticalAlign="middle"
    creationComplete="onCreationComplete();">

    <mx:Metadata>
        [Event(name="save", type="flash.events.Event")]
        [Event(name="requestAddress", type="flash.events.Event")]
        [Event(name="requestLocations", type="flash.events.Event")]
    </mx:Metadata>

    <mx:Script>
        <![CDATA[
            import com.aircmr.locator.data.LocatorDataManager;
            import com.aircmr.locator.services.DBService;
            import mx.binding.utils.BindingUtils;
            import mx.collections.ArrayCollection;

            [Bindable] private var _data:LocatorDataManager;
            private var _mode:String;
            private var _locations:ArrayCollection;

            public static const SAVE:String = "save";
            public static const REQUEST_ADDRESS:String = "requestAddress";
            public static const REQUEST_LOCATIONS:String = "requestLocations";

            private function onCreationComplete():void
            {
                _data = LocatorDataManager.getInstance();
                BindingUtils.bindSetter( invalidateMode, this, "mode" );
            }

            private function invalidateMode( arg:* ):void
            {
                locationCtrl.selectedChild = ( mode == ModeType.ONLINE )
                                                    ? onlineCtrl : offlineCtrl;
                saveField.text = "";
            }

            private function validateAddress( str:String ):Boolean
            {
                return ( str != '' && str != null && str != "Select..." );
            }

            private function requestLocations():void
            {
                dispatchEvent( new Event( LocationControls.REQUEST_LOCATIONS ) );
            }
```

```
        private function onLocationSearch():void
        {
            dispatchEvent( new Event( LocationControls.REQUEST_ADDRESS ) );
        }

        private function onLocationSave():void
        {
             // if we have changed the name, mark for new entry...
            if( saveField.text != _data.location.name )
            {
                _data.location.id = -1;
                _data.location.name = saveField.text;
            }
            dispatchEvent( new Event( LocationControls.SAVE ) );
        }

        private function onInputChange():void
        {
            searchButton.enabled = addressField.text != '';
        }
        private function onComboChange():void
        {
            onLocationSearch();
        }

        [Bindable]
        public function get mode():String
        {
            return _mode;
        }
        public function set mode( str:String ):void
        {
            _mode = str;
        }

        [Bindable]
        public function get locations():ArrayCollection
        {
            return _locations;
        }
        public function set locations( arr:ArrayCollection ):void
        {
            _locations = arr;
            _locations.addItemAt( "Select...", 0 );
        }

        public function get currentAddress():String
        {
            return ( _mode == ModeType.ONLINE ) ?
                        addressField.text :
                        locationCB.selectedLabel;
        }

    ]]>
```

```
    </mx:Script>

    <mx:Label text="Locate:" />
    <mx:HBox width="100%" height="30">
        <mx:ViewStack id="locationCtrl"
            width="100%" height="100%">
            <mx:HBox id="onlineCtrl"
                width="100%" height="100%"
                hide="{addressField.text = ''}">
                <mx:TextInput id="addressField"
                    width="100%"
                    change="onInputChange();"
                    />
                <mx:Button id="searchButton"
                    label="go"
                    click="onLocationSearch();"
                    />
            </mx:HBox>
            <mx:Canvas id="offlineCtrl"
                width="100%" height="100%"
                show="requestLocations();"
                hide="{locationCB.selectedIndex = 0}">
                <mx:ComboBox id="locationCB"
                    width="100%"
                    dataProvider="{locations}"
                    change="onComboChange();"
                    />
            </mx:Canvas>
        </mx:ViewStack>
    </mx:HBox>

    <mx:HRule width="100%" />
    <ui:MarkerBank id="bank"
        enabled="{validateAddress(_data.currentAddress)}"
        />
    <mx:HRule width="100%" />

    <mx:HBox width="100%" height="30">
        <mx:Label text="Save as:" />
        <mx:TextInput id="saveField"
            width="100%"
            enabled="{validateAddress(_data.currentAddress)}"
            text="{_data.location.name}"
            />
        <mx:Button label="save"
            enabled="{saveField.text != ''}"
            click="onLocationSave();"
            />
    </mx:HBox>

</mx:VBox>
```

2. Save the file as `LocationControls.mxml` in the directory `com/aircmr/locator/ui` within your working directory.

3. Create a new document and enter the following markup:

```
<?xml version="1.0" encoding="utf-8"?>
<mx:HBox
    xmlns:mx="http://www.adobe.com/2006/mxml"
    xmlns:ui="com.aircmr.locator.ui.*"
    width="100%" height="30"
    verticalAlign="middle">

    <mx:Script>
        <![CDATA[
            import com.aircmr.locator.data.MarkerVO;

            import mx.containers.Canvas;
            import mx.core.DragSource;
            import mx.managers.DragManager;

            private function onMarkerStart( evt:MouseEvent ):void
            {
                var pt:Point = marker.localToGlobal( new Point( evt.localX,
                                                                evt.localY ) );
                var source:DragSource = new DragSource();
                source.addData( new MarkerVO(), "marker" );
                var bmp:BitmapData = new BitmapData( marker.width, marker.height );
                bmp.draw( marker );
                DragManager.doDrag( this, source, evt, marker,
                                    pt.x - 5, evt.localY - marker.height );
            }
        ]]>
    </mx:Script>

    <mx:Label text="Click and drag marker to map:" />
    <ui:Marker id="marker" mouseDown="onMarkerStart(event);" />
</mx:HBox>
```

4. Save the file as `MarkerBank.mxml` in the directory `com/aircmr/locator/ui` within your working directory.

The `LocationsControls` class holds controls for navigating to locations and adding destination markers. Depending on the mode type in which the application is running, you can enter or select an address to forward requests either to the Yahoo! Maps AJAX API or to the local database. When working in online mode, an input field and Submit button are displayed; while in offline mode, a `ComboBox` is shown with a list of locations held in the local database.

The main purpose of the `LocationControls` component is to dispatch events upon user interaction to notify a client about a request. The `LocationControls` component dispatches a request for an address based on the `text` property of the `addressField` or the `selectedLabel` property of the `locationCB` instance. When entering offline mode, `LocationControls` also dispatches an event to request all locations held in the local database.

Within the `click` event handler for the Save button, the `LocationsControl` class also dispatches a `save` event to indicate that the user has opted to save the current location and destinations:

```
private function onLocationSave():void
{
    // if we have changed the name, mark for new entry...
    if( saveField.text != _data.location.name )
    {
        _data.location.id = -1;
        _data.location.name = saveField.text;
    }
    dispatchEvent( new Event( LocationControls.SAVE ) );
}
```

Because locations entered into the database have a unique ID consisting of a positive integer associated with the location, setting the `id` property on the current `LocationVO` object to a value of `-1` will flag the data as not having been previously saved locally. The `if` statement in the `onLocationSave()` handler checks whether the user has been working with data received from the database and has chosen a new associative name for that data — prompting a client who will handle communicating with the database to add a new entry, rather than override any existing data.

The `MarkerBank` component displays a `Marker` instance enabled to be dragged and dropped onto any display object with drag-and-drop capability enabled — in the case of this application, that is the display of the `LocationDisplay` component. Though the `MarkerBank` component from this example currently displays a single marker with generic graphics, it can be updated to handle additional markers that may have specific graphics based on destination types — such as places to eat or places to stay.

With the appropriate value objects available and the view classes set for interacting with destinations-based locations, in the next section you will create the main file, which communicates with the local database, handles events coming from these control views, and interfaces with the database service classes.

Bringing It All Together

You have come a long way! The following examples get you started on managing the events coming from the view classes you created in the previous sections.

Create a new document and enter the following markup:

```
<?xml version="1.0" encoding="utf-8"?>
<mx:WindowedApplication
    xmlns:mx="http://www.adobe.com/2006/mxml"
    xmlns:ui="com.aircmr.locator.ui.*"
    layout="absolute"
    applicationComplete="onAppComplete();"
    networkChange="checkConnection();">
```

```
<mx:Style>
    .displayHolder {
        padding-left: 5px;
        padding-right: 5px;
        padding-top: 5px;
        padding-bottom: 5px;
        border-style: 'solid';
        border-color: #DDDDDD;
        border-thickness: 2;
        background-color: #FFFFFF;
    }
</mx:Style>

<mx:Script>
    <![CDATA[
        import com.aircmr.locator.data.MarkerVO;
        import com.aircmr.locator.data.LocationVO;
        import com.aircmr.locator.services.DBService;
        import com.aircmr.locator.events.DBResultEvent;
        import com.aircmr.locator.data.LocatorDataManager;
        import com.aircmr.locator.ui.ModeType;
        import mx.binding.utils.BindingUtils;
        import mx.collections.ArrayCollection;
        import mx.controls.ProgressBar;
        import mx.managers.PopUpManager;

        private var _service:DBService;
        private var _isAvailable:Boolean;
        private var _progressBar:ProgressBar;
        private var _markerIndex:int;

        private static const MAP_HTML:String = "ymap.html";
        private static const CONN_URL:String =
          "http://www.wiley.com/WileyCDA/WileyTitle/productCd-0470182075.html";

        private function onAppComplete():void
        {
            _service = new DBService();
            BindingUtils.bindSetter( invalidateResource, this, "isAvailable" );

            checkHTMLFile();
            checkConnection();
            createProgress();
        }

        private function invalidateResource( bool:Boolean ):void
        {
            modeControl.isAvailable = bool;
        }

        private function checkHTMLFile():void
        {
```

```
        var tFile:File = File.applicationDirectory.resolvePath( MAP_HTML );
        tFile.copyTo(
          File.applicationStorageDirectory.resolvePath( MAP_HTML ), true );
        // apply html map...
        locationDisplay.htmlLocation = "app-storage:/" + MAP_HTML;
    }

    private function checkConnection():void
    {
        modeControl.mode = ModeType.OFFLINE;
        var request:URLRequest = new URLRequest();
        request.method = URLRequestMethod.HEAD;
        request.url = CONN_URL;
        var loader:URLLoader = new URLLoader();
        loader.addEventListener( HTTPStatusEvent.HTTP_STATUS,
                                                    onHTTPStatus );
        loader.addEventListener( IOErrorEvent.IO_ERROR, onStatusError );
        loader.addEventListener( SecurityErrorEvent.SECURITY_ERROR,
                                                    onStatusError );
        loader.load( request );
    }

    private function createProgress():void
    {
        _progressBar = new ProgressBar();
        _progressBar.indeterminate = true;
        _progressBar.labelPlacement = "top";
       }
       private function showProgress( msg:String ):void
       {
            _progressBar.label = msg;
        PopUpManager.addPopUp( _progressBar, this, true );
        PopUpManager.centerPopUp( _progressBar );
       }
       private function hideProgress():void
       {
           PopUpManager.removePopUp( _progressBar );
       }

    private function onHTTPStatus( evt:HTTPStatusEvent ):void
    {
        isAvailable = evt.status < 400;
    }
    private function onStatusError( evt:IOErrorEvent ):void
    {
        isAvailable = false;
    }

    private function onDisplayChange():void
    {
        status = "Locating map...";
        if( modeControl.mode == ModeType.ONLINE )
            locationControl.enabled = false;
    }
```

```
private function onDisplayComplete():void
{
    status = "Map located.";
    if( modeControl.mode == ModeType.ONLINE )
        locationControl.enabled = true;
}

private function onModeChanged():void
{
    LocatorDataManager.getInstance().refresh();
    locationControl.mode = modeControl.mode;
    locationDisplay.mode = modeControl.mode;
}

private function onAddressRequest():void
{
    LocatorDataManager.getInstance().refresh();
    LocatorDataManager.getInstance().currentAddress =
                                locationControl.currentAddress;
}

private function onLocationRequest():void
{
    _service.addEventListener( DBResultEvent.LOCATION_RETRIEVED,
                                                onLocationResult );
    _service.retrieveLocation(
                LocatorDataManager.getInstance().currentAddress );
}
private function onLocationResult( evt:DBResultEvent ):void
{
    _service.removeEventListener( DBResultEvent.LOCATION_RETRIEVED,
                                                onLocationResult );
    if( evt.result.data == null ) return;
    var result:LocationVO = evt.result.data[0] as LocationVO;
    result.deserialize();
    LocatorDataManager.getInstance().location = result;

    _service.addEventListener( DBResultEvent.MARKER_RETRIEVED_ALL,
                                                onMarkersResult );
    _service.retrieveMarkersFromLocation( result.id );
}

private function onLocationsRequest():void
{
    _service.addEventListener( DBResultEvent.LOCATION_RETRIEVED_ALL,
                                                onLocationsResult );
    _service.retrieveAllLocations();
}
private function onLocationsResult( evt:DBResultEvent ):void
{
    _service.removeEventListener( DBResultEvent.LOCATION_RETRIEVED_ALL,
                                                onLocationsResult );
    var result:Array = evt.result.data;
    var dp:ArrayCollection = new ArrayCollection();
```

```
        if( result != null )
        {
            for( var i:int = 0; i < result.length; i++ )
            {
                dp.addItem( {label:unescape( result[i].name )} );
            }
        }
        locationControl.locations = dp;
    }

    private function onMarkersResult( evt:DBResultEvent ):void
    {
        _service.removeEventListener( DBResultEvent.MARKER_RETRIEVED_ALL,
                                                          onMarkersResult );
        var result:Array = evt.result.data;
        if( result != null )
        {
            var marker:MarkerVO;
            for( var i:int = 0; i < result.length; i++ )
            {
                marker = result[i] as MarkerVO;
                if( marker == null ) continue;
                marker.deserialize();
                locationDisplay.addMarker( marker );
            }
        }
    }

    private function saveNextMarker( evt:DBResultEvent = null ):void
    {
        var markers:ArrayCollection =
                            LocatorDataManager.getInstance().markers;
        if( evt != null )
        {
            markers.getItemAt( _markerIndex ).id = evt.result.data[0].id;
            _markerIndex++;
        }

        if( _markerIndex < markers.length )
        {
            markers.getItemAt( _markerIndex ).locationId =
                            LocatorDataManager.getInstance().location.id;
            _service.saveMarker( markers.getItemAt( _markerIndex )
                                                          as MarkerVO );
        }
        else
        {
            _service.removeEventListener( DBResultEvent.MARKER_SAVED,
                                                          saveNextMarker );
            hideProgress();
        }
    }

    private function onSaveLocation():void
```

```
        {
            showProgress( "Saving Location..." );
            locationDisplay.prepareForSave();
        }
        private function onLocationSaved( evt:DBResultEvent ):void
        {
            LocatorDataManager.getInstance().location.id =
                                                    evt.result.data[0].id;
            _service.addEventListener( DBResultEvent.MARKER_SAVED,
                                                        saveNextMarker );
            _markerIndex = 0;
            saveNextMarker();
        }

        public function saveLocation():void
        {
            _service.addEventListener( DBResultEvent.LOCATION_SAVED,
                                                        onLocationSaved );
            _service.saveLocation( LocatorDataManager.getInstance().location );
        }

        [Bindable]
        public function get isAvailable():Boolean
        {
            return _isAvailable;
        }
        public function set isAvailable( bool:Boolean ):void
        {
            _isAvailable = bool;
        }

    ]]>
</mx:Script>

<mx:VBox width="100%" height="100%">
    <mx:HBox width="100%" height="100%">
        <ui:LocationControls id="locationControl"
            width="300"
            styleName="displayHolder"
            requestAddress="onAddressRequest();"
            requestLocations="onLocationsRequest();"
            save="onSaveLocation();"
            />
        <ui:LocationDisplay id="locationDisplay"
            width="100%" height="100%"
            change="onDisplayChange();"
            complete="onDisplayComplete();"
            prepared="saveLocation();"
            requestLocation="onLocationRequest();"
            styleName="displayHolder"
            />
    </mx:HBox>
    <ui:ModeControls id="modeControl"
        width="100%" height="34"
```

```
            styleName="displayHolder"
            modeChanged="onModeChanged();"
            />
    </mx:VBox>

</mx:WindowedApplication>
```

Save the file as `Locator.mxml` in the root of your working directory alongside the previously created file `ymap.html`.

The layout of the main application file displays the `LocationControls` and `LocationDisplay` views next to each other horizontally, with the `ModeControls` component added to the display list vertically, below. Notice that all the events fired from these components are handled in `Locator` to update the data model and make requests to the database service you created in the section "Querying the Database."

After the application is initialized and added to the display list, the `onAppComplete()`event handler creates an instance of the `DBService`, which in turn creates a local database in the application storage directory if it does not already exist. Also added to the application storage directory is a copy of the `ymap.html` file found in the application resource directory:

```
private function checkHTMLFile():void
{
    var tFile:File = File.applicationDirectory.resolvePath( MAP_HTML );
    tFile.copyTo( File.applicationStorageDirectory.resolvePath( MAP_HTML ), true );
    // apply html map...
    locationDisplay.htmlLocation = "app-storage:/" + MAP_HTML;
}
```

Along with these operations, the `Locator` also establishes a binding to the `isAvailable` property to a function that updates the property on the `ModeControls` instance. The `ModeControls` class allows a user to work in offline or online mode when an Internet connection is available. Without a connection, the user is restricted access to data available offline. This restriction is a result of an update to the `isAvailable` property of the `ModeControls` instance, whose value is governed by the operations run by the `checkConnection()`event handler for the `networkChange` event declared in the `<mx:Windowed Application>` application root tag:

```
private function checkConnection():void
{
    modeControl.mode = ModeType.OFFLINE;
    var request:URLRequest = new URLRequest();
    request.method = URLRequestMethod.HEAD;
    request.url = CONN_URL;
    var loader:URLLoader = new URLLoader();
    loader.addEventListener( HTTPStatusEvent.HTTP_STATUS, onHTTPStatus );
    loader.addEventListener( IOErrorEvent.IO_ERROR, onStatusError );
    loader.addEventListener( SecurityErrorEvent.SECURITY_ERROR, onStatusError );
    loader.load( request );
 }
```

An HTTP `HEAD` request is made to establish that an Internet connection is available for the application as long as the status code is below 400. The status code is checked within the `onHTTPStatus()`event handler, and the isAvailable property is valued as true if less than 400; and false if it is 400 or over. The onStatusError() event handler sets the isAvailable property to false directly. This property drives the mode property of the ModeControls component and in turn dictates the display of the other components. You are free to use the monitoring API of AIR discussed in previous chapters (air.net.URLMonitor and air.net.ServiceMonitor) as you see fit. However, for the purposes of this application, the Locator is only concerned about a direct change to the network connection, rather than continually polling to check its availability.

Aside from responding to changes from the network, the Locator plays an important part in handling events from the LocationControls and LocationDisplay components, which require communication with the database service class. Though most calls to the database service are simple requests with corresponding DBService result handlers, how locations and markers are saved deserves a closer look. When the save event is dispatched from the LocationControls component, the application instructs the LocationDisplay component to run operations appropriate for saving. When ready, the saveLocation() method is invoked:

```
public function saveLocation():void
{
    _service.addEventListener( DBResultEvent.LOCATION_SAVED, onLocationSaved );
    _service.saveLocation( LocatorDataManager.getInstance().location );
}
private function onLocationSaved( evt:DBResultEvent ):void
{
    LocatorDataManager.getInstance().location.id = evt.result.data[0].id;
    _service.addEventListener( DBResultEvent.MARKER_SAVED, saveNextMarker );
    _markerIndex = 0;
    saveNextMarker();
}
```

The current LocationVO object held on the LocatorDataManager is handed to the DBService instance to add or update an entry into the database. Upon a successful result, the onLocationSaved() method is invoked, which in turn updates the id property of the LocationVO object based on the resulting data. Because the database is set up to assign a unique ID to each entry of a location, that ID is available on the SQLResult object and updates the current property on the location. Also within the onLocationSaved() method, the saveNextMarker() method is called to begin sending each MarkerVO object held on the LocationDataManager instance to the database service:

```
private function saveNextMarker( evt:DBResultEvent = null ):void
{
    var markers:ArrayCollection = LocatorDataManager.getInstance().markers;
    if( evt != null )
    {
        markers.getItemAt( _markerIndex ).id = evt.result.data[0].id;
        _markerIndex++;
    }

    if( _markerIndex < markers.length )
    {
        markers.getItemAt( _markerIndex ).locationId =
                                    LocatorDataManager.getInstance().location.id;
        _service.saveMarker( markers.getItemAt( _markerIndex ) as MarkerVO );
    }
```

```
        else
        {
            _service.removeEventListener( DBResultEvent.MARKER_SAVED, saveNextMarker );
            hideProgress();
        }
    }
```

As each marker is successfully added to the database, the `id` property of each `MarkerVO` object held on the `LocationDataManager` is updated based on the resulting data. Just as the ID for a location is updated based on the ID returned in the `SQLResult` as it pertains to the ID of the field entry, so is the ID for each marker entered into the marker table of the local database. If the IDs of the locations and markers were not updated after they were entered into the application, then the `DBService` would treat each instance as a new entry and quickly fill with duplicate data.

With the main application complete and responding to a change in network and request events from the display components, you have the capability to navigate to locations and add destinations using either the Yahoo! Maps AJAX API or data stored in a local database. Looks like you are all set! The next section covers creating the descriptor file and deploying the map application.

Deploying the Application

Now that you've got the map application built it is time to create the descriptor file so you can deploy and start planning your next trip.

The Descriptor File

Open your favorite text editor, create a new document and enter the following markup:

```
<?xml version="1.0" encoding="UTF-8"?>
<application xmlns="http://ns.adobe.com/air/application/1.0">

    <id>com.aircmr.Locator</id>
    <filename>Locator</filename>
    <version>0.1</version>
    <name>Locator</name>
    <description>A destinations-based map application</description>
    <copyright>2007</copyright>

      <initialWindow>
        <title>Locator</title>
        <content>Locator.swf</content>
        <systemChrome>standard</systemChrome>
        <transparent>false</transparent>
        <visible>true</visible>
        <width>760</width>
        <height>540</height>
      </initialWindow>

    <installFolder>AIRCMR/Locator</installFolder>
    <programMenuFolder>AIRCMR</programMenuFolder>

</application>
```

Save the file as `Locator-app.xml` in the root of your working directory along with the `Locator.mxml` and `ymap.html` files.

This file will serve as the application descriptor file. The element values from this snippet are somewhat generic and should be changed as you see fit. When the Locator application is installed, the application directory will be found within the `AIRCMR` folder of the application directory of your operating system. When the database is created and the `ymap.html` file is copied over to the application storage directory, they can be found in a folder named `com.aircmr.Locator`, which is the node value of the `id` element for the application descriptor file.

With the descriptor file in place, you're set to compile and package the Locator AIR executable.

Compiling and Packaging

Recall that two files are necessary to package an AIR application — the main SWF file and the XML application descriptor file. In this section you will produce the SWF file using the command-line tools and package the AIR application.

The graphic asset `marker_red.png` *is an embedded graphic in the* `Marker` *class and can be found in the /*`assets` *folder included with the source code for this chapter on the accompanying website, or you can create your own. If you are following along with the examples in this chapter, the graphic asset needs to reside in a folder named* `assets` *in order to compile the source.*

Open a command prompt, navigate to the working directory for the Locator map application, enter the following command, and press Enter:

```
> amxmlc Locator.mxml
```

If you have purchased a certificate from a certificate authority, such as VeriSign or Thawte, then you can use that certificate, rather than create the self-signed certificate, and can skip the following operation. To create a self-signed certificate within the working directory, enter the following command:

```
> adt -certificate -cn Locator 1024-RSA certificate.pfx password
```

With the command prompt still pointing to the working directory, enter the following command to package the Locator application:

```
> adt -package -storetype pkcs12 -keystore certificate.pfx Locator.air Locator-
app.xml Locator.swf ymap.html
```

You will be prompted to enter the password for the certificate. If you created a self-signed certificate from the second command, enter **password**. Running these commands, a `Locator.swf` file, a `certificate.pfx` file, and the `Locator.air` installer file are generated within your working directory.

Once the installer has been created, navigate to your working directory and double-click on the AIR installer to install and run the Locator. If all goes well, the application will launch and be ready to navigate to locations and start adding destination markers. Figure 9-1 shows what the application looks like in online mode.

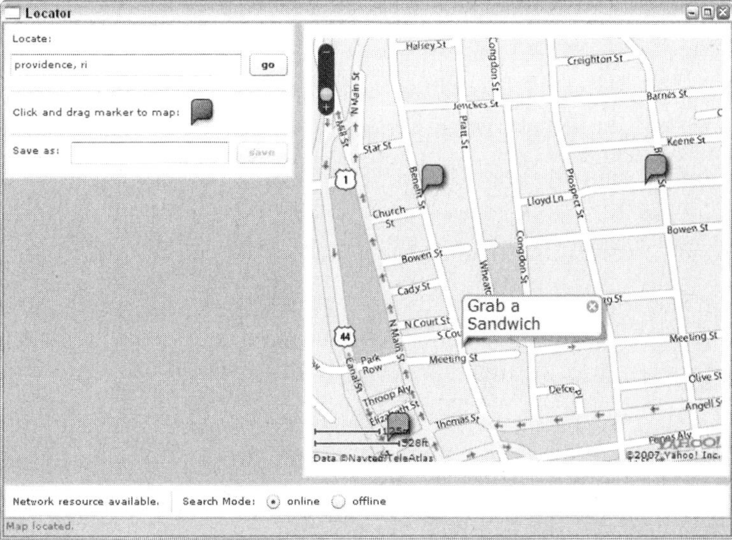

Figure 9-1

Figure 9-2 shows what the application looks like in offline mode.

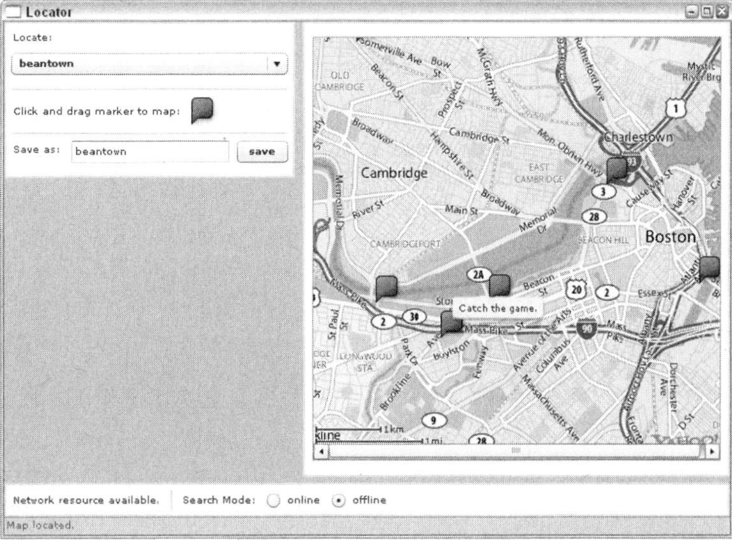

Figure 9-2

If you are seeing something similar to these two displays, then a local database has been created with the appropriate tables in your application storage directory. To locate the storage directory in Windows, navigate to `C:\Documents and Settings\<username>\Application Data\com.apolloir.Locator\Local Store`. On a Mac, navigate to `/Users/<username>/Library/Preferences/com.apolloir.Locator/Local Store`.

If you have already saved a location, you will see an image file in that directory, named for the timestamp string when the file was created.

Experiment with looking up locations and adding markers, and marvel at the power of not having to remember that you parked at 42.358028 latitude and –71.0060417 longitude!

Summary

This chapter delved deeper into working with the database engine included in Adobe AIR, introduced you to the `HTML` control and script bridging ActionScript and JavaScript, all while building a map application to navigate to locations while interfacing with the Yahoo! Maps AJAX API and the local database.

From here, you can modify the map application to incorporate other online services, build your own mashups, and even serialize saved database entries to pass on to anyone else with the Locator installed on their machine. It's a big world! Get out there and start finding new destinations.

10

Blogger Agent

If you've ever wanted to write a blog entry when your computer wasn't connected to the Internet, you wouldn't be alone. To get around this situation, you've probably written your entry and saved it to some sort of text file for later posting. When your computer was connected to the Internet again, you probably logged into your blogging service, navigated to the compose entry page, opened your text file, and then finally copied and pasted the text into the form. That certainly doesn't feel very efficient. Surely there is a better way.

Luckily, most blogging services and blogging software offer some sort of web services that enable third-party software and applications to communicate with them. This chapter will utilize Google's Blogger service (`www.blogger.com`). Blogger is a simple blogging service that has a very useful data API that enables third-party applications to retrieve and send various pieces of data through simple GET and POST requests. The application you will build in this chapter utilizes this service combined with functionality available in Adobe AIR to avoid the inefficient process described in the previous paragraph. If you do not already have an account with Blogger, it would be best to create one before you begin this chapter.

The following section discusses the design of the application. This includes the logistics of managing the data and the components that are necessary for the user interface. After design, you'll get into the code and learn about the important classes and functions that tie everything together.

Design

If you've ever worked with browser-based Flash content that attempts to communicate with servers other than the one your content is running on, no doubt you have run into some security concerns. Normally, in order for a web service to allow browser/plug-in based Flash content to access it, a cross-domain file (`crossdomain.xml`) must reside at the root level of the application's domain. This would be an issue when developing an application such as the one in this chapter.

However, in contrast to browser-based Flash content, Adobe AIR content does not need a cross-domain file to be present in order to access it. In other words, you don't have to worry about any security issues, and this application will take advantage of that fact.

Additionally, it's a good idea to make a list of items that your application aims to fulfill. The following list outlines the most important functionality of the Blogger Agent application:

- Allow users to manage all of their Blogger accounts/blogs.
- Allow users to compose and publish blog entries.
- Allow users to add blog entries to a publish queue.
- Allow users to preview their blog.
- Display a list of saved accounts.
- Display a list of queued blog entries.
- Store account information in a local database.
- Store queued blog entries in a local database.
- Encrypt all saved account passwords.

These are the main features of the Blogger Agent application. The application is relatively simple and will utilize some great features available in Adobe AIR. In the following sections you will learn how to approach the application and the specific Adobe AIR features that will be utilized to create the functionality outlined above.

Managing Accounts

This application will enable users to manage all of their blogs associated with any Blogger account. In order to achieve this, the Blogger Data API will be utilized to enable users to retrieve a list of blogs associated with their Blogger username and password. Users can then choose a blog from the returned list and save the blog information to a local database.

You will first create a service class called `BloggerService` to manage the communication between the Blogger Data API. This class performs user authentication and retrieves the list of blogs for that user's credentials. Second, in order to save the blog information to the user's hard drive for later use, you will create another service class called `DBService`. This class utilizes Adobe AIR's native SQLite support to create and manage a small database. The use of these two classes is illustrated in Figure 10-1.

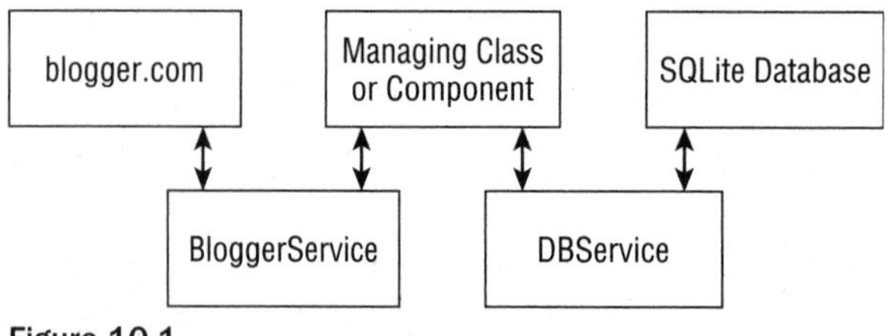

Figure 10-1

Within the database a table titled `blogs` holds the necessary information about the blog and the user's account. Additionally, this class utilizes the native Adobe AIR class called `LocalEncryptedStore` to store the user's password in an encrypted state. The `DBService` class requires a custom event class named `DBServiceEvent`. Lastly, you will create a simple object class called `Blog`. This class serves as an ActionScript representation of the information stored in the SQLite database.

Managing Blog Entries

In addition to managing accounts, users will be able to manage blog entries. Blog entries, composed of a title and body, will be allowed to be published immediately if the user is connected to the Internet, or they will be saved in a queue to be published after the user has reconnected. Publishing blog entries will be managed by the aforementioned `BloggerService` class. Furthermore, the `DBService` class, also previously mentioned, will take care of managing the saved blog entries. To represent a blog entry, you will create a simple object class called `BlogEntry`. This class serves as an ActionScript representation of the information stored in the database.

Lastly, in order to publish the saved blog entries in a queued manner, you will create two classes. The `PublishQueueItem` class holds a reference to a `BlogEntry` object and the entry's corresponding `Blog` object. The other class you will write is a service class called `QueueService`. This class manages the subsequent publishing of all the blog entries saved in the database.

Utility Classes

This application will utilize two utility classes, the first being the `NetworkConnection` class. This class will utilize the Adobe AIR `NativeApplication` class to detect when the user's connection status has changed. This is useful for activating or deactivating particular functionality. For example, users should not be able to publish a blog entry or start the publish queue if their computer is not connected to the Internet. The second utility class will aid in formatting XML documents for the `BloggerService` class. The Blogger Data API supplies and expects XML documents using the standardized Atom 1.0 XML schema. Thus, you will create a class called `AtomUtil` to aid in the parsing and formatting of XML for the Blogger Data API.

User Interface

The user interface is relatively simple for this application, composed of five components, including the main application component. The user has the choice of selecting one of three screens. Each screen enables the user to perform a different operation. The first screen the user is presented with is the `BlogManager` component. This panel displays a list of all the currently saved blogs, as shown in Figure 10-2. From this screen users can add a blog, which brings up the `AddBlogPrompt` component. This prompt is where users enter their username and password to retrieve a list of blogs.

The second screen the user may open is the `ComposeEntryPanel` component. This screen includes a drop-down of available blogs to publish to and a form in which to enter the blog entry. From this screen the user is also able to publish the entry or add it to the queue, as shown in Figure 10-3.

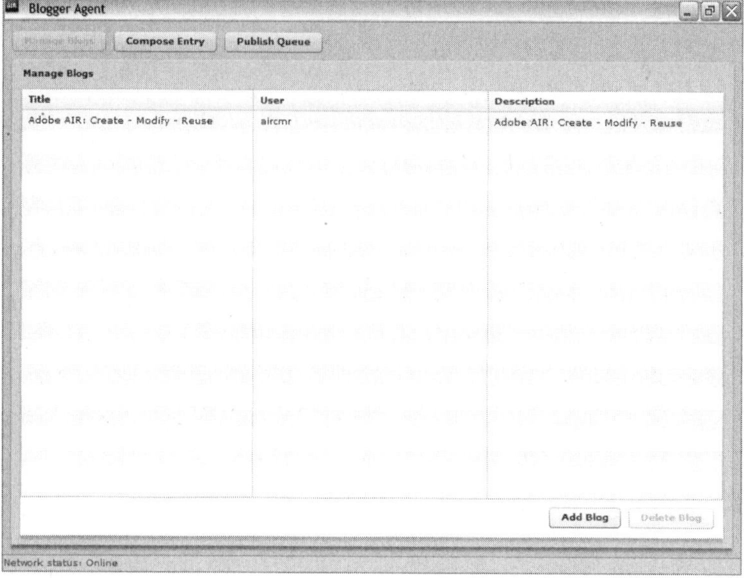

Figure 10-2

Figure 10-3

The third screen the user may open is the `PublishQueuePanel` component. This screen displays a list of all the blog entries currently in the queue, as shown in Figure 10-4. From here, users may start the queue so long as they are connected to the Internet.

This completes the overview of the design of the application. The next section covers the specific functionality of each class and component.

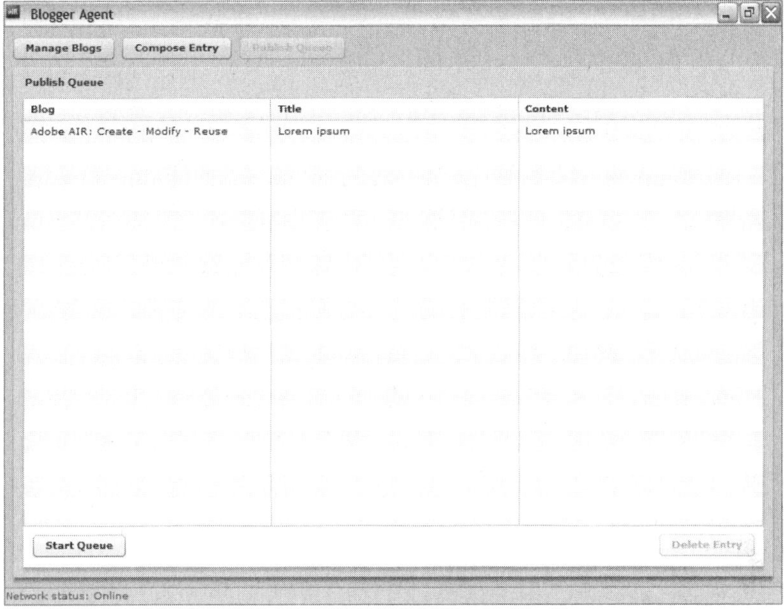

Figure 10-4

Code and Code Explanation

This section dives into the code of each class and component of the application. Throughout the remaining sections, you will create each class and component required by the application and will be briefed upon the important functionality of each, focusing on the Adobe AIR functionality and classes relating to the application. At the end of the chapter, you will bring it all together by creating the main application file. If you have not done so already, create a new working directory for this application.

Data Objects

The data objects for this application are the simplest pieces, so why not get them out of the way first. As mentioned in the previous section, this application requires three basic data object classes.

1. Create a new document and enter the following markup:

```
package com.aircmr.bloggeragent.data
{
    public class Blog
    {
        public var id:int;
        public var title:String;
        public var description:String;
        public var username:String;
        public var password:String;
```

```
        public var publishURL:String;


        public function Blog()
        {

        }
    }
}
```

2. Save the file as `Blog.as` in the directory `com/aircmr/bloggeragent/data/` within your working directory.
3. Create a new document and enter the following markup:

```
package com.aircmr.bloggeragent.data
{
    public class BlogEntry
    {
        public var id:int;
        public var blogID:int;
        public var content:String;
        public var title:String;

        public function BlogEntry()
        {

        }
    }
}
```

4. Save the file as `BlogEntry.as` in the directory `com/aircmr/bloggeragent/data/` within your working directory.
5. Create a new document and enter the following markup:

```
package com.aircmr.bloggeragent.data
{
    public class PublishQueueItem
    {
        public var blog:Blog;
        public var blogEntry:BlogEntry;
        public var blogTitle:String;
        public var blogEntryTitle:String;
        public var blogEntryContent:String;

        public function PublishQueueItem()
        {

        }
    }
}
```

6. Save the file as `PublishQueueItem.as` in the directory `com/aircmr/bloggeragent/data/` within your working directory.

In the previous six steps, you created the necessary data object classes. These classes will serve as ActionScript representations of the information stored in the database. The `Blog` and `BlogEntry` classes contain the necessary properties that need to be transferred throughout the application. The property names should be self-explanatory. The `PublishQueueItem` class will be used to pair a `Blog` and a `BlogEntry` together when managing the publish queue.

Event Objects

This application will make use of one custom event class. Specifically, it will be used by the `DBService` class to notify any listening objects of a few key events. This custom event class is necessary because any actions performed on a local SQLite database occur asynchronously. The event class enables the application to send result data to any listening objects when the operation has completed.

Create a new document and enter the following markup:

```
package com.aircmr.bloggeragent.events
{
    import flash.events.Event;

    public class DBServiceEvent extends Event
    {
        public static const BLOG_ADDED:String = "blogAdded";
        public static const BLOG_DELETED:String = "blogDeleted";
        public static const BLOG_ENTRY_ADDED:String = "blogEntryAdded";
        public static const BLOG_ENTRY_DELETED:String = "blogEntryDeleted";
        public static const GET_BLOGS:String = "getBlogs";
        public static const GET_BLOG_ENTRIES:String = "getBlogEntries";

        private var _data:Object;

        public function DBServiceEvent( type:String, data:Object = null )
        {
            super( type );
            _data = data;
        }

        public function get data():Object
        {
            return _data;
        }
    }
}
```

Save the file as `DBServiceEvent.as` in the directory `com/aircmr/bloggeragent/events/` within your working directory.

The `DBServiceEvent` class will be used by the `DBService` class to notify any listeners of particular database-related events. This event has six different types that correspond to a particular action that will be performed on the database. For example, the `BLOG_ADDED` event will notify any listeners when the information for a blog has been successfully stored in the database. This event class should also give you an idea of what types of methods will be available in the `DBService` class.

Utility Classes

Two utility classes are needed in this application. One will detect whether the user's computer is connected to the Internet, and the other will aid in creating and parsing Atom 1.0 XML feeds for use with the Blogger Data API.

1. Open your editor and create a new document. Enter the following markup:

```
package com.aircmr.net
{
    import flash.errors.IllegalOperationError;
    import flash.events.Event;
    import flash.events.EventDispatcher;
    import flash.events.HTTPStatusEvent;
    import flash.events.IOErrorEvent;
    import flash.events.SecurityErrorEvent;
    import flash.net.URLLoader;
    import flash.net.URLRequest;
    import flash.desktop.NativeApplication;

    final public class NetworkDetection extends EventDispatcher
    {
        private static var _instance:NetworkDetection = new NetworkDetection();

        private var _loader:URLLoader;
        private var _request:URLRequest;
        private var _autoPingOnChange:Boolean = true;
        private var _httpSuccessful:Boolean = false;
        private var _connected:Boolean = false;

        private static const HTTP_SUCCESS:int = 200;
        private static const REQ_URL:String = "http://www.wrox.com";
        public static const SUCCESS:String = "success";
        public static const FAILURE:String = "failure";
        public static const PROGRESS:String = "progress";
        public static const PAGE_FAILURE:String = "pageFailure";
        public static const CONNECTION_CHANGE:String = "connectionChange";

        public static function getInstance():NetworkDetection
        {
            return _instance;
        }

        public function NetworkDetection()
        {
            if( _instance == null )
                init();
            else
            {
                throw new IllegalOperationError( "Error at NetworkDetection. " +
                        "NetworkDetection is a Singletion and should be " +
                        "accessed through NetworkDetection:getInstance." );
            }
        }
```

```
private function init():void
{
    _request = new URLRequest();
    _request.method = "HEAD";
    _loader = new URLLoader();
    _loader.addEventListener( HTTPStatusEvent.HTTP_STATUS, onHttpStatus );
    _loader.addEventListener( Event.COMPLETE, onComplete );
    _loader.addEventListener( IOErrorEvent.IO_ERROR, onError );
    _loader.addEventListener( SecurityErrorEvent.SECURITY_ERROR, onError );
    NativeApplication.nativeApplication.addEventListener(
        Event.NETWORK_CHANGE, onNetworkChange );
}

private function onNetworkChange( evt:Event ):void
{
    dispatchEvent( new Event( Event.NETWORK_CHANGE ) );
    if( _autoPingOnChange ) checkConnection();
}

private function onHttpStatus( evt:HTTPStatusEvent ):void
{
    _httpSuccessful = ( evt.status == HTTP_SUCCESS );
}

private function onComplete( evt:Event ):void
{
    connected = _httpSuccessful;
    dispatchEvent( new Event( ( _connected ) ? SUCCESS : PAGE_FAILURE ) );
}

private function onError( evt:IOErrorEvent ):void
{
    connected = false;
    dispatchEvent( new Event( FAILURE ) );
}

public function checkConnection():void
{
    checkConnectionTo( ( _request.url != null ) ? _request.url : REQ_URL );
}

public function checkConnectionTo( url:String ):void
{
    dispatchEvent( new Event( PROGRESS ) );
    _request.url = url;
    _loader.load( _request );
}

public function get autoPingOnChange():Boolean
{
    return _autoPingOnChange;
}
public function set autoPingOnChange( bool:Boolean ):void
{
```

```
            _autoPingOnChange = bool;
        }

        [Bindable]
        public function get connected():Boolean
        {
            return _connected;
        }
        private function set connected( bool:Boolean ):void
        {
            _connected = bool;
            dispatchEvent( new Event( CONNECTION_CHANGE ) );
        }
    }
}
```

2. Save the file as `NetworkDetection.as` in the directory `com/aircmr/net/` within your working directory.

3. Create a new document and enter the following markup:

```
package com.aircmr.bloggeragent.utils
{
    import com.aircmr.bloggeragent.data.Blog;
    import com.aircmr.bloggeragent.data.BlogEntry;

    public class AtomUtil
    {
        namespace atom = "http://www.w3.org/2005/Atom"

        public static const CONTENT_TYPE:String = "application/atom+xml";

        public static function serializeBlogEntry( entry:BlogEntry ):XML
        {
            var result:String = new String();
            result += '<entry xmlns="http://www.w3.org/2005/Atom">';
            result += '<title type="text">' + entry.title + '</title>';
            result += '<content type="html">' + entry.content + '</content>';
            result += '</entry>';
            return new XML( result );
        }

        public static function parseBlogList( feed:XML,
            username:String, password:String ):Array
        {
            use namespace atom;
            var entries:XMLList = feed.entry;
            var result:Array = new Array();

            for each( var entryItem:XML in entries )
            {
                var blog:Blog = new Blog();
                blog.title = entryItem.title.toString();
```

```
                blog.description = entryItem.summary.toString();
                blog.publishURL = entryItem.link.(
                    @rel.indexOf("#post") > -1 ).@href;
                blog.username = username;
                blog.password = password;
                result.push( blog );
            }

            return result;
        }
    }
}
```

4. Save the file as `AtomUtil.as` in the directory `com/aircmr/bloggeragent/utils/` within your working directory.

In steps 1 and 2 you created the `NetworkDetection` class. This class enables various parts of the application to determine both whether the user is connected to the Internet and whether their connection status ever changes. The following snippet shows the `init` function within the `NetworkDetection` class:

```
private function init():void
{
    _request = new URLRequest();
    _request.method = "HEAD";
    _loader = new URLLoader();
    _loader.addEventListener( HTTPStatusEvent.HTTP_STATUS, onHttpStatus );
    _loader.addEventListener( Event.COMPLETE, onComplete );
    _loader.addEventListener( IOErrorEvent.IO_ERROR, onError );
    _loader.addEventListener( SecurityErrorEvent.SECURITY_ERROR, onError );
    NativeApplication.nativeApplication.addEventListener( Event.NETWORK_CHANGE,
onNetworkChange );
}
```

Notice the use of the `NativeApplication` class. This native Adobe AIR class provides application information, application-wide functions, and dispatches application-level events. One of the events that it dispatches is a `NETWORK_CHANGE` event. This event is dispatched by the static `nativeApplication` property of the class when a network resource on the user's computer becomes available or an existing connection is lost. When the event is dispatched, this utility class checks whether a remote resource is available, which in this case is the Wrox website. If the website is successfully loaded, the `_connection` property is set and a `CONNECTION_CHANGE` event is redispatched. It is this event that the components of the application will listen for to determine whether the connection has changed from `true` to `false` or vice versa.

In steps 3 and 4 you created the `AtomUtil` class. This class will be used by the `BloggerService` class to help parse and create Atom 1.0 feeds.

The Blogger Service Class

In this section you will create the class that communicates with the Blogger Data API. While this class does not utilize any native Adobe AIR functionality, it is still one of the most important pieces of this application. This class makes the required requests to the Blogger Data API and handles the responses.

Open your editor and create a new document. Enter the following markup:

```
package com.aircmr.bloggeragent.services
{
    import com.aircmr.bloggeragent.data.Blog;
    import com.aircmr.bloggeragent.data.BlogEntry;
    import com.aircmr.bloggeragent.utils.AtomUtil;
    import flash.errors.IllegalOperationError;
    import flash.events.ErrorEvent;
    import flash.events.Event;
    import flash.events.EventDispatcher;
    import flash.events.HTTPStatusEvent;
    import flash.events.IOErrorEvent;
    import flash.net.URLLoader;
    import flash.net.URLRequest;
    import flash.net.URLRequestHeader;
    import flash.net.URLRequestMethod;
    import flash.net.URLVariables;
    import mx.utils.StringUtil;

    public class BloggerService extends EventDispatcher
    {

        private static var _instance:BloggerService = new BloggerService();

        public static const BLOG_LIST_RETURNED:String = "blogListReturned";
        public static const BLOG_ENTRY_PUBLISHED:String = "blogEntryPublished";
        public static const HTTP_SUCCESS:int = 200;
        public static const HTTP_CREATED:int = 201;
        public static const AUTH_END_POINT:String =
            "https://www.google.com/accounts/ClientLogin";
        public static const BLOG_LIST_END_POINT:String =
            "http://www.blogger.com/feeds/default/blogs";
        public static const SERVICE_NAME:String = "blogger";

        private var _appID:String;
        private var _authCallback:Function;
        private var _authCallbackArgs:Array;
        private var _authToken:String;
        private var _authHeader:URLRequestHeader;
        private var _blogList:Array;
        private var _httpStatus:int;
        private var _username:String;
        private var _password:String;

        public static function getInstance():BloggerService
        {
            return _instance;
        }

        public function BloggerService()
        {
            if( _instance != null )
            {
```

```
            throw new IllegalOperationError( "Error at :: BloggerService. " +
                    "BloggerService is a Singleton and should be accessed " +
                    "through BloggerService.getInstance()." );
        }
    }

    private function onLoaderHTTPStatus( event:HTTPStatusEvent ):void
    {
        if( event.status != HTTP_SUCCESS && event.status != HTTP_CREATED )
        {
            dispatchEvent( new ErrorEvent( ErrorEvent.ERROR, false, false,
                "HTTP Error: " + event.status.toString() ) );
        }
        _httpStatus = event.status;
    }

    private function onLoaderIOError( event:IOErrorEvent ):void
    {
        dispatchEvent( new ErrorEvent(
            ErrorEvent.ERROR, false, false, event.text ) );
    }

    private function onAuthResponse( event:Event ):void
    {
        if( _httpStatus == BloggerService.HTTP_SUCCESS )
        {
            var response:String = String( event.target.data );
            var authIndex:Number = response.indexOf("Auth");
            _authToken = response.substr( authIndex ).split("=")[1];
            _authToken = StringUtil.trim( _authToken );
            _authHeader = new URLRequestHeader( "Authorization",
                "GoogleLogin auth=" + _authToken );

            if( _authCallback != null )
            {
                if( _authCallbackArgs )
                    _authCallback.apply( null, _authCallbackArgs );
                else
                    _authCallback();
            }
        }
    }

    private function onBlogFeedResponse( event:Event ):void
    {
        if( event.target.data != null )
        {
            var xmlData:XML = new XML( String( event.target.data ) );
            _blogList = AtomUtil.parseBlogList(
                xmlData, _username, _password );
            dispatchEvent( new Event( BLOG_LIST_RETURNED ) );
        }
    }
```

```
    private function onPublishComplete( event:Event ):void
    {
        if( _httpStatus == BloggerService.HTTP_CREATED )
        {
            dispatchEvent( new Event( BLOG_ENTRY_PUBLISHED ) );
        }
    }

    private function createNewRequest( url:String, method:String,
        contentType:String = null ):URLRequest
    {
        var request:URLRequest = new URLRequest( url );
        request.requestHeaders.push( _authHeader );
        request.method = method;
        if( contentType != null ) request.contentType = contentType;
        return request;
    }

    private function authenticate( callback:Function,
        callbackArgs:Array = null ):void
    {
        _authCallback = callback;
        _authCallbackArgs = callbackArgs;

        var vars:URLVariables = new URLVariables();
        vars.Email = _username;
        vars.Passwd = _password;
        vars.source = _appID;
        vars.service = SERVICE_NAME;

        var request:URLRequest = new URLRequest();
        request.method = URLRequestMethod.POST;
        request.url = AUTH_END_POINT;
        request.data = vars;

        makeRequest( request, onAuthResponse );
    }

    private function makeRequest( request:URLRequest, callback:Function ):void
    {
     var loader:URLLoader = new URLLoader();
        loader.addEventListener(
            HTTPStatusEvent.HTTP_STATUS, onLoaderHTTPStatus );
        loader.addEventListener( IOErrorEvent.IO_ERROR, onLoaderIOError );
        loader.addEventListener( Event.COMPLETE, callback );
        loader.load( request );
    }

    public function getBlogs():void
    {
        if( _authToken )
        {
```

```
            _blogList = new Array();
            var request:URLRequest = createNewRequest( BLOG_LIST_END_POINT,
                URLRequestMethod.GET );
            makeRequest( request, onBlogFeedResponse );
        }
        else authenticate( getBlogs, null );
    }

    public function publishBlogEntry( blog:Blog, blogEntry:BlogEntry ):void
    {
        if( _authToken )
        {
            var request:URLRequest = createNewRequest( blog.publishURL,
                URLRequestMethod.POST, AtomUtil.CONTENT_TYPE );
            request.data = AtomUtil.serializeBlogEntry(
                blogEntry ).toXMLString();
            makeRequest( request, onPublishComplete );
        }
        else authenticate( publishBlogEntry, [blog, blogEntry] );
    }

    public function setCredentials( username:String,
        password:String, appID:String ):void
    {
        _username = username;
        _password = password;
        _appID = appID;
        _authToken = null;
    }

    public function get blogList():Array { return _blogList; }
  }
}
```

Save the file as `BloggerService.as` in the directory `com/aircmr/bloggeragent/services/` within your working directory.

The `BloggerService` class is designed to get a list of blogs and publish a blog entry. There are only three public methods in this class, two of which correspond to a method call to the Blogger Data API. Before any of those two methods may be called, the other public method, `setCredentials`, must be called. Three parameters are required, the first two being the username and password of the user's Blogger account. The third parameter, `appID`, is necessary for when the application communicates with the Blogger Data API. When called, this parameter is simply a string that represents your application, and is used by the Blogger Data API when authenticating a user.

Note that this method does not authenticate the user right away, but rather stores the authentication information for later use. Authentication does not take place until the first method call is made. Each method checks to see whether the user has been authenticated yet, and if not, attempts to authenticate the user by calling the `authenticate` method. Once the user has been authenticated, the previously attempted method call is made. This process is meant to streamline the process of getting information from the Blogger Data API.

> **This class is based on the latest Blogger Data API as of the publish date of this book. For more information concerning the Blogger Data API, visit `http://code.google.com/apis/blogger/overview.html`. This class is a very limited representation of the available methods. If you have a related project and require a more comprehensive code library for communicating with the Blogger Data API, visit `http://as3bloggerlib.googlecode.com`.**

The two other main methods in this class are `getBlogs` and `publishBlogEntry`. These self-explanatory methods perform exactly as you would expect. Each method will subsequently make the class dispatch a corresponding event, notifying any listeners of when the method call has completed and either data has been returned or a blog entry has successfully been published. Last but not least, notice that this class makes use of the previously constructed data objects, `Blog` and `BlogEntry`, and the `AtomUtil` utility class.

The Database Service Class

In this section you will create the `DBService` class. The `DBService` class manages the application's local SQLite database. This is another very important piece of the application, which in this case utilizes some of the great features of Adobe AIR.

Open your editor and create a new document. Enter the following markup:

```
package com.aircmr.bloggeragent.services
{
    import com.aircmr.bloggeragent.data.Blog;
    import com.aircmr.bloggeragent.data.BlogEntry;
    import com.aircmr.bloggeragent.data.PublishQueueItem;
    import com.aircmr.bloggeragent.events.DBServiceEvent;
    import flash.data.EncryptedLocalStore;
    import flash.data.SQLConnection;
    import flash.data.SQLResult;
    import flash.data.SQLStatement;
    import flash.errors.IllegalOperationError;
    import flash.events.EventDispatcher;
    import flash.events.SQLErrorEvent;
    import flash.events.SQLEvent;
    import flash.filesystem.File;
    import flash.utils.ByteArray;

    public class DBService extends EventDispatcher
    {
        private static var _instance:DBService = new DBService();

        private static const DB:String = "BloggerAgent.db";

        private var _dbFile:File;
        private var _connection:SQLConnection;
        private var _initCallback:Function;
        private var _initCallbackArgs:Array;
        private var _passwordToEncrypt:String;
```

```
        public static function getInstance():DBService
        {
            return _instance;
        }

        public function DBService()
        {
            if( _instance != null )
            {
                throw new IllegalOperationError( "Error at :: DBService. " +
                        "DBService is a Singleton and should be accessed " +
                        "through DBService:getInstance." );
            }
        }

        private function init( callback:Function = null, callbackArgs:Array = null
):void
        {
        }

        private function onConnectionError( event:SQLErrorEvent ):void
        {
            trace( "Database connection error:" + event.text );
        }

        private function onConnectionOpen( evt:SQLEvent ):void
        {
            createBlogsTable();
        }

        private function onBlogsTableCreation( event:SQLEvent ):void
        {
            createPublishQueueTable();
        }

        private function onPublishQueueTableCreation( event:SQLEvent ):void
        {
            if( _initCallback != null )
            {
                if( _initCallbackArgs )
                    _initCallback.call( null, _initCallbackArgs );
                else
                    _initCallback();
            }
        }

        private function onGetBlogs( event:SQLEvent ):void
        {
        }

        private function onGetPublishQueue():void
        {
        }
```

```
private function onAddBlog():void
{
}

private function onAddBlogEntry( event:SQLEvent ):void
{
    dispatchEvent( new DBServiceEvent( DBServiceEvent.BLOG_ENTRY_ADDED ) );
}

private function onBlogDeleted( event:SQLEvent ):void
{
    dispatchEvent( new DBServiceEvent( DBServiceEvent.BLOG_DELETED ) );
}

private function onBlogEntryDeleted( event:SQLEvent ):void
{
    dispatchEvent(
        new DBServiceEvent( DBServiceEvent.BLOG_ENTRY_DELETED ) );
}

private function onQueryError( event:SQLErrorEvent ):void
{
    trace("SQL Error: " + event.text );
}

private function executeStatement():void
{
}

private function createBlogsTable():void
{
    var q:String = "CREATE TABLE IF NOT EXISTS blogs (" +
                   "id    INTEGER    PRIMARY KEY," +
                   "title    TEXT    NOT NULL," +
                   "description    TEXT    NOT NULL," +
                   "publishURL  TEXT  NOT NULL," +
                   "username    TEXT    NOT NULL);";
    executeStatement( q, [], [], onBlogsTableCreation );
}

private function createPublishQueueTable():void
{
    var q:String = "CREATE TABLE IF NOT EXISTS publish_queue (" +
                   "id    INTEGER PRIMARY KEY," +
                   "blog_id  TEXT  NOT NULL," +
                   "title  TEXT  NOT NULL," +
                   "content  TEXT  NOT NULL);";
    executeStatement( q, [], [], onPublishQueueTableCreation );
}

private function encryptPassword():void
{
}
```

```
private function unencryptPassword():void
{
}

public function addBlog():void
{
}

public function addBlogEntry( blogEntry:BlogEntry ):void
{
    if( _connection )
    {
        var q:String = "INSERT INTO publish_queue VALUES (null," +
            ":blogID, :title, :content);";
        var paramNames:Array =
            [":blogID", ":title", ":content"];
        var paramValues:Array =
            [blogEntry.blogID, blogEntry.title, blogEntry.content];
        executeStatement( q, paramNames, paramValues, onAddBlogEntry );
    }
    else init( addBlogEntry, [blogEntry] );
}

public function getBlogs():void
{
    if( _connection )
    {
        var q:String = "SELECT * FROM blogs ORDER BY id DESC;";
        executeStatement( q, [], [], onGetBlogs );
    }
    else init( getBlogs );
}

public function deleteBlog( id:int ):void
{
    if( _connection )
    {
        var q:String = "DELETE FROM blogs WHERE id='" + id + "';";
        executeStatement( q, [], [], onBlogDeleted );
    }
    else init( deleteBlog, [id] );
}

public function getPublishQueue():void
{
    if( _connection )
    {
        var q:String = "SELECT blogs.id AS blogid, " +
            "blogs.title AS blogtitle, blogs.description, " +
            "blogs.username, blogs.publishURL, " +
            "publish_queue.id, publish_queue.blog_id, " +
            "publish_queue.title, publish_queue.content " +
            "FROM blogs, publish_queue WHERE " +
            "blogs.id=publish_queue.blog_id;";
```

```
                executeStatement( q, [], [], onGetPublishQueue );
            }
            else init( getPublishQueue );
        }

        public function deleteBlogEntry( id:int ):void
        {
            if( _connection )
            {
                var q:String = "DELETE FROM publish_queue WHERE id='" + id + "';";
                executeStatement( q, [], [], onBlogEntryDeleted );
            }
            else init( deleteBlogEntry, [id] );
        }

        public function close():void
        {
            if( _connection )
                _connection.close();
        }
    }
}
```

Save the file as `DBService.as` in the directory `com/aircmr/bloggeragent/services/` within your working directory.

Now you've just begun to create the `DBService` class. This class will create and manage the local SQLite database for the application. This database will store the user's blog information — specifically, the blog's title, a description, the publish URL, and the username that owns the blog. The database will also store any queued blog entries. Please keep in mind that the class is not yet complete. In the following steps you will add some crucial functionality that takes advantage of some of the native AIR API.

Make the following changes and additions to the markup of the `init` function of the `DBService` class:

```
private function init( callback:Function = null, callbackArgs:Array = null ):void
{
    _initCallback = callback;
    _initCallbackArgs = callbackArgs;
    _dbFile = File.applicationStorageDirectory.resolvePath( DB );
    _connection = new SQLConnection();
    _connection.addEventListener( SQLEvent.OPEN, onConnectionOpen );
    _connection.addEventListener( SQLErrorEvent.ERROR, onConnectionError );
    _connection.open( _dbFile );
}
```

The init function is set to `private` because here it is essentially the equivalent of the `authenticate` method in the `BloggerService` class. In the `BloggerService` class, the user must be authenticated before any method calls can be made. Similarly, the `DBService` class must be initialized first before any method calls may be made. Initialization ensures that the database is created and the connection is opened.

Notice the use of the `SQLConnection` class. This is a native Adobe AIR class that is used to manage a connection to a local SQLite database. A SQLite database is a flat file located on the user's hard drive. This file can already exist, or it is automatically created when the `open` method is called. The `open` method requires a File object that points to the location of the database. In this case, the database is stored in the application's storage directory. This is ensured by using the applicationStorageDirectory property of Adobe AIR's File object. This property is also of type File and is a reference to — you guessed it — the application's storage directory. By utilizing the property's resolvePath method, the application specifies a file with the name BloggerAgent.db, which is hard-coded into the DBService class as a private static variable. After the database connection is opened, the two database tables must be created. Two methods create these tables: createBlogsTable and createPublishQueueTable, respectively. These methods are called in a brief event chaining sequence once the SQLConnection instance dispatches an OPEN event. Notice the use of the specific SQLEvent and SQLErrorEvent classes. These events will help you manage the connection. After the OPEN event is dispatched, the onConnectionOpen event handler is called.

Make the following changes and additions to the markup of the executeStatement function of the DBService class:

```
private function executeStatement( query:String, paramNames:Array,
    paramValues:Array, resultHandler:Function ):void
{
    var newStatement:SQLStatement = new SQLStatement();
    newStatement.sqlConnection = _connection;
    newStatement.addEventListener( SQLEvent.RESULT, resultHandler );
    newStatement.addEventListener( SQLErrorEvent.ERROR, onQueryError );
    newStatement.text = query;

    for( var i:int = 0; i < paramNames.length; i++ )
        newStatement.parameters[paramNames[i]] = paramValues[i];

    newStatement.execute();
}
```

This method is used throughout the class to execute statements on the local SQLite database. The four parameters of this function are used to construct a SQLStatement object. A SQLStatement instance is used to execute a SQLite statement against a local SQLite database that is open through an SQLConnection instance. In this case, the connection property is set to the local class variable _connection, which was created in the init function. Then the result handler for the statement is set by the resultHandler parameter, and the text property is set by the query parameter.

The statement is nearly ready to be executed; however, one more step is necessary. As a precaution, the parameters of the statement are defined by modifying the statement's parameters property. This property serves as an associative array to which you add values for the parameters specified in the statement's text property. The array keys are the names of the parameters. Setting the parameters of the statement in this manner is a defensive measure to prevent a malicious technique known as *SQL injection*. In an SQL injection attack, a user attempts to insert his or her own SQL statements through user-accessible locations. Finally, to execute the statement, the execute method is called.

Make the following changes and additions to the markup of the addBlog function of the DBService class:

```
public function addBlog( blog:Blog ):void
{
    if( _connection )
    {
        _passwordToEncrypt = blog.password;
        var q:String = "INSERT INTO blogs VALUES (null, " +
```

```
            ":title, :description, :publishURL, :username);";
        var paramNames:Array =
            [":title",":description",":publishURL",":username"];
        var paramValues:Array =
            [blog.title, blog.description, blog.publishURL, blog.username];
        executeStatement( q, paramNames, paramValues, onAddBlog );
    }
    else init( addBlog, [blog] );
}
```

This method serves as an example to illustrate how the class utilizes the `executeStatement` function to execute statements on the local SQLite database. This function accepts one parameter: an object of type `Blog`. This `Blog` object will be created outside this class, but when provided will provide all the relevant information needed to add the blog to the database. If the connection is set, the function stores the blog's password into the `_passwordToEncrypt` class variable. This will be used after the other blog data has been successfully stored in the database. Afterward, a SQLite statement string is created. The values for this particular `INSERT` statement are not specifically set in the string, but rather are represented using parameter keys. The keys all begin with a colon and will eventually be replaced with valid values in the `executeStatement` function. In order for this to happen, two arrays are created. The first is an array containing the names of the keys. The second is an array containing the values for each key. Once this is done, the statement string, the arrays, and a corresponding event handler are then sent to the `executeStatement` function for processing.

Make the following changes and additions to the markup of the `onGetBlogs`, `onGetPublishQueue`, and `onAddBlog` event handlers of the `DBService` class:

```
private function onGetBlogs( event:SQLEvent ):void
{
    var statement:SQLStatement = event.target as SQLStatement;
    var result:SQLResult = statement.getResult();
    var typedData:Array = new Array();

    if( result.data != null )
    {
        var data:Array = result.data;
        for( var i:int = 0; i < data.length; i++ )
        {
            var blog:Blog = new Blog();
            blog.id = data[i].id;
            blog.title = data[i].title;
            blog.description = data[i].description;
            blog.publishURL = data[i].publishURL;
            blog.username = data[i].username;
            blog.password = unencryptPassword( blog.id );
            typedData.push( blog );
        }
    }

    dispatchEvent( new DBServiceEvent( DBServiceEvent.GET_BLOGS, typedData ) );
}
private function onGetPublishQueue( event:SQLEvent ):void
{
    var statement:SQLStatement = event.target as SQLStatement;
```

```
    var result:SQLResult = statement.getResult();
    var typedData:Array = new Array();

    if( result.data != null )
    {
        var data:Array = result.data;
        for( var i:int = 0; i < data.length; i++ )
        {
            var blog:Blog = new Blog();
            blog.id = data[i].blogid;
            blog.title = data[i].blogtitle;
            blog.description = data[i].description;
            blog.publishURL = data[i].publishURL;
            blog.username = data[i].username;
            blog.password = unencryptPassword( blog.id );

            var blogEntry:BlogEntry = new BlogEntry();
            blogEntry.id = data[i].id;
            blogEntry.blogID = data[i].blogID;
            blogEntry.title = data[i].title;
            blogEntry.content = data[i].content;

            var publishQueueItem:PublishQueueItem = new PublishQueueItem();
            publishQueueItem.blogTitle = blog.title;
            publishQueueItem.blogEntryTitle = blogEntry.title;
            if( blogEntry.content.length > 30 )
            {
                publishQueueItem.blogEntryContent =
                    blogEntry.content.substr( 0, 30 ) + "..."
            }
            else publishQueueItem.blogEntryContent = blogEntry.content;
            publishQueueItem.blog = blog;
            publishQueueItem.blogEntry = blogEntry;

            typedData.push( publishQueueItem );
        }
    }

    dispatchEvent(
       new DBServiceEvent( DBServiceEvent.GET_BLOG_ENTRIES, typedData ) );
}
private function onAddBlog( event:SQLEvent ):void
{
    encryptPassword( _connection.lastInsertRowID, _passwordToEncrypt );
    dispatchEvent( new DBServiceEvent( DBServiceEvent.BLOG_ADDED ) );
}
```

These functions handle the events that are dispatched from executing a `SQLStatement` object. In the case of the `onGetBlogs` and `onGetPublishQueue` functions, information from a `SELECT` query is parsed and converted to the application's specific data objects. However, in the case of the `onAddBlog` function, there isn't much to do except for encrypting the password associated with that blog. To do this, the `encryptPassword` method is called, passing it the ID of the last inserted blog record and the blog's password. The ID of the last inserted blog is retrieved by accessing the `lastInsertRowID` property of the `SQLConnection` instance named `_connection`.

Make the following changes and additions to the markup of the encryptPassword method and the unencryptPassword method of the DBService class:

```
private function encryptPassword( blogID:int, password:String ):void
{
    var data:ByteArray = new ByteArray();
    data.writeUTFBytes( password );
    EncryptedLocalStore.setItem( "blog-" + blogID, data );
}
```

```
private function unencryptPassword( blogID:int ):String
{
    var passwordData:ByteArray = EncryptedLocalStore.getItem( "blog-" + blogID );
    return passwordData.readUTFBytes( passwordData.bytesAvailable );
}
```

These methods perform as you would expect. Specifically, in this application, both functions utilize Adobe AIR's EncryptedLocalStore class to encrypt and unencrypt passwords. The EncryptedLocalStore class provides methods for setting and getting objects in the encrypted local data store for an AIR application. Items in the encrypted local data store are identified with a string, and all items are stored as byte array data. Anything stored in this manner is only available to Adobe AIR application content. It is the perfect place for storing sensitive information such as a user's Blogger password.

Here, the blogID parameter in each function relates the id column of a record in the blog table of the database. This ID is used to create a string that specifies the name of the item to store or retrieve from the encrypted local store. To retrieve an item, the static getItem method is used. This method requires a string specifying the item to retrieve. The method will return a ByteArray object. Using the byte array's readUTFBytes method, the password is extracted from the byte information and returned as a useful String. To save an item, the static setItem method is called. Two parameters, a String and a ByteArray, are required to save the data to the encrypted local store.

That covers the main functionality of the DBService class. In the next section, you will create a class to manage the publishing of blog entries in the publish queue.

The Queue Service Class

In this section you will create the QueueService class. This is a relatively simple class that manages the subsequent publishing of blog entries stored in the publish queue.

Create a new document and enter the following markup:

```
package com.aircmr.bloggeragent.services
{
    import com.aircmr.bloggeragent.data.Blog;
    import com.aircmr.bloggeragent.data.BlogEntry;
    import com.aircmr.bloggeragent.data.PublishQueueItem;
    import flash.events.Event;
    import flash.events.EventDispatcher;
```

```
    public class QueueService extends EventDispatcher
    {

        private var _items:Array;
        private var _currentItem:PublishQueueItem;
        private var _dbService:DBService;
        private var _bloggerService:BloggerService;

        public function QueueService( items:Array )
        {
            _items = items;
            _dbService = DBService.getInstance();
            _bloggerService = BloggerService.getInstance();
        }

        private function onBlogEntryPublished( event:Event ):void
        {
            _dbService.deleteBlogEntry( _currentItem.blogEntry.id );
            _bloggerService.removeEventListener(
                BloggerService.BLOG_ENTRY_PUBLISHED, onBlogEntryPublished );

            if( _items.length > 0 )
                nextItem();
            else
                dispatchEvent( new Event( Event.COMPLETE ) );
        }

        private function nextItem():void
        {
            _currentItem = _items.shift() as PublishQueueItem;

            var blog:Blog = _currentItem.blog;
            var blogEntry:BlogEntry = _currentItem.blogEntry;

            _bloggerService.addEventListener(
                BloggerService.BLOG_ENTRY_PUBLISHED, onBlogEntryPublished );
            _bloggerService.setCredentials( blog.username, blog.password,
                BloggerAgent.APPLICATION_ID );
            _bloggerService.publishBlogEntry( blog, blogEntry );
        }

        public function startQueue():void
        {
            nextItem();
        }

    }
}
```

Save the file as `QueueService.as` in the directory `com/aircmr/bloggeragent/services/` within your working directory.

You just created the `QueueService` class. As mentioned earlier, this class manages the subsequent publishing of blog entries stored in the publish queue. This class is designed to take an array of `PublishQueue` objects and publish the blog entry of each item to the appropriate blog. As you can see, the constructor of this class accepts one parameter: an `Array`. This `Array` should consist of one or more `PublishQueueItem` objects. After the `QueueService` object is constructed, the `startQueue` function will be used to start publishing.

The following snippet is from the `nextItem` function:

```
private function nextItem():void
{
    _currentItem = _items.shift() as PublishQueueItem;

    var blog:Blog = _currentItem.blog;
    var blogEntry:BlogEntry = _currentItem.blogEntry;

    _bloggerService.addEventListener( BloggerService.BLOG_ENTRY_PUBLISHED,
onBlogEntryPublished );
    _bloggerService.setCredentials( blog.username, blog.password,
BloggerAgent.APPLICATION_ID );
    _bloggerService.publishBlogEntry( blog, blogEntry );
}
```

Here you can see use of the `BloggerService` class. Within this class, the `BloggerService` class is used to publish a blog entry to a particular blog. The `Blog` and `BlogEntry` objects are pulled from the `currentItem` variable by accessing the `PublishQueueItem` object's `blog` and `blogEntry` properties. Once this is done, the `onBlogEntryPublished` event handler is configured for the `BLOG_ENTRY_PUBLISHED` event. This event enables the class to determine when to move on to the next `PublishQueueItem`.

Finally, the blog entry is published by first calling the `setCredentials` function and then the `publishBlogEntry` function of the `BloggerService` class. The `setCredentials` function accepts three parameters, the first two being the username and password for the blog account. In this case, they are taken from the current `Blog` object. The third is a string representing the application that is accessing the Blogger Data API. This parameter is taken from the static property of the main application file (which you will create in the following section).

After the credentials are set, its safe to call the `publishBlogEntry` function, passing it the current `Blog` and `BlogEntry` objects as the two parameters. When the blog entry has published, the `onBlogEntryPublished` function is called and the entry is deleted from the queue by calling the `deleteBlogEntry` function of the `DBService` class and passing it the ID number of the blog entry to delete.

At this point, you have created all the ActionScript classes necessary for this application. It's now time to move on to the user interface.

Creating the User Interface

In this section you will create the user interface elements for the application. The user interface consists of the five components. Three of these components will serve as the main views. The remaining two will serve as prompts for the main views. With the following code you will create the user interface components, starting with the `AddBlogPanel` component.

Create a new document and enter the following markup:

```
<?xml version="1.0" encoding="utf-8"?>
<mx:Panel xmlns:mx="http://www.adobe.com/2006/mxml"
    width="412" height="258" title="Add Account"
    creationComplete="init();">
    <mx:Script><![CDATA[

    import com.aircmr.bloggeragent.data.Blog;
    import com.aircmr.bloggeragent.services.BloggerService;
    import com.aircmr.net.NetworkDetection;
    import mx.controls.Alert;
    import mx.managers.CursorManager;
    import mx.managers.PopUpManager;

    private static var NO_BLOGS:Array = [{title:"No blogs available for this user"}];

    private var _bloggerService:BloggerService;
    private var _netDetect:NetworkDetection;

    public static function show():AddBlogPanel
    {
        var prompt:AddBlogPanel =
            AddBlogPanel( PopUpManager.createPopUp(
            DisplayObject( mx.core.Application.application ),
            AddBlogPanel, true ) );

        PopUpManager.centerPopUp( prompt );
        return prompt;
    }

    private function init():void
    {
        _bloggerService = BloggerService.getInstance();
        _netDetect = NetworkDetection.getInstance();

        _bloggerService.addEventListener( BloggerService.BLOG_LIST_RETURNED,
            onBlogListReturned );
        _bloggerService.addEventListener( ErrorEvent.ERROR,
            onBloggerError );
        _netDetect.addEventListener( NetworkDetection.CONNECTION_CHANGE,
            onConnectionChange );

        onConnectionChange( null );
    }

    private function onConnectionChange( event:Event ):void
    {
        listBlogsBtn.enabled = _netDetect.connected;
    }
```

```
private function onBlogListReturned( event:Event ):void
{
    var blogList:Array = _bloggerService.blogList;

    if( blogList.length > 0 )
    {
        blogListComboBox.dataProvider = blogList;
        addBlogBtn.enabled = true;
    }
    else
    {
        blogListComboBox.dataProvider = NO_BLOGS;
        addBlogBtn.enabled = false;
    }
    enable();
}

private function onBloggerError( event:ErrorEvent ):void
{
    blogListComboBox.dataProvider = null;
    addBlogBtn.enabled = false;
    Alert.show( "Login failed. Try again.", "Error", (Alert.OK), this );
    enable();
}

private function getBlogs( event:Event ):void
{
    disable();
    _bloggerService.setCredentials( usernameInput.text, passwordInput.text,
        BloggerAgent.APPLICATION_ID );
    _bloggerService.getBlogs();
}

private function addBlog( event:MouseEvent ):void
{
    dispatchEvent( new Event( Event.SELECT ) );
}

public function enable():void
{
    this.enabled = true;
    CursorManager.removeBusyCursor();
}

public function disable():void
{
    this.enabled = false;
    CursorManager.setBusyCursor();
}

public function close():void { PopUpManager.removePopUp( this ); }

public function get selectedItem():Blog
{
```

```
        return blogListComboBox.selectedItem as Blog;
    }

    public function get username():String { return usernameInput.text; }
    public function get password():String { return passwordInput.text; }

    ]]></mx:Script>
    <mx:Canvas width="100%" height="100%">
        <mx:Text text="Username:" x="10" y="24" width="86"
            fontWeight="bold" textAlign="right"/>
        <mx:TextInput id="usernameInput" x="113" y="22" enter="getBlogs(event)"/>
        <mx:Text text="Password:" x="10" y="58" width="86"
            fontWeight="bold" textAlign="right"/>
        <mx:TextInput id="passwordInput" x="113" y="54"
            displayAsPassword="true" enter="getBlogs(event)"/>
        <mx:Button id="listBlogsBtn" x="281" y="54"
            label="List Blogs" click="getBlogs(event)"/>
        <mx:Text text="Blog Title:" x="10" y="117" width="86"
            fontWeight="bold" textAlign="right"/>
        <mx:ComboBox id="blogListComboBox" x="113" y="115"
            width="248" labelField="title"/>
        <mx:Button id="cancelBtn" x="207" y="174"
            label="Cancel" click="close()"/>
        <mx:Button id="addBlogBtn" x="284" y="174" label="Add Blog"
            enabled="false" click="addBlog(event)"/>
    </mx:Canvas>
</mx:Panel>
```

Save the file as `AddBlogPanel.mxml` in the directory `com/aircmr/bloggeragent/ui/` within your working directory.

The `AddBlogPanel` component acts as a prompt. When displayed, it enables users to enter their Blogger login information, retrieve a list of blogs for that account, and then select a blog to add to the application. The following snippet is from the `AddBlogPanel` component's `init` function:

```
private function init():void
{
    _bloggerService = BloggerService.getInstance();
    _netDetect = NetworkDetection.getInstance();

    _bloggerService.addEventListener( BloggerService.BLOG_LIST_RETURNED,
onBlogListReturned );
    _bloggerService.addEventListener( ErrorEvent.ERROR, onBloggerError );

    _netDetect.addEventListener( NetworkDetection.CONNECTION_CHANGE,
onConnectionChange );

    onConnectionChange( null );
}
```

Here you can see use of the `BloggerService` class and the `NetworkDetection` class. Within this component, the `BloggerService` class will be used to retrieve a list of blogs; thus, the `BLOG_LIST_RETURNED` event is configured to be handled by the `onBlogListReturned` function. This function grabs the list of blogs from the service class to use as the `dataProvider` of the combo box. Additionally, the `CONNECTION_CHANGE` event of the `NetworkDetection` class is configured to be handled by the `onConnectionChange` function. This function activates or deactivates particular interface elements depending on whether the user is connected to the Internet or not.

This component will be used within the `BlogManagerPanel` component, created next:

```
<?xml version="1.0" encoding="utf-8"?>
<mx:Panel xmlns:mx="http://www.adobe.com/2006/mxml"
    width="800" height="600" top="40" right="10"
    bottom="10" left="10" title="Manage Blogs"
    creationComplete="init();">
    <mx:Script><![CDATA[

    import com.aircmr.bloggeragent.ui.AddBlogPanel;
    import com.aircmr.bloggeragent.services.DBService;
    import com.aircmr.bloggeragent.events.DBServiceEvent;
    import com.aircmr.net.NetworkDetection;
    import mx.managers.CursorManager;

    [Bindable]
    private var _blogs:Array;

    private var _addBlogPanel:AddBlogPanel;
    private var _dbService:DBService;
    private var _netDetect:NetworkDetection;

    private function init():void
    {
        _dbService = DBService.getInstance();
        _netDetect = NetworkDetection.getInstance();
        _dbService.addEventListener( DBServiceEvent.GET_BLOGS, onGetBlogs );
        _dbService.addEventListener( DBServiceEvent.BLOG_ADDED, onBlogsModified );
        _dbService.addEventListener( DBServiceEvent.BLOG_DELETED, onBlogsModified );
        _netDetect.addEventListener( NetworkDetection.CONNECTION_CHANGE,
onConnectionChange );
        onConnectionChange( null );
    }

    private function onConnectionChange( event:Event ):void
    {
        addBlogBtn.enabled = _netDetect.connected;
    }

    private function onBlogsModified( event:DBServiceEvent ):void
    {
        _dbService.getBlogs();
    }

    private function onGetBlogs( event:DBServiceEvent ):void
    {
        _blogs = event.data as Array;
    }
```

```
        private function onAddBlogSelect( event:Event ):void
        {
            _dbService.addBlog( _addBlogPanel.selectedItem );
            _addBlogPanel.close();
        }

        private function openAddBlogPanel( event:MouseEvent ):void
        {
            _addBlogPanel = AddBlogPanel.show();
            _addBlogPanel.addEventListener( Event.SELECT, onAddBlogSelect );
        }

        private function deleteBlog( event:MouseEvent ):void
        {
            _dbService.deleteBlog( blogDataGrid.selectedItem.id );
        }

        public function update():void
        {
            _dbService.getBlogs();
        }

        ]]></mx:Script>
        <mx:Canvas width="100%" height="100%">
            <mx:DataGrid id="blogDataGrid" dataProvider="{_blogs}"
                top="0" bottom="40" left="0" right="0">
                <mx:columns>
                    <mx:DataGridColumn headerText="Title" dataField="title"/>
                    <mx:DataGridColumn headerText="User" dataField="username"/>
                   <mx:DataGridColumn headerText="Description" dataField="description"/>
                </mx:columns>
            </mx:DataGrid>
            <mx:Button id="addBlogBtn" label="Add Blog"
                right="110" bottom="10" click="openAddBlogPanel(event)"/>
            <mx:Button label="Delete Blog" right="10" bottom="10"
                enabled="{(blogDataGrid.selectedItem != null)}"
                click="deleteBlog(event)"/>
        </mx:Canvas>
    </mx:Panel>
```

Save the file as `BlogManagerPanel.mxml` in the directory `com/aircmr/bloggeragent/ui/` within your working directory.

The `BlogManagerPanel` component displays the accounts (or blogs) that the user has added to the application. It also enables the user to add a new blog (by using the previously created `AddBlogPrompt` component) or delete an existing blog. When adding or deleting a blog, the component utilizes the `DBService` class to store or modify the account information within the local database.

The following snippet is from the `BlogManagerPanel` component's `init` function. Here you can see use of the `DBService` class and, similar to that of the `AddBlogPrompt` component, the `NetworkDetection` class:

```
private function init():void
{
```

```
        _dbService = DBService.getInstance();
        _netDetect = NetworkDetection.getInstance();

        _dbService.addEventListener( DBServiceEvent.GET_BLOGS, onGetBlogs );
        _dbService.addEventListener( DBServiceEvent.BLOG_ADDED, onBlogsModified );
        _dbService.addEventListener( DBServiceEvent.BLOG_DELETED, onBlogsModified );

        _netDetect.addEventListener( NetworkDetection.CONNECTION_CHANGE,
    onConnectionChange );

        onConnectionChange( null );
    }
```

Within this component, the `DBService` class is used to retrieve a list of blogs, add a blog, and delete a blog from the local database. Each of these methods causes a corresponding event to be dispatched when the operation has completed. These events are configured with an appropriate handler function. Note that whenever a blog is added or deleted, the list of blogs is again retrieved from the `DBService` class by calling the `getBlogs` function. This ensures that the data within the database is synchronized with the user interface.

This component, paired with the `AddBlogPrompt` component, enables users to manage their blog accounts. The next component necessary enables users to compose a blog entry.

Create a new document and enter the following markup:

```
    <?xml version="1.0" encoding="utf-8"?>
    <mx:Panel xmlns:mx="http://www.adobe.com/2006/mxml"
        width="800" height="600" top="40" right="10" bottom="10" left="10"
        title="Compose Blog Entry" creationComplete="init();">
        <mx:Script><![CDATA[

        import com.aircmr.bloggeragent.data.Blog;
        import com.aircmr.bloggeragent.data.BlogEntry;
        import com.aircmr.bloggeragent.events.DBServiceEvent;
        import com.aircmr.bloggeragent.services.BloggerService;
        import com.aircmr.bloggeragent.services.DBService;
        import com.aircmr.net.NetworkDetection;
        import mx.controls.Alert;
        import mx.managers.CursorManager;

        private static var NO_BLOGS:Array = [{title:"Add an account first!"}];

        [Bindable]
        private var _blogs:Array;

        private var _bloggerService:BloggerService;
        private var _dbService:DBService;
        private var _netDetect:NetworkDetection;

        private function init():void
        {
            _bloggerService = BloggerService.getInstance();
            _dbService = DBService.getInstance();
```

```
        _dbService.addEventListener( DBServiceEvent.GET_BLOGS, onGetBlogs );
        _netDetect = NetworkDetection.getInstance();
        _netDetect.addEventListener(
            NetworkDetection.CONNECTION_CHANGE, onConnectionChange );
        blogSelector.dataProvider = NO_BLOGS;
        updateButtons();
    }

    private function onConnectionChange( event:Event ):void
    {
        updateButtons();
    }

    private function onBloggerError( event:ErrorEvent ):void
    {
        Alert.show( event.text, "Error", (Alert.OK), this );
        enable();
    }

    private function onBlogEntryPublished( event:Event ):void
    {
        _bloggerService.removeEventListener( BloggerService.BLOG_ENTRY_PUBLISHED,
            onBlogEntryPublished );
        _bloggerService.removeEventListener( ErrorEvent.ERROR, onBloggerError );
        titleInput.text = contentInput.htmlText = "";
        Alert.show( "Entry published successfully", "Success!", (Alert.OK), this );
        enable();
    }

    private function onGetBlogs( event:DBServiceEvent ):void
    {
        var data:Array = event.data as Array;
        _blogs = ( data.length > 0 ) ? data : NO_BLOGS;
        updateButtons();
    }

    private function onTextFieldChange( event:Event ):void
    {
        updateButtons();
    }

    private function updateButtons():void
    {
        if( _blogs != NO_BLOGS )
        {
            if( titleInput.text.length > 0 && contentInput.text.length > 0 )
            {
                addToQueueBtn.enabled = true;
                publishBtn.enabled = _netDetect.connected;
            }
            else addToQueueBtn.enabled = publishBtn.enabled = false;
        }
        else publishBtn.enabled = addToQueueBtn.enabled = false;
    }
```

```
private function publishNow( event:MouseEvent ):void
{
    var blog:Blog = blogSelector.selectedItem as Blog;
    var blogEntry:BlogEntry = new BlogEntry();
    blogEntry.title = titleInput.text;
    blogEntry.content = contentInput.text;
    _bloggerService.addEventListener( BloggerService.BLOG_ENTRY_PUBLISHED,
        onBlogEntryPublished );
    _bloggerService.addEventListener( ErrorEvent.ERROR, onBloggerError );
    _bloggerService.setCredentials(
        blog.username, blog.password, BloggerAgent.APPLICATION_ID );
    _bloggerService.publishBlogEntry( blog, blogEntry );
    disable();
}

private function addToQueue( event:MouseEvent ):void
{
    var blogEntry:BlogEntry = new BlogEntry();
    blogEntry.blogID = blogSelector.selectedItem.id;
    blogEntry.title = titleInput.text;
    blogEntry.content = contentInput.text;
    _dbService.addBlogEntry( blogEntry );
    titleInput.text = contentInput.text = "";
}

private function enable():void
{
    this.enabled = true;
    CursorManager.removeBusyCursor();
}

private function disable():void
{
    this.enabled = false;
    CursorManager.setBusyCursor();
}

public function update():void
{
    _dbService.getBlogs();
}

]]></mx:Script>
<mx:Canvas width="100%" height="100%">
    <mx:Text text="Publish to:" x="10" y="10"/>
    <mx:ComboBox id="blogSelector" x="10" y="30" width="327"
        labelField="title" dataProvider="{_blogs}"/>
    <mx:Text text="Title" x="10" y="61"/>
    <mx:TextInput id="titleInput" x="10" y="78" width="580"
        change="onTextFieldChange(event)"/>
    <mx:Text text="Content" x="10" y="110"/>
    <mx:TextInput id="contentInput"
        left="10" right="10" top="129" bottom="50"
        change="onTextFieldChange(event)"/>
```

```
            <mx:Button id="publishBtn" label="Publish Now"
                left="10" bottom="10" click="publishNow(event)"/>
            <mx:Button id="addToQueueBtn" label="Add to Publish Queue"
                right="10" bottom="10" click="addToQueue(event)" />
        </mx:Canvas>
    </mx:Panel>
```

Save the file as `ComposeEntryPanel.mxml` in the directory `com/aircmr/bloggeragent/ui/` within your working directory.

The `ComposeEntryPanel` component enables users to compose a blog entry and either publish it immediately by using the `BloggerService` class or place it in the publish queue by using the `DBService` class. The `NetworkDetection` class is used here again to keep track of the user's connection status and update user interface elements accordingly.

The following snippet is from the `ComposeEntryPanel` component's `publishNow` function. Here you can see how the `BloggerService` class is used to publish a blog entry:

```
private function publishNow( event:MouseEvent ):void
{
    var blog:Blog = blogSelector.selectedItem as Blog;
    var blogEntry:BlogEntry = new BlogEntry();
    blogEntry.title = titleInput.text;
    blogEntry.content = contentInput.text;
    _bloggerService.addEventListener( BloggerService.BLOG_ENTRY_PUBLISHED,
       onBlogEntryPublished );
    _bloggerService.addEventListener( ErrorEvent.ERROR, onBloggerError );
    _bloggerService.setCredentials( blog.username, blog.password,
        BloggerAgent.APPLICATION_ID );
    _bloggerService.publishBlogEntry( blog, blogEntry );
    disable();
}
```

First, the blog to which the entry should be published is specified by accessing the `selectedItem` property of the combo box component named `blogSelector`. Note that the data provider for the combo box is an array of `Blog` objects that have been retrieved from the `DBService` class. Second, a `BlogEntry` object is created. This object needs only two properties to be set, `title` and `content`, in order for it to be prepared for posting. These properties are set to the input values from the corresponding input components.

Now that the `BlogEntry` object is prepared, the `BloggerService` class is configured with two events. The `BLOG_ENTRY_PUBLISHED` event is dispatched when the blog entry has been successfully published, and the `ERROR` event is dispatched if there's any sort of problem while attempting to publish. Next, the `BloggerService` class is configured with the appropriate login credentials by calling the `setCredentials` function and passing it the `username` and `password` properties from the previously saved `Blog` object. Lastly, an attempt is made to publish the blog entry by calling the `publishBlogEntry` function of the `BloggerService` class, passing it the `Blog` and `BlogEntry` objects.

The following snippet is from the `addToQueue` function. Here you can see how the `DBService` class is used to add a blog entry to the publish queue:

```
private function addToQueue( event:MouseEvent ):void
{
```

```
        var blogEntry:BlogEntry = new BlogEntry();
        blogEntry.blogID = blogSelector.selectedItem.id;
        blogEntry.title = titleInput.text;
        blogEntry.content = contentInput.text;
        _dbService.addBlogEntry( blogEntry );
        titleInput.text = contentInput.text = "";
    }
```

First, a new `BlogEntry` object is created and is prepared similarly to how one is prepared for publishing. The only difference here is that in addition to setting the `title` and `content` properties, the `blogID` property is set as well. This is set equal to the `id` property of the currently selected blog in the combo box. Now, the only thing left to do is call the `addBlogEntry` function of the `DBService` class, passing the `BlogEntry` object as the only parameter.

This covers the main functionality of the `ComposeEntryPanel` component. Next up is the `PublishQueuePanel` component.

Create a new document and enter the following markup:

```
<?xml version="1.0" encoding="utf-8"?>
<mx:Panel xmlns:mx="http://www.adobe.com/2006/mxml"
    width="800" height="600" top="40" right="10" bottom="10" left="10"
    title="Publish Queue" creationComplete="init();">
    <mx:Script><![CDATA[
        import flash.net.navigateToURL;

    import com.aircmr.bloggeragent.services.QueueService;
    import com.aircmr.bloggeragent.events.DBServiceEvent;
    import com.aircmr.bloggeragent.services.DBService;
    import com.aircmr.net.NetworkDetection;
    import mx.controls.Alert;
    import mx.managers.CursorManager;

    [Bindable]
    private var _publishQueueItems:Array;

    private var _dbService:DBService;
    private var _netDetect:NetworkDetection;
    private var _queueService:QueueService;

    private function init():void
    {
        _dbService = DBService.getInstance();
        _netDetect = NetworkDetection.getInstance();
        _dbService.addEventListener( DBServiceEvent.GET_BLOG_ENTRIES,
            onGetBlogEntries );
        _dbService.addEventListener( DBServiceEvent.BLOG_ENTRY_DELETED,
            onBlogEntryDeleted );
        _netDetect.addEventListener( NetworkDetection.CONNECTION_CHANGE,
            onConnectionChange );
        onConnectionChange( null );
    }
```

```
private function onConnectionChange( event:Event ):void
{
    startQueueBtn.enabled = _netDetect.connected;
}

private function onGetBlogEntries( event:DBServiceEvent ):void
{
    _publishQueueItems = event.data as Array;
}

private function onBlogEntryDeleted( event:DBServiceEvent ):void
{
    _dbService.getPublishQueue();
}

private function onQueueServiceComplete( event:Event ):void
{
    this.enabled = true;
    CursorManager.removeBusyCursor();
    Alert.show( "Publish queue complete!", "Success!", (Alert.OK), this );
}

private function startQueue( event:MouseEvent ):void
{
    _queueService = new QueueService( _publishQueueItems );
    _queueService.addEventListener( Event.COMPLETE, onQueueServiceComplete );
    _queueService.startQueue();

    this.enabled = false;
    CursorManager.setBusyCursor();
}

private function deleteEntry( event:MouseEvent ):void
{
    var blogEntryID:int = publishQueueGrid.selectedItem.blogEntry.id;
    _dbService.deleteBlogEntry( blogEntryID );
}

public function update():void
{
    _dbService.getPublishQueue();
}

]]></mx:Script>
<mx:Canvas width="100%" height="100%">
    <mx:DataGrid id="publishQueueGrid" dataProvider="{_publishQueueItems}"
        top="0" right="0" left="0" bottom="40">
        <mx:columns>
            <mx:DataGridColumn headerText="Blog" dataField="blogTitle"/>
            <mx:DataGridColumn headerText="Title" dataField="blogEntryTitle"/>
            <mx:DataGridColumn headerText="Content"
               dataField="blogEntryContent"/>
        </mx:columns>
    </mx:DataGrid>
```

```
            <mx:Button id="startQueueBtn" click="startQueue(event)"
                label="Start Queue" left="10" bottom="10"
                enabled="{(_publishQueueItems.length > 0)}"/>
            <mx:Button id="deleteBtn" click="deleteEntry(event)"
                label="Delete Entry" right="10" bottom="10"
                enabled="{(publishQueueGrid.selectedItem != null)}"/>
        </mx:Canvas>
    </mx:Panel>
```

Save the file as `PublishQueuePanel.mxml` in the directory `com/aircmr/bloggeragent/ui/` within your working directory.

The `PublishQueuePanel` component displays a list of blog entries currently in the queue to be published. From here, the user can either delete an entry from the queue or start the queue.

The following snippet is of the `startQueue` function within the `PublishQueuePanel` component. This function is called when the user clicks the Start Queue button. Here, a `QueueService` object is created, passing the `publishQueueItems` property into the constructor as the only parameter. Simply enough, the `QueueService` object is configured with an event handler for the `COMPLETE` event and the queue is started by calling the object's `startQueue` method:

```
private function startQueue( event:MouseEvent ):void
{
    _queueService = new QueueService( _publishQueueItems );
    _queueService.addEventListener( Event.COMPLETE, onQueueServiceComplete );
    _queueService.startQueue();

    this.enabled = false;
    CursorManager.setBusyCursor();
}
```

This component uses the `DBService` class as well, but you should be familiar with the usage of this class by now, having created the other components already. The `PublishQueuePanel` component is the last component necessary for this application. It's now time to tie everything together and create the main application file.

The Main Application File

In this section you will create the main application file. This file will tie everything together by creating a simple navigation that enables users to utilize the four main components created in the previous section.

Create a new document and enter the following markup:

```
<?xml version="1.0" encoding="utf-8"?>
<mx:WindowedApplication xmlns:mx="http://www.adobe.com/2006/mxml"
    layout="absolute" width="800" height="600"
    applicationComplete="onAppInit()" closing="onAppClosing()"
    xmlns:ui="com.aircmr.bloggeragent.ui.*">

    <mx:Script><![CDATA[
```

```
import com.aircmr.bloggeragent.services.DBService;
import com.aircmr.net.NetworkDetection;
import mx.managers.CursorManager;

public static const APPLICATION_ID:String = "com.aircmr.bloggeragent";

private var _currentPanel:Object;
private var _currentButton:Button;
private var _dbService:DBService;
private var _netDetect:NetworkDetection;

private function onAppInit():void
{
    this.systemManager.stage.nativeWindow.width = 800;
    this.systemManager.stage.nativeWindow.height = 600;
    _currentButton = accountManagerBtn;
    _currentPanel = accountManagerPanel;
    _dbService = DBService.getInstance();
    _netDetect = NetworkDetection.getInstance();
    _netDetect.addEventListener( NetworkDetection.CONNECTION_CHANGE,
        onConnectionChange );
    _netDetect.checkConnection();
    onConnectionChange( null );
    setSelection( accountManagerBtn, accountManagerPanel );
}

private function onAppClosing():void
{
    _dbService.close();
}

private function onButtonClick( event:MouseEvent, panel:Object ):void
{
    if( CursorManager.currentCursorID == 0 )
        setSelection( event.target as Button, panel );
}

private function onConnectionChange( event:Event ):void
{
    var msg:String = "Network status: ";
    this.status = ( _netDetect.connected ) ? msg + "Online" : msg + "Offline";
}

private function setSelection( button:Button, panel:Object ):void
{
    _currentButton.enabled = true;
    _currentButton = button;
    _currentButton.enabled = false;
    _currentPanel.visible = false;
    _currentPanel = panel;
    _currentPanel.visible = true;
    _currentPanel.update();
}
]]></mx:Script>
```

```
    <mx:Button id="accountManagerBtn" x="10" y="10" label="Manage Blogs"
        click="onButtonClick(event, accountManagerPanel)"/>
    <mx:Button id="composeEntryBtn" x="122" y="10" label="Compose Entry"
        click="onButtonClick(event, composeEntryPanel)"/>
    <mx:Button id="publishQueueBtn" x="242" y="10" label="Publish Queue"
        click="onButtonClick(event, publishQueuePanel)"/>
    <ui:BlogManagerPanel id="accountManagerPanel" visible="true"/>
    <ui:ComposeEntryPanel id="composeEntryPanel" visible="false"/>
    <ui:PublishQueuePanel id="publishQueuePanel" visible="false"/>
</mx:WindowedApplication>
```

Save the file as `BloggerAgent.mxml` within your working directory.

You just created the main application file. This file utilizes the `BlogManagerPanel`, `ComponseEntryPanel`, and `PublishQueuePanel` components that you created in the previous section. Each panel has a corresponding button that calls the `onButtonClick` function when the user clicks it. This function simply changes which panel is visible to the user and calls the panel's `update` function. Each panel's `update` function ensures that its own user interface elements are synchronized with the latest data within the database. Lastly, the main application file utilizes the `NetworkDetection` class to perform a small detail:

```
private function onConnectionChange( event:Event ):void
{
    var msg:String = "Network status: ";
    this.status = ( _netDetect.connected ) ? msg + "Online" : msg + "Offline";
}
```

The previous snippet is from the `onConnectionChange` function within the main application file. This function is called when the `NetworkDetection` class dispatches a `CONNECTION_CHANGE` event. Here, the only user interface element that needs to be updated is the status bar of the main application window. The main application file for an AIR application always starts out as a `WindowedApplication` component. This component has a simple property named `status` that determines what text should be displayed in the application's status bar. Because the status bar is always visible, it's the perfect place to display the network connection status.

Other than managing the display of the main panels, the main application file doesn't have to do very much. At this point, the application is essentially finished. The only tasks left are to package and deploy the application.

Deploying the Application

Your application is almost complete. It's now time to package and deploy the application so that your users may install it.

The Descriptor File

Open your editor and create a new document. Enter the following markup:

```
<?xml version="1.0" encoding="UTF-8"?>
<application xmlns="http://ns.adobe.com/air/application/1.0">
    <id>com.aircmr.bloggeragent</id>
    <name>Blogger Agent</name>
    <filename>Blogger Agent</filename>
    <version>v1</version>
    <initialWindow>
        <content>BloggerAgent.swf</content>
        <title>Blogger Agent</title>
    </initialWindow>
</application>
```

Save the file as `BloggerAgent-app.xml` in your working directory.

This file will serve as the application descriptor file. The element values from this snippet are mostly placeholders and should be changed as appropriate. With the descriptor file in place, you are set to compile and package the application's AIR executable.

Compiling and Packaging

Two files are necessary to package an AIR application: the main SWF file and the XML application descriptor file. However, in the case of this application, a third file must also be included. In this section you will produce the SWF file using the command-line tools and package the AIR application.

Open a command prompt, navigate to the working directory for this application, enter the following, and press Enter:

```
> amxmlc BloggerAgent.mxml
```

If you have purchased a certificate from a certificate authority, such as VeriSign or Thawte, you may use that certificate, rather than create the self-signed certificate, and skip the following operation. To create a self-signed certificate within the working directory, enter the following command:

```
> adt -certificate -cn BloggerAgent 1024-RSA certificate.pfx password
```

With the command prompt still pointing to the working directory, enter the following command and press Enter:

```
> adt -package -storetype pkcs12 -keystore certificate.pfx BloggerAgent.air
BloggerAgent-app.xml BloggerAgent.swf
```

After the installer has been created, navigate to your working directory and double-click on `BloggerAgent.air` to install and run the application. If all goes well, the application will launch and look very similar to what is shown in Figure 10-2. The only difference will be the absence of an account, but go ahead and add your own!

Summary

In this chapter you learned how to create an application that enables users to publish blog entries to a Blogger account. The application also enables users to save entries to be published later, perhaps because they are not currently connected to the Internet. You accomplished this by learning how to utilize AIR's SQLite API to create and use a local SQLite database. This database is used to store and manage blog accounts and blog entries to be published at a later time. In addition, you also learned how to utilize the `EncryptedLocalStore` class to safely store sensitive information on a user's computer for later retrieval.

This application utilizes the Blogger Data API, but that's not to say it could not be modified to interface with other blogging services that have a public API. For instance, you could create a `WordPressService` class to post to your WordPress blog instead. If you wanted to get really creative, you could create a proxy class that enables you to publish one entry to more than one blog service at once. Think of all the possibilities!

11

Slideshow Maker

Since the dawn of what is commonly referred to as the Projector Age, vacations and slideshows have gone hand in hand. While the popularity of taking pictures of the same object from different angles did not coincide with this period, being able to show them singled out and blown up has. In this chapter you will build an AIR application that enables you to create individual slides and organize slideshows to capture those very special moments in a sequence. (While slideshows are fun to create, they are not always fun to be subjected to. The examples in this chapter do not present an algorithm for keeping people from wondering whether the slideshow will ever end.)

The application will enable you to save your work on that ovation-inspiring slideshow, to continue working either from the same computer at a later date or on another computer with the application installed. This program introduces invoking your application using associated file types as well as OS-level notifications. In continuing with your knowledge of the AIR file system API, you will also learn how to serialize objects to a file.

Along with creating individual slides and organizing the order of a slideshow, the application has multiple displays as they pertain to creating and presenting a slideshow. With this in mind, the Slideshow Maker will handle the following actions:

- Switching between a workspace and a presentation
- Navigating through a slideshow presentation
- Alerting a user to unsaved changes in a slideshow prior to closing the application

The capability to save and open individual slides and slideshows is also a crucial part of the application and entails the following:

- Opening and saving slideshows
- Importing and exporting single slides
- Invoking the application to open slide and slideshow files associated with the application

The next section discusses the plan to achieve these goals.

Design

Spawning operating system (OS) native windows enables you to separate different presentation layers on the desktop. In breaking from the mold of a web-based Flex application, an AIR application can present any number of native windows that are not confined to the visible bounds of the main application window. The Slideshow Maker uses the AIR windowing API to present the *workspace* in the main application window from which you can launch a full-screen slideshow presentation and spawn notification windows of unsaved data prior to closing the workspace.

Using the AIR file system API, you can write an object to the buffer of a filestream that is serialized using the ActionScript Messaging Format (AMF). AMF encodes objects to a binary format, and writing that data to a filestream outputs a compact file on your hard drive. Most built-in object types, such as `Boolean` and `String`, are automatically serialized.

The custom data objects that you will create for the Slideshow Maker will not be automatically serialized with their associated custom type. Though public properties of a built-in type can be serialized, any properties of a custom type are not inherently serialized as well. As such, you will register each data object with a class-alias in order to map the object read into the filestream to a custom type.

The serialization of custom objects will be used to save files associated with individual slides and sets of slides, or slideshows. The slide and slideshow files have unique file extensions that will register the Slideshow Maker as the default application. This enables you to open a slide or slideshow file in the Slideshow Maker whether or not the application is currently running. This operation addresses the invocation goal of the previous section and involves handling an event from the `NativeApplication` instance of the AIR application.

The next section covers the data objects that the application serializes to a file and how the Slideshow Maker manages that data during an opened session.

Handling Data

A slideshow is just a series of slides, and each slide has its own data. As addressed in the previous section, the data objects will be serialized to files. You will expose public properties to be serialized along with the object and mark some properties to not be serialized. Properties tagged to not be encoded along with the object are considered *session-related* and are remembered only while the application is open.

Creating Serializable Data Objects

The slides you create in the Slideshow Maker application are relatively simple in that they present an image and a caption. The image held on the slide model is itself a serializable data object as well, and holds the graphical data pertaining to that slide. In this section you will create those two data objects.

Within your development directory, create a folder titled SlideshowMaker. This will be your working directory for the application. With that set, you can get to work:

1. Open your favorite text editor and enter the following ActionScript:

```
package com.aircmr.slideshow.data
{
    import flash.events.Event;
    import flash.events.EventDispatcher;

    [Bindable]
    [RemoteClass]
    public class Slide extends EventDispatcher
    {
        public var title:String;
        public var caption:String;
        public var backgroundColor:uint;
        public var textColor:uint;
        private var _image:SlideImage;

        public static const IMAGE_CHANGE:String = "imageChange";

        public function Slide( title:String = "Enter Title",
                               caption:String = "Enter Caption",
                               image:SlideImage = null,
                               backgroundColor:uint = 0xFFFFFF,
                               textColor:uint = 0x000000 )
        {
            this.title = title;
            this.caption = caption;
            this.image = image;
            this.backgroundColor = backgroundColor;
            this.textColor = textColor;
        }

        public function clean():void
        {
            if( _image != null ) _image.clean();
        }

        public function serialize():void
        {
            if( this.image != null ) image.serialize();
        }
        public function deserialize():void
        {
            if( this.image != null ) image.deserialize();
        }

        [Bindable("imageChange")]
        public function get image():SlideImage
        {
            return _image;
        }
```

```
        public function set image( vo:SlideImage ):void
        {
            if( _image != null ) _image.clean();
            _image = vo;
            dispatchEvent( new Event( Slide.IMAGE_CHANGE ) );
        }
    }
}
```

2. Save the file as `Slide.as` in the directory `com/aircmr/slideshow/data` in your working directory.

3. Create a new document and enter the following ActionScript:

```
package com.aircmr.slideshow.data
{
    import flash.display.Bitmap;
    import flash.display.BitmapData;
    import flash.display.Loader;
    import flash.events.Event;
    import flash.events.EventDispatcher;
    import flash.filesystem.File;
    import flash.filesystem.FileMode;
    import flash.filesystem.FileStream;
    import flash.net.URLRequest;
    import flash.utils.ByteArray;

    import mx.graphics.codec.PNGEncoder;

    [RemoteClass]
    public class SlideImage extends EventDispatcher
    {
        [Bindable] public var _width:Number;
        [Bindbale] public var _height:Number;

        private var _data:ByteArray;
        private var _filepath:String;
        private var _bitmapData:BitmapData;

        private var _tempFile:File;
        private var _loader:Loader;

        public static const DATA_CHANGE:String = "dataChange";
        public static const FILEPATH_CHANGE:String = "filepathChange";

        public function SlideImage( bmp:BitmapData = null,
                                    filepath:String = "" ):void
        {
            if( bmp != null ) this.bitmapData = bmp;
            this.filepath = filepath;
        }

        private function writeTempFile( byteArray:ByteArray ):void
        {
```

```
        _tempFile = File.createTempFile();
        filepath = _tempFile.url;
        var stream:FileStream = new FileStream();
        stream.open( _tempFile, FileMode.WRITE );
        stream.writeBytes( byteArray );
        stream.close();
    }

    public function clean():void
    {
        if( _tempFile != null ) _tempFile.deleteFile();
        if( bitmapData != null ) bitmapData.dispose();
    }

    public function serialize():void
    {
        _data = new ByteArray();
        if( _filepath.indexOf( "http://" ) != -1 )
            writeTempFile( new PNGEncoder().encode( bitmapData ) );

        var stream:FileStream = new FileStream();
        stream.open( new File( _filepath ), FileMode.READ );
        stream.readBytes( _data );
        _data.compress();
    }
    public function deserialize():void
    {
        _data.uncompress();
        _data.position = 0;
        writeTempFile( _data );

        _loader = new Loader();
        _loader.contentLoaderInfo.addEventListener( Event.COMPLETE,
                                                          onOpenComplete );
        _loader.load( new URLRequest( _tempFile.url ) );
    }

    private function onOpenComplete( evt:Event ):void
    {
        var bitmap:Bitmap = _loader.content as Bitmap;
        bitmapData = bitmap.bitmapData;
    }

    [Bindable]
    public function get data():ByteArray
    {
        return _data;
    }
    public function set data( barr:ByteArray ):void
    {
        _data = barr;
    }

    [Bindable("filepathChange")]
```

```
        [Transient]
        public function get filepath():String
        {
            return _filepath;
        }
        public function set filepath( str:String ):void
        {
            _filepath = str;
            dispatchEvent( new Event( SlideImage.FILEPATH_CHANGE ) );
        }

        [Bindable("dataChange")]
        [Transient]
        public function get bitmapData():BitmapData
        {
            return _bitmapData;
        }
        public function set bitmapData( bmd:BitmapData ):void
        {
            _bitmapData = bmd;
            _width = _bitmapData.width;
            _height = _bitmapData.height;
            dispatchEvent( new Event( SlideImage.DATA_CHANGE ) );
        }
    }
}
```

4. Save the file as `SlideImage.as` in the directory `com/aircmr/slideshow/data` in your working directory.

The first snippet, saved as `Slide.as`, represents the data associated with an individual slide. The `RemoteClass` meta-tag above the class definition registers an alias with the fully qualified class name. By registering a class alias with a class, the custom type is preserved when encoded to AMF and is recognized by the Flash Player serializer/deserializer. This enables you to open that object in the application and have it deserialized to a `Slide` instance.

The various properties of a `Slide` object are fairly basic, as they pertain to display, with attributes for background color, caption string, and so on. One property of note is the `image` property. The `image` property is of type `SlideImage` — the second snippet created in this section. The `SlideImage` also has a registered class alias to preserve its type upon serialization.

Two properties of note on the `SlideImage` class, `filepath` and `bitmapData`, are marked with the `Transient` meta-tag. Properties tagged as `[Transient]` are not included in the serialization process of that instance. The values of these properties are only relevant to a `SlideImage` instance when the application is open. That may seem odd. If the properties of a `SlideImage` instance are associated with the graphical data for an image on a slide, why would you not want to encode that data?

The reason is that slides created in the Slideshow Maker are saved to files that can be moved from computer to computer and opened at a later date. The `SlideImage` does not hold a reference to the file path of an image file held on any single machine. One option is to store the `bitmapData` of that image file, but that property is marked as `[Transient]` as well. While it is possible to generate a `ByteArray` of pixel data from a `BitmapData` instance, storing that `ByteArray` along with the object will significantly increase the file's size when that object is saved to the hard drive. To get around saving large files of graphical data using a ByteArray object, the application will actually serialize the image file itself to unpack when the slide file is reopened. This is where the serialize() and deserialize() methods of the SlideImage come into play.

Prior to encoding the Slide object, the serialize() method is called on the SlideImage instance held on that Slide instance:

```
public function serialize():void
{
    _data = new ByteArray();
    if( _filepath.indexOf( "http://" ) != -1 )
        writeTempFile( new PNGEncoder().encode( bitmapData ) );

    var stream:FileStream = new FileStream();
    stream.open( new File( _filepath ), FileMode.READ );
    stream.readBytes( _data );
    _data.compress();
}
```

The serialize() method encodes the currently held bitmapData of the SlideImage instance and writes that data to a temporary file. That image file is then written to the buffer of the function-local FileStream instance and the image file itself is stored as a ByteArray on the SlideImage instance.

Upon opening the saved file, the deserialize() method is called to write that stored file data back out to a temporary file and load it:

```
public function deserialize():void
{
    _data.uncompress();
    _data.position = 0;
    writeTempFile( _data );

    _loader = new Loader();
    _loader.contentLoaderInfo.addEventListener( Event.COMPLETE,
                                                onOpenComplete );
    _loader.load( new URLRequest( _tempFile.url ) );
}
```

The handler for the complete event dispatched from the contentLoaderInfo of the Loader instance assigns the bitmapData property value, which in turn dispatches a dataChange event for any listening clients.

The SlideImage data object holds more than just property values, and plays an important role in keeping the files associated with the Slideshow Maker relatively small. In the next section, you will create the client that manages the sequence of slides.

Managing Slides

The class you will create in this section has two distinct roles. It manages the organization of slides while the application is open and it stores that set of slides to be serialized to a file representing a slideshow.

Like the previously created data objects in this chapter, the object representing the slideshow itself has a registered class alias.

Create a new document and enter the following ActionScript:

```
package com.aircmr.slideshow.data
{
    import flash.events.Event;
    import flash.events.EventDispatcher;

    [Event(name="indexChange", type="flash.events.Event")]
    [Event(name="slidesChange", type="flash.events.Event")]
    [RemoteClass]
    public class SlideGallery extends EventDispatcher
    {
        [ArrayElementType("com.aircmr.slideshow.data.Slide")]
        private var _slides:Array = [];
        private var _currentIndex:int;

        public static const INDEX_CHANGE:String = "indexChange";
        public static const SLIDES_CHANGE:String = "slidesChange";

        public function SlideGallery() {}

        public function clean():void
        {
            while( _slides.length > 0 )
            {
                Slide( _slides.shift() ).clean();
            }
        }
        public function serialize():void
        {
            var i:int = _slides.length;
            while( --i > -1 )
            {
                Slide( _slides[i] ).serialize();
            }
        }
        public function deserialize():void
        {
            var i:int = _slides.length;
            while( --i > -1 )
            {
                Slide( _slides[i] ).deserialize();
            }
        }

        public function addSlide( slide:Slide, fromBeginning:Boolean = false ):void
        {
            slides = _slides.concat( slide );
            currentIndex = fromBeginning ? 0 : _slides.length - 1;
        }
```

```
        public function removeSlide( slide:Slide ):void
        {
            var arr:Array = _slides.concat();
            for( var i:int = 0; i < arr.length; i++ )
            {
                if( Slide( _slides[i] ) == slide )
                {
                    arr.splice( i, 1 );
                    break;
                }
            }
            if( arr.length == 0 ) arr.push( new Slide() );
            slides = arr;
            currentIndex = ( _currentIndex > arr.length - 1 ) ? 0 : _currentIndex;
        }

        public function get length():int
        {
            return _slides.length;
        }

        public function get currentSlide():Slide
        {
            return _slides[_currentIndex];
        }

        [Bindable("indexChange")]
        [Transient]
        public function get currentIndex():int
        {
            return _currentIndex;
        }
        public function set currentIndex( n:int ):void
        {
            _currentIndex = n;
            dispatchEvent( new Event( SlideGallery.INDEX_CHANGE ) );
        }

        [Bindable("slidesChange")]
        public function get slides():Array
        {
            return _slides;
        }
        public function set slides( arr:Array ):void
        {
            _slides = arr;
            dispatchEvent( new Event( SlideGallery.SLIDES_CHANGE ) );
        }
    }
}
```

Save the file as `SlideGallery.as` in the directory `com/aircmr/slideshow/data` along with the previous model classes created in this section.

The SlideGallery manages the order of a set of slides. Slide instances can be added and removed, and the index of the current slide being viewed in the Slideshow Maker can be set and obtained.

You will notice that the currentIndex property is tagged as [Transient]. Like the filepath and bitmapData properties of the SlideImage, the currentIndex value is not going to be stored with an AMF-encoded SlideGallery object. The currentIndex value only pertains to the current elemental index of the slide being viewed from the slides array while the application is open, and is accessed from both the workspace and presentation displays. The current index prior to saving the slideshow has no relevance in the example for this chapter, but you are free to unmark the property as being transient if you intend to use it — for instance, to take the user back to the last slide viewed upon opening a slideshow.

In the next section you will build the visual components that enable you to preview and modify slides.

Building the User Interface

The Slideshow Maker application has a workspace and presentation display. The slideshow presentation is launched from the workspace, which enables you to create and modify individual slides and the order in which they are presented. As such, the workspace has the following three main components:

- **A slide canvas**: The slide canvas will display a preview of the current slide being modified and maintains an aspect ratio of the screen dimensions.
- **A Properties panel**: The Properties panel enables you to modify the current slide by updating property values of the underlying Slide data object.
- **A slide carousel**: The carousel displays a list of slides in the current slideshow and enables you to reorder and remove slides.

In the next section you will build the view class that represents a slide.

Viewing Slides

The view representing a slide is available in multiple displays. The view that is presented when modifying a slide is the same one that is used for displaying a slide during a slideshow and previewing a slide in the gallery carousel. Having a versatile view for a slide enables you to make modifications to a single set of classes that represent the same view in different displays. Now you can get to work on the slide view:

1. Create a new document in your favorite text editor and enter the following markup:

```
<?xml version="1.0" encoding="utf-8"?>
<mx:Box xmlns:mx="http://www.adobe.com/2006/mxml"
    xmlns:ui="com.aircmr.slideshow.ui.*"
    width="100%" height="100%"
    verticalAlign="middle" horizontalAlign="center"
    verticalScrollPolicy="off" horizontalScrollPolicy="off"
    resize="onResize();">
    <mx:Style>
        .caption {
            font-size: 20px;
        }
```

```
    </mx:Style>
    <mx:Script>
        <![CDATA[
            import com.aircmr.slideshow.data.Slide;
            import com.aircmr.slideshow.data.SlideImage;
            import com.aircmr.slideshow.util.Settings;
            import mx.binding.utils.ChangeWatcher;
            import mx.binding.utils.BindingUtils;

            private var _canvasScale:Number = 1.0;
            private var _includeView:Boolean = true;
            private var _scaleWatcher:ChangeWatcher;
            [Bindable] private var _slide:Slide;

            private static const PADDING:int = 20;

            private function onViewCreate():void
            {
                var bounds:Rectangle = Settings.getScreenSize();
                view.width = bounds.width;
                view.height = bounds.height;
                _scaleWatcher = BindingUtils.bindSetter( invalidateViewScale, this,
                                                        'canvasScale', true );
            }

            private function onResize():void
            {
                var bounds:Rectangle = Settings.getScreenSize();
                var scale:Number = Math.min( ( width - PADDING ) / bounds.width,
                                            ( height - PADDING ) / bounds.height );
                canvasScale = scale;
            }

            private function invalidateViewScale( arg:* = null ):void
            {
                view.scaleX = view.scaleY = _canvasScale;
                view.x = ( width - view.width * _canvasScale ) / 2;
                view.y = ( height - view.height * _canvasScale ) / 2;
            }

            public function clean():void
            {
                _scaleWatcher.unwatch();
            }

            [Bindable]
            public function get slideData():Slide
            {
                return _slide;
            }
            public function set slideData( slide:Slide ):void
            {
                _slide = slide;
            }
```

```
            [Bindable]
            public function get canvasScale():Number
            {
                return _canvasScale;
            }
            public function set canvasScale( n:Number ):void
            {
                _canvasScale = n;
            }

            [Bindable]
            public function get includeViewInLayout():Boolean
            {
                return _includeView;
            }
            public function set includeViewInLayout( bool:Boolean ):void
            {
                _includeView = bool;
            }
        ]]>
    </mx:Script>
    <mx:Binding source="{_slide.image.bitmapData}" destination="image.source" />
    <mx:VBox id="view"
        backgroundColor="{_slide.backgroundColor}"
        creationComplete="onViewCreate();"
        includeInLayout="{includeViewInLayout}"
        paddingLeft="10" paddingRight="10"
        paddingTop="10" paddingBottom="10"
        filters="{[new DropShadowFilter()]}">
        <ui:SlideGraphic id="image"
            width="100%" height="100%"
            />
        <mx:Text id="captionField"
            width="100%" height="30"
            styleName="caption"
            text="{_slide.caption}"
            color="{_slide.textColor}"
            textAlign="center"
            />
    </mx:VBox>
</mx:Box>
```

2. Save the file as `SlideCanvas.mxml` in the directory `com/aircmr/slideshow/ui` in your working directory.

3. Create a new document and enter the following ActionScript:

```
package com.aircmr.slideshow.ui
{
    import flash.display.Bitmap;
    import flash.display.BitmapData;
```

```
    import flash.events.Event;
    import flash.geom.Matrix;

    import mx.core.UIComponent;

    public class SlideGraphic extends UIComponent
    {
        private var _source:BitmapData;
        private var _image:Bitmap;

        public function SlideGraphic() {}

        override protected function createChildren():void
        {
            super.createChildren();
            _image = new Bitmap();
            addChild( _image );
        }

        override protected function updateDisplayList(unscaledWidth:Number,
                                                      unscaledHeight:Number):void
        {
            super.updateDisplayList( unscaledWidth, unscaledHeight );
            invalidateImage();
        }

        private function invalidateImage():void
        {
            if( _source == null ) return;
            if( unscaledWidth == 0 || unscaledHeight == 0 ) return;
            var scale:Number = 1.0;
            var matrix:Matrix = new Matrix();
            if( _source.width > unscaledWidth || _source.height > unscaledHeight )
            {
                scale = Math.min( unscaledWidth / _source.width,
                                  unscaledHeight / _source.height );
            }
            matrix.scale( scale, scale );
            _image.bitmapData = new BitmapData( _source.width * scale,
                                                _source.height * scale );
            _image.bitmapData.draw( _source, matrix );
            _image.x = ( unscaledWidth - _image.width ) / 2;
            _image.y = ( unscaledHeight - _image.height ) / 2;
        }

        public function get source():BitmapData
        {
            return _source;
        }
        public function set source( bmp:BitmapData ):void
        {
```

```
                _source = bmp;
                if( _source == null ) _image.bitmapData = null;
                else invalidateImage();
            }
        }
    }
```

4. Save the file as `SlideGraphic.as` in the directory `com/aircmr/slideshow/ui` in your working directory.

The first snippet, saved as `SlideCanvas.mxml`, displays the visual elements that make up a slide. The `VBox` container held on a `SlideCanvas` instance encompasses the graphical representation of a slide, with properties bound to the supplied `Slide` instance. The scale of the container is updated based on the current bounds of the screen and in response to a `resize` event from the `SlideCanvas`. The handler for the `creationComplete` event of the `view` container is the `onViewCreate()` method:

```
private function onViewCreate():void
{
        var bounds:Rectangle = Settings.getScreenSize();
        view.width = bounds.width;
        view.height = bounds.height;
        _scaleWatcher = BindingUtils.bindSetter( invalidateViewScale, this,
                                                        'canvasScale', true );
}

private function onResize():void
{
        var bounds:Rectangle = Settings.getScreenSize();
        var scale:Number = Math.min( ( width - PADDING ) / bounds.width,
                                     ( height - PADDING ) / bounds.height );
        canvasScale = scale;
}
```

Within the `onViewCreate()` method, the `view` container is set to the size of the current screen bounds, as that will be the dimensions of a slide being viewed during a slideshow presentation. The `onResize()` method is the event handler for the `resize` event dispatched from `SlideCanvas`. The `onResize()` method evaluates the scale at which to set the `view` container based on the current dimensions and the screen dimensions.

The `invalidateViewScale()` method is bound to the `canvasScale` property and is invoked when the scale value has changed and after the creation of the `view` container. This ensures that any resizing that may have occurred on the `SlideCanvas` prior to the `view` container being created is applied and its scale and position updated through the instantiation of the `ChangeWatcher` instance `_scaleWatcher`.

```
private function invalidateViewScale( arg:* = null ):void
{
    view.scaleX = view.scaleY = _canvasScale;
    view.x = ( width - view.width * _canvasScale ) / 2;
    view.y = ( height - view.height * _canvasScale ) / 2;
}
```

With the scale of the view container based on the screen resolution, you can be assured of an accurate representation of how a slide will look when presented during an actual slideshow.

The view container holds an instance of a SlideGraphic — the snippet saved as SlideGraphic.as. The SlideGraphic presents the graphical data associated with an image for a Slide instance. The bitmap data of the Bitmap instance held on SlideGraphic updates based on the source property. When the value of the source property has changed from not being null (a null value represents a Slide with image), the invalidateImage() method is invoked:

```
private function invalidateImage():void
{
    if( _source == null ) return;
    if( unscaledWidth == 0 || unscaledHeight == 0 ) return;
    var scale:Number = 1.0;
    var matrix:Matrix = new Matrix();
    if( _source.width > unscaledWidth || _source.height > unscaledHeight )
    {
        scale = Math.min( unscaledWidth / _source.width,
                          unscaledHeight / _source.height );
    }
    matrix.scale( scale, scale );
    _image.bitmapData = new BitmapData( _source.width * scale,
                                        _source.height * scale );
    _image.bitmapData.draw( _source, matrix );
    _image.x = ( unscaledWidth - _image.width ) / 2;
    _image.y = ( unscaledHeight - _image.height ) / 2;
}
```

The invalidateImage() method handles drawing a scaled representation of the supplied BitmapData and centers the Bitmap instance based on the unscaled dimensions of the SlideGraphic container. Since the SlideCanvas is used in multiple displays varying in size, the bitmap data of an associated image is drawn to scale to fit the display, rather than scaling the Bitmap instance itself.

With the view set for displaying a slide, you can get to work on building the control view to modify that slide. The next section addresses just that.

Modifying Slides

A slideshow with all the same slides is not very exciting. The Properties panel in the workspace display of the Slideshow Maker application enables you to modify the visual makeup of each slide. In this section you will create the Properties panel that exposes controls for modifying slides.

Create a new document and enter the following markup:

```
<?xml version="1.0" encoding="utf-8"?>
<mx:VBox xmlns:mx="http://www.adobe.com/2006/mxml"
    width="100%" height="100%"
    creationComplete="onCreationComplete();">

    <mx:Script>
        <![CDATA[
```

```
import com.aircmr.slideshow.data.Slide;
import com.aircmr.slideshow.data.SlideImage;

private var _loader:Loader;
private var _importFile:File;
private var _url:String;
private var _hasChanged:Boolean = false;
[Bindable] private var _slide:Slide;

private function onCreationComplete():void
{
    _loader = new Loader();
    _loader.contentLoaderInfo.addEventListener( Event.COMPLETE,
                                                onImageLoad );
}

private function onBrowseForFile():void
{
    _importFile = new File();
    _importFile.addEventListener( Event.SELECT, onImageSelect );
    _importFile.browseForOpen( "Choose Image",
        [new FileFilter( "Image File", "*.jpg;*.png;*.jpeg;" )] );
}

private function onImageSelect( evt:Event ):void
{
    loadImage( _importFile.url );
}

private function onImageLoad( evt:Event ):void
{
    _slide.image = new SlideImage(
                    ( _loader.content as Bitmap ).bitmapData, _url );
    hasChanged = true;
}

private function onSlideColorChange():void
{
    _slide.backgroundColor = backgroundPicker.selectedColor
    hasChanged = true;
}
private function onSlideTitleChange():void
{
    _slide.title = titleInput.text;
    hasChanged = true;
}
private function onSlideCaptionChange():void
{
    _slide.caption = captionInput.text;
    hasChanged = true;
}
private function onSlideCaptionColorChange():void
{
```

```
                _slide.textColor = captionPicker.selectedColor;
                hasChanged = true;
            }

            private function loadImage( url:String ):void
            {
                _url = url;
                _loader.load( new URLRequest( url ) );
            }

            public function get slideData():Slide
            {
                return _slide;
            }
            public function set slideData( slide:Slide ):void
            {
                _slide = slide;
            }

            [Bindable]
            public function get hasChanged():Boolean
            {
                return _hasChanged;
            }
            public function set hasChanged( bool:Boolean ):void
            {
                _hasChanged = bool;
            }

        ]]>
    </mx:Script>

    <mx:Binding source="{_slide.image.filepath}" destination="imageInput.text" />
    <mx:Form paddingTop="0" paddingBottom="0">
        <mx:FormItem label="Background:">
            <mx:ColorPicker id="backgroundPicker"
                selectedColor="{_slide.backgroundColor}"
                change="onSlideColorChange();"
                />
        </mx:FormItem>
        <mx:FormItem label="Title:">
            <mx:TextInput id="titleInput" width="300"
                text="{_slide.title}" maxChars="25"
                change="onSlideTitleChange();"
                />
        </mx:FormItem>
        <mx:FormItem label="Caption:">
            <mx:HBox>
                <mx:TextInput id="captionInput" width="300"
                    text="{_slide.caption}" maxChars="70"
                    change="onSlideCaptionChange();"
                    />
                <mx:ColorPicker id="captionPicker"
                    selectedColor="{_slide.textColor}"
```

```
                        change="onSlideCaptionColorChange();"
                        />
                </mx:HBox>
            </mx:FormItem>
            <mx:FormItem label="Image:">
                <mx:HBox>
                    <mx:TextInput id="imageInput" width="300"
                        enter="{loadImage( imageInput.text )}"
                        />
                    <mx:Button label="Browse"
                        click="onBrowseForFile();"/>
                </mx:HBox>
            </mx:FormItem>
        </mx:Form>

    </mx:VBox>
```

Save the file as `PropertiesPanel.mxml` in the directory `com/aircmr/slideshow/ui` of your working directory.

The `PropertiesPanel` object holds controls laid out in column, and row constraints that relate to the property values held on the supplied `Slide` instance. It also keeps track of any changes made to any of the slides by updating the `hasChanged` property. Knowing whether a slideshow has changed will come in handy when a user is alerted to save changes prior to closing, which is addressed in the "Bringing It All Together" section.

Along with displaying the properties of a slide, the `PropertiesPanel` serves as a controller in updating the property values of the `Slide` instance when one of the control fields has changed. Each of the event handlers held on `PropertiesPanel` updates the associated property value of the slide and sets the `hasChanged` flag to a value of `true`. Of note among these event handlers is the `onImageLoad()` method:

```
private function onImageLoad( evt:Event ):void
{
    _slide.image = new SlideImage(
                    ( _loader.content as Bitmap ).bitmapData, _url );
    hasChanged = true;
}
```

The `onImageLoad()` method is the handler for the "complete" event dispatched from the `contentLoadInfo` of the class-local `Loader` instance. This method updates the `image` value of the `Slide` instance with a new `SlideImage` instance and is invoked upon the success of loading an image file either from entering a new file path or browsing for a file. The arguments passed into the constructor for the `SlideImage` object set the `bitmapData` and `filepath` property values, respectively, for that instance. With client properties bound to those `SlideImage` properties, including the `text` property of the `imageInput` field of `PropertiesPanel`, displays are refreshed and stay consistent between multiple views.

In the next section you will build the display that holds the current slides for a slideshow being created.

Previewing Slides

As you amass slides to be presented in a slideshow, you may find that some are in the wrong order or don't belong in the show at all. The slide carousel you build in this section will enable you to reorder and remove slides while displaying a thumbnail preview of each.

1. Create a new document and enter the following markup:

```
<?xml version="1.0" encoding="utf-8"?>
<mx:VBox xmlns:mx="http://www.adobe.com/2006/mxml"
    xmlns:ui="com.aircmr.slideshow.ui.*"
    verticalGap="0" height="130"
    horizontalScrollPolicy="off"
    creationComplete="onCreationComplete();">
    <mx:Metadata>
        [Event(name="deleteSlide", type="flash.events.Event")]
    </mx:Metadata>
    <mx:Style>
        .deleteButton {
            font-size: 8px;
        }
    </mx:Style>
    <mx:Script>
        <![CDATA[
            import com.aircmr.slideshow.data.Slide;

            [Bindable] private var _data:Slide;
            public static const DELETE:String = "deleteSlide";

            private function onCreationComplete():void
            {
                slide.invalidateProperties();
                slide.invalidateSize();
            }

            private function onDeleteSlide():void
            {
                dispatchEvent( new Event( CarouselItem.DELETE, true ) );
            }

            override public function set data(value:Object):void
            {
                _data = value as Slide;
                super.data = value;
            }
            override public function get data():Object
            {
                return _data;
            }
```

```
            ]]>
        </mx:Script>
        <mx:Binding source="{_data}" destination="slide.slideData" />
        <mx:HBox width="100%">
            <mx:Spacer width="100%" />
            <mx:Text text="delete X" mouseChildren="false"
                buttonMode="true" useHandCursor="true"
                styleName="deleteButton" toolTip="Delete Slide?"
                click="onDeleteSlide();"
                />
        </mx:HBox>
        <ui:SlideCanvas id="slide"
            width="100%" height="100%"
            backgroundColor="0x333333"
            slideData="{_data}" />
        <mx:Text id="titleField"
            width="100%" textAlign="center"
            selectable="false"
            text="{_data.title}"
            />
    </mx:VBox>
```

2. Save the file as `CarouselItem.mxml` in the directory `com/aircmr/slideshow/ui` along with the slide view classes created previously.

3. Create a new document and enter the following markup:

```
<?xml version="1.0" encoding="utf-8"?>
<mx:VBox xmlns:mx="http://www.adobe.com/2006/mxml"
    width="135" height="100%">
    <!-- bubbled -->
    <mx:Metadata>
        [Event(name="deleteSlide", type="flash.events.Event")]
    </mx:Metadata>
    <mx:Script>
        <![CDATA[
            import com.aircmr.slideshow.data.SlideGallery;

            [Bindable] private var _gallery:SlideGallery;

            private function onSlideSelect():void
            {
                _gallery.currentIndex = slideList.selectedIndex;
            }

            public function get gallery():SlideGallery
            {
                return _gallery;
            }
            public function set gallery( glry:SlideGallery ):void
            {
                _gallery = glry;
            }
        ]]>
```

```
    </mx:Script>
    <mx:List
        id="slideList"
        width="100%" height="100%"
        paddingRight="2"
        dataProvider="{_gallery.slides}"
        dragEnabled="true" dropEnabled="true"
        dragMoveEnabled="true"
        selectedIndex="{_gallery.currentIndex}"
        itemRenderer="com.aircmr.slideshow.ui.CarouselItem"
        change="onSlideSelect();"
        />
</mx:VBox>
```

4. Save the file as `Carousel.mxml` in the directory `com/aircmr/slideshow/ui` in your working directory.

The first snippet, saved as `CarouselItem.mxml`, is a thumbnail preview of a slide and the item renderer for an instance of the second snippet — saved as `Carousel.mxml`. The `CarouselItem` contains a control to delete the instance and displays a `SlideCanvas` and a `Text` control for the title of a slide. With the `slideData` property of the `SlideCanvas` instance bound to the supplied `Slide` instance, updates to the properties of that `Slide` instance are reflected in the display of the `CarouselItem`.

The `Carousel` displays a list of `CarouselItems` that are rendered based on the supplied slide gallery data. Two properties of the `List` control are bound to properties of the supplied `SlideGallery` instance:

```
<mx:List
    id="slideList"
    width="100%" height="100%"
    paddingRight="2"
    dataProvider="{_gallery.slides}"
    dragEnabled="true" dropEnabled="true"
    dragMoveEnabled="true"
    selectedIndex="{_gallery.currentIndex}"
    itemRenderer="com.aircmr.slideshow.ui.CarouselItem"
    change="onSlideSelect();"
    />
```

As the set of slides held on the supplied `SlideGallery` instance changes, so does the `dataProvider` of the `slideList`. The `selectedIndex` property updates in response to a change of the `currentIndex` of the `SlideGallery` as well. However, the `Carousel` container acts as a controller in setting the `currentIndex` of the slide gallery by handling the `change` event dispatched from `slideList`. The `onSlideSelect()` method updates the `currentIndex` value based on the selected index of the list when a change occurs:

```
private function onSlideSelect():void
{
    _gallery.currentIndex = slideList.selectedIndex;
}
```

Not terribly interesting, but by allowing the `Carousel` to control updates to the `currentIndex` of a `SlideGallery` rather than explicitly setting that value on the in-line "change" handler of `slideList`, the `Carousel` can, for example, later check for changes to the slide and prevent a user from selecting another slide without saving first.

The versatility of `SlideCanvas` was mentioned previously, and the `CarouselItem` is the first place you see it being added to the display in the examples of this chapter. As this chapter continues, `SlideCanvas` will be added to more views and its versatility will be seen as the slide display scales based on the bounds of the main screen — particularly in the next section, where you will build the view screen for playing a slideshow.

Presenting Slides

It's time to get those slides up and covering the screen for the big show! As mentioned previously, the Slideshow Maker has two main displays — the workspace and the presentation. These two displays are separate containers and both make use of the AIR windowing API. In this section, you will create the presentation display that is used to present a slideshow.

Create a new document and enter the following markup:

```
<?xml version="1.0" encoding="utf-8"?>
<mx:Window xmlns:mx="http://www.adobe.com/2006/mxml"
    xmlns:ui="com.aircmr.slideshow.ui.*"
    layout="vertical"
    backgroundColor="0x000000"
    systemChrome="none"
    transparent="true"
    type="lightweight"
    showGripper="false"
    showStatusBar="false"
    showTitleBar="false"
    creationComplete="onInit();">

    <mx:Script>
        <![CDATA[
            import mx.binding.utils.ChangeWatcher;
            import mx.binding.utils.BindingUtils;
            import com.aircmr.slideshow.data.Slide;

            [ArrayElementType("com.aircmr.slideshow.data.Slide")]
            private var _slides:Array;
            private var _index:int;
            private var _slideWatcher:ChangeWatcher;
            private var _indexWatcher:ChangeWatcher;

            private function onInit():void
            {
                setFocus();
                nativeWindow.stage.addEventListener( KeyboardEvent.KEY_UP,
                                                                onKeyUp );
                contextMenu = getContextMenu();
                _slideWatcher = BindingUtils.bindSetter( initiateShow, this,
                                                        "slides", true );
```

```
        _indexWatcher = BindingUtils.bindSetter( initiateSlide, this,
                                                "index", true );
    }
    private function initiateShow( arg:* = null ):void
    {
        index = 0;
    }
    private function initiateSlide( arg:* = null ):void
    {
        slide.slideData = _slides[_index] as Slide;
    }

    private function getContextMenu():NativeMenu
    {
        var menu:NativeMenu = new NativeMenu();
        menu.addItem( new NativeMenuItem( "Close" ) );
        menu.addEventListener( Event.SELECT, onMenuItemSelect );
        return menu;
    }

    private function onMenuItemSelect( evt:Event ):void
    {
        exit();
    }

    private function onKeyUp( evt:KeyboardEvent ):void
    {
        switch( evt.keyCode )
        {
            case Keyboard.LEFT:
                index = ( ( _index - 1 ) < 0 ) ?
                            _slides.length - 1 : _index - 1;
                break;
            case Keyboard.RIGHT:
                index = ( ( _index + 1 ) > _slides.length - 1 ) ?
                            0 : _index + 1;
                break;
            case Keyboard.ESCAPE:
                exit();
                break;
        }
    }

    public function exit():void
    {
        _slideWatcher.unwatch();
        _indexWatcher.unwatch();
        _slides = null;
        nativeWindow.stage.removeEventListener( KeyboardEvent.KEY_UP,
                                                            onKeyUp );
        close();
    }
```

```
            [Bindable]
            public function get index():int
            {
                return _index;
            }
            public function set index( n:int ):void
            {
                _index = n;
            }

            [Bindable]
            public function get slides():Array
            {
                return _slides;
            }
            public function set slides( arr:Array ):void
            {
                _slides = arr;
            }
        ]]>
    </mx:Script>
    <ui:SlideCanvas id="slide" width="100%" height="100%" />
</mx:Window>
```

Save the file as `SlideshowWindow.mxml` in the directory `com/aircmr/slideshow/windows` of your working directory.

The `SlideshowWindow` display extends the `Window` container of the AIR windowing API. The `Window` component acts as a container to which you can add components to its display directly, and it has properties related to the characteristics of a window — such as chrome — that can be set only upon creation, as is done in the `<mx:Window>` tag of `SlideshowWindow`:

```
<mx:Window xmlns:mx="http://www.adobe.com/2006/mxml"
   xmlns:ui="com.aircmr.slideshow.ui.*"
   layout="vertical"
   backgroundColor="0x000000"
   systemChrome="none"
   transparent="true"
   type="lightweight"
   showGripper="false"
   showStatusBar="false"
   showTitleBar="false"
   show="onShow();">
```

The `SlideshowWindow` has the `type` value of `"lightweight"`, with `systemChrome` set to `"none"`, and the action to display other window characteristics set to `"false"`. In essence, when the `SlideshowWindow` is called to open for a presentation, the `SlideCanvas` on its display list will be the only visible item presented and scaled to the dimensions set by the client opening it.

The "show" event handler is of note, as once this window has been called to open and appears, a `Keyboard` event handler is set and a `NativeMenu` is added:

```
private function onShow():void
{
    setFocus();
    nativeWindow.stage.addEventListener( KeyboardEvent.KEY_UP,
                                                        onKeyUp );
    contextMenu = getContextMenu();
    _slideWatcher = BindingUtils.bindSetter( initiateShow, this,
                                                "slides", true );
    _indexWatcher = BindingUtils.bindSetter( initiateSlide, this,
                                                "index", true );
}
```

An event listener for the keyUp event dispatched from the stage of the NativeWindow instance of SlideshowWindow is set to move forward and backward through a slide show and to close the slideshow. Two ChangeWatcher instances are created to bind methods based on a change to the slides and index properties of the SlideshowWindow. The slides property is updated upon the presentation of a new slideshow, which in turn updates the index at which to start displaying slides. Along with being updated upon a change of slideshow, the index value is also changed in response to the arrow keys.

A native context menu is also set for the SlideshowWindow in the onShow()method. The NativeMenu created and assigned to the contextMenu property of the window contains a single action item:

```
private function getContextMenu():NativeMenu
{
    var menu:NativeMenu = new NativeMenu();
    menu.addItem( new NativeMenuItem( "Close" ) );
    menu.addEventListener( Event.SELECT, onMenuItemSelect );
    return menu;
}
```

While the Esc key has been set in the keyUp event handler to exit the slideshow, the option to exit is also presented when the context menu of the SlideshowWindow is accessed. The NativeMenu created and returned from getContextMenu()can have any number of command items, but for the purpose of this example presents an easy way to exit the slideshow.

You have created the views to display, modify, and present slides. In the next section, you will create the workspace from which you can access these views in creating and presenting a slideshow.

Bringing It All Together

The classes you will create in this section address the creation of a slideshow in the main workspace, alerting users to unsaved data prior to exiting the application, and providing an entry point for accessing file and screen data used by multiple clients.

Save Alert Window

Up to this point, you have addressed the data objects associated with the Slideshow Maker application and the views for displaying and modifying that data. In this section you will create the notification window that is presented to a user who has instructed the application to close with unsaved slide data.

Create a new document and enter the following markup:

```
<?xml version="1.0" encoding="utf-8"?>
<mx:Window xmlns:mx="http://www.adobe.com/2006/mxml"
    title="Save Slideshow?"
    showStatusBar="false"
    resizable="false"
    maximizable="false" minimizable="false"
    layout="vertical"
    verticalAlign="middle" horizontalAlign="center"
    width="270" height="100"
    creationComplete="addActivationListeners();">
    <mx:Metadata>
        [Event(name="submit", type="flash.events.Event")]
        [Event(name="cancel", type="flash.events.Event")]
        [Event(name="close", type="flash.events.Event")]
    </mx:Metadata>
    <mx:Script>
        <![CDATA[
            private var _message:String;
            public static const SUBMIT:String = "submit";
            public static const CANCEL:String = "cancel";
            public static const CLOSE:String = "close";

            private function addActivationListeners():void
            {
                addEventListener( Event.CLOSING, removeActivationListeners );
                nativeWindow.addEventListener( Event.DEACTIVATE,
                                                        onDeactivate );
            }
            private function removeActivationListeners( evt:Event ):void
            {
                removeEventListener( Event.CLOSING, removeActivationListeners );
                nativeWindow.removeEventListener( Event.DEACTIVATE,
                                                        onDeactivate );
            }

            private function onDeactivate( evt:Event ):void
            {
                this.activate();
                if( NativeApplication.supportsDockIcon )
                {
                    DockIcon( NativeApplication.nativeApplication.icon ).bounce(
                                                NotificationType.INFORMATIONAL );
                    this.close();
                }
                else
                {
                    nativeWindow.notifyUser( NotificationType.INFORMATIONAL );
                    nativeWindow.activate();
                }
            }
```

```
            private function onSubmit():void
            {
                dispatchEvent( new Event( SaveWindow.SUBMIT ) );
            }
            private function onCancel():void
            {
                dispatchEvent( new Event( SaveWindow.CANCEL ) );
            }
            private function onClose():void
            {
                dispatchEvent( new Event( SaveWindow.CLOSE ) );
            }

            [Bindable]
            public function get message():String
            {
                return _message;
            }
            public function set message( str:String ):void
            {
                _message = str;
            }
        ]]>
    </mx:Script>
    <mx:Text text="{message}" textAlign="center" />
    <mx:HBox width="100%" horizontalAlign="center"
        paddingLeft="10" paddingRight="10"
        paddingTop="10" paddingBottom="10">
        <mx:Button label="yes" width="100%" click="onSubmit();" />
        <mx:Button label="no" width="100%" click="onCancel();" />
        <mx:Button label="cancel" width="100%" click="onClose();" />
    </mx:HBox>
</mx:Window>
```

Save the file as `SaveWindow.mxml` in the directory `com/aircmr/slideshow/windows` in your working directory, alongside the `SlideshowWindow.mxml` file created previously.

The `SaveWindow` will serve as an alert to users that modifications to the slideshow have been made prior to closing the application. Just as the `SlideshowWindow` extends the `mx.core.Window` class for customization, so too does the `SaveWindow`. The `SaveWindow` and `SlideshowWindow` differ not only in the roles they play within the application, but also in window properties. Whereas the `SlideshowWindow` hides all chrome and fills the screen, the `SaveWindow` acts more as a modal alert for the application. It does so by alerting the user of information through an operating system–specific notification:

```
private function onDeactivate( evt:Event ):void
{
    this.activate();
    if( NativeApplication.supportsDockIcon )
    {
        DockIcon(NativeApplication.nativeApplication.icon ).bounce(
                                                    NotificationType.INFORMATIONAL );
```

```
            this.close();
        }
        else
        {
            nativeWindow.notifyUser( NotificationType.INFORMATIONAL );
            nativeWindow.activate();
        }
    }
```

The `onDeactivate()` method is the event handler for the "deactivate" event dispatched by the `nativeWindow` instance of the window. This event is dispatched when a user has removed the focus from the Slideshow Maker application while the `SaveWindow` is open and present. The notification action of the Max OS X operating system is to bounce the application icon in the dock. The notification action of the Windows operating system is a blinking of the application icon in the application tray. To determine what system the AIR application is running under, the `SaveWindow` checks the `supportsDockIcon` property of the `NativeApplication` instance created upon application startup.

When a `SaveWindow` instance has been notified that the native window of the application is no longer the active window on the system, the appropriate notification action is presented to the user. When the window has been instructed to close, the event handler for deactivation is removed within the `removeActivateListeners()` method.

Notification of unsaved data within the Slideshow Maker application only occurs when a user has not addressed how to handle unsaved data. When the user chooses an option indicating how unsaved data should be handled, the `SaveWindow` dispatches events based on the user's selection. These events are handled by the client opening an instance of the `SaveWindow`.

In the next section, you will create the client that presents the `SaveWindow` and complete the Slideshow Maker application.

The Main File

It is time to bring together the display views and windows previously created in the chapter and make them accessible from a main workspace. That workspace will be the main application class. Without further ado, create a new document in your favorite text editor and enter the following markup:

```
<?xml version="1.0" encoding="utf-8"?>
<mx:WindowedApplication
    xmlns:mx="http://www.adobe.com/2006/mxml"
    xmlns:ui="com.aircmr.slideshow.ui.*"
    layout="absolute"
    showStatusBar="false"
    initialize="onAppInit();"
    invoke="onAppInvoke(event);"
    applicationComplete="onAppComplete();"
    closing="onAppClosing(event);">

    <mx:Script>
        <![CDATA[
            import com.aircmr.slideshow.windows.SaveWindow;
            import com.aircmr.slideshow.windows.SlideshowWindow;
```

```
import com.aircmr.slideshow.util.Settings;
import com.aircmr.slideshow.data.SlideGallery;
import com.aircmr.slideshow.data.Slide;

private var _importFile:File;
private var _exportFile:File;
private var _saveWindow:SaveWindow;
private var _slideshowWindow:SlideshowWindow;
private var _invokedGallery:SlideGallery;
private var _isInitialized:Boolean = false;
private var _exportAsSlide:Boolean = false;
[Bindable] private var _gallery:SlideGallery;
[Bindable] private var _currentSlide:Slide;

private function onAppInit():void
{
    setGallery( new SlideGallery() );
}

private function onAppInvoke( evt:InvokeEvent ):void
{
    if( evt.arguments.length <= 0 ) return;
    var file:File = new File( evt.arguments[0] );
    var ext:String = file.extension;
    if( ext == Settings.getSlideExtension()
        || ext == Settings.getShowExtension() )
    {
        openItem( file );
    }
}

private function onAppComplete():void
{
    initializeView();
    if( _invokedGallery != null )
    {
        setGallery( _invokedGallery );
        _gallery.currentIndex = 0;
        _invokedGallery = null;
    }
    if( _gallery.length == 0 )    addNewSlide();
    addMenu();
}

private function initializeView():void
{
    visible = true;
    view.createComponentsFromDescriptors();
    _isInitialized = true;
}

private function addMenu():void
{
    var fItem:NativeMenuItem = new NativeMenuItem( "File" );
```

```
        var vItem:NativeMenuItem = new NativeMenuItem( "View" );
        var fileMenu:NativeMenuItem;
        var viewMenu:NativeMenuItem;
        if( NativeWindow.supportsMenu )
        {
            stage.nativeWindow.menu = new NativeMenu();
            fileMenu = stage.nativeWindow.menu.addItem( fItem );
            viewMenu = stage.nativeWindow.menu.addItem( vItem );
        }
        else if( NativeApplication.supportsMenu )
        {
            NativeApplication.nativeApplication.menu = new NativeMenu();

            var appMenu:NativeMenuItem = new NativeMenuItem(
                                                "Slideshow Maker" );
            appMenu.submenu = createAppMenu();

            appMenu = NativeApplication.nativeApplication.menu.addItem(
                                                             appMenu );

            fileMenu = NativeApplication.nativeApplication.menu.addItem(
                                                                fItem );
            viewMenu = NativeApplication.nativeApplication.menu.addItem(
                                                                vItem );
        }
        fileMenu.submenu = createFileMenu();
        viewMenu.submenu = createViewMenu();
    }

    public function createFileMenu():NativeMenu
    {
        var menu:NativeMenu = new NativeMenu();
        var openSlideshowCmd:NativeMenuItem =
                menu.addItem( new NativeMenuItem( "Open Slideshow" ) );
        openSlideshowCmd.addEventListener( Event.SELECT,
                                    browseForSlideshow );
        var saveSlideshowCmd:NativeMenuItem =
                menu.addItem( new NativeMenuItem( "Save Slideshow" ) );
        saveSlideshowCmd.addEventListener( Event.SELECT, saveSlideshow );
        var importSlideCmd:NativeMenuItem =
                menu.addItem( new NativeMenuItem( "Import Slide" ) );
        importSlideCmd.addEventListener( Event.SELECT, browseForSlide );
        var exportSlideCmd:NativeMenuItem =
                menu.addItem( new NativeMenuItem( "Export Slide" ) );
        exportSlideCmd.addEventListener( Event.SELECT, saveSlide );
        var newSlideCmd:NativeMenuItem =
                menu.addItem( new NativeMenuItem( "New Slide" ) );
        newSlideCmd.addEventListener( Event.SELECT, addNewSlide );

        return menu;
    }

    private function createViewMenu():NativeMenu
    {
```

```
        var menu:NativeMenu = new NativeMenu();
        var viewSlideshowCmd:NativeMenuItem =
                menu.addItem( new NativeMenuItem( "View Slideshow" ) );
        viewSlideshowCmd.addEventListener( Event.SELECT, viewSlideshow );
        var viewSlideCmd:NativeMenuItem =
                menu.addItem( new NativeMenuItem( "View Slide" ) );
        viewSlideCmd.addEventListener( Event.SELECT, viewSlide );
        return menu;
    }

    private function createAppMenu():NativeMenu
    {
        var menu:NativeMenu = new NativeMenu();
        var quitCmd:NativeMenuItem =
             menu.addItem( new NativeMenuItem( "Quit Slideshow Maker" ) );
        quitCmd.addEventListener( Event.SELECT, onAppClosing );
        return menu;
    }

    private function openItem( file:File ):void
    {
        var stream:FileStream = new FileStream();
        stream.open( file, FileMode.READ );
        switch( file.extension )
        {
            case Settings.getSlideExtension():
                openSlide( stream.readObject() as Slide );
                break;
            case Settings.getShowExtension():
                openSlideshow( stream.readObject() as SlideGallery );
                break;
        }
        stream.close();
    }
    private function openSlide( slide:Slide ):void
    {
        slide.deserialize();
        _gallery.addSlide( slide );
    }
    private function openSlideshow( gallery:SlideGallery ):void
    {
        gallery.deserialize();
        if( !_isInitialized )
        {
            _invokedGallery = gallery;
        }
        else
        {
            setGallery( gallery );
            _gallery.currentIndex = 0;
        }
    }

    private function setGallery( gallery:SlideGallery ):void
    {
```

```
        _gallery = gallery;
        _gallery.addEventListener( SlideGallery.INDEX_CHANGE,
                                   onGalleryIndexChange );
    }

    private function browseForSlideshow( evt:Event = null ):void
    {
        var ext:String = Settings.getShowExtension();
        _importFile = new File();
        _importFile.addEventListener( Event.SELECT, onImportSelect );
        _importFile.browseForOpen( "Open Slideshow", [new FileFilter(
                    "Slideshow (*." + ext + ")", "*." + ext )] );
    }
    private function browseForSlide( evt:Event = null ):void
    {
        var ext:String = Settings.getSlideExtension();
        _importFile = new File();
        _importFile.addEventListener( Event.SELECT, onImportSelect );
        _importFile.browseForOpen( "Open Slide", [new FileFilter(
                "Slideshow Slide (*." + ext + ")" , "*." + ext )] );
    }
    private function saveSlideshow( evt:Event = null ):void
    {
        _exportFile = new File();
        _exportFile.addEventListener( Event.SELECT, onExportSelect );
        _exportFile.browseForSave( "Save Slideshow" );
    }
    private function saveSlide( evt:Event = null ):void
    {
        _exportAsSlide = true;
        _exportFile = new File();
        _exportFile.addEventListener( Event.SELECT, onExportSelect );
        _exportFile.browseForSave( "Save Slide" );
    }
    private function addNewSlide( evt:Event = null ):void
    {
        _gallery.addSlide( new Slide() );
    }
    private function viewSlideshow( evt:Event = null ):void
    {
        showSlideshowWindow( _gallery.slides );
    }
    private function viewSlide( evt:Event = null ):void
    {
        showSlideshowWindow( [_currentSlide] );
    }

    private function showSlideshowWindow( slides:Array ):void
    {
        _slideshowWindow = new SlideshowWindow();
        _slideshowWindow.width = Settings.getScreenSize().width;
        _slideshowWindow.height = Settings.getScreenSize().height;
        _slideshowWindow.alwaysInFront = true;
```

```
        _slideshowWindow.addEventListener( Event.CLOSING,
                                            onSlideshowWindowClosing );
        _slideshowWindow.open();
        _slideshowWindow.move( 0, 0 );
        _slideshowWindow.slides = slides;
    }

    private function showSaveWindow():void
    {
        if( _saveWindow != null ) _saveWindow.close();
        _saveWindow = new SaveWindow();
        _saveWindow.addEventListener( SaveWindow.SUBMIT, closeSaveWindow );
        _saveWindow.addEventListener( SaveWindow.CLOSE, closeSaveWindow );
        _saveWindow.addEventListener( SaveWindow.CANCEL, onSaveCancel );
        _saveWindow.message = "You have unsaved changes.\n" +
                               "Would you like to save your work?";
        _saveWindow.open();
        var cx:Number = ( nativeWindow.width - _saveWindow.width ) / 2;
        var cy:Number = ( nativeWindow.height - _saveWindow.height ) / 2;
        _saveWindow.move( nativeWindow.x + cx, nativeWindow.y + cy );
        _saveWindow.nativeWindow.orderToFront();
    }

    private function closeSaveWindow( evt:Event = null ):void
    {
        _saveWindow.close();
        _saveWindow.removeEventListener( SaveWindow.SUBMIT,
                                            closeSaveWindow );
        _saveWindow.removeEventListener( SaveWindow.CLOSE,
                                            closeSaveWindow );
        _saveWindow.removeEventListener( SaveWindow.CANCEL, onSaveCancel );
        _saveWindow = null;
    }

    private function onImportSelect( evt:Event ):void
    {
        openItem( _importFile );
    }

    private function onExportSelect( evt:Event ):void
    {
        Settings.checkExtension( _exportFile, _exportAsSlide );
        var stream:FileStream = new FileStream();
        stream.open( _exportFile, FileMode.WRITE );
        switch( _exportFile.extension )
        {
            case Settings.getShowExtension():
                _gallery.serialize();
                stream.writeObject( _gallery );
                properties.hasChanged = false;
                break;
            case Settings.getSlideExtension():
                _currentSlide.serialize();
```

```
                    stream.writeObject( _currentSlide );
                    break;
            }
            stream.close();
            _exportAsSlide = false;
        }

        private function onSlideDelete():void
        {
            _gallery.removeSlide( _currentSlide );
        }

        private function onGalleryIndexChange( evt:Event ):void
        {
            _currentSlide = _gallery.currentSlide;
        }

        private function onSlideshowWindowClosing( evt:Event ):void
        {
            _slideshowWindow.removeEventListener( Event.CLOSING,
                                                onSlideshowWindowClosing );
            _slideshowWindow = null;
        }

        private function onSaveCancel( evt:Event ):void
        {
            closeSaveWindow();
            shutDown();
        }

        private function onAppClosing( evt:Event ):void
        {
            evt.preventDefault();
            if( properties.hasChanged ) showSaveWindow();
            else shutDown();
        }

        private function shutDown():void
        {
            _gallery.clean();
            NativeApplication.nativeApplication.exit();
        }
    ]]>
</mx:Script>

<mx:Canvas id="view"
    width="100%" height="100%"
    creationPolicy="none">
    <mx:HBox width="100%" height="100%"
        paddingTop="10" paddingBottom="10"
        paddingLeft="10" paddingRight="10">
        <mx:VBox width="100%" height="100%">
            <ui:SlideCanvas id="canvas"
```

```
                    width="100%" height="100%"
                    includeViewInLayout="false"
                    slideData="{_currentSlide}"
                    backgroundColor="0xCDCDCD"
                    borderColor="0x999999" borderStyle="solid"
                    />
                <ui:PropertiesPanel id="properties"
                    height="130"
                    paddingLeft="10" paddingRight="10"
                    paddingTop="10" paddingBottom="10"
                    backgroundColor="0xDEDEDE"
                    borderColor="0x999999" borderStyle="solid"
                    slideData="{_currentSlide}"
                    />
            </mx:VBox>
            <ui:Carousel id="carousel"
                borderColor="0x999999" borderStyle="solid"
                gallery="{_gallery}" deleteSlide="onSlideDelete();"
                />
        </mx:HBox>
    </mx:Canvas>
</mx:WindowedApplication>
```

Save the file as `SlideshowMaker.mxml` in your working directory.

The `SlideshowMaker` is the main application class. `SlideshowMaker` handles the importing and exporting of single slides and slideshows as well as supplying current data to the display views and responding to the invocation event of the application. Along with handling these actions, the `SlideshowMaker` also serves as the workspace display and provides access to the presentation display. There's a lot going on in the main application class, so dive right in and look at the "invoke" event handler:

```
private function onAppInvoke( evt:InvokeEvent ):void
{
    if( evt.arguments.length <= 0 ) return;
    var file:File = new File( evt.arguments[0] );
    var ext:String = file.extension;
    if( ext == Settings.getSlideExtension()
        || ext == Settings.getShowExtension() )
    {
        openItem( file );
    }
}
```

The `invoke` event of the `<mx:WindowedApplication>` application container is dispatched upon invocation of the application. The event is dispatched when you open the application directly or when the application is requested to open a file whether the application is open or not. The `arguments` property of the `InvokeEvent` is an array of string values. When invoked to open files in the Slideshow Maker, that array supplied through invocation will be a set of file paths.

The first evaluation in the `onAppInvoke()` method checks whether any arguments where passed along during invocation of the application. If arguments are available upon invocation, then the application requests to open the first file in the list, as the Slideshow Maker will only open one file at a time upon invocation. If the extension of the file is valid for this application, then it is instructed to open that file by calling the `openItem()` method:

```
private function openItem( file:File ):void
{
    var stream:FileStream = new FileStream();
    stream.open( file, FileMode.READ );
    switch( file.extension )
    {
        case Settings.getSlideExtension():
            openSlide( stream.readObject() as Slide );
            break;
        case Settings.getShowExtension():
            openSlideshow( stream.readObject() as SlideGallery );
            break;
    }
    stream.close();
}
```

In the `openItem()` method, the supplied file is read into the buffer and is type-cast to the appropriate data object. In the previous section, "Handling Data," you created the data objects used in the Slideshow Maker to preserve their custom type upon serialization. In this snippet, those data objects are deserialized when the `readObject()` method of the `FileStream` instance is invoked and then typed to their associated class based on the extension of the file being read.

How those data objects are serialized to a file is shown in the `onExportSelect()` method:

```
private function onExportSelect( evt:Event ):void
{
    Settings.checkExtension( _exportFile, _exportAsSlide );
    var stream:FileStream = new FileStream();
    stream.open( _exportFile, FileMode.WRITE );
    switch( _exportFile.extension )
    {
        case Settings.getShowExtension():
            _gallery.serialize();
            stream.writeObject( _gallery );
            properties.hasChanged = false;
            break;
        case Settings.getSlideExtension():
            _currentSlide.serialize();
            stream.writeObject( _currentSlide );
            break;
    }
    stream.close();
    _exportAsSlide = false;
}
```

The `onExportSelect()` method is invoked from a `select` event of a file browser when a user chooses to export a slide or a whole slideshow. In this method, the extension is checked and a `FileStream` instance opened to write the appropriate data object to a file — either the current `SlideGallery` or the current `Slide` being worked on. Prior to being written to the file stream, the `serialize()` method is called on the data objects. This results in the creation of a temporary file to be held in the serialized SlideImage instance of a Slide object, as discussed in the section "Handling Data." The writeObject() method writes the supplied object in AMF serialized format and, in this example, saves that object out to the specified path held on _exportFile.

While the option to import a file is available by handling the "invoke" event of the SlideshowMaker, that action is also available as a command item on the NativeMenu of the main application:

```
private function addMenu():void
{
    var fItem:NativeMenuItem = new NativeMenuItem( "File" );
    var vItem:NativeMenuItem = new NativeMenuItem( "View" );
    var fileMenu:NativeMenuItem;
    var viewMenu:NativeMenuItem;
    if( NativeWindow.supportsMenu )
    {
        stage.nativeWindow.menu = new NativeMenu();
        fileMenu = stage.nativeWindow.menu.addItem( fItem );
        viewMenu = stage.nativeWindow.menu.addItem( vItem );
    }
    else if( NativeApplication.supportsMenu )
    {
        NativeApplication.nativeApplication.menu = new NativeMenu();
        var appMenu:NativeMenuItem = new NativeMenuItem( "Slideshow Maker" );
        appMenu.submenu = createAppMenu();

        appMenu = NativeApplication.nativeApplication.menu.addItem( appMenu );
        fileMenu = NativeApplication.nativeApplication.menu.addItem( fItem );
        viewMenu = NativeApplication.nativeApplication.menu.addItem( vItem );
    }
        fileMenu.submenu = createFileMenu();
        viewMenu.submenu = createViewMenu();
}
```

The call to addMenu() is made in the event handler for the creationComplete event dispatched from SlideshowMaker and assigns two submenus to the native menu of the application based on the operating system. Native menus within an application differ between operating systems. Under Windows, only window menus are supported, while under Mac OS X only application menus are supported. As such, within the addMenu() method, the current operating system is determined using the supportsMenu property of the NativeWindow class and the NativeApplication class.. In Windows, menus are added to the NativeWindow instance and the first if statement is entered. If the NativeWindow instance does not support menus and the NativeApplication instance does, the second statement is entered — this will occur when running in the Mac OS X environment. When you supply a new NativeMenu object as the application menu for applications running in Mac OS X, you overwrite the default menu given to the application by the operating system. As such, an extra menu is added to the application menu that is not added to the window menu for applications running in the Windows environment. The appMenu created within the addMenu() method is a relatively simple menu with a submenu command allowing you to quit the application.

The command items added to the File menu relate to the actions of opening and saving a single slide and slideshows. The importing and exporting of AMF serialized data objects will occur from commands invoked from this submenu. The command items added to the View menu relate to previewing a slide or presenting a slideshow in full screen. Each of the options will open a slideshow presentation with the appropriate slide data:

```
private function showSlideshowWindow( slides:Array ):void
{
    _slideshowWindow = new SlideshowWindow();
    _slideshowWindow.width = Settings.getScreenSize().width;
    _slideshowWindow.height = Settings.getScreenSize().height;
    _slideshowWindow.alwaysInFront = true;
    _slideshowWindow.addEventListener( Event.CLOSING,
                                        onSlideshowWindowClosing );
    _slideshowWindow.open();
    _slideshowWindow.move( 0, 0 );
    _slideshowWindow.slides = slides;
}
```

The `showSlideshowWindow()` method is called from the select event handlers of menu items in the View menu. In this method, the `SlideshowWindow` is created, resized to the bounds of the screen, and brought to the front of the z-order of windows displayed. After the `SlideshowWindow` instance is called to open, it is moved to the upper left corner of the screen and supplied an array of `Slide` data objects. In the creation of the `SlideshowMaker`, key events and a context menu are set, so once the slide data is supplied you are off and running with a presentation.

The display of `SlideshowMaker` is composed of a `SlideCanvas`, a `PropertiesPanel`, and a `Carousel` — view classes created previously in the section "Building the User Interface." Another instance of the versatile `SlideCanvas` makes an appearance in the `SlideshowMaker` with its `slideData` property bound to the `_currentSlide` of the application. The `slideData` property of the `PropertiesPanel` instance is also bound to this value, allowing any updates made to the slide through the `PropertiesPanel` to be updated on the `SlideCanvas` instance. The `Carousel` instance displays the current set of slides held on the application through data binding as well, and sets the `onSlideDelete()` method as the event handler for the removal of a `Slide` instance from the gallery.

Within these display classes, static method calls are made on a `Settings` class to obtain the dimensions of the screen and operations related to valid file extensions, as shown in the `openItem()` and `onExportItem()` methods discussed in this section. In the next section, you will create the utility class that is used to retrieve and evaluate that data.

Settings Utility

The utility class you create in this section provides access to the current screen bounds and validation of associated file types. It also handles parsing the application descriptor file to evaluate associated file types.

Create a new document and enter the following ActionScript:

```
package com.aircmr.slideshow.util
{
    import flash.desktop.NativeApplication;
    import flash.display.Screen;
    import flash.filesystem.File;
```

```
    import flash.geom.Rectangle;

    public class Settings
    {
        private static var ns:Namespace;
        private static const SLIDE_NAME:String = "com.aircmr.slideshow.Slide";
        private static const SHOW_NAME:String = "com.aircmr.slideshow.Slideshow";

        public static function getScreenSize():Rectangle
        {
            return Screen.mainScreen.bounds;
        }

        public static function getExtensionType( typeName:String ):String
        {
            var descriptor:XML =
                     NativeApplication.nativeApplication.applicationDescriptor;
            ns = new Namespace( String ( descriptor.namespace() ) );
            default xml namespace = ns;
            return descriptor..fileType.(name == typeName).extension.toString();
        }

        public static function getSlideExtension():String
        {
            return Settings.getExtensionType( SLIDE_NAME );
        }

        public static function getShowExtension():String
        {
            return Settings.getExtensionType( Settings.SHOW_NAME );
        }

        public static function checkExtension( file:File,
                                               isSlide:Boolean = false ):void
        {
            if( isSlide )
            {
                if( file.extension != Settings.getSlideExtension() )
                    file.nativePath += "." + Settings.getSlideExtension();
            }
            else
            {
                if( file.extension != Settings.getShowExtension() )
                    file.nativePath += "." + Settings.getShowExtension();
            }
        }
    }
}
```

Save the file as `Settings.as` in the directory `com/aircmr/slideshow/util` in your working directory.

Receiving the current screen size is relatively easy but has been centralized to the `Settings` file so all clients that display containers relative to the bounds of the screen are working with data from a single source.

```
public static function getScreenSize():Rectangle
{
    return Screen.mainScreen.bounds;
}
```

The `Screen` class of the AIR API provides access to system screen information. In this example, the `Settings` utility class returns the bounds of the main display screen from the static `getScreenSize()` method. In following with the examples in this chapter, the `getScreenSize()` value is used in scaling the view of a `SlideCanvas` instance and the dimension display for a slideshow presentation.

Access to the associated file extensions for a slide and slideshow file is gained through the `getSlideExtension()` and `getShowExtension()` static methods. Both methods call the `getExtensionType()` method with the relative file type name:

```
public static function getExtensionType( typeName:String ):String
{
    var descriptor:XML = NativeApplication.nativeApplication.applicationDescriptor;
    ns = new Namespace( String ( descriptor.namespace() ) );
    default xml namespace = ns;
    return descriptor..fileType.(name == typeName).extension.toString();
}
```

The contents of the application descriptor file — which is in XML format and created in the next section, "Deploying the Application" — is obtained from the `applicationDescriptor` property of the `NativeApplication` Singleton. The `NativeApplication` instance is created upon startup of the application and enables the application to interact with the operating system GUI shell — the Explorer in Windows, and Finder in Mac OS X. In the `getExtensionType()` method of the `Settings` class, the `default xml namespace` directive sets the default `Namespace` to use in parsing the descriptor file with the namespace URI held on the descriptor XML. The return value is that of the extension string relative to the `fileType` element, with a child node `name` value that matches the supplied argument.

With the `Settings` utility class serving as a main access point for multiple clients who deal with screen bounds and file types complete, you can get to work on creating the application descriptor file that will associate file types with the Slideshow Maker.

Deploying the Application

With the application in place, it's time to set up the application descriptor file to associate file types with the Slideshow Maker, and deploy it to begin working on a slideshow.

The Descriptor File

Create a new document in your favorite text editor and enter the following markup:

```
<?xml version="1.0" encoding="UTF-8"?>
<application xmlns="http://ns.adobe.com/air/application/1.0">

    <id>com.aircmr.SlideshowMaker</id>
```

```
    <filename>SlideshowMaker</filename>
    <version>0.1</version>
    <name>Slideshow Maker</name>
    <description>A way to make slideshows</description>
    <copyright>2007</copyright>

      <initialWindow>
        <title>SlideshowMaker</title>
        <content>SlideshowMaker.swf</content>
        <systemChrome>standard</systemChrome>
        <transparent>false</transparent>
        <visible>true</visible>
        <width>720</width>
        <height>540</height>
      </initialWindow>

    <installFolder>AIRCMR/SlideshowMaker</installFolder>
    <programMenuFolder>AIRCMR</programMenuFolder>

  <fileTypes>
     <fileType>
        <name>com.aircmr.slideshow.Slide</name>
        <extension>slide</extension>
        <description>Slideshow Maker slide file</description>
        <contentType>application/x-amf</contentType>
     </fileType>
     <fileType>
        <name>com.aircmr.slideshow.Slideshow</name>
        <extension>show</extension>
        <description>Slideshow Maker slideshow file</description>
        <contentType>application/x-amf</contentType>
     </fileType>
  </fileTypes>

</application>
```

Save the file as `SlideshowMaker-app.xml` in your working directory along with the previously created `SlideshowMaker.mxml` file.

While the property values for the application and initial window in the application descriptor file have the usual generic values you have come to know and love while creating applications in this book, the `SlideshowMaker-app.xml` file has some elements not yet addressed. The term *associated file types* has been peppered throughout this chapter without really addressing what that means.

Within the `<fileTypes>` element of the application descriptor file, you can list any number of `<fileType>` elements to associate with your application. In the example for this chapter, you have added two file types — one related to individual slides and one related to a slideshow, or a set of slides:

```
<fileType>
    <name>com.aircmr.slideshow.Slide</name>
    <extension>slide</extension>
    <description>Slideshow Maker slide file</description>
```

```
        <contentType>application/x-amf</contentType>
    </fileType>
```

The child elements of a `<fileType>` declaration represent the name, extension, description, and content-type associated with the file. In looking at the values associated with a slide file:

- The `<name>` element value represents the file type name that identifies the extension on the operating system. The format for this example is a dot-delimited reversed-DNS string with the file type at the end.
- The `<extension>` element value is the extension for the file without the preceding period character. When the application is installed, files with this extension will be associated with the application.
- The `<description>` element value is the description of the file type. This will appear in the properties views of a selected file.
- The `<contentType>` element value specifies the MIME type for the file. Because the Slideshow Maker serializes objects to a file using AMF, `application/x-amf` is specified as the known content-type of the files.

Files with the extension of `.slide` and `.show` will register the Slideshow Maker as the default system application for handling those files when the application is installed. This enables you to export slides and slideshows from the workspace and open them with the Slideshow Maker by choosing File ➪ Open With and double-clicking on the file itself, whether the application is currently open or not — the `invoke` event handler of the main application will handle that for you.

In the next section, you will break out the command prompt and deploy the Slideshow Maker application for installation.

Compiling and Packaging

Two files are necessary to package the Slideshow Maker AIR application — the main SWF file and the XML application descriptor file. In this section you will produce the SWF file and package the application using the command-line tools from the AIR SDK.

Open a command prompt, navigate to the working directory for the Slideshow Maker map application, enter the following command, and press Enter:

```
> amxmlc SlideshowMaker.mxml
```

If you have purchased a certificate from a certificate authority, such as VeriSign or Thawte, you may use that certificate, rather than create the self-signed certificate, and skip the following operation. To create a self-signed certificate within the working directory, enter the following command:

```
> adt -certificate -cn SlideshowMaker 1024-RSA certificate.pfx password
```

With the command prompt still pointing to the working directory, enter the following command to package the SlideshowMaker application:

```
> adt -package -storetype pkcs12 -keystore certificate.pfx SlideshowMaker.air
SlideshowMaker -app.xml SlideshowMaker.swf
```

You will be prompted to enter the password for the certificate. If you created a self-signed certificate from the second command, enter "**password**." Running these commands, a `SlideshowMaker.swf` file, a `certificate.pfx` file and the `SlideshowMaker.air` installer file are generated within your working directory.

Once the installer has been created, navigate to your working directory and launch the Slideshow Maker application. If all goes well, you'll be presented with the workspace to begin creating slideshows. After a few slides have been created, the application should look something like Figure 11-1.

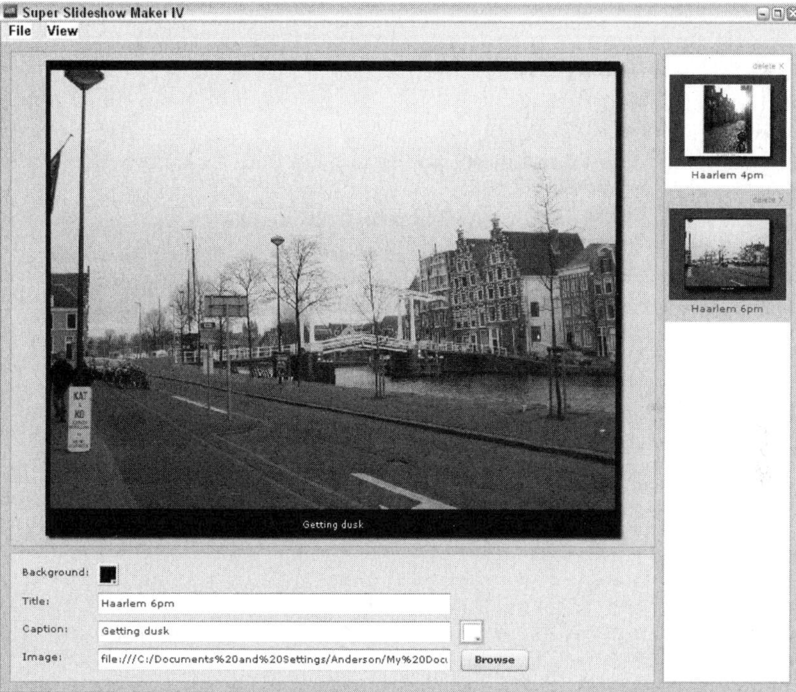

Figure 11-1

Click View ➪ View Slideshow and the slideshow will begin displaying slides to the full bounds of your system's main screen (see Figure 11-2), which you can navigate through and close.

Figure 11-2

Save out individual slides and slideshows. Open them when you are ready, or install the Slideshow Maker on another computer and pass those files over to continue working.

Summary

In this chapter, you have created a working Slideshow Maker while delving deeper into the AIR file system API as it pertains to serializing custom objects to a file. You have also learned how to associate file types with an application from the application descriptor file, and spawn Window objects used for full-screen presentations and notification alerts.

From here, you can set up keystroke commands that coincide with the menu commands for saving and viewing slideshows, and add more commands as you see fit. You can also add more properties to the Properties panel and extra controls to make more engaging slides.

In the next chapter, you will continue to add to your toolbox of AIR knowledge by learning how to create a video player.

12

AIR Video Player

The past ten years have seen many attempts at bringing video to the Internet. Both web-based and desktop-based applications have risen and fallen with usage trends, while a few competitors have stood their ground. However, with every new player, there is a new data format and another sector of people supporting only that technology. The result is a machine that has far too many applications that do the same thing. The latest release of Flash Player's support of the H.264 codec in combination with Flex 3 and AIR will, with any luck, push the Internet industry into using one video format.

In this chapter, you will build a desktop video player that supports both FLV and H.264 video formats. It will have all the basic functionality of a desktop video player such as play, pause, rewind, full-screen support, volume, and timeline scrubbing controls. The intention of this chapter isn't necessarily to create a video player with a lot of bells and whistles, but to familiarize you with some of the main features of the AIR API. It is hoped that this gives you some ideas for adding your own touch to this application.

While building the video player, the following features in the AIR and Flex APIs are discussed:

- Utilizing the Flex `VideoDisplay` component
- Creating contextual and application menus
- Accessing files from both a system browser window and drag-and-drop events
- Switching between normal and full-screen display states

The next section discusses the design of the video player.

Design

The design of a video player may seem pretty intuitive, and for the most part it is. After all, with the success of a website like YouTube, you end up looking at a video player every time a friend or colleague sends you another humorous or absurd video. At this point, you probably have an idea of the core functionality, such as playback controls, and you could jump right into building the player. However, mixing in the AIR functionality while not cluttering your application may take some more planning.

You could create one giant class file that contains everything: the video display, the video controls, and the integration with AIR. However, you'll probably want to reuse some of the functionality of the player itself at some point. Therefore, it would be nice to have a standalone video player that can be used on and off the web, one that you can instantiate in either a Flex `<mx:Application>` container or an AIR `<mx:WindowedApplication>` container.

The standalone video player will contain all of the core playback functionality for the AIR Video Player. This functionality will be separated into two separate classes, one for the video display and the other for the video controls. It will consist of functionality such as the following:

- **Playback controls:** Every video player has, at a minimum, a play button and a rewind button. The play button will toggle between pause and play states, and will change the button's graphical view (skin) accordingly. Along with the play, pause, and rewind controls, you will include a timeline scrubber for jumping to different sections of the video, a time stamp indicator that tracks progress, and a volume controller.
- **Liquid layout:** One key feature of the AIR Video Player is the capability to display the video full-screen. In order to accommodate this, you need to create a layout that adjusts with the size of the video. For instance, if the video display expands from 300×250 to 640×480 or full-screen, the playback controls need to resize accordingly with the expanded display.
- **Webcam capture:** This isn't necessarily needed, but it's a simple and fun feature to add to the video player. Of course, feel free to exclude this if you do not have a webcam.

After the video player component has been created, you will instantiate it in the main `<mx:WindowedApplication>` container. The main application container will feature all AIR functionality, including the following:

- **Drag and drop:** You will enable users to drag and drop FLV or H.264 encoded files onto the AIR Video Player. Once the file is accepted, you will then pass the native path to the video player component as its source.
- **Full-screen support:** The Flash Player supports a full-screen display state. This is especially useful for an application like the AIR Video Player and is easy to do. Enabling this feature will turn the user's computer into a virtual cinema.
- **Context and window menus:** Outside of the drag-and-drop support, the other way to open a video file is through the window menu. Additionally, it is helpful to set up a basic context menu that offers playback controls such as play and pause, along with the full-screen toggle.

Now that the basic design and functionality have been defined, you can begin building the AIR Video Player. The next section will help you set up the directory structure and gather the accompanying files.

Building the Directory Structure

Before discussing *how* the video player is built, it is important to properly set up the directory structure for this chapter. Begin by creating a new directory in your local development directory called `VideoPlayer`. This directory will be your working directory for this application.

Next, create the package structure for this application by creating three new directories, `com`, `aircmr`, and `videoplayer`, in your working directory. The video player package structure should look like the following: *`working directory`*`/com/aircmr/videoplayer`.

Lastly, download the corresponding `assets` from the accompanying website and place them in the root of the working directory. These files will be used throughout the development of the video player. They include graphical skins for the buttons, and two sample videos.

The two videos included in the `assets` *directory will be helpful in testing the AIR Video Player. One is an Apple QuickTime movie encoded with the H.264 codec, and the other is a standard Flash FLV.*

Now that the directory structure has been set up, you can jump right into building the AIR Video Player. The next section, jumps right into developing the first component in the AIR Video Player.

Building the UIVideoPlayer Component

As discussed in the design section, the `UIVideoPlayer` component will include all video playback functionality. This functionality is dispersed throughout two separate Flex component files, `UIVideoPlayer.mxml` and `UIVideoControls.mxml`. In order to the functionality of the `UIVideoPlayer`, first you need to set up the two component classes:

1. Open a new editor window and insert the following markup:

```
<?xml version="1.0" encoding="utf-8"?>
<mx:VBox xmlns:mx="http://www.adobe.com/2006/mxml"
    width="300" height="290" verticalGap="0"
    xmlns:ui="com.aircmr.videoplayer.ui.*">
    <mx:Metadata>
        [Event(name="videoResize", type="flash.events.Event")]
        [Event(name="metadataReceived", type="mx.events.MetadataEvent")]
        [Event(name="stateChange", type="mx.events.VideoEvent")]
    </mx:Metadata>
    <mx:Script>
        <![CDATA[
            import mx.events.VideoEvent;
            import mx.events.MetadataEvent;

            public static const VIDEO_RESIZE:String = "videoResize";

            private var _source:String;
            private var _autoPlay:Boolean = true;
            private var _autoRewind:Boolean = true;
            private var _maintainAspectRatio:Boolean = true;
            private var _resizeToVideo:Boolean = false;
            private var _showVideoControls:Boolean = false;
            private var _playing:Boolean = false;

            public function play( event:Event = null ):void
            {
                videoDisplay.play();
            }
```

```
public function pause( event:Event = null ):void
{
    videoDisplay.pause();
}

public function enableCamera( event:Event = null ):void
{
    var camera:Camera = Camera.getCamera();
    videoDisplay.attachCamera( camera );
}

public function setDoubleSize( event:Event = null ):void
{
    this.width = videoDisplay.videoWidth * 2;
    this.height = videoDisplay.videoHeight * 2 + videoControls.height;
    dispatchEvent( new Event( UIVideoPlayer.VIDEO_RESIZE ) );
}

public function setNormalSize( event:Event = null ):void
{
    this.width = videoDisplay.videoWidth;
    this.height = videoDisplay.videoHeight + videoControls.height;
    dispatchEvent( new Event( UIVideoPlayer.VIDEO_RESIZE ) );
}

private function handleMetaData( event:MetadataEvent ):void
{
    if( _resizeToVideo )
    {
        width = event.info.width;
        height = event.info.height + videoControls.height;

        dispatchEvent( new Event( UIVideoPlayer.VIDEO_RESIZE));
    }

    dispatchEvent( event );
}

private function handleVideoDisplayStateChange( event:VideoEvent ):void
{
    playing = videoDisplay.playing;
    dispatchEvent( event );
}

[Bindable]
public function get source():String
{
    return _source;
}

public function set source( val:String ):void
{
    _source = val;
}
```

```
[Bindable]
public function get autoPlay():Boolean
{
    return _autoPlay;
}

public function set autoPlay( bool:Boolean ):void
{
    _autoPlay = bool;
}

[Bindable]
public function get autoRewind():Boolean
{
    return _autoRewind;
}

public function set autoRewind( bool:Boolean ):void
{
    _autoRewind = bool;
}

[Bindable]
public function get maintainAspectRatio():Boolean
{
    return _maintainAspectRatio;
}

public function set maintainAspectRatio( bool:Boolean ):void
{
    _maintainAspectRatio = bool;
}

[Bindable]
[Inspectable(defaultValue="false")]
public function get resizeToVideo():Boolean
{
    return _resizeToVideo;
}

public function set resizeToVideo( bool:Boolean ):void
{
    _resizeToVideo = bool;
}

public function get showVideoControls():Boolean
{
    return _showVideoControls;
}

public function set showVideoControls( bool:Boolean ):void
{
    _showVideoControls = bool;
```

```
                if( bool )
                {
                    if( !contains( videoControls ) ) addChild( videoControls );
                }
                else
                {
                    if( contains( videoControls ) ) removeChild( videoControls );
                }
            }

            [Bindable]
            public function get playing():Boolean
            {
                return _playing;
            }

            public function set playing( bool:Boolean ):void
            {
                _playing = bool;
            }

        ]]>
    </mx:Script>
    <mx:VideoDisplay id="videoDisplay"
        width="100%" height="100%"
        backgroundAlpha="0"
        source="{ source }"
        autoRewind="{autoRewind}"
        autoPlay="{autoPlay}"
        maintainAspectRatio="{maintainAspectRatio}"
        stateChange="handleVideoDisplayStateChange( event );"
        metadataReceived="handleMetaData( event );"
    />

    <ui:UIVideoControls id="videoControls"
        playheadTime="{videoDisplay.playheadTime}"
        playheadTimeTotal="{videoDisplay.totalTime}"
        playing="{videoDisplay.playing}"
        playheadTimeChange="{videoDisplay.playheadTime =
            videoControls.newPlayheadTime}"
        volumeChange="{videoDisplay.volume = videoControls.volume}"
        playVideo="{videoDisplay.play();}"
        pauseVideo="{videoDisplay.pause();}" />
</mx:VBox>
```

2. Save this class as `UIVideoPlayer.mxml` in the directory `/com/aircmr/videoplayer/ui/` within the working directory.

3. Open a new editor window and insert the following markup:

```
<?xml version="1.0" encoding="utf-8"?>
<mx:Canvas xmlns:mx="http://www.adobe.com/2006/mxml"
    width="100%" height="50" backgroundColor="0xFFFFFF"
    resize="onResizeHandler( event );"
    borderColor="0x0000000"
```

```
    borderStyle="inset"
    borderThickness="1"
    xmlns:ui="com.aircmr.videoplayer.ui.*" >

    <mx:Metadata>
        [Event(name="volumeChange", type="flash.events.Event")]
        [Event(name="playheadTimeChange" , type="flash.events.Event")]
        [Event(name="pauseVideo" , type="flash.events.Event")]
        [Event(name="playVideo" , type="flash.events.Event")]
    </mx:Metadata>

    <mx:Script>
        <![CDATA[
            import mx.events.SliderEvent;
            import mx.events.VideoEvent;

            public static const VOLUME_CHANGE:String = "volumeChange";
            public static const PLAYHEADTIME_CHANGE:String = "playheadTimeChange";
            public static const PAUSE_VIDEO:String = "pauseVideo";
            public static const PLAY_VIDEO:String = "playVideo";

            private var _newPlayheadTime:Number = 0;
            private var _playheadTimeTotal:Number = 0
            private var _playheadTime:Number = 0;
            private var _volume:Number = 1;
            private var _playing:Boolean = false;
            private var _wasPlaying:Boolean = false;
            private var _updateTime:Boolean = false;

            private function onResizeHandler( event:Event ):void
            {
                scrubber.width = this.width - 90;
            }

            private function handleRewind( event:MouseEvent ):void
            {
                newPlayheadTime = 0;
            }

            private function handlePlay( event:MouseEvent ):void
            {
                dispatchEvent( new Event( playing ?
                    UIVideoControls.PAUSE_VIDEO :  UIVideoControls.PLAY_VIDEO ));
            }

            private function handleVolumeChange( event:SliderEvent ):void
            {
                 volume = event.value;
            }

            private function handleVideoPlayheadUpdate():void
            {
                if( !_updateTime ) scrubber.value = _playheadTime;
```

```
        timelabel.text = String( timeFormatter.format(
            new Date( _playheadTime * 1000) ))
             + "/"+ String( timeFormatter.format(
                new Date( _playheadTimeTotal * 1000) ));

        if( timelabel.text == "/" ) timelabel.text = "00:00/00:00";
    }

    private function handleSliderThumbEvent( event:SliderEvent ):void
    {
        switch( event.type )
        {
            case SliderEvent.THUMB_PRESS : _wasPlaying = playing;
                dispatchEvent( new Event( UIVideoControls.PAUSE_VIDEO ));
                _updateTime = true;
                break;

            case SliderEvent.THUMB_RELEASE : if( _wasPlaying )
                    dispatchEvent(new Event( UIVideoControls.PLAY_VIDEO ));
                newPlayheadTime = event.value;
                _updateTime = false;
                break;
        }
    }

    private function formatTimelineValue( num:Number ):String
    {
        return String( timeFormatter.format( new Date( num * 1000) ));
    }

    private function formatVolume( num:Number ):String
    {
        return String( Math.round( num * 100 ));
    }


    [Bindable]
    public function get playheadTimeTotal():Number
    {
        return _playheadTimeTotal;
    }

    public function set playheadTimeTotal( val:Number ):void
    {
        _playheadTimeTotal = val;
    }

    [Bindable]
    public function get playheadTime():Number
    {
        return _playheadTime;
    }

    public function set playheadTime( val:Number ):void
```

```
            {
                _playheadTime = val;
                handleVideoPlayheadUpdate();
            }

            [Bindable("playheadTimeChange")]
            public function get newPlayheadTime():Number
            {
                return _newPlayheadTime;
            }

            public function set newPlayheadTime( val:Number ):void
            {
                _newPlayheadTime = val;
                dispatchEvent( new Event("playheadTimeChange") );
            }

            [Bindable("volumeChange")]
            public function get volume():Number
            {
                return _volume;
            }

            public function set volume( val:Number ):void
            {
                _volume = val;

                dispatchEvent( new Event( "volumeChange" ) );
            }

            [Bindable]
            public function get playing():Boolean
            {
                return _playing;
            }

            public function set playing( bool:Boolean ):void
            {
                _playing = bool;

                play.styleName = bool ? "pauseBtn" :  "playBtn";
            }
        ]]>
    </mx:Script>

    <mx:DateFormatter id="timeFormatter" formatString="NN:SS" />

    <mx:VBox width="100%" verticalGap="0">
        <mx:Canvas width="100%" height="15" id="timeTracker" >
            <mx:HSlider id="scrubber"
                width="100%" height="4"
                x="5" y="5"
                dataTipFormatFunction="formatTimelineValue"
                allowTrackClick="false"
```

```
                liveDragging="false"
                tickInterval="0"
                minimum="0"
                   maximum="{ playheadTimeTotal }"
                   thumbPress="handleSliderThumbEvent( event );"
                thumbRelease="handleSliderThumbEvent( event );"
                />
            <mx:Label id="timelabel" x="{timeTracker.width - timelabel.width}"
                styleName="timeText" text="00:00/00:00" />
        </mx:Canvas>

        <mx:Canvas width="100%" height="100%" id="toggle">
            <mx:HBox horizontalGap="0" x="2">
                <mx:Button styleName="toStartBtn" id="rewind"
                    click="handleRewind( event );" />
                <mx:Button styleName="playBtn" id="play"
                    click="handlePlay( event );"/>
            </mx:HBox>

            <mx:HBox horizontalGap="0" x="{toggle.width - 90}" y="10">
                <mx:Image source="@Embed('/assets/images/volumeLow.png')" />
                <mx:HSlider id="volumeController"
                    width="70" height="4"
                    allowTrackClick="true"
                    invertThumbDirection="true"
                    dataTipFormatFunction="formatVolume"
                    liveDragging="true"
                    change="handleVolumeChange( event );"
                    maximum="1"
                    minimum="0"
                    tickInterval="0"
                    value="{volume}"
                />
                <mx:Image source="@Embed('/assets/images/volumeHigh.png')" />
            </mx:HBox>
        </mx:Canvas>
    </mx:VBox>
</mx:Canvas>
```

4. Save this class as `UIVideoControls.mxml` in the directory `/com/aircmr/videoplayer/ui/` within the working directory.

To properly test this component, you may want to create the main application file and instantiate the `UIVideoPlayer` component. To do so, open a new editor window and insert the following stripped-down markup:

```
<?xml version="1.0" encoding="utf-8"?>
<mx:WindowedApplication width="300" height="290"
    xmlns:mx="http://www.adobe.com/2006/mxml"
    layout="absolute" verticalScrollPolicy="off"
```

```
        xmlns:ui="com.aircmr.videoplayer.ui.*">
    <mx:Style source="assets/style/app.css" />
    <ui:UIVideoPlayer width="100%" height="100%"
        source="assets/Redline_Renegades.mov" />
</mx:WindowedApplication>
```

Save this class as `AIRVideoPlayer.mxml` in the root of your working directory.

Both `AIRVideoPlayer.mxml` *and* `UIVideoControls.mxml` *reference assets found in the* `/assets` *directory. You can find these assets on the included CD. If you choose to not use them, be sure to comment out the references.*

At this point, if you were to compile and run this application, you would have a basic video player with the included video playing, as illustrated in Figure 12-1.

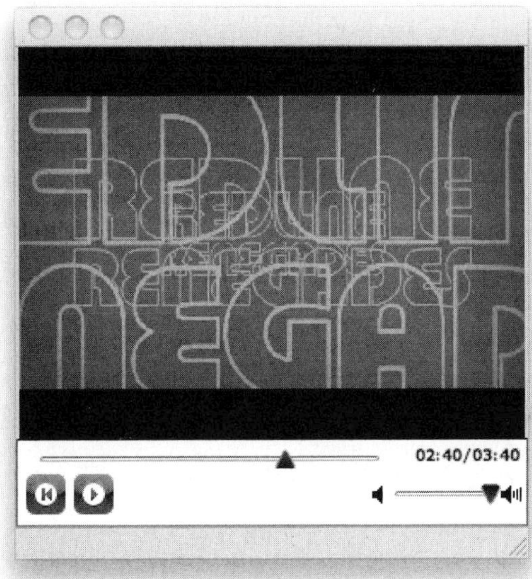

Figure 12-1

Begin reviewing the code by opening the `UIVideoControls` component class.

UIVideoControls Explained

The `UIVideoControls` class is the interface for the video player. It features a play button, a rewind button, a volume control, a timeline scrubber, and time-stamp labels. The component functionality is nested within an `<mx:Canvas>` container that has a controlled height and a variable width. The width is variable so that the controls will contract and expand along with the video player's size.

Public Variables

Before jumping into how the interface is created, review the public variables that control the UIVideoControls component:

- playheadTime: Once the video has started playing, the UIVideoPlayer component updates this property every time the playhead has changed. When the variable is set, the handleVideoPlayheadUpdate method is accessed. This method changes the time stamps and adjusts the marker location on the video scrubber.
- playheadTimeTotal: Once the video has been loaded, this value is set. You use this to display how long the video is versus the current playheadTime. This also acts as the maximum value for the timeline scrubber.
- newPlayheadTime: Any time the user moves the marker on the video scrubber, or hits rewind, you want to update this value. By doing so, a playheadTimeChange event is thrown, telling the UIVideoPlayer that the video's playheadTime must be updated.
- volume: This value is updated by the volume controller and dispatches the volumeChange event. Once the event is thrown, the volume is updated in the UIVideoPlayer.
- playing: This Boolean value is bound to the VideoDisplay component instantiated by the UIVideoPLayer. As the value changes from true to false, you update the styleName to match either a play icon or a pause icon.

Handling Timestamps

The playheadTime value is represented in seconds. Unfortunately, most video time stamps are represented in minutes, such as 01:30 rather than 90 seconds. In order to format the time in such a manner, you will use a Flex DateFormatter:

```
<mx:DateFormatter id="timeFormatter" formatString="NN:SS" />
```

This DateFormatter will format the playheadTime into NN:SS, which represent minute minute : second second. You access this formatter by calling the following:

```
timeFormatter.format( new Date( playheadTime * 1000 ) )
```

The DateFormatter class looks for a Date object to be sent through the format method. First it multiplies the playheadTime by 1000 to convert to milliseconds, and then it passes the playheadTime in milliseconds to a new Date object. The result is a String that looks like 01:30.

Video Scrubber Controller

Most video players have some sort of timeline scrubbing controls. As the video's time progresses, there is some graphical representation that can also serve as a way to seek (scrub) positions in the video. Flex's HSlider component will work for the video scrubber. The scrubber is called in the <mx:HSlider> markup with the ID scrubber.

As the playheadTime is updated, the position of the HSlider's value property is updated, moving the slider thumb along the slider track. This is accomplished in handleVideoPlayheadUpdate method. The maximum property of the HSlider is bound to the playheadTimeTotal property; therefore, the thumb marker's position on the slider will represent the position of playheadTime in relation to the playheadTimeTotal. This gives the user an accurate view of the video's progress.

Lastly, the user should be able to scrub through the video by moving the thumb on the slider. This is accomplished by the `handleSliderThumbEvent` method, which is called by the `thumbPress` and `thumbRelease` events. On press, the `handleSliderTumbEvent` records whether the video was playing before the thumb was pressed. On release, the `newPlayheadTime` property is set to the value of the thumb marker and an event is dispatched to the `UIVideoPlayer` component, which updates the `VideoDisplay` component. If the video was playing before the thumb press, then the video resumes play.

On Live Scrubbing Updates

The `newPlayheadTime` property is only updated on release for the same reason why there is no fast-forward or rewind functionality to the video player. The Flex `VideoDisplay` component's `playheadTime` property can continually receive new values. However, if the position in the `NetStream` object of `VideoDisplay` is being updated, new values will be queued and executed in order. Therefore, if the `newPlayheadTime` value was updated when the user drags the thumb, the video display would visually skip until it reaches the next `playheadTime` value in the queue.

Play, Pause, and Rewind

The play button acts as both the play and pause button, depending on whether the video is playing. When pressed, it calls the `handlePlay` method, which checks the playing `property` and dispatches either a `play` or `pause` event:

```
dispatchEvent( new Event( playing ? UIVideoControls.PAUSE_VIDEO :
UIVideoControls.PLAY_VIDEO ));
```

The rewind button calls the `handleRewind` method, which sets the `newPlayheadTime` property to zero.

UIVideoPlayer Explained

Now that there is the `UIVideoControls` component, it can be instantiated by the `UIVideoPlayer` component along with the Flex `VideoDisplay` component. The `UIVideoPlayer` consists of the two components, nested in a `VBox` container.

The `videoDisplay` and `videoControls` components interface directly with each other through public properties in events. For example, the `videoControls` `playing` property is bound to the `playing` property of the `videoDisplay`. Likewise, when the `volumeChange` event is dispatched, the inline code setting the `volume` property of `videoDisplay` is set:

```
<ui:UIVideoControls id="videoControls"
    playheadTime="{videoDisplay.playheadTime}"
    playheadTimeTotal="{videoDisplay.totalTime}"
    playing="{videoDisplay.playing}"
    playheadTimeChange="{videoDisplay.playheadTime = videoControls.newPlayheadTime}"
    volume="{videoDisplay.volume}"

    volumeChange="{videoDisplay.volume = videoControls.volume}"

    playVideo="{videoDisplay.play();}"
    pauseVideo="{videoDisplay.pause();}" />
```

The same applies to the `playheadTimeChange` event thrown by the `videoControls`.

Public Variables

The UIVideoPlayer has public variables that affect either the videoDisplay directly or the functionality of the UIVideoPlayer component. These variables include the following:

- source: This property is set by the parent class instantiating the UIVideoPlayer component. Once set, the URL is passed to the source property of the VideoDisplay component.
- autoPlay: Like source, this property is passed directly to the VideoDisplay component and affects whether the video automatically plays once loaded.
- autoRewind: Like source, this property is passed directly to the VideoDisplay component and affects whether the video automatically rewinds once the playhead has reached the end of the video.
- maintainAspectRatio: Like source, this property is passed directly to the VideoDisplay component and affects the aspect ratio of the video on resize.
- resizeToVideo: If set to true, when the video has been loaded, the UIVideoPlayer will resize to fit the height and width of the source. Otherwise, the video will be resized to fit inside of the UIVideoPlayer.
- showVideoControls: The videoControls component can be added and removed from the UIVideoPlayer by setting this Boolean property. This is used to turn the controls off when the player is set to full-screen.
- playing: This property is set by the VideoDisplay component and can be used to monitor whether the video is playing.

Handling Resizing

One key feature of the UIVideoPlayer is its ability to resize based on either the content or the setDoubleSize and setNormalSize public methods. For instance, once the source has been set and the VideoDisplay has received the metadata containing the height and width of the video, the handleMetaData method is called:

```
private function handleMetaData( event:MetadataEvent ):void
{
    if( _resizeToVideo )
    {
        width = event.info.width;
        height = event.info.height + videoControls.height;

        dispatchEvent( new Event( "videoResize" ) );
    }
    dispatchEvent( event );
}
```

In the preceding code snippet, if _resizeToVideo is set to true, then the width and height of the UIVideoPlayer is set to the height and width of the video, and the height of the videoControls is taken into account. Once set, the videoResize event is thrown. Otherwise, the MetaDataEvent is dispatched and can be received by the parent class.

Because UIVideoPlayer extends the VBox container class, any resizing will keep the videoControls below the VideoDisplay component. As the VBox resizes, so will the videoControls accordingly.

Capturing Camera Input

As previously mentioned, one small bell and whistle to be added to the UIVideoPlayer is the ability to display the feed from a webcam, should the user have one. This is done by the enableCamera method:

```
public function enableCamera( event:Event = null ):void
{
    var camera:Camera = Camera.getCamera();
    videoDisplay.attachCamera( camera );
}
```

This method creates a new Camera object and calls the getCamera method. If a camera is present, then it assigns the Camera object to the VideoDisplay component through the attachCamera method. If a webcam is present, the VideoDisplay component will automatically start to display the input.

play and pause Methods

The last feature in the UIVideoPlayer component is the capability to play and pause the video from outside of the component. This is offered in case something other than the UIVideoControls component needs to start and stop the video. Both methods call the play and pause methods of the VideoDisplay component.

Now that the UIVideoPlayer has been created, a source can be assigned to it and it can be tested. One huge section of the AIR Video Player has been created. The next section demonstrates how to implement the UIVideoPlayer component.

Bringing It All Together

Now that the standalone video player has been developed, AIR functionality can be added to the application. In the previous section, you created the main application file, AIRVideoPlayer.mxml. If you have already created this file, open it and overwrite its contents with the following markup. If you have yet to create this file, open a new editor window and insert the following:

```
<?xml version="1.0" encoding="utf-8"?>
<mx:WindowedApplication
    xmlns:mx="http://www.adobe.com/2006/mxml"
    layout="absolute" width="320" height="290"
    backgroundColor="0x000000"
    verticalScrollPolicy="off"
    horizontalScrollPolicy="off"
    applicationComplete="handleAppCreationComplete( event )"
    resizing="handleResizingMainApp( event );"
    xmlns:ui="com.aircmr.videoplayer.ui.*">

    <mx:Style source="assets/style/app.css" />

    <mx:Script>
        <![CDATA[
            import mx.events.VideoEvent;
            import mx.events.ResizeEvent;
            import mx.events.MetadataEvent;
```

```
        private var _activeNativeMenu:NativeMenu;

        private function handleAppCreationComplete( event:Event ):void
        {
            this.addEventListener( NativeDragEvent.NATIVE_DRAG_ENTER,
                onDragEnterHandler );
            this.addEventListener( NativeDragEvent.NATIVE_DRAG_DROP,
                onDragDropHandler );

            this.contextMenu = buildContextMenu();

            stage.addEventListener( FullScreenEvent.FULL_SCREEN,
                handleResizeFullScreen );

            if( NativeApplication.supportsMenu )
                NativeApplication.nativeApplication.menu = buildAppMenu();
            if( NativeWindow.supportsMenu )
                stage.nativeWindow.menu = buildAppMenu();
        }

        private function buildContextMenu( isNormal:Boolean = true ):NativeMenu
        {
            var menu:NativeMenu = new NativeMenu();

            var fileMenu:NativeMenuItem =
                menu.addItem( new NativeMenuItem( "File" ) );
            fileMenu.submenu = buildFileMenu();

            menu.addItem( new NativeMenuItem( "seperator" , true ));

            if( isNormal )
            {
                var fullScreen:NativeMenuItem = menu.addItem(
                    new NativeMenuItem("ENTER FULLSCREEN") );
                fullScreen.addEventListener( Event.SELECT,
                    handleFullScreen );
            }
            else
            {
                var exitFullScreen:NativeMenuItem =
                    menu.addItem( new NativeMenuItem("EXIT FULLSCREEN") );
                exitFullScreen.addEventListener( Event.SELECT,
                    handleExitFullScreen );
            }

            var playVideoMenuItem:NativeMenuItem =
                menu.addItem( new NativeMenuItem( "PLAY" ) );
            playVideoMenuItem.addEventListener( Event.SELECT,
                videoPlayer.play );

            var pauseVideoMenuItem:NativeMenuItem =  menu.addItem(
                new NativeMenuItem( "PAUSE" ) );
            pauseVideoMenuItem.addEventListener( Event.SELECT,
                videoPlayer.pause );
```

```
        return menu;
    }

    private function buildAppMenu():NativeMenu
    {
        var appMenu:NativeMenu = new NativeMenu();
        var fileMenu:NativeMenuItem = appMenu.addItem(
            new NativeMenuItem( "File" ) );
        fileMenu.submenu = buildFileMenu();

        var viewMenu:NativeMenuItem = appMenu.addItem(
            new NativeMenuItem( "View" ) );
        viewMenu.submenu = buildViewMenu();

        return appMenu;
    }

    private function buildFileMenu():NativeMenu
    {
        var fileSubMenu:NativeMenu = new NativeMenu();
        var openVideo:NativeMenuItem = fileSubMenu.addItem(
            new NativeMenuItem( "Open Video" ));
        openVideo.addEventListener( Event.SELECT , handleOpenVideo );

        var closePlayer:NativeMenuItem = fileSubMenu.addItem(
            new NativeMenuItem( "Close Player" ));
        closePlayer.addEventListener( Event.SELECT , handleClosePlayer );

        return fileSubMenu;
    }

    private function buildViewMenu():NativeMenu
    {
        var viewSubMenu:NativeMenu = new NativeMenu();
        var fullScreen:NativeMenuItem = viewSubMenu.addItem(
            new NativeMenuItem("Enter FullScreen") );
        fullScreen.addEventListener( Event.SELECT , handleFullScreen );

        var doubleSize:NativeMenuItem = viewSubMenu.addItem(
           new NativeMenuItem("Double Size") );
        doubleSize.addEventListener( Event.SELECT,
            videoPlayer.setDoubleSize );

        var normalSize:NativeMenuItem = viewSubMenu.addItem(
            new NativeMenuItem("Normal Size") );
        normalSize.addEventListener( Event.SELECT,
            videoPlayer.setNormalSize );

        var seperator:NativeMenuItem = viewSubMenu.addItem(
            new NativeMenuItem("SEPERATOR" , true ));

        var viewCamera:NativeMenuItem = viewSubMenu.addItem(
            new NativeMenuItem("View Camera") );
        viewCamera.addEventListener( Event.SELECT,
```

```
            videoPlayer.enableCamera );

        return viewSubMenu;
    }

    private function handleOpenVideo( event:Event ):void
    {
        var videoFilter:FileFilter = new FileFilter("Video",
            "*.flv;*.mp4;*.mov;*.mpg;*.m4a;*.mp4v;*.3gp;*.3g2");
        var file:File = new File();
        file.addEventListener( Event.SELECT , handleVideoSelection );
        file.browseForOpen("Video" , [videoFilter] );
    }

    private function handleClosePlayer( event:Event ):void
    {
        stage.nativeWindow.close();
    }

    private function handleVideoSelection( event:Event ):void
    {
        var prefix:String =
           ( Capabilities.os.search("Mac") >= 0 ) ? "file://" : "";
        videoPlayer.source = prefix + event.target.nativePath;

        openLabel.visible = false;
    }

    private function onDragEnterHandler( event:NativeDragEvent ):void
    {
        NativeDragManager.dropAction = NativeDragActions.LINK;
        NativeDragManager.acceptDragDrop( this );
    }

    private function onDragDropHandler( event:NativeDragEvent ):void
    {
        if( event.clipboard.hasFormat(ClipboardFormats.FILE_LIST_FORMAT) )
        {
            var fileArray:Array = event.clipboard.getData(
                ClipboardFormats.FILE_LIST_FORMAT ) as Array;
            for each( var file:File in fileArray )
            {
                var prefix:String =
                    (Capabilities.os.search("Mac") >= 0) ? "file://" : "";

                switch( file.extension )
                {
                    case "flv" :  videoPlayer.source =
                        prefix + file.nativePath;
                                  break;
                    case "mp4" :  videoPlayer.source =
                        prefix + file.nativePath;
                                  break;
                    case "mov" :  videoPlayer.source =
```

```
                prefix + file.nativePath;
                        break;
            case "mpg" :  videoPlayer.source =
                prefix + file.nativePath;
                        break;
            case "m4a" :  videoPlayer.source =
                        prefix + file.nativePath;
                        break;
            case "mp4v" :  videoPlayer.source =
                        prefix + file.nativePath;
                        break;
            case "3gp" :  videoPlayer.source =
                        prefix + file.nativePath;
                        break;
            case "3g2" :  videoPlayer.source =
                        prefix + file.nativePath;
                        break;

        }

        openLabel.visible = false;
    }
  }
}

private function handleVideoPlayerResize( event:Event ):void
{
    this.width = videoPlayer.width;
    this.height = videoPlayer.height + 18;
}

private function handleMetaData( event:MetadataEvent ):void
{
    this.title = videoPlayer.source.split('/').pop();
}


private function handleResizingMainApp(
    event:NativeWindowBoundsEvent = null ):void
{
    videoPlayer.width = this.width;
    videoPlayer.height = this.height - 18;
}

private function handleResizeFullScreen( event:FullScreenEvent ):void
{
    if(stage.displayState == StageDisplayState.FULL_SCREEN_INTERACTIVE)
    {
        videoPlayer.showVideoControls = false;
        videoPlayer.width = this.width;
        videoPlayer.height = this.height;

        this.contextMenu = buildContextMenu( false );
    }
```

```
                if( stage.displayState == StageDisplayState.NORMAL )
                {
                    videoPlayer.showVideoControls = true;
                    handleResizingMainApp();

                    this.contextMenu = buildContextMenu();
                }
            }

            private function handleFullScreen( event:Event ):void
            {
                stage.displayState = StageDisplayState.FULL_SCREEN_INTERACTIVE;
            }

            private function handleExitFullScreen( event:Event ):void
            {
                stage.displayState = StageDisplayState.NORMAL;
            }
        ]]>
    </mx:Script>

    <mx:Label id="openLabel" color="0xFFFFFF"
        text="DRAG VIDEO INTO PLAYER TO START"
        x="{this.width / 2 - openLabel.width / 2}" y="{this.height / 2}" />

    <ui:UIVideoPlayer
        id="videoPlayer"
        width="100%" height="100%"
        resizeToVideo="true"
        metadataReceived="handleMetaData( event );"
        videoResize="handleVideoPlayerResize( event );"
      />
</mx:WindowedApplication>
```

Save this class as `AIRVideoPlayer.mxml` in the root of your working directory.

At this point, the AIR Video Player can be compiled and tested. The result is illustrated in Figure 12-2.

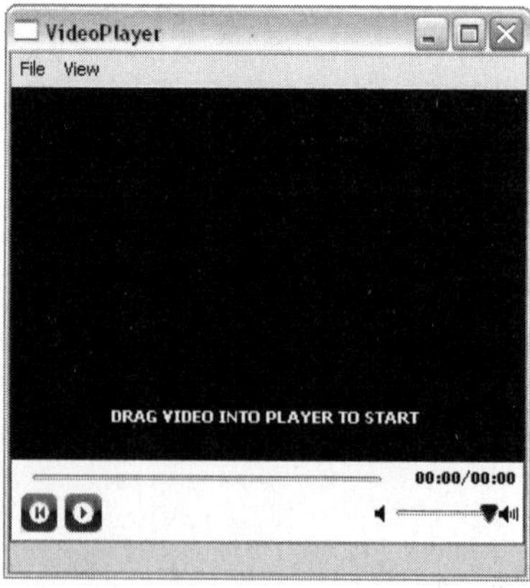

Figure 12-2

AIRVideoPlayer.mxml Explained

The AIRVideoPlayer instantiates the UIVideoPlayer components and acts as a controller between it and the AIR capabilities. It extends the <mx:WindowedApplication> container and controls the initially displayed height, width, and backgroundColor.

Implementing the UIVideoPlayer Component

The AIRVideoPlayer instantiates the UIVideoPlayer component and assigns values and methods to the properties and events of the component:

```
<ui:UIVideoPlayer
    id="videoPlayer"
    width="100%" height="100%"
    resizeToVideo="true"
    metadataReceived="handleMetaData( event );"
    videoResize="handleVideoPlayerResize( event );"
/>
```

Looking through the properties, the width and height are set to 100% in order for the player to take up all available window real estate. Likewise, the height and width affect the size of the AIRVideoPlayer when the videoResize event is dispatched. This is discussed in more detail later in this section.

The public property resizeToVideo is set to true in order for the UIVideoPlayer to expand and contract to the loaded video content.

Once the metadataReceived event is dispatched, the handleMetaData method is accessed. In here, any properties pertaining to the video file's metadata can be set on the application level. For instance, the window title is set to the name of the file once it has been loaded:

```
this.title = videoPlayer.source.split('/').pop();
```

Although this could be assigned when the File object has been created, it is better to assign it after the video has been initialized.

Adding Drag and Drop Capabilities

One excellent feature of AIR is the capability it provides to drag and drop content from the desktop to the AIR application. In this situation, FLV and H.264 encoded files can be dropped into the AIR Video Player and automatically played. This is attained by adding NativeDragEvent.NATIVE_DRAG_ENTER and NativeDragEvent.NATIVE_DRAG_DROP listeners to the handleAppCreationComplete method. This method is called after the application has finished instantiation.

Dragging

When the user drags a video onto the AIR Video Player, the following method is called:

```
private function onDragEnterHandler( event:NativeDragEvent ):void
{
    NativeDragManager.dropAction = NativeDragActions.LINK;
    NativeDragManager.acceptDragDrop( this );
}
```

This method references the NativeDragManager and assigns the dropAction property to link, meaning only a reference to the file will be created, versus copying or moving the file to another directory location. In addition, AIRVideoPlayer lets the NativeDragManager know that it is OK to allow drag and drop by passing a reference of itself to the acceptDragDrop method of the NativeDragManager.

Dropping

When the user drops a file onto the AIRVideoPlayer, the onDragDropHandler method is called. This method is passed a NativeDragEvent that contains the reference information for the dropped file. The reference information is located in the event.clipboard container.

The method first ensures that the clipboard has file information by calling the hasFormat method on the clipboard container. The hasFormat method accepts a format String. In this case, because this method is checking for a file format, the String ClipboardFormats. FILE_LIST_FORMAT is passed.

Once the clipboard information is determined to be file data, the onDragDropHandler method creates a new array and assigns it the data from the clipboard using the clipboard.getData method:

```
var fileArray:Array =
    event.clipboard.getData(ClipboardFormats.FILE_LIST_FORMAT) as Array;
```

It then loops through each File object in the Array and determines whether the file extension is either an FLV or another acceptable H.264 encoded format such as .MOV. If the file is an acceptable format, its NativePath is assigned to the source property of the UIVideoPlayer and the video is loaded. If the user is running Mac OS X, then the prefix file:// needs to be added:

```
var prefix:String = (Capabilities.os.search("Mac")>=0) ? "file://" : "";
```

Adding Context and Window Menus

Even though accessing files through drag and drop is an acceptable way to open a video file, the AIRVideoPlayer will need a more intuitive way to open files. In order to do so, a NativeMenu object will be assigned to application.

Window and Application Menus

There are actually two different types of window menus, and they are determined by which operating system the user is on. For instance, OS X has one stationary menu bar at the top of the screen, separate from the application window, whereas Windows has a menu that resides within the application window. In the case of the AIRVideoPlayer, this is decided in the handleAppCreationComplete method:

```
if( NativeApplication.supportsMenu )
    NativeApplication.nativeApplication.menu = buildAppMenu();
if( NativeWindow.supportsMenu )
    stage.nativeWindow.menu= buildAppMenu();
```

If this application is run in OS X, then NativeApplication.supportsMenu will be true, whereas in Windows, NativeWindow.supportsMenu would be true. In either case, the same menu set is assigned to either the nativeApplication (OS X) or the nativeWindow (Windows).

The method buildAppMenu creates the menu set and returns a NativeMenu object:

```
var menu:NativeMenu = new NativeMenu();
var fileMenu:NativeMenuItem = menu.addItem(new NativeMenuItem("File") );
fileMenu.submenu = buildFileMenu();
```

The preceding snippet of code is taken from buildAppMenu. In this example, a new NativeMenu object is created and a new NativeMenuItem named fileMenu is added to it. Once fileMenu has been added, the fileMenu submenu is assigned through buildFileMenu, which returns a NativeMenu. The result is a menu entitled File that contains a drop-down with options for Open Video and Close Player. The same is applied to the View menu. Figure 12-3 illustrates the window menu running in Windows.

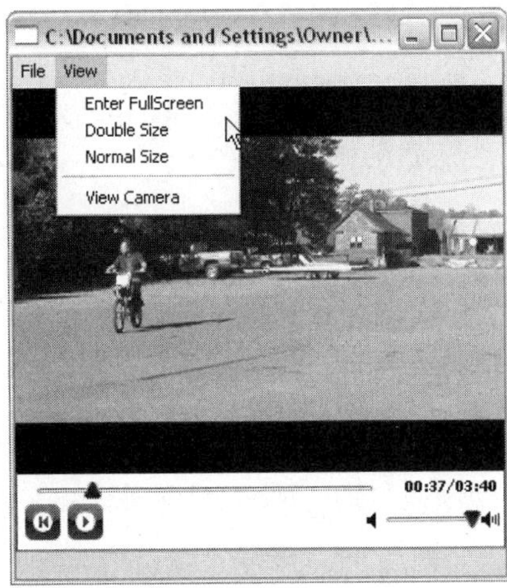

Figure 12-3

Context Menus

Context menus will be added to enable users to switch between full-screen and normal windowed views. Basic play and pause functionality will be added, as well as the fileMenu that was added in the last section. The context menu is added to the application in the handleAppCreationComplete method:

```
this.contextMenu = buildContextMenu();
```

The buildContextMenu is set up similarly to the buildAppMenu method and also returns a NativeMenu object. A new NativeMenu object titled menu is created and the NativeMenuItems are assigned to it. The only exception is when the application checks to determine whether or not it is in full-screen mode:

```
if( isNormal )
{
    var fullScreen:NativeMenuItem = menu.addItem( new
        NativeMenuItem("ENTER FULLSCREEN") );
    fullScreen.addEventListener( Event.SELECT , handleFullScreen );
```

```
}
else
{
    var exitFullScreen:NativeMenuItem = menu.addItem( new
        NativeMenuItem("EXIT FULLSCREEN") );
    exitFullScreen.addEventListener( Event.SELECT , handleExitFullScreen );
```

If the application is in full-screen mode, then `isNormal` will be false. Once this is determined, either Enter Fullscreen or Exit Fullscreen options are added accordingly. The result of the context menu is illustrated in Figure 12-4 and can also be viewed in Figure 12-6 in the following section.

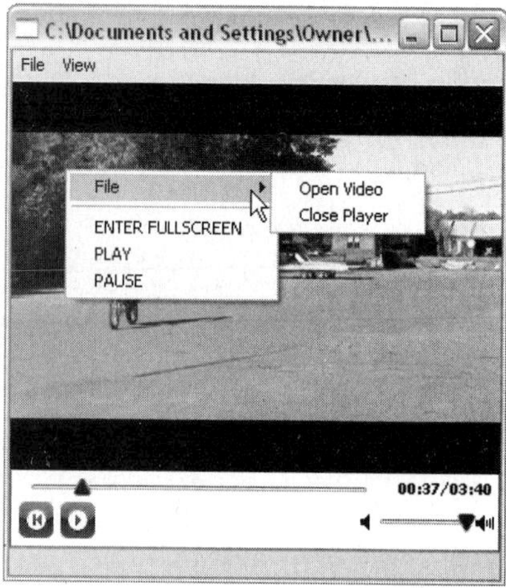

Figure 12-4

Supporting Full-Screen and Resizing

Viewing a video full-screen is almost a necessity in a full-featured video player, as is the capability to resize the player to either the set size of the loaded video or to a size specified by the user. Luckily, all three component files that make up the AIR Video Player are coded to accommodate resizing.

Resizing

Resizing (without full-screen) happens in two places. The first is declared in the `resizing` event dispatched by the `WindowedApplication`. When `resizing` is dispatched, the method `handleResizingApp` is called. This method adjusts the `UIVideoPlayer` to the `height` and `width` of the window as the user drags the window's size to a larger or smaller height and width, all while the video's aspect ratio is preserved unless `UIVideoPlayer.maintainAspectRatio` is set to `false`.

The second place is declared in the `UIVideoPlayer` component instantiation markup. The `videoResize` event is assigned the `handleVideoPlayerResize` method. This event is dispatched once the video's metadata has been received. From there, `handleVideoPlayerResize` readjusts the application's `height` and `width` to the `height` and `width` of the `UIVideoPlayer`. This is illustrated in Figure 12-5.

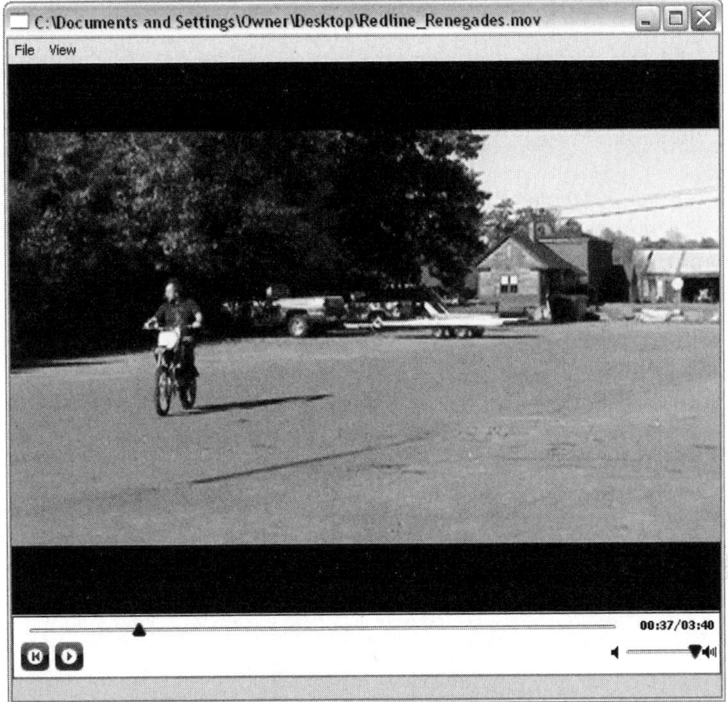

Figure 12-5

Going Full-Screen

The toggles for full-screen were set up in the section "Adding Context and Window Menus." Users can enter full-screen either from the View menu or by right-clicking on the player and selecting Enter Full-Screen.

To enter full-screen mode, the method `handleFullScreen` is called, which sets the `stage.displayState` to `StageDisplayState.FULL_SCREEN_INTERACTIVE`. This effectively sets the application to full-screen.

To exit full-screen mode, the method `handleExitFullScreen` is called, which sets the `stage.displayState` to `StageDisplayState.NORMAL`. This effectively sets the application back to the normal size, which is the height and width of the application before entering full-screen.

The application listens for the display state change by adding a listener to the `stage` in `handleAppCreationComplete`, which listens for `FullScreenEvent.FULL_SCREEN`. Once this event is dispatched, the `handleResizeFullScreen` method is called:

```
private function handleResizeFullScreen( event:FullScreenEvent ):void
{
    if(stage.displayState == StageDisplayState.FULL_SCREEN_INTERACTIVE)
    {
        videoPlayer.showVideoControls = false;
        videoPlayer.width = this.width;
```

```
        videoPlayer.height = this.height;

        this.contextMenu = buildContextMenu( false );
    }

    if(stage.displayState == StageDisplayState.NORMAL)
    {
        videoPlayer.showVideoControls = true;
        handleResizingMainApp();

        this.contextMenu = buildContextMenu();
    }
}
```

This method is called when either going into or coming out of full-screen mode. The display state can be detected by checking the value of `stage.displayState` against any of the public constants contained in the `StageDisplayState` class.

If the `stage.displayState` is equal to `StageDisplayState.FULL_SCREEN_INTERACTIVE`, then the `height` and `width` properties of `UIVideoPlayer` are adjusted to fit the full screen. Additionally, the context menu is changed to enable the user to exit full screen, and the controls in the `UIVideoPlayer` are removed, as illustrated in Figure 12-6. Likewise, the interface and the size of `UIVideoPlayer` are restored if the `stage.displayState` is equal to `StageDisplayState.NORMAL`.

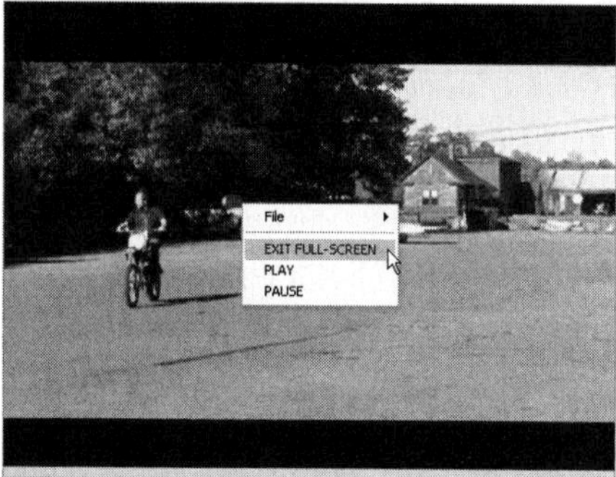

Figure 12-6

Now that the `AIRVideoPlayer` application class has been completed, it is time to sew up any loose ends and deploy the application. Proceed to the next section to finish up this application.

Deploying the Application

The AIR Video Player is nearing completion. The last step is to create a descriptor file and package everything as a deployable AIR file.

The Descriptor File

The final file needed in the creation of your AIR Video Player is the application descriptor file. This XML file contains properties for the application, such as for the initial window settings, copyright, and title. It is packaged and distributed with the final deployable file.

Create a new document and enter the following markup:

```
<?xml version="1.0" encoding="UTF-8"?>
<application xmlns="http://ns.adobe.com/air/application/1.0">
    <id>com.aircmr.VideoPlayer</id>
    <filename>VideoPlayer</filename>
    <version>0.1</version>
    <name>AIR VideoPlayer</name>
    <description></description>
    <copyright>2008</copyright>

  <initialWindow>
       <title/>
       <content>AIRVideoPlayer.swf</content>
       <systemChrome>standard</systemChrome>
       <transparent>false</transparent>
       <visible>true</visible>
   </initialWindow>

    <installFolder>AIRCMR/AIRVideoPlayer</installFolder>
    <programMenuFolder>AIRCMR</programMenuFolder>
</application>
```

Save the file as `AIRVideoPlayer-app.xml` in the root of your working directory along with the `AIRVideoPlayer.mxml` file.

Once the descriptor is created, move on to compiling and packaging the application.

Compiling and Packaging

The last step in creating the AIR Video Player is to compile and package it. Begin packaging your application by first compiling the `AIRVideoPlayer.mxml` file into a SWF.

Open a command prompt, navigate to the working directory for the AIR Video Player, enter the following, and press Enter:

```
> amxmlc AIRVideoPlayer.mxml
```

With the command prompt still pointing to the working directory, package the widget as an AIR installer by entering the following and pressing Enter:

```
> adt -package AIRVideoPlayer AIRVideoPlayer-app.xml AIRVideoPlayer.swf
```

Once the package is created, navigate to your working directory. If the video player packaged correctly, you should have an `AIRVideoPlayer.air` file. Execute the `AIRVideoPlayer.air` package in order to install the application on your hard drive. Once it is installed, open it, drag and drop the included video into your new video player, and enjoy the show.

Summary

This chapter covered how to utilize the `VideoDisplay` component included in the Flex API in combination with other components and classes such as the `HSlider` and `DataFormatter` to create a fully featured video player component capable of playing FLV or H.264 encoded video. It introduced the idea of creating a liquid component layout that allows for resizing to any video content width and height. In building the video player component, the chapter discussed how to create a player that can be used with or without the AIR SDK.

Once the video player was created, you learned how to implement the component in an AIR application. The AIR Video Player uses the `NativeDragManager` and `NativeMenu` to provide users with access to playing videos. Lastly, you learned how to enable full-screen video support through setting the `stage.displayState`, and how to adjust the layout of the application accordingly. As a result of all these features, the AIR Video Player is capable of playing multiple formats and can be customized and distributed cross-platform.

As stated earlier in this chapter, the intention of this player wasn't necessarily to create a video player with a lot of bells and whistles, but to create a good base for you to improve on. You could take this application and add features such as playlist support, custom skins, a custom slider (in place of the `HSlider`), multiple window support, controller effects such as fading in and out when full-screen, or anything else that you can think of. The video player is yours to utilize either in Flex or in AIR; it is left to you to perhaps create the next QuickTime killer app.

Index

A

B

C

D

E

F

G

O

P

Q

R

S

T

U

V

W